THE EARLY WORKS
OF ORESTES A. BROWNSON

VOLUME II:
THE FREE THOUGHT
AND UNITARIAN YEARS, 1830-35

Edited by Patrick W. Carey

MARQUETTE
UNIVERSITY

PRESS
2001

MARQUETTE STUDIES IN THEOLOGY NO. 27
Andrew Tallon, Series Editor

Library of Congress Cataloguing in Publication Data

Brownson, Orestes Augustus, 1803-1876.
  [Selections. 2000]
  The early works of Orestes A. Brownson: Volume II: The Free
    Thought and Unitarian Years, 1830-35 / edited by Patrick W. Carey.
    p. cm. — (Marquette studies in theology ; no. 27)
  Includes indexes.
  ISBN 0-87462-676-5 (v. 2 : pbk. : alk. paper)
  1. Philosophy. 2. Theology. I. Carey, Patrick W., 1940- II. Title.
  III. Marquette studies in theology ; #27.
B908 .B612 2000
191—dc21
                                                        99-050779

Member, THE ASSOCIATION OF AMERICAN UNIVERSITY PRESSES

MARQUETTE UNIVERSITY PRESS
MILWAUKEE

The Association of Jesuit University Presses

MARQUETTE UNIVERSITY PRESS
MILWAUKEE WISCONSIN USA
2001

ii

THE EARLY WORKS OF ORESTES A. BROWNSON
VOLUME II: THE FREE THOUGHT
AND UNITARIAN YEARS, 1830=35

TABLE OF CONTENTS

ACKNOWLEDGMENTS

This volume is indebted to some of the same persons and institutions that helped to make the first volume possible. Two graduate research assistants, Anne Slakey and Jeffrey Barbeau, have been particularly helpful throughout the years that volume two was in preparation, formatting the text and locating biblical and philosophical citations. Jeffrey Barbeau also helped proofread the texts. Constance Nielsen, another graduate research assistant, helped prepare the indexes. Karen Krueger and Aldemar Hagen, too, provided clean typed copies of original texts that were very difficult to read.

Over the years this project has been aided by the staffs of various archives and libraries, including those of the University of Notre Dame, where the Brownson papers are located, Harvard University, the American Antiquarian Society (Worcester, Mass.), Cornell University, and the Leroy House in Leroy, New York. I am especially grateful to Lynne Belloscio of the Leroy House for providing me with the only extant issues of the *Genesee Republican and Herald of Reform*, which Brownson edited in 1830. I am also indebted to Joan Sommers and the Reference and Interlibrary Loan staffs of Memorial Library at Marquette University. I have pestered them numerous times over the past twenty years for various requests, and they have graciously responded to them. Father Thaddeus Burch, S.J., Dean of Marquette's Graduate School, has supplied me with a number of summer research grants to complete this project. Dr. Andrew Tallon, director of Marquette University Press, has provided encouragement and expert advice throughout the preparation of this and the previous volume. His associate Joan Skocir has also been very helpful during the final stages in providing technical assistance for the publication of this volume.

vi

INTRODUCTION

Volume one of Orestes A. Brownson's early writings marked his years as a Universalist minister and concluded with his with drawal from the ministry and Universalism. This second volume covers the period from 1830, immediately after his departure from Universalism, to 1836, the beginning of his ministry with the working classes in Boston—a period of intellectual ferment and transition for Brownson. He began 1830 as a skeptic and a supporter of the workingmen's cause, but by the end of 1830, under the influence of William Ellery Channing's works, he abandoned his self-acknowledged skepticism and returned to the Christian ministry. In 1831 and thereafter he aligned himself with Channing's Unitarianism and gradually moved toward a Romantic world view that rejected or modified some of the Enlightened (or quasi-rationalist) religious perspectives of his Universalist years.

Throughout this intellectual sojourn, Brownson and his family, which grew from two to four sons, moved from Auburn to Leroy to Ithaca, New York (1830-32), to Walpole, New Hampshire (1832-34), to Canton, Massachusetts (1834-36), and finally to Mount Bellingham in Chelsea, Massachusetts (1836). His movement intellectually and geographically prepared him for the Transcendentalist battles that were to take place in Boston during 1836. Indeed these years of study and preparation were a significant part of his development as a Christian thinker. Gradually he became more widely known in urban Unitarian circles and eventually he became one of the young Unitarian ministers who participated in the Transcendentalist Club of Boston—even though he remained an outsider to the social and educated elite of Boston.

Brownson was a part of that generation of Americans who, born around the turn of the century, separated themselves from what they called the stationary party in favor of their own movement party, the party of reform and change in things religious, political, and social. They envisioned themselves as participants in a new American reformation in sensibilities, and called for a renewal of church and society that reflected these new feelings. This volume contains something of the intellectual struggle that Brownson underwent in moving toward a new set of religious and social affections.

INFIDEL AND ADVOCATE
OF THE WORKINGMEN'S PARTY, 1830

Brownson claimed that during his last two years as a Universalist and for another year thereafter he was an infidel.[1] He used the term "infidelity" very broadly and did not mean by it what many in the twentieth century would take it to mean—namely, atheism. For Brownson the term generally meant skepticism, or referred to someone who protested against religious establishments because they were untrue to the religious spirit, or alluded to anyone who had serious doubts about specific religious doctrines held by the churches. Available evidence suggests that immediately after leaving the editorship of the *Gospel Advocate* and Universalism, Brownson wrote almost nothing about religious issues and tried to avoid all religious questions. As in the late 1820s, however, he remained opposed to Dr. Ezra Stiles Ely's Christian Party in politics and any attempts to prohibit sending mail on Sundays,[2] an issue that was hotly contested in the religious press of the day.

Most of Brownson's biographers, including his son Henry, have had little to say about his so-called period of infidelity and his association with the workingmen's movement in 1830 after he left Universalism—primarily because there was little evidence to indicate what in fact he thought and did. Brownson himself relates that after he left the ministry he associated himself for a few months with the New York *Daily Sentinel*, a newspaper like the *Free Enquirer* that supported the workingmen's cause. He also founded a paper, the *Genesee Republican and Herald of Reform*, to advance the cause of the Workingmen's Party in western New York.[3] It is now clear from at least one extant issue of the *Genesee Republican*[4] that Brownson moved his family from

[1]Henry F. Brownson, ed., *The Works of Orestes A. Brownson*, [hereafter *Works*] 20 vols. (Detroit: Thorndike Nourse, 1882-87), 5:47.

[2]On Ely's Christian Party in politics, see the Introduction to volume 1 of *The Early Works of Orestes A. Brownson: The Universalist Years, 1826-29*, [hereafter EW, 1], ed. Patrick W. Carey (Milwaukee: Marquette University Press, 2000), 21-22.

[3]*Works* 5:63. In *The Convert* Brownson did not identify the paper he established, but he had done so in his "The Workingmen," *Philanthropist* 2 (March 13, 1832): 156, where he referred to it as the Genesee *Herald of Reform*, published at Leroy, New York.

[4]The August 18, 1830 issue that Brownson edited has been preserved in the Leroy House, Leroy, New York. Five of Brownson's articles from that issue are reprinted here ("Necessity of Reform. No. 2," "Common Schools," "Public Education. Essay 6," "Cayuga Patriot," "Workingmen's Convention"); his review of "Paul Clifford" is not republished. I would like to thank Ms. Lynne Belloscio of the

Auburn to Leroy, New York sometime in early 1830 and that he founded and began to edit the paper in early July. Brownson continued to publish and edit the paper until after the November elections when he sold his share of the paper to his co-publisher, Henry S. Freeman of Leroy. Brownson apparently went to Leroy to support and foster the cause of a large number of farmers, workers and mechanics in Genesee County who had associated themselves with the workingmen's movement that had originated in New York City in the previous year under the sponsorship, among others, of Thomas Skidmore (1790-1832),[5] the *Free Enquirer*, and the *Daily Sentinel*.

As editor of the Genesee workingmen's paper Brownson became an advocate of universal public education, the movement against all monopolies, the abolition of imprisonment for debts and all laws on the collection of debts, the election of representatives from the useful (i.e., producing) classes, the destruction of the aristocratic caucus system in politics, and the separation of religion from politics—issues that were central to the workingmen's movement.[6] The workingmen, Brownson's prospectus for the *Genesee Republican* declared, aimed to "regenerate society" by destroying its anti-social institutions and replacing them with ones that were more sympathetic to all citizens, not just to the non-productive classes (i.e., the lawyers, priests, doctors, bankers and speculators—all those who lived on the sweat of others' brows).[7] The paper reflected a class consciousness that was clearly a threat to the established order in politics and religion.

Leroy House for providing me with a copy of that issue and the other thirteen extant issues from December 29, 1830 to August 31, 1831 (these thirteen issues Brownson did not edit). In my *Orestes A. Brownson: A Bibliography, 1826-1876* (Milwaukee: Marquette University Press, 1997), I indicated that I was unable to locate any copies of the *Genesee Republican*. The discovery of the Leroy House copies will make it necessary to revise that bibliography in the future.

[5] On Skidmore, see Gary M. Fink, ed., *Biographical Dictionary of American Labor* (Westport, Conn.: Greenwood Press, 1984), 521.

[6] On the Workingmen's movement and Party, see Sean Wilentz, *Chants Democratic: New York City & the Rise of the American Working Class, 1788-1850* (New York: Oxford University Press, 1984), Edward Pessen, *Most Uncommon Jacksonians: The Radical Leaders of the Early Labor Movement* (Albany, NY: State University of New York Press, 1967), and Walter Hugins, *Jacksonian Democracy and the Working Class: A Study of the New York Workingmen's Movement* (Stanford, CA: Stanford University Press, 1960).

[7] The most extensive outline of the prospectus was published in the New York *Daily Sentinel* of July 7, 1830; that version of the prospectus is also published in this volume.

For Brownson the lack of an adequate education was the root of most problems in society and so the question of education loomed large during his editorship of the *Genesee Republican*. Like others in the workingmen's movement, he supported free universal public education and in this he was part of the much larger free school movement.[8] Although he supported universal and equal education, and more rigorous standards of accountability in the curriculum and in the hiring of teachers, he did not agree with Robert Dale Owen's and Fanny Wright's more radical proposals to make children the wards of the state in the educational process. Like many in the workingmen's movement and the free school movement, however, he perceived education to be a panacea for solving most individual and social problems; the responsibility for education, moreover, belonged to the entire society—not just schools, but churches, lyceums, newspapers, parents, teachers, politicians, workers and manufacturers—all had a role to play in providing education for the moral and intellectual improvement of the individual and the society.

Although we cannot be sure that Brownson was entirely silent on the religious questions in 1830 because we have only one extant issue of his *Genesee Republican*, we do know that that issue published nothing on religion except for its resistance to Dr. Ely's Christian Party in politics. Brownson asserted that the paper would not interfere in religious matters, that those issues were best left to individual consciences, and that it respected the clergy as long as they kept out of politics; but it contained nothing on Brownson's own religious perspectives at the time. Brownson had soured on all organized religion by the beginning of 1830, as his published correspondence of the period indicates.[9] After he left Universalism, he wanted a clean break with religious traditions because he considered them all, even Universalism, intolerant and uninterested in the social concerns he had for the working class.

While in Leroy Brownson campaigned for the election of those who supported the principles of the workingmen's movement for

[8]On the free school movement and its association with the workingmen's movement, see Rena L. Vassar, ed., *Social History of American Education*, volume 1: *Colonial Times to 1860* (Chicago: Rand McNally and Co., 1965), 153-94, especially pp. 153-63, and Lawrence A. Cremin, *American Education: The National Experience, 1783-1876* (New York: Harper and Row, 1980), 130-33.

[9]See, in particular, various letters to Universalists, Robert Dale Owen, Ulysses F. Doubleday, the editors of the *Free Enquirer*, and untitled correspondence in *Free Enquirer* 2 (November 28, 1829): 38; (December 12, 1829): 55-56; (December 26, 1829), 409, 417; (January 2, 1830): 79; (January 16, 1830): 95-96; (January 23, 1830): 103.

justice. But it was on the issue of the elections that he eventually separated himself from the Workingmen's Party. Although he clearly supported the workingmen's issues, he maintained repeatedly during the 1830s (and for the rest of his life) that he abhorred party politics and partisan political bickering because it generally put self-promotion and the seeking of political power in the place of principles. Brownson became disgusted, moreover, with the contentions within the Workingmen's Party during 1830 and especially with the workingmen's politicians who had "a stronger desire to pull down the party in power than they have to build up correct principles."[10] He was particularly skeptical, too, about the politicians who were chosen to advance the workingmen's cause, asking "how far may we rely on these individuals [General Erastus Root and General Nathaniel Pitcher, workingmen's candidates for Governor and Lieutenant Governor in the 1830 elections] to support the great measures of reform for which we are now contending."[11] It was clear to Brownson by September of 1830, that the contending factions within a separate third party were doomed to political failure.

The 1830 political campaign in New York State unmasked three major divisions within the workingmen's movement: one group supported Thomas Skidmore's radical perspective on equal distribution of property, another backed Robert Dale Owen's and Fanny Wright's *Free Enquirer* emphasis upon an emancipating education as the means for establishing the rights of the workingmen, and a third group, perhaps the majority of workingmen, followed Noah Cook, editor of the New York *Evening Journal*, who had criticized both the Skidmorites and the *Free Enquirer*s for their radical, "fanatic," and infidel solutions. Cook eventually championed Henry Clay (1777-1852) as the politician most likely to protect and foster the workingmen's industry.[12] Support for Clay disclosed Cook's and the National Republicans' anti-Jacksonianism and revealed their advocacy of the financial and mercantile classes' interests.

Brownson became disgusted with the internal political divisions within the Workingmen's Party in 1830 and eventually supported a Jacksonian candidate for governor, believing that a major party candidate committed to workingmen's principles would have a more

[10]On this, see on the editorial page of the New York *Daily Sentinel* (September 1, 1830), 2, an article reprinted from the *Genesee Republican*.
[11]*Daily Sentinel* (September 8, 1830), 2, quoting the *Genesee Republican*. See also *Daily Sentinel* (September 29, 1830), 1.
[12]On the divisions within the New York City Workingmen's Party in 1830, see Sean Wilentz, 172-219.

realistic chance of initiating much needed reforms than a third-party candidate. He asserted during a later political campaign, that of 1839, that the failure of the Workingmen's Party, not the movement itself, was "that there was no general and permanent demand [among the voting public] for such a party." The fundamental doctrines of the workingmen's movement, he also believed, were practically parallel to those of the Democratic Party. Third parties, Brownson had learned by 1839, were utterly impractical and inefficient, and would never be a significant force in American politics.[13]

Once he gave his political allegiance to Enos Thompson Throop (1784-1874), the Jacksonian candidate for governor of New York, against the anti-Masonic candidate, Frank Granger (1792-1868), he lost the support of the Workingmen's Party and had to give up his paper.[14] Prior to 1830 the Jacksonian politicians who supported the so-called common man had not represented the workingman's cause, but once the divisions erupted within the newly formed Workingmen's Party, the Jacksonians stepped into the breech and claimed to support the workingmen's cause. Brownson's promotion of Troop was his acknowledgment that the Workingmen's Party was dead politically and that other means had to be tried to represent their cause. After the election in the autumn of 1830, Brownson left the Workingmen's Party, he wrote, but not the cause of the laboring and poorer classes, a cause he continued to advocate throughout his life.

Brownson was burned by party politics, but once the twenty-seven year old ex-Universalist minister left the political arena as an editor he had no means by which he could support his wife and two young sons, and it is not evident how he did so. In late 1830, he moved his family from Leroy, where they were apparently living, to Ithaca, where he sought a pastorate and where the family had previously lived in 1827 and 1828. Sometime in early February of 1830, moreover, he founded and edited at Ithaca a bi-weekly periodical,

[13]See "Democracy and Reform," *Boston Quarterly Review* 2 (October, 1839): 478-517, see especially, 488-90.

[14]*Works* 5:63-64. Troop was acting governor of New York in 1829 when President Jackson appointed Governor Martin Van Buren Secretary of State. In 1830 Troop was elected governor. See *Dictionary of American Biography* (hereafter DAB 18:510-11). In 1828 Francis Granger made himself spokesman for the anti-Masonic excitement that swept the State of New York and became associated with Thurlow Weed. In 1830 Granger was the unanimous choice of both the National Republicans and the Anti-Masons to run for the governor's race, which he lost to Troop. See DAB 7:482-83. According to Sean Wilentz, 190, anti-Masonry helped to gather together the anti-Jacksonian forces in the raw canal towns and farming hamlets of upstate New York.

the *Philanthropist*, which he continued to publish until July of 1832.[15] In the first issue of the second volume of the *Philanthropist* Brownson outlined the journal's aims. The paper, as its title indicated, was not a sectarian journal, but a "friend of man." Brownson unwaveringly dedicated it "to effect some reform, to do something to restore the gospel to its pristine purity, to reconcile man to man, and to promote peace on earth." The paper, though, appealed directly and decidedly to the "friends of liberal sentiments," those interested in rescuing "this State from the thraldom of barbarous sectaries." The paper was explicitly religious and clearly within the liberal tradition of Christianity. As editor of the *Philanthropist* Brownson had returned to his career as a religious writer and by November of 1831 he was referring to the journal as the only Unitarian paper in the State of New York.[16] After starting the paper, Brownson sought a parish to serve and in February of 1831 he was hired as pastor of a church in Ithaca.

An Independent Ministry, 1831-32

What possessed Brownson to return to the ministry and to some form of organized religion, which he swore in late 1829 he had given up to become a "friend of man"? For a year or so he tried living without organized religion and focused on the reform of society through the political propaganda of his workingmen's newspaper. But he found those efforts fruitless. Sometime in late 1830 or early 1831 he had a "joyful conversion" from his former skepticism.[17] The religious conversion surprised Brownson as well as his friends, but he attributed it to his reading of and reflection on the works (especially the published sermons) of William Ellery Channing (1780-1842), which Henry Brownson tells us his father began reading in 1829.[18]

As editor of the *Philanthropist*, Brownson republished one of Channing's sermons, "Discourse at the Installation of the Rev. M. I.

[15]Extant copies of the *Philanthropist* include a single issue from volume 1 (July 23, 1831) and most the issues from volume 2 (November 5, 1831 to June 26, 1832). Volume 1 probably covered the period from November of 1830 to October of 1831. The single issue of volume 1 is available at Cornell University Library and volume 2 is available at the University of Notre Dame Archives.
[16]"To Our Patrons," *Philanthropist* 2 (November 5, 1831): 10-11.
[17]See "Essay on Reform," *Philanthropist* 2 (February 14, 1832): 115.
[18]Henry F. Brownson, *Orestes A. Brownson's Early Life: From 1803 to 1844* (Detroit: H. F. Brownson, 1898), 88. Hereafter, *Early Life*.

Motte" (Boston, 1828),[19] which outlined Channing's view of the glory and purpose of Christianity. Christ came, Channing argued, to set the mind free, cleanse it from evil, breathe love of virtue into it, and to call forth its noblest faculties and affections, giving it moral power and restoring it to order, health, and liberty. He came to purify human character, elevate the soul, and lift up the mind. Such aims, though, had been perverted in the course of the history of Christianity and must now be restored. Brownson praised Channing profusely in 1832, judging that he stood "at the head of the brightest geniuses of our country,"[20] and thought so much of him in fact that he named his third son William Ellery Channing Brownson (born 4 January 1834).

Channing's *Likeness to God* (1828),[21] which Brownson probably read in the late autumn of 1830, had the most profound affect upon his religious life. Brownson asserted that his reading and reflection upon that published sermon ended his infidelity and converted him to the "mysteries of Christianity."[22] In 1829 Brownson had periodically written about the light within and about the presence of an immediate, pre-reflective internal witness to the divine, but that theme

[19]Republished as "A Discourse by W. E. Channing," *Philanthropist* 2 (April 10, 1832): 177-90. The sermon, originally published in 1828, was printed in William Ellery Channing, *Discourses, Reviews, and Miscellanies* (Boston: Carter and Hendee, 1830), 435-53, which was more than likely the source of Brownson's republication.

[20]"W. E. Channing, D.D.," *Philanthropist* 2 (April 10, 1832): 190.

[21]On Brownson's reading of Channing, see *Works* 5:69-70, 4:141-42; "W. E. Channing, D.D.," *Philanthropist* 2 (April 10, 1832): 190-91, and especially "Channing's Discourses," *Christian Register* 12 (January 19, 1833): 10, which was a review of Channing's *Discourses, Reviews, and Miscellanies*.

[22]In November or December of 1832, Brownson began writing a book tentatively entitled "Letters to an Unbeliever in Answer to Some Objections to Religion" (see Roll # 10 of the microfilm edition of the "Orestes Augustus Brownson Papers"). The Brownson Papers are located in the Archives of the University of Notre Dame; for a microfilm edition of these papers, see Thomas McAvoy and Lawrence J. Bradley, ed., *A Guide to the Microfilm Edition of the Orestes Augustus Brownson Papers* (Notre Dame, Ind.: University of Notre Dame Press, 1966). The preface to that unpublished manuscript of the "Letters" acknowledged Brownson's indebtedness to Channing: "It was his sermon [i.e., "Likeness to God"] delivered in 1829 [sic] at Providence in R.I. at the ordination of Mr. [Frederick]Farley that first initiated me into the mysteries of Christianity, & led to that train of reflections which ended in my [indecipherable] love for religion, and my belief in the gospel. That sermon and the conversation of the pastor [i.e., Isaac B. Peirce whose numerous letters to Brownson are located on microfilm Roll # 1 of the Brownson Papers] of the Reformed Christian Church in Trenton, N.Y. were the means, under God, of giving me that full faith in the gospel which I now believe myself to have."

emerged with new force in 1831 and 1832 after he read Channing's *Likeness to God*, which emphasized the divinity within humanity as the source of human perfectability. The emphasis upon the dignity of humanity, the internal revelation, and the soul's instinct for God, found in Channing's writings, gave Brownson a new enthusiasm for and a new perspective on Christianity. He would assert time and again during 1831 and 1832 that this interior impulse for the divine could be covered up for a time, it could wither or be smothered, and it could even be denied, but it remained even under the conscious experience of doubt. Once attended to, however, it brought an immediate perception of truth and produced a sense of joy that was incomparable to any other human experience. Channing's sermons became the occasion for Brownson's awakening to the divine within and for his return to the Christian ministry as his vocation.

Channing had influenced many young men of Brownson's generation and helped move the generation of the 1830s into a more Romantic and less rationalistic view of reality. Like Ralph Waldo Emerson (1803-82), Theodore Parker (1810-60), and others, Brownson eventually moved toward Transcendentalism, but for Brownson Channing's influence was originally a form of liberation from skepticism, not an emancipation from Unitarianism (as it was, for example, for Emerson). Throughout his life, even after he had parted ideological company with Channing and Unitarianism, Brownson expressed his gratitude to Channing for bringing him out of infidelity.

In Ithaca Brownson became an independent minister, meaning that he was not identified with any specific religious denomination and was freed from any creeds or traditions. Such a non-denominational Christianity, he believed, allowed him to speak his mind freely. But he did acknowledge that he was becoming more and more impressed with the writings of Unitarians. Prior to 1830, he had little direct knowledge of Unitarianism, even though it had been the subject of hot debate in Boston since 1805. But Brownson lived outside the cultural circle of the intellectual elites in the United States and had no formal collegiate education that would have familiarized him with the debate.

During his ministry in Ithaca, from February 1831 to July 1832, Brownson tried to work out in pulpit and press a new direction for his religious and political beliefs. His Ithaca pastorate aimed to develop a Christian social responsibility for the benefit of the poor and working class, define his own religious philosophy vis-á-vis dogmatism and infidelity, and defend Unitarianism.

Brownson continued to support workingmen and their cause and did not abandon the political doctrines he advanced while editor of the *Genesee Republican* in 1830. Nor had he despaired of the reform he attempted to promote through that journal.[23] For him poverty, which the working class experienced, was not part of the divine design; it was the result of individual and social ignorance and injustice, and therefore it could be overcome by individual and social effort and reform.

In his late twenties Brownson had complained that Christians and especially those in the Christian ministry were indifferent if not hostile to the workingmen's cause. He saw in that apathy one of the causes of the workingmen's unbelief. The New York workingmen's movement was periodically identified with agrarianism and infidelity, a charge some in the movement denied. Others admitted that a minority in the movement, i.e., those who associated themselves with Thomas Skidmore and the *Free Enquirers*, were indeed unbelievers. Brownson was most closely identified with the *Free Enquirer* and *Daily Sentinel* crowd and he indeed saw them as either deists or atheists. Christians, Brownson complained, had done nothing to demonstrate that Christianity itself had a solid foundation for social and political reforms that could assist the workingmen's cause. After his own period of infidelity ended, he began to write about the necessity of promoting a Christian dimension of social reform to overcome the problems of poverty and injustice that were imbedded in political and economic structures. In this he tried to articulate a new relationship between Christianity and social justice, referring repeatedly to Christ as the great social reformer and advocate for the poor.

In 1832, Isaac B. Peirce, a Unitarian pastor of the Reformed Christian Church in Trenton, New York, and one of Brownson's frequent correspondents, drew his attention to an article in the *Daily Sentinel*, which described the doctrines of the Saint-Simonians,[24] a group of Frenchmen who had instituted a new religion that focused on the social dimensions of Christianity, emphasizing, at least, the inherent connection between religious belief and social justice.[25] It

[23]See "Poverty," *Philanthropist* 2 (March 27, 1832): 161-63.

[24]Peirce to Brownson, 1 February 1832. See also Peirce to Brownson, 13 March 1834, where Peirce quotes large sections of an article on the St. Simonians from *Encyclopaedia Americana*, 13 vols. (Philadelphia: Carey, Lea & Carey, 1833), 11:414. Both letters are in microfilm roll #1 of the Brownson papers.

[25]On the Saint-Simonians, see Frank E. Manuel, *The Prophets of Paris* (Cambridge, Mass.: Harvard University Press, 1962), 103-94; David Owen Evans, *Social Romanticism in France 1830-1848* (New York: Octagon Books, 1969); Paul Bénichou, *Le temps des prophètes: Doctrines de l'âge romantique* (Paris: Gallimard,

was obvious that Brownson had no prior acquaintance with the Saint-Simonians, but also that he saw in the new religion a hope for the cause of the workingmen and the poor. One of the Saint-Simonians' pivotal doctrines proposed that "All social institutions should have for their object, the melioration of the moral and physical condition of the poorest and most numerous class."[26] Although he did not make much of this first acquaintance with the Saint-Simonians, he was to be greatly influenced by them in the future. In the early 1830s, however, he was drawn to their message because of their attempts to unite religious and social issues.

Brownson's concern for social issues was not limited to issues of poverty and the workingmen's cause. He was also troubled with the issue of capital punishment, and not so much with the state's right to execute a criminal as with the criminal effects such actual executions had upon the society as a whole. On 3 February 1832, he witnessed in Ithaca, New York, the execution of Guy Clark, who had killed his wife in a fit of rage. Clark requested that Brownson prepare an address to the crowd on the day of execution, an address he indeed prepared but the sheriff refused to let him deliver it, probably out of fear of arousing the drunken crowd who had come to witness the public event. After the day of execution, however, Brownson published the address. Although the address tried to explain (not justify) the mental circumstances that precipitated the murder, it was obvious that Brownson used the occasion to call into question the evil effects of public executions upon those who witnessed such events in upstate New York. Clark's crime was itself bad enough, but the vengeance it brought forth in the public was worse and indeed, if possible, more criminal than the murder itself because the public "crime" never came to a judicial decision. According to Brownson's account, over 20,000 people of all ages came to witness the man hanged to death. "Our village," he wrote, "and places of resort on the roads leading to it were rife with drunkenness, gambling, fighting, and the like. The iniquity committed by Clark was nothing in comparison to the moral evil occasioned by this public spectacle of killing a man according to law." Brownson protested against this savage law and

---

1977), 248-358; Martin U. Martel, "Saint-Simon," *International Encyclopedia of the Social Sciences*, ed. David L. Sills, 18 vols. (New York: Macmillan Company, 1968), 13:591-94.

[26]See "Doctrines of the St. Simonians," *Philanthropist* 2 (February 14, 1832): 125-26.

"the more savage feelings which sustain it in force."[27] Such a position was not a popular one and, like his support of the workingmen's cause, alienated him from a large segment of American frontier society.

Although Brownson took issue with some values in his frontier society, he could at times also articulate issues that were close to the heart of the American people whether on the frontier or elsewhere. This became clear in his Fourth of July addresses, some of which were published at the request of those who heard them. One of them was an address delivered at Ovid in Seneca County, New York, in 1831. In that address Brownson celebrated in florid fashion the political liberty that had created the United States and that sustained it during the previous fifty-five years. But Brownson wanted to see liberty extended into the social dimension of American life and therefore he called for a new emphasis on liberty, an emphasis that focused on the emancipation of all Americans from ignorance, poverty, superstition, and bigotry—the evils that still needed to be overcome before Americans would be truly free. This emphasis upon social liberty was not new with Brownson, but it did demonstrate that he like a number of other leaders in American society had expanded notions of American liberty; the Fourth of July celebrations became occasions for reminding Americans of what needed to be accomplished in the future if America was to live up to its dedication to freedom.

The emphasis upon religious liberty, free inquiry, and the use of reason had been constant themes in Brownson's writings since his early twenties. These emphases were consistent with his own view of liberal Christianity, whether identified with Universalism or Unitarianism. And, for him, the liberal form of Christianity was certainly closer to central American values than were either dogmatic orthodoxy or infidelity.

As in the immediate past, Brownson continued to attack bigotry, Presbyterianism, revivalism, and protracted meetings—all of which he identified with dogmatic orthodoxy. Neither Calvinism (which he always associated with dogmatic bigotry) nor Universalism, he argued, provided grounds and incentives for moral living. For Brownson morality became almost the sole criterion in the early 1830s for his view of true Christianity. Calvinism failed to provide ideological grounds for moral living because of its emphasis upon divine election and irresistible grace, and Universalism was equally

---

[27]See *Philanthropist* 2 (February 14, 1832): 127.

inadequate because of its extreme emphasis upon the inevitable salvation of all.

These two extremes within the Christian tradition had previously driven Brownson into what he had repeatedly called infidelity
or unbelief. But infidelity, too, Brownson soon discovered, had no
power to motivate him or his culture to moral living. Although the
infidels he knew were concerned with issues of justice and morality,
they could not provide the powerful incentives needed to make human beings choose the good. Something deeper than reason was
needed to sustain human efforts to reform society especially when
reformers had to face opposition to their efforts. Only religion could
inspire humans to the long term struggle that was necessary to regenerate society.

Unitarianism, Brownson gradually learned, had been able to steer
a path between the two extremes of Calvinism and Universalism.
Unitarianism also avoided the pitfalls of infidelity by emphasizing
the inherent moral and religious affections that were necessary for
moral living. In a series of essays (included in this volume)—e.g.,
"Patrick O'Hara," "Infidel and Priest," and "Calvanism [*sic*] and Infidelity"—Brownson struggled to redefine himself and to come to
terms with the extremes, tensions and experiences of skepticism and
belief in his own life and in that of American culture.

It was already clearly evident during his "independent" ministry
in Ithaca, New York, that he had come to identify most closely with
the Unitarianism of William Ellery Channing whose works had freed
him from the trap of unbelief. In his first sermon as an independent
minister, he indicated that of all the denominations the one most
congenial to his new religious perspective was Unitarianism.[28] In a
series of articles—"Unitarianism," "Letters to Rev. Wm. Wisner," and
"Unitarians Not Deists"[29]—Brownson defended the Unitarian perspective, arguing that it provided solid ideological grounds for the
religious affections, for involvement in issues of social justice, and
for the preservation of religious freedom, free inquiry, and the use of
reason in religion. Unitarianism was to be, he asserted, as Thomas
Jefferson had before him (though not for exactly the same reasons),

---

[28]See his "A Sermon on Righteousness," *Philanthropist* 2 (January 14, 1832):
85-94. This sermon was delivered February 31, 1831, his first sermon as an "independent" minister.

[29]See *Philanthropist* 2 (November 5, 1831): 3-5; ibid., 11-14; (November 19,
1831): 20-24; (December 3, 1831): 37-42; (December 17, 1831): 55-59; (January
31, 1832): 109-11; (February 14, 1832): 115-19; (February 28, 1832): 141-44;
(May 15, 1832): 193-95; (June 12, 1832): 228-36.

the religion of America's future because it corresponded so perfectly to the demands of democratic culture and the religious aspirations of the human heart.

For Brownson Unitarianism emphasized that the "essence of Christianity is moral freedom and enlargement of soul."[30] Human beings, created in the image of God, had the religious affections that led them to perfect themselves and their society. Thus, Unitarianism had re-captured the essence of Christianity and had abandoned the historical accretions that tended to cover up the core of the Christian moral tradition. The mission of the Christ of Unitarianism, more-over, was to demonstrate and illustrate divine love, to bring to light immortality, to teach righteousness by precepts and example, and to lead human beings confidently in a triumph over individual and so-cial sin. In this Christ was the true reformer who unveiled the Fa-therhood of God.

Such a view of Christianity could not be proven, Brownson ar-gued, by the defective methods used by John Tillotson (1630?-94), John Locke (1632-1704), Samuel Clarke (1675-1729), and William Paley (1743-1805). They all in one way or another appealed to some form of external evidence to demonstrate the validity or divinity of Christianity. Christianity, Brownson asserted, could not be proven by historical records, external forms of revelation, or by miracles and prophecy. Such forms of evidence were unconvincing because they were unreliable forms of human testimony, subject to human decep-tion and external to human experience. The only convincing proof of Christianity was found within the human heart where the divine dwelt; the God within, moreover, made the external records and the miracles themselves intelligible and meaningful. "My own faith," Brownson asserted in early 1832, "rests on this internal revelation from God to the inner man. I have thus a witness within; and, hav-ing this witness, I can find its testimony corroborated by the whole of external nature."[31]

Long before the "Miracles Controversy" (1836 to 1840) between Boston Unitarians and Transcendentalists,[32] Brownson was saying that miracles do not authenticate the divine message; it is the inter-nal revelation in the human soul that bears witness to the truth of

[30]"Letter to Rev. Wm. Wisner," *Philanthropist* 2 (November 19, 1831): 20.

[31]"Essay on Reform," *Philanthropist* 2 (February 14, 1832): 115. See also ibid., (February 28, 1832): 129-35.

[32]On the miracles question, see William R. Hutchison, *The Transcendentalist Ministers: Church Reform in the New England Renaissance* (New Haven: Yale University Press, 1959), 52-97.

what Christ taught and what Christianity teaches.[33] What enables human beings to acknowledge a miracle as indeed a divine communication, Brownson would say in 1836, is not the miracle itself but the internal witness within. Already in 1832 Brownson had carried the emphasis upon the internal witness much further than some Unitarians were willing to go. He had clearly separated himself from the evidentiary tradition of Locke and Paley, and was moving in a more overtly Romantic direction by emphasizing the internal experience of the divine.

Brownson's defense of Unitarian Christianity did not go unchallenged in upstate New York. Ithaca's Presbyterian pastor, Rev. William Wisner (1782-1871), had charged that Unitarianism was the "devil's doctrine"; others asserted that it was a form of deism. Brownson countered that Unitarianism was the earliest historical form of Christianity, and its reassertion in the nineteenth century was a return to primitive Christianity.[34] Although Unitarians shared many ideas with deists (particularly the emphasis upon religious liberty, the use of reason in religion, and free inquiry), they were not deists because they emphasized the internal revelation, the inner light, that allowed them to interpret and see in the Bible an authentic communication from God. Unitarians, moreover, unlike deists, confessed their faith in divine providence over all creation and all history, and acknowledged the necessity of personal and communal prayer. Unitarians also believed in a future state of righteous retribution; the deist of the day, Brownson claimed, did not. Unitarianism needed to be defended in upstate New York because few had any correct idea of what Unitarianism claimed. Thus, by 1832, Brownson saw himself as an apologist for Unitarianism, as he had been an apologist for Universalism in the mid-1820s.

Brownson's Unitarianism was as foreign to the dominant orthodox Christian tradition in upstate New York as was his former Universalism and therefore he could not find the patronage for his form

[33]"Essay on Reform," (February 28, 1832): 134.
[34]Brownson's assertion about the historical priority of Unitarianism did not go unchallenged by his fellow Unitarians. George Wannay told Brownson that his history was just wrong. He informed Brownson that Tertullian, about the year 200, had spoken to Praxeas about the Trinity. See Wannay to Brownson, December 13, 1831, Brownson papers, roll #1. Brownson's historical knowledge of Christianity was very thin and his periodic careless historical statements made his essays incredible to some. Gradually, through corrections from correspondents like Wannay and through his reading, he became more familiar with the historical tradition, but he was never really as interested in history as he was in the philosophy and theology of history.

of liberal Christianity that would sustain his periodical, his ministry
and his family in Ithaca. By early June of 1832 it was becoming clear
to him that he had little support for his *Philanthropist*, that subscrib-
ers were not paying their dues, and that public opinion was turning
against him again because of his liberal Christian leanings. Again,
too, he had failed to gain sufficient financial resources for himself
and his family. On 26 June 1832, therefore, he ceased publishing his
journal and traveled throughout the East during the next three months
looking for a new Unitarian pastorate where he could preach and
find sufficient funds for his family. In October of 1832 he received a
call to a pastorate in Walpole, New Hampshire, about ninety miles
north of Boston.

THE WALPOLE YEARS, 1832 TO 1834

The Unitarian congregation in Walpole offered Brownson a salary of $500 per year, a larger salary than he had received at any of the
previous congregations he served.[35] He and his family had been no
strangers to poverty, as he admitted occasionally in his writings, but
the Walpole pastorate gave him sufficient funds to survive and would
be the first time he did not have to serve as an editor of a paper to
supplement his parish income.

The Walpole pastorate also gave Brownson the time needed for a
more systematic study of philosophy and theology than he had had
in the immediate past. At Walpole, moreover, he taught himself French
and a little German and began reading some French sources, the first
of which was Benjamin Constant's (1767-1830) *De la religion
considérée dans sa source, ses formes et ses développements* (1824-31), a
text, as he indicates in his "Letters to an Unbeliever," that was conso-
nant with his own emerging views of religion as a natural instinct or
sentiment.[36] Constant has been called a "contributor to modern liberalism" because of his emphasis upon the necessity of safeguarding
the freedom of the individual against a despotic political authority
and the tyranny of the majority. His views on religion, like those on

[35]$500 was a decent salary. Isaac B. Peirce, Unitarian pastor in Trenton, had a
salary of $212 for the year 1836. On this, see *Early Life*, 62. On the other hand
William Ellery Channing's salary was over $1600 per year in 1824, but was re-
duced to $800 per year in 1830 when Channing decided to decrease his work load
at Federal Street Church in Boston. In 1830, too, his assistant, Ezra Gannett, received $800 per year. On this, see Madeleine Hooke Rice, *Federal Street Pastor: The
Life of William Ellery Channing* (New York: Bookman Associates, 1961), 156.
[36]*Christian Register* 12 (November 30, 1833): 190.

politics, stressed the progress and freedom of the individual within a social context, reflecting motifs in Romantic as well as Enlightenment thought.[37] Constant provided Brownson with a language for distinguishing the permanent in religion (i.e., a natural religious sentiment) from the transitory (i.e., the culturally, historically, and ideologically conditioned forms of religion) and for seeing the religious dynamic itself as progressive—that is, from age to age the religious sentiment itself became an agent for purifying its forms.

Some time in 1833, Brownson also began reading the French eclectic philosopher Victor Cousin (1792-1867) whose works would have a fundamental shaping influence on his philosophical and religious perspectives.[38] Initially Brownson read Cousin's 1828 and 1829 introductory lectures on the history of philosophy and the *Fragments philosophiques* (1826).[39] Although he did not write anything explicitly on Cousin's philosophy until September of 1836, he did refer to Cousin periodically in his articles of 1834 and 1835. Brownson's writings show that what he saw in Cousin was consistent with what he had already learned from Constant about the foundation and history of religion; but Cousin provided Brownson with a philosophically grounded psychological method that better equipped him to analyze the relationship between the permanent and the transient in religious tradition.[40] It was not until the middle of 1836, however,

[37]On Constant, see Pierre Deguise, *Benjamin Constant méconnu: Le livre "De la Religion"* (Geneva: Droz, 1966).

[38]Cousin was a significant figure in the development of philosophy as a professional discipline in early nineteenth-century France. Influenced by Kant, Hegel, Schelling, and the Scottish Common Sense tradition, Cousin tried to bring together in a synthetic whole the best of the four schools of philosophy that he had identified: sensationalism, idealism, skepticism, and mysticism. For him, moreover, philosophy was the highest of all forms of knowledge because it translated into pure rational truths the intuitions or inspirations of God that religion and art expressed only in symbols. On Cousin, see A. B. Spitzer, *The French Generation of 1820* (Princeton, NJ: Princeton University Press, 1987), George Boas, *French Philosophers of the Romantic Period* (Baltimore: Johns Hopkins University Press, 1925), and Jules Simon, *Victor Cousin*, trans. Gustave Masson (London: George Routledge, and Sons, 1888).

[39]A translation of some of Cousin's introductory lectures was published in Boston in 1832. See Victor Cousin, *Introduction to the History of Philosophy*, trans. Henning Gotfried Linberg (Boston: Hilliard, Gray, Little, and Wilkins, 1832). Brownson may have used this text in addition to the French. For the original editions, see *Cours de philosophie . . . Introduction a l'histoire de philosophie*, 2 vols. (Paris: Pichon and Didier, 1828), and *Fragments philosophiques* (Paris: A Sautelet & Cie, 1826).

[40]See *Works* 5:85, 125-29, for Brownson's own assessment of the influence of Cousin on his intellectual development.

before Brownson became interested in Cousin's metaphysical and psychological perspectives. But even before the middle of 1836, Brownson was developing a psychology that acknowledged a distinction between reason and understanding, or between what Cousin called "spontaneous reason" and "reflective reason."[41] In the period prior to his move to Boston, however, Brownson was primarily interested in Cousin's eclecticism, becoming particularly enamored with Cousin's view that all systems of philosophy are "true in what they affirm, false only in what they deny."[42] He applied Cousin's eclecticism to religious systems, as is clear from his writings on belief and unbelief during the early 1830s, and to the question of reconciling the spiritual and the material orders of human existence.

Brownson's interest in the Saint-Simonians, sparked already when he was in upstate New York, continued at Walpole and later at Canton, Massachusetts. Like the Saint-Simonians he became interested in developing a new form of Christianity that would transcend the weaknesses of Catholicism and Protestantism, incorporate their strengths, and create a new synthetic form of religion that would be more consistent with the basic religious sentiment.

Still, Brownson filtered his reading of Constant, Cousin, and the Saint-Simonians through his American Unitarian experience. The move to Walpole definitely cemented his formal relationship with Unitarianism, but it also brought him close to Boston, the intellectual center of Unitarianism. From Walpole, he had easier access than in the past to the intellectual currents of the day and to Unitarian magazines like the *Christian Register*, the *Unitarian*, and the *Christian Examiner*, all of which became outlets for his developing thought.

Brownson's American Unitarian experience was one that was particularly sensitive to the problems of skepticism and the workingmen's cause and therefore his published writings during this period focused upon a new Christian apologetic for unbelievers, and a reform of society for the benefit of the poor laboring class. In the late 1820s Brownson began to consider the nature of unbelief and it would continue to be an intellectual interest for him for the remainder of his life, culminating in his "Essay in Refutation of Atheism" in 1873 and 1874.[43] It was obvious, particularly in his "Letters to an

---

[41]Later in this Introduction I will examine Brownson's understanding of both the Coleridgean distinction between reason and understanding and the Cousinian distinction between spontaneous and reflective reason.

[42]*Works* 5:85.

[43]*Brownson's Quarterly Review* 27 (October 1873): 433-65; 28 (January 1874): 1-37; 28 (April 1874): 145-79.

Unbeliever,"[44] which were written in 1832 and 1833, that the issue of infidelity was highly personal and in fact his developing apologetic for Christianity emerged from his own experience with skepticism. During his Walpole pastorate, moreover, Brownson would begin writing a novel, which was in reality a thinly disguised autobiographical account of his emergence from infidelity. Though he finished writing *Charles Elwood* while at Canton, Massachusetts, it remained unpublished until 1840.

Brownson's personal experience with religious doubt and unbelief preceded his reading of Cousin's *Cours de philosophie* (1828), but Brownson could find in that text a systematic philosophical analysis of skepticism that would help him to understand his own experience and to place it in a context that transcended his individual experience. According to Cousin, doubt or skepticism was one of the observable primitive elements of the human mind that manifested itself periodically in the history of Western thought as one of the four cardinal philosophical systems (the others being sensualism or empiricism, idealism, and mysticism). Historically skepticism arose or could arise out of a sensualism that had become dogmatical (i.e., when an empirical approach to reality "believes only in the authority of the senses and in the existence of matter").[45] During the late 1820s Brownson had indeed experienced some of this kind of empirical dogmatism, a kind of extreme reductionism that, Cousin asserted, the human mind ultimately finds unsatisfactory. Brownson's own dogmatism in the late 1820s was in reaction, he thought, to an excessively spiritualized Christianity that had no place for matter or the daily affairs of this world. This war between an extreme empiricism and an equally excessive spiritualism produced, naturally according to Cousin, doubt or the "first rise of common sense upon the stage of philosophy."[46] Skepticism—like sensualism, idealism, and mysticism—tended to end in an extreme position, asserting that everything was false in the other systems or that there was no attainable truth for human beings. Such a dogmatic skepticism was also unsatisfactory because it was at war with the mind's natural, and pre-reflective, mystical or religious tendency. Such a Cousinian eclectic method of interpreting the history of philosophy resonated with Brownson's own confusing and simultaneous experiences of doubt and belief. After reading Cousin Brownson would himself begin to

[44]*Christian Register* 12 (October 5, 1833): 158.
[45]Victor Cousin, *Introduction to the History of Philosophy*, trans. Henning Gotfried Linberg, 353.
[46] Ibid.

analyze more seriously than before the mind's inherent and conflicting experiences of doubt and belief.

Editors of Unitarian papers took note of Brownson's interest and
personal acquaintance with issues of unbelief and his understanding
of the influence of infidelity among the working class. Some, like
Bernard Whitman (1796-1834), editor of the *Unitarian*, for example,
feared that infidelity was growing among the working class in Boston.[47] Brownson's articles on unbelief and the working class in the
Boston Unitarian magazines, moreover, helped to increase his reputation among some Boston intellectuals; at least, he was someone
who had personal knowledge of both areas, an experience most of
the Boston Brahmins did not possess.

Brownson had been emancipated from the prison of unbelief, he
asserted, by reading Channing who had demonstrated that the religious sentiment was the noblest part of human nature. What, then,
was the origin of unbelief or why were people attracted to it? Brownson
sought during these years to explain the origins of infidelity. He focused on three major sources of contemporary unbelief: (1) Calvinism, because its extreme views of God and human nature had driven
many away from Christianity; (2) the Christians' and particularly
the clergy's indifference and even hostility to the poor and the working class; and (3) the divisions, the quarrels, and even the wars within
Christianity.

In the eighteenth century, Brownson asserted, unbelief was primarily an issue for the intellectual elites; in the nineteenth century it
was becoming much more an issue for the masses. It had the poten-
tial of becoming a widespread cultural phenomenon and Christians
and believers had to address the issue or they would find themselves
with little influence in the culture. Unitarians certainly had to define
themselves not only vis-à-vis Calvinism, which had become their
primary focus in the immediate past, but also vis-à-vis deism and the
growing unbelief in the culture. The old eighteenth century apologetic met the objections of the intellectual elites, but it was inadequate to meet the objections of the uninstructed masses of the nineteenth century who thought for themselves, distrusted antiquity, and
had little regard for history or miracle. Brownson recognized the need
for a new apologetic for the untutored nineteenth-century masses
who were beginning to trust their own experiences.[48]

[47]See, in particular, B. Whitman to Brownson, December 26, 1833, in Henry
Brownson, *Early Life*, 100-03, and Brownson papers, Roll #1.
   [48]On this see, "Channing's Discourses," *Christian Register* 12 (January 19,
1833): 10.

By 1833 and 1834, that is, by the time he had read Benjamin Constant, Brownson was trying to point out the positive as well as the negative sides of what he called unbelief or infidelity. Doubt and skepticism were natural to human beings and a necessary part of the inquiring mind and the search for truth. Disbelief, one of the sources of the so-called movement party in the modern world, protested against the outmoded forms of religion and against antiquated social values, manifested the incompleteness and inadequacy of the status quo, and pointed to the power of the progressive human mind. It was in fact a partial realization that there was something more to human existence than existed in contemporary institutions. To some extent, therefore, infidelity was a source of historical and cultural progress. In this sense, Protestantism itself represented infidelity, as Brownson was defining it in the early 1830s. But, infidelity, in this meaning of the term, was the result of the exercise of human "understanding" (that is, it came from that part of the human mind that perceived only the external forms of religion); it was not the result of the exercise of "reason," which had the capacity to perceive the "idea of the holy."[49] Reason was that faculty that did not rely on the mediation of the senses but had an immediate intuitive grasp of reality that the understanding could not always reach. Though necessary for human progress, infidelity became a temporary and not a permanent phenomenon. Nonetheless, it had to be addressed in the contemporary world or the masses would begin to identify religion or Christianity with its external forms. The contemporary apologetical task, therefore, was a defense of Christianity in its essence and a search for contemporary forms and idioms that would translate that essence for the modern world.

Brownson's objective in the early 1830s was to develop an apologetic for Christianity that would meet the needs and the difficulties that unbelievers experienced, one that made Christianity not only intelligible, but desirable and applicable to the needs of all individuals. A sound apologetic had to focus upon Christianity's universal appeal and truth, but first of all it had to treat all unbelievers with charity and not as moral cripples. Unbelievers had experiences that were deeply human and the Christian apologist had to pay close attention to those experiences. It was of little value, Brownson argued, to present the authoritative historical documents that authenticate

---

[49]The use of "reason" and "understanding" in this context is certainly Coleridgean language, but the explanation of the distinction comes from Cousin in Brownson's "Remarks on G. E. E.," *Boston Observer and Religious Intelligencer* 1 (May 1835): 146-47.

the truth of Christianity; it would be much more effective to demonstrate the intrinsic truth of Christianity and show how that intrinsic truth relates to the unbelievers' fundamental human experiences: "When I propose Christianity to an unbeliever, I refer him to the workings of his own soul, to what passes in his own mind, for proofs of its truth. When I bring the evidences of a matter of fact to a man's senses, I suppose my labor of proof is done; so when I bring the proofs of a moral or religious proposition home to man's own consciousness, I suppose I have done all that can be asked of me."[50] This apologetical appeal to inner consciousness was based on Brownson's own experience of deliverance from skepticism and upon his reading of Channing, Constant and Cousin. He formulated the steps of his own apologetic in the following way: "I would begin, not with the facts of Christianity, not with the genuineness and authenticity of the Scriptures, but with the excellence of the moral precepts; from this, I would proceed to the reasonableness, then to the desirableness, and then to the truth of the doctrinal propositions."[51] The apologetic was basically a moral apologetic, demonstrating the consciousness of moral living as the center of the Christian tradition.

In "Letters to an Unbeliever," a series of essays Brownson wrote in 1832 and 1833 when he was coming out of his period of skepticism,[52] he outlined something of his own experience with unbelief. He also defined his understanding of religion, its universality, and its origin as a sentiment of the heart that needed to be distinguished from its forms. Religion arose from a natural sentiment—not from education, priestcraft, or imagination—but the sentiment originated either from revelation or instinct. Although he did not deny the role of revelation in the origin of religion, Brownson believed, at this point in his career, that a natural religious instinct provided the best explanation for the origin and universality of the religious experience. Brownson noted that these ideas were certainly similar to Constant's, but that he had developed them before he had read Constant.[53] Natural instinct could explain the universality of religion in its different forms—and this universal cultural consent of the human race became one of Brownson's primary arguments against unbelief and helped to explain how he argued himself out of infidelity.

[50]"Treatment of Unbelievers," *Christian Register* 11-12 (February 2, 1833): 18.
[51]Ibid.
[52]The "Letters" were published in *Christian Register* between October and December of 1833, and are republished in this volume.
[53]"Letters to an Unbeliever," *Christian Register* 12 (November 30, 1833): 190.

There he distinguished clearly between the religious sentiment—which was a natural instinct and therefore a "fundamental law of human nature," an irresistible feeling of awe superior to speculation that periodically overcomes doubt and unbelief—and the forms of religion, which originated in human imagination and appeared in diverse manifestations, as diverse as the humans who created them. The religious sentiment was as necessary to the soul as food and drink were necessary to the body, and its evidence as certain as that of one's own existence.

During his Walpole pastorate Brownson took up again the issue of social reforms. He perceived Christianity as a "level of reform" because it was infused with a religious sentiment that was inherently social. In revealing the character of God as Father, Jesus had demonstrated that divine love not only penetrated an individual's interior experience but instilled a responsibility for the outcast of society, especially for the poor, weak, needy, and sick. Of its very nature therefore Christianity was a reform movement, seeking to cultivate the individual mind for the benefit of the entire society. Jesus came to reform society by reforming individuals, making them sensitive to the needs of others and making them responsible for the general welfare of their society.[54]

Brownson continued to work for a variety of social reforms during his pastorate in Walpole. Although he had an aversion to benevolent societies, he supported the Walpole Temperance Society because he saw it as one way to reinforce public opinion against intemperance, which not only diseased the individual soul but contaminated the society. An address to the Society in 1833 outlined four causes of intemperance (idleness, debt, melancholy, and example), delineated the evil effects, and suggested remedies to overcome those effects. Individuals were responsible for intemperance but so were social institutions such as the credit system that maintained, promoted and profited from it. Intemperance could be overturned, therefore, not just by reforming the individual drunkard but by attacking the public support system. Temperance societies could help to change the situation by developing a strong public opinion against the institutions that profited from intemperance.[55]

[54]See "Christianity and Reform," *Unitarian* 1 (January 1834): 30-39; (February 1834): 51-58.
[55]*An Address on Intemperance. Delivered in Walpole, NH, February 26, 1833* (Neene, NH: J. & J. W. Prentiss, 1833).

Brownson also continued to support the workingmen's movement and tried to explain the causes for the rise of the Workingmen's Party. He saw that social movement as a necessary and inevitable result of democracy and a developing consciousness of equality among the working class that was consistent with the gospel. In two essays, one on the Workingmen's Party and one on social evils,[56] Brownson wrote of the rising consciousness of the working class and of the need for Christians, especially those in the ministry, to support the movement. It was clear in those two essays, though, that he saw a class war on the horizon unless the Christian ministry supported the legitimate aims of the workingmen. Education, popular and universal (not just education for the elites), was the one indispensable remedy for the social evils of the day. One could no longer accept the widely shared religious view that human beings were destined by their divinely established gifts and capacities to be forever placed into upper and lower classes in society. There were indeed different natural capacities and gifts, but that was, Brownson argued, no excuse for denying just rewards to laborers. Brownson held to a labor theory of value and reasserted the necessity of giving laborers their fair share of the profits of the rising industrial system.

Brownson's views on the necessity of social reforms, especially those reforms that would benefit the workingmen, were not widely shared and in fact were resisted by those Unitarians and others who were "hardly friends of social democracy."[57] Brownson, unlike many of the Boston Unitarian elites, was a Jacksonian democrat who emphasized social as well as political equality. To someone in the early twenty-first century Brownson's views on social equity seem harmless, but they were a radical challenge to those who perceived social inequalities to be part of the divine design.

Brownson had identified himself with the working class, sympathized with their cause, and saw American society as divided into two classes—the possessing class of powerful elites and the dispossessed class, without power and resources. The church had to stand on the side of the dispossessed—to educate them, to cultivate their minds and hearts, to reform their attitudes, but also to provide them with articulate voices and power in society. Such a view threatened some Unitarian ministers who eventually indicted Brownson as a

---

[56]"The Workingmen's Party," and "Social Evils and Their Remedy," *Unitarian* 1 (April 1834): 170-77; (May 1834): 238-44.

[57]On this, see Charles Robert Crowe, *George Ripley, Transcendentalist and Utopian Socialist* (Athens, Ga.: University of Georgia Press, 1967), 51.

social radical. While still in Walpole, however, Brownson did not meet any opposition to his social views, probably because they were not yet widely known in the Boston area.

Some Boston Unitarian ministers, however, did know, follow, and appreciate Brownson's social views and his understanding of the relationship between Christianity and social reform. George Ripley, acting editor of the *Christian Register* in 1833, was one of them. By 1833 Ripley too had called for the elevation of the working class and had supported the Unitarian ministry-at-large in Boston, a Unitarian effort, under the pioneering leadership of Joseph Tuckerman (1786-1840), to meet the religious, educational, and social needs of the poor working class in Boston.[58] On 26 March 1834, Ripley wrote to Brownson inviting him to come to Boston to serve the needs of the unchurched working class. He thought that Brownson might be able to attract those "persons who are disgusted with orthodoxy and insensible to liberal Christianity in any of its modes." He encouraged Brownson to come to Boston to preach the gospel of Jesus "in a way to meet their intellectual and moral needs." Ripley's attempt to entice Brownson to Boston appealed to Brownson's own desire to serve a larger audience than he was capable of serving in Walpole where his parishioners were primarily farmers. Brownson, according to Ripley, had "rare advantages from your former relations with skepticism, and it appears to me [that you are] designed in Providence to act upon larger and different classes of men from those to whom you now have access. A large city presents the true field of your labors where you would meet with congenial spirits, and infuse your soul into them."[59]

Ripley and Brownson had become close friends during the previous two years, but Brownson was not in a position to accept Ripley's tempting offer.[60] Brownson had been searching for a place closer to Boston for about two months and, in fact, was negotiating with a parish in Canton, Massachusetts (fourteen miles from Boston), at the time he received the Ripley letter.

---

[58]On Tuckerman, see Daniel T. McColgan, *Joseph Tuckerman: Pioneer in American Social Work* (Washington, D.C.: The Catholic University of America Press, 1940).

[59]*Early Life*, 104-6, and Brownson papers, Roll #1.

[60]In his autobiography, *Works* 5:81, Brownson acknowledged Ripley's friendship: "One man, and one man only, shared my entire confidence, and knew my most secret thought. Him, from motives of delicacy, I do not name; but, in the formation of my mind, in systematizing my ideas, and in general development and culture, I owe more to him than to any other man among Protestants."

Brownson wanted closer access to the Boston libraries and a wider field for his influence. It was also clear from the Walpole parish's testimonial letter of dismissal that "some differences in opinions" had erupted in the parish between Brownson and a few in the parish, but the nature of those differences are not evident.[61] Brownson's growing family of three sons also needed more adequate resources than the Walpole parish was able to provide. Brownson left Walpole sometime in April of 1834 and became pastor of the Unitarian parish in Canton, Massachusetts.

CANTON UNITARIAN MINISTRY, 1834 TO 1836

Brownson was installed as pastor in Canton on 14 May 1834. George Ripley preached the installation sermon, "Jesus Christ, the Same Yesterday, Today, and Forever." Perry Miller called the sermon, which Ripley repeated numerous times after Brownson's installation, "one of the finest expressions of the new doctrine."[62] The "new doctrine" was Ripley's demonstration of the necessity, universality, eternity, and immutability of religious sentiments and ideas, and the transitoriness of all human life and all human and corruptible religious forms—a perspective Brownson shared and one that he articulated clearly in an article on Benjamin Constant in the September 1834 issue of the *Christian Examiner*. Ripley told Brownson's congregation that the biblical phrases attributed to Jesus Christ did not refer to the person of Christ, who was as subject to change as all other human beings, but to the eternal ideas and religious truths that resided in his mind and which he preached with power to all who would hear. The biblical phrases did not mean that Jesus Christ was a "partaker of the Immutability which belongs to God alone."[63] It did mean, though, that his religious ideas did indeed partake of the immutability of the Divine mind from which they had emanated.[64] Brownson's choice of Ripley for this sermon indicated Brownson's unofficial membership in the new school of thought and signaled to his congregation where his ideological sympathies lay.

[61]Testimonial signed by Thomas Bellows, chairman of the parish committee, March 10, 1834. See *Early Life*, 109-10, and Brownson papers, Roll #1.

[62]*The Transcendentalists: An Anthology* (Cambridge, Mass.: Harvard University Press, 1950), 284. The sermon itself is on pp. 284-93.

[63]Ibid., 285.

[64]Ibid., 286, 290.

A number of Unitarian ministers were present at the installation. The sermon itself was consistent with the spiritual tradition of Unitarianism, but there was a germ of newness in the sermon. The seeds of a changing sensibility were clearly present in the sermon, but they had not yet been developed in ways that contravened Unitarian traditions or forms of Christian life. The Unitarian ministers who were present apparently saw nothing strange in the sermon. Adin Ballou, a former Universalist like Brownson and at the time a Unitarian minister, attended the ceremony and described it in his autobiography, but made no notice of any new spirit in Ripley's address. He did comment on Brownson, though, saying that he was a "ripe scholar, an able preacher, and a writer of rare ability." But, he complained, "in theology, metaphysics, ethics, and ecclesiasticism, his convictions, positions, and associations underwent strange vicissitudes." These comments were written long after Brownson had converted to Catholicism,[65] but they reveal a general opinion about Brownson's intellectual instability. Like Ripley and a few other young ministers of the time, Brownson was undergoing a series of changes in his intellectual and religious life, searching for a more satisfying philosophy of religion than he found available in much contemporary Unitarian thought. Like a number of others in their early thirties, he was trying to work out his own religious positions in the midst of a variety of new influences upon his life. Most importantly he and Ripley were both at the time coming under the influence of Constant and Victor Cousin.

Brownson stayed in Canton for about two years. During his Canton pastorate his wife Sarah gave birth to their fourth son, Henry Francis (born 7 August 1835). Canton was a small town of about 2000 in 1834. Boston had a population of about 78,000. In Canton Brownson had the unanimous support of his parish in 1834. He became immediately active in the community—delivering a Fourth of July address in Dedham (the Canton county seat), becoming a member of the town school board, lecturing before the Canton Lyceum, organizing a debating club for the young people of his parish, and giving addresses to youth groups in Boston as well as Canton. He also continued to write for Boston Unitarian periodicals and newspapers, finished his novel *Charles Elwood*, and began his *New Views of Christianity*, which was not published until he moved to Boston in 1836. *New Views* would establish his reputation as a principal par-

---

[65]Adin Ballou, *The Autobiography of Adin Ballou, 1803-1890* (Lowell, Mass.: The Vox Populi Press, 1896), 254-55.

ticipant in Boston intellectual circles, but before that work was published he continued to read the works of the French eclectics and to publish addresses, lecturers and sermons that revealed his emerging Romantic and Transcendentalist world view.

Brownson, a popular public lecturer, was invited almost as soon as he arrived in Canton to address the Boston Young Men's Bible Society. That April 1834 address, excerpts of which were published in the *Christian Register*,[66] concentrated on the rising generation, a new focus in Brownson's ministry. During the Canton years he put much energy in developing a new tradition among the younger generation and this speech was one of those efforts. He hoped to bring them into what he called the movement or the reform party in church and society. As he interpreted it, the Young Men's Bible Society was formed to assist the poor and his address emphasized the Christian youth's role in coming to the aid of the poor, not just by almsgiving (the way of the past) but by establishing conditions that would allow the poor to help themselves. "Christianity is emphatically a religion of the poor" and the "grand lever of reform," he told the young people, and if they were to be true to their Christian calling they had to raise the moral tone of the poor and to cultivate their minds and hearts. They could help the poor develop a sense of their own moral worth and dignity by providing them with Bibles because where the Bible and Christianity were effectively communicated reform was sure to follow.

Brownson also worked to bring the young people of his parish into the movement party by establishing a debating club within the parish and by frequently lecturing to them. One of those lectures was published and widely distributed in Canton.[67] It was based upon Matthew 6:33, "seek you first the kingdom of God." Here Brownson first asked the young people to scrutinize the great object of their own desires: pleasure, power, wealth, etc., and then spoke of what should be the ultimate desire for the Christian, the kingdom or reign of God. Young people were not to seek such a kingdom in the world beyond, but here and now, in their own hearts. The reign of God was primarily in the heart and they should learn to discern that divine presence within; they should learn to seek the "reign of his [God's] moral attributes or perfections." To come under the reign of God was to desire and love what God desires and loves. This stirring ad-

---

[66] 13 (June 28, 1834): 101; (July 5, 1834): 105; (July 19, 1834): 114.

[67] *A Sermon, Delivered to the Young People of the First Congregational* [Unitarian] *Society in Canton, on Sunday, May 24th, 1835* (Dedham, Mass.: H. Mann, Printer, 1835).

dress reflected again the influence of Channing and Constant. Young
people, like others, needed to concentrate upon the two great, inherently related concerns of Christianity: the divine within and service
to the poor.

Brownson gave other public addresses that were eventually published and distributed. Shortly after arriving in Canton, he delivered
the Fourth of July address at the County seat in Dedham, Massachusetts. He gave a barn-burner that alarmed some of his Unitarian col-
leagues in Boston who were unacquainted with his social views and
unsympathetic, to say the least, to the kind of social democracy
Brownson promoted in this address. Although many Fourth of July
addresses lectured on American freedoms and independence,
Brownson's addresses would increasingly be devoted to equality—
political, social, and economic equality or equity in American society. The Dedham address[68] acknowledged the spirit of progress behind the American Revolution and praised the development of political freedom and equality, but, he asserted, the Revolution needed
to be continued because no real social equality existed in the United
States. A new revolution was necessary to rid the country of the continuing social disparities that were indeed fostered by unjust laws
and practices in the United States. The real remedy for social inequality, though, was not legislation, but a universal education that
would raise the consciousness of freedom and equality. The entire
community, not just the elites of society, needed a formative education that developed them morally, religiously, intellectually, and physi-
cally. A truly republican education could elevate the masses and bring
about the social equity that would make America a better society and
carry out the destiny of the American Revolution.

The Unitarian editor of the *Christian Register* in 1834, David
Reed (1790-1870), took issue with the Dedham address, calling
Brownson's views of social democracy radical. The editor feared that
Brownson would use legislation to bring about the social equality he
envisioned and that his harping on social inequalities and his articu-
lation of the grievances of the lower classes would raise undue expectations. He also asserted what many believed: namely, that the divisions and separations in society were "the ordination of Providence."
Behind his critique of Brownson's address, too, lay a fear of an even-
tual class warfare between the lower and higher orders of society.[69]

---

[68]*An Address, Delivered at Dedham, on the Fifty-Eighth Anniversary of American
Independence, July 4, 1834* (Dedham, Mass.: H. Hamm, 1834).
[69]See "Mr. Brownson's Oration," *Christian Register* 14 (August 23, 1834): 6.

Brownson protested against the criticism, claiming that he was only trying to elevate the poor and not bring down the rich.[70] But, there was no doubt where Brownson's sympathies lay, and few who heard or read the address would have missed the point.

During the Canton pastorate Brownson also continued to develop his religious philosophy in conjunction with his reading of Constant and the eclectics Cousin and Théodore Jouffroy (1796-1842), one of Cousin's principal disciples. His reading of the French Romantics led him more and more in the direction of what would become Transcendentalism. The most significant publication of his religious philosophy during the Canton period was his review of Benjamin Constant's *De la religion*, published in the *Christian Examiner*, one of the chief journals of Unitarian opinion.[71] Constant helped Brownson to systematize the direction his thought had taken since 1831 and provided Brownson with a language, a clarity, and historical evidence for understanding the distinction between religious sentiment and religious forms.[72]

Certainly, the distinction between religious sentiment and religious forms had surfaced in "Christianity and Reform," "Social Evils and Their Remedy," and "Spirituality of Religion," but in "Benjamin Constant *on Religion*" he clearly and systematically defined the differences. Brownson's distinction adumbrated the more famous and more radical 1841 Transcendentalist essay by Theodore Parker on "The Transient and the Permanent in Christianity."[73] The distinction served many purposes for Brownson. It helped to demonstrate the reason for the universality of religious experience, the variety of the different historical religious traditions and institutions, and the progressive movements within history to purify, transform, and improve the forms and institutions of religion by adapting them to the cultural and ideological advances of various nations. For Brownson the interior religious sentiment "determined" human beings to the worship and veneration of God. It was a fundamental law of human nature, "a law [that was] invariable, eternal, indestructible."[74] The history of religion, as Constant had demonstrated, was, in a nutshell, a history of the breakdown of the "variable and transitory" forms of

[70]"Letter to Rev. Mr. R[ipley]," *Christian Register* 14 (August 30, 1834): 10.

[71]"Benjamin Constant *on Religion*," *Christian Examiner and General Review* 17 (September 1834): 63-77.

[72]On his self-confessed debt to Constant, see *Works* 5:70-74.

[73]See Theodore Parker, *A Discourse on the Transient and Permanent in Christianity . . . May 19, 1841* (Boston: Printed by the Author, 1841).

[74]"Benjamin Constant on Religion," 64.

the religious sentiment.[75] It was not only permanent but progressive and manifested itself in three distinct historical stages of development: (1) human beings establish a religion by giving the sentiment a regular and determinate form; (2) eventually the forms (e.g., old religious institutions and formulas of the faith) lose their life and inevitably a conflict arises within the religious institution between the progressive religious sentiment and the forms; (3) the conflict ultimately annihilates the old forms, bringing about a crisis of complete unbelief; but the crisis is always followed by new forms of religious ideas that are better suited to the faculties of the progressive human mind, and "religion comes forth from its ashes, with a new youth, purer, and more beautiful."[76] And so the process continues in an ever more purifying direction. Judaism and Christianity, the monotheist traditions, are the highest development of this process, but even in Christianity, which is the religious sentiment itself,[77] stages of development exist. Catholicism represented the first historical stage, Protestantism the second, and the third stage is manifested in the contemporary groping for new religious institutions that transcend both Protestantism and Catholicism in the attempt to obey the religious sentiment more perfectly than in the past. This search for a new religious form would occupy Brownson until early 1842, and would be systematically diagramed for the first time in his *New Views of Christianity* (1836). But, there was no doubt that during his Canton pastorate he was already moving in that direction, under the influence of Constant.

Two other French influences were evident during the Canton period. His published articles reveal that he was increasingly coming under the influence of Victor Cousin and Théodore Jouffroy although he did not write an explicit review of their works until September of 1836 and May of 1837 respectively.[78] Like Cousin and Jouffroy, he criticized the materialism and rationalism of the Enlightenment and sought within the soul the source of all life and thought. Moreover, like Cousin, he tried to discover a way of reconciling the spiritual and the material orders of existence, seeking a synthesis in life as well as in thought. The subject of the reconciliation of the two orders, in fact, became a dominant concern in the essays he published during these years.

[75]Ibid., 65.
[76]Ibid., 67.
[77]Ibid., 70.
[78]"Cousin's Philosophy," *Christian Examiner and Gospel Review* 21 (September, 1836): 33-64; "Jouffroy's Contributions to Philosophy," *Christian Examiner and Gospel Review* 22 (May, 1837): 181-217.

As already mentioned, Cousin had a significant influence upon Brownson's philosophical development in the mid-1830s. In fact, of the generation of young men who eventually became Transcendentalists, Brownson was a major player in communicating Cousin's eclectic philosophy to American intellectuals.[79] Brownson's writings for 1834 and 1835 do not come to grips explicitly with Cousin's philosophy, but there is evidence that he was applying Cousin's eclecticism to the issues of belief and unbelief.[80] In trying to explain his own definition of infidelity (as the rejection of inadequate or outdated religious forms), for example, Brownson used Cousin to distinguish between the religious ideal and its historical realization, arguing that no one rejected religion as an ideal; the infidel rejected only the false or misleading manifestations of religion. That rejection alone constituted unbelief or infidelity. Using Cousin, he argued that the "idea of the holy" existed within absolute or impersonal reason. This idea of the holy was ideal, subjective, "inseparable from the being we call man," and thus invariable, eternal, indestructible.

The ideal, however, had a tendency to realize itself in some form, outward expression, or symbol. The form itself was constructed by the human understanding (not reason), and "constitutes religion for the understanding, as the idea of the holy constitutes religion for the reason."[81] Religion, as it related to the understanding, was changing, variable, and inherently progressive as it attempted to realize ever more perfectly the idea of the holy in history. Infidelity, for Brownson, related to the rejection of historical forms, symbols, and institutional manifestations of the religious idea. It was only the outward form or the ideological construction of religion that could be rejected; infidelity never struck at the ideal. But, infidelity was a necessary movement within history to destroy worn-out forms of religion and to purify and develop the idea of the holy in history. The infidel's dissent was a manifestation, moreover, of the freedom of the human mind in its progressive movement to seek the truth.

By 1834 and 1835, as was evident in earlier paragraphs, Brownson used Samuel Taylor Coleridge's (1772-1834) distinction between "rea-

[79]On this, see René Wellek, "The Minor Transcendentalists and German Philosophy," and Georges J. Joyaux, "Victor Cousin and American Transcendentalism," both of which are reprinted in *American Transcendentalism: An Anthology of Criticism*, ed. Brian M. Barbour (Notre Dame: University of Notre Dame Press, 1973), 103-24; 125-38.

[80]On this, see in particular "Remarks on G. E. E.," *The Boston Observer and Religious Intelligencer* 1 (May 7, 1835): 146-47.

[81]Ibid., 147.

son" and "understanding," emphasizing the priority of reason in the immediate or intuitive grasp of the idea of the holy. Brownson had read some of Coleridge's poetry in the early 1830s, as is evident in this volume, but, as far as I am aware, he never explicitly referred to the distinction as it was articulated in James Marsh's (1794-1842) edition of Coleridge's *Aids to Reflection* (1829). More than likely Brownson had read *Aids* and in September of 1836, as a charter member of the so-called Transcendentalist Club, he took part in a discussion of *Aids* and of the Coleridgean distinction.[82] Throughout the early 1830s he used the Coleridgean language, but increasingly he came to fill that language with Cousinian content and would in the period after 1836 reject the American appropriations of the Coleridgean distinction, especially as they were found in Emerson's writings. After 1836 he preferred Cousin's distinction between spontaneous reason and reflective reason, as two modes of the operation of one and the same reason.

Cousin as well as Constant, moreover, had supplied Brownson with a philosophical perspective for making intelligible much of modern Christian history, especially history since the Protestant Reformation. As he tried to interpret Christian history in the Cousinian-Hegelian dialectic, he looked for a new historical synthesis in the struggle between Protestantism (a form of infidelity) and Catholicism. That project, however, became the explicit objective of his Boston period. While he remained in Canton, these ideas were simply germinating in his mind and occasionally broke forth in an essay here and there.

Both "Essays for Believers and Disbelievers" and "Remarks on G. E. E." reveal that the issue of unbelief remained foremost in Brownson's mind and that Constant and Cousin were helping him come to terms with the issue. In the "Essays," in fact, Brownson applied Cousin's eclecticism to the systems of belief and unbelief, seeking to affirm what both believers and unbelievers affirmed and to deny what they denied. Brownson argued that both believers and unbelievers affirmed some truth, but not the whole truth, and that both needed to be attune to the feelings and perspectives of the other. Following Cousin, Brownson asserted that infidelity, like belief, was founded in human nature. The Christian could learn something of the truth and of human nature from the infidel just as the infidel could learn from the believer.

---

[82]See Frederick Henry Hedge's recollection of that meeting in James Elliot Cabot, *A Memoir of Ralph Waldo Emerson* (Boston and New York: Houghton, Mifflin and Co., 1887), 244-45.

Brownson identified the infidels with the movement party in contemporary society because they were governed by a sentiment of the insufficiency of the present. The believers belonged to the stationary party because they were generally satisfied with the status quo and abhorred change, and because they thought it better to submit to what is painful in the present insufficiencies than to hazard the good by attempting to remove them. Brownson's division of the world into these two ideological models helped him, moreover, to explain historical developments of religion.

Brownson was so fascinated by his ideological models that he thought of writing an entire history of unbelief, and in fact, as stated above, in 1832 he had started writing a manuscript on infidelity. In April of 1835, he wrote Abner Kneeland (1774-1844), editor of the *Boston Investigator* and a former Universalist who had by this time disassociated himself from organized Christianity, that he was preparing for publication a philosophical history of "modern infidelity," a project that Brownson never published.[83]

Brownson's understanding of social reform was also maturing during his Canton period. Much like William Ellery Channing, Brownson saw the cultivation and education of the individual mind as the primary means for social regeneration. Reform of the individual was the best method of reforming society as a whole. Alongside this emphasis on the individual, however, was a parallel movement in his thought—one that emphasized the need to change social structures that impeded the progress of individual and social reform. Although, like Channing, Brownson emphasized individual self-cultivation, he could not limit himself to it as the sole means of reform because he knew since the days of his association with the workingmen's movement that there were societal structural problems (like the credit system) that could not be reformed solely by self-culture. Structural abuses demanded more than personal reform. This emphasis on the social structures of human existence, already evident in "Progress of Society,"[84] would eventually sublate his individualism and modify it to such an extent after 1836 that he would gradually separate himself from Channing's dominating influence. The emphasis on the social dimension would also eventually separate Brownson from the individualism of some Transcendentalists

---

[83]"Correspondence," *Boston Investigator* 4 (April 17, 1835): 157. On Kneeland, see Russell E. Miller, *The Larger Hope: The First Century of the Universalist Church in America, 1770-1870* (Boston: Unitarian Universalist Association, 1979), 185-96.

[84]*Christian Examiner and General Review* 18 (July, 1835): 345-68.

like Ralph Waldo Emerson and Henry David Thoreau (1817-62). During the Canton period, however, his views of the impact of social structures were unsystematic and undeveloped.

Toward the beginning of 1836, as Brownson was contemplating a move to Boston, Henry Thoreau, a nineteen-year-old Harvard student who needed a break from his studies, came to Canton to teach before finishing his college education. He stayed there about six weeks. While there he attended some of Brownson's lectures and sermons, read German with Brownson, and entered into some long conversations that were perhaps the subject of Brownson's *New Views*. This experience with Brownson was, by Thoreau's own later admission, memorable.[85] It is strange, however, that Brownson never, as far as I know, explicitly reviewed any of Thoreau's works once Thoreau became a distinguished American author—strange because Brownson generally reviewed the works of prominent American authors.

Brownson had been well received in 1834 when he began his Canton pastorate and his ministry had generally been successful. A year later, however, a minority of ten members of the parish, those most under the influence of Calvinism (according to his successor), voted against retaining him as pastor. He had a way of irritating people and always spoke his mind without consideration of the consequences. Whether or not he had alienated some of his parishioners, he was himself itching to get to Boston where he would have a wider field of influence. He had been invited there in 1834 and again in 1836.[86] Even though he had the support of the majority in his parish, he wanted to leave Canton, he told the parish committee, because of "my pecuniary embarrassments."[87] His growing family of four young boys, no doubt, needed greater resources than he was able to command at Canton, where he received a salary of $700 a year. By the end of May 1836 he had moved his family to Mount Bellingham, Chelsea, Massachusetts, across the Charles River from Boston, to take on a new effort to reach the unchurched working class in Boston.

The editorial principles and procedures for this volume are the same as those for volume one.[88]

[85]On Thoreau's relationship with Brownson at Canton, see Kenneth Walter Cameron, "Thoreau and Orestes Brownson," *Emerson Society Quarterly* 51 (1968): 53-74, especially 61-65 for Cameron's construction of an imaginary conversation between the two men.

[86]*Works* 5:82.

[87]On Brownson's relationship with the Canton parish and on his reasons for leaving, see Kenneth W. Cameron, "Thoreau and Orestes Brownson," 60.

[88]On the editorial principles, see EW, 1:30-34.

WORKS

1.

PROSPECTUS OF THE GENESEE REPUBLICAN AND HERALD OF REFORM[1]

New York Daily Sentinel (July 17, 1830)[2]

TO THE PUBLIC

Fellow Citizens: In coming before you with a moral and political journal, it is due to you and to ourselves to state explicitly our objects and the rules by which you may expect us to be governed.

The farmer, the mechanic, and the working man, after ages of patient submission to the burdens imposed upon them by the privileged orders, have at length awaked. Casting their eyes around and surveying the condition of society, they ask, "Why have we, who are the many, been made to bow at the feet of the few? Why have we toiled, and, others reaped the fruits of our labors? Why is it those who labor not are rich, while we are poor—respected while we are despised—honored and caressed while we are trampled to the earth we cultivate? Why is the sigh of poverty heard in the midst of wealth? Why in the midst of plenty does want writhe his haggard brow?"

These may be startling questions to the privileged few. They are big with meaning; they are put with emphasis; they will not be withdrawn till the wrongs which have extorted them be redressed. The working men have suffered; their rights have been abridged; their interests have been betrayed and neglected. They have discovered it and resolved no longer to endure it. They have too long trusted to others, hereafter they will take the management of affairs in their

---

[1][Ed. A weekly paper Brownson published and edited at Le Roy, Genesee County, New York, from July to November of 1830. The paper continued from November of 1830 to at least August of 1831, but under the sole proprietorship of Henry S. Freeman, Brownson's co-owner during its first six months of existence. The prospectus here should be compared to the much shorter one published in the *Genesee Republican and Herald of Reform* (August 18, 1830): 4. The shorter one is even more egalitarian than the one republished here. It is not clear why there are two separate editions of the prospectus for the paper.]

[2][Ed. Brownson was associated with the *Daily Sentinel* in 1830 and had the prospectus for his paper regularly published in the New York paper in exchange for publishing its prospectus.]

own hands, and attend to their own interests. Powerful from their numbers, strong in the justness of their cause, they are no longer to be met with trifles, or lulled to sleep by flattering speeches. They have aroused in behalf of suffering humanity, and they will not rest till their object is accomplished.

Their objects are neither trivial nor few. They bring forward measures of important bearing. Their aim is high. They seek not palliatives—ask not to be amused by lopping the branches of the tree of evil. They would strike deep to its root, and having brushed it, trunk and branch, out of the way, they would build up social order on a solid and lasting basis. They aim high; they would regenerate society, destroy its anti-social institutions, banish its artificial distinctions, and make of mankind but one class—that of human beings.

Even in this republican country, honest industry is viewed rather as a badge of servitude, as a low calling; and almost every boy, soon as old enough to look around, is enquiring for some means to live by his wits, and not by his hands. Hence it is that all professions are crowded—the land deluged with lawyers, priests, doctors, bankers and speculators, who rack their invention to discover means to live on the sweat of others' brow. Hence the burden under which the people groan—hence the cry of distress—of hard times.

The evil is a great one; to remove it is the object of the working-men in the spirited efforts they have commenced. They want that rank to which their importance to community entitles them. But they are aware that without education, equal to that which the non-productive classes received, they would not be able to maintain it were they to claim it. Hence their first measure is a system of equal education—a system that will "train up in the way they should go" [Prov. 22:6], alike the child of the poor man and of the rich—that will provide for the equal maintenance and instruction of all the children of the state—educate, side by side, under the same roof, the child of your first magistrate, with the child of your poorest working man—the widow's charge and the unprotected orphan. Let all the children of the state be trained to the same habits of industry—bred in the discharge of the same moral duties; let the child of the workingman have the same opportunity to obtain knowledge and respectability as has the child of the wealthy citizen, and useful industry will lose that badge of servitude and degradation which it has so long worn, and all would pursue it, no less for pleasure than for interest, we should then have an intelligent and virtuous community. Our republic would be safe, and our example would triumphantly refute the often repeated slander, "man is incapable of self-government."

The workingmen have suffered from monopolies; they cannot believe that it is consistent with the genius of our government to allow an individual, or a number of individuals to accumulate wealth under the sanction of the law, when the same law forbids others to pursue the same course. Whatever state physicians may allege to the contrary, all laws, to be just, should be equal in their operation; protecting the rights of all—granting special favors to none. The workingmen declare against all monopolies; they require that every just and honorable pursuit should be open to every citizen who chooses to follow it; and that all of a different description should be tolerated by the law in favor of none. This, it is intended, the legislature shall remember.

Another measure we shall advocate is the abolishment of imprisonment for debt. Our statute books have been too long disgraced with that barbarian law. Humanity calls loudly for its repeal. It does no good; it makes the unfortunate debtor more unfortunate, and benefits not the creditor. We shall also advocate the abolition of all laws for the collection of debts; leaving every man to his debtor's sense of honor. The credit system which now keeps us in this county one or two years behind hand, would be broken up; and enough would be saved, in time and costs now occasioned by lawsuits, to defray the expenses of a system of state education for all the children of the state.

We shall oppose the machinery now in use among politicians, to deceive or control the people. We dislike the caucus system; it is essentially aristocratic, and only answers to enable a few political "trimmers" to control a county, a state, and the nation. We wish the people to select their own candidates, and every elector select for himself. This might not build up a party, but it would give the voice of the people. But as long as a few men in Albany and New York are able to cut out our politics and control our suffrages by the magic influence of the caucus system, it is vain to talk of liberty.

Another measure we shall advocate is that our representatives and all intrusted with the administration of public affairs should be chosen from the useful classes—should have interests in common with the great body of the people—should be men who will regard those interests; who will remember they are the agents—not the masters of the people—who will understand their duty to be, not to tell us what laws we must have, but to make such as we tell them we want. Our officers have been prone to forget these plain republican maxims, and chosen, as they have usually been, from the non-productive classes, they forget, with particular injury to the workingmen.

Such, fellow citizens, are some of the measures we shall advocate—measures which, in our estimation, involve the great interests of the nation—measures which strike deep; and which, in their operation, will have an important bearing upon the present, and all future ages. We have heard of reform, but where is it? Farmers, mechanics, and workingmen of Genesee, you have been noted for your high toned democracy, for the spirit with which you have uniformly resisted whatever you deemed an invasion of your rights; behold now a subject which may give full play to all the noble energies of your minds, and to all the republicanism of your hearts—you are called upon to support measures for which ages yet unborn will bedew your names with tears of gratitude for having supported them. You are called upon to aid a reform nobly commenced, which if once completed will render man universally enlightened, free and able to sit down in peace with his brother.

In reference to existing parties, we have only to say, our object is to promote the interests of the nation, without regard to sect or party. The interests of the workingmen we believe to be the interests of the nation. Ours is, therefore, a working man's paper, and will fearlessly advocate the working man's interest, let him belong to what party he may. We shall cooperate with either of the existing parties, so far as they advocate our measures; further than that, no party will receive our aid.

With religion we shall not interfere. We wish to leave every man to the full enjoyment of his own religious views and feelings. It is a subject on which good citizens do and may differ. To avoid contention, the only way we know, is to keep religion out of politics, and leave it to its appointed guardians. Our paper is not designed for religious discussions and will meddle with no man's creed, except it perceive that creed abridging some fellow citizen's rights. The clergy we shall treat with respect, though we shall not advocate Dr. Ely's[3] Christian Party in politics, nor the project of stopping the Sabbath mail.

Fellow citizens, we come not to make war against what you deem sacred, and dear to your hearts, as you have dreamed. We come with the olive branch of peace; appealing to your best and noblest feelings, we entreat you calmly and dispassionately to enquire if we can-

---

[3][Ed. On Ezra Stiles Ely, see my Introduction to EW, 1:21-22.]

not, after so many ages of suffering, find out the means of making society virtuous, and man happy. Relying on the patronage of genuine republicans, disguised by whatever name they may be, we give the Genesee Republican and Herald of Reform to the public, confident of its success and the final triumph of the cause it advocates.

2.

NECESSITY OF REFORM. NO. 2

Genesee Republican and Herald of Reform
1 (August 18, 1830): 1

As Reformer closed his remarks, as given by our last, he was startled by the twang of a new voice. Publicus, unobserved by Reformer had edged himself into the room and had been listening with both ears open.

Publicus is about a third rate attorney—though, thanks to his partner, he is considered something more. He is about thirty years of age, of full middling size, very prominent bones, a crooked and somewhat shaking figure, of a dark and lowering complexion, a black, but spiteful eye, none of the horse or alligator, but a little spice of the "snapping turtle." His *tout ensemble* is far from prepossessing, and a physiognomist would pronounce him a compound of about equal quantities of avarice, ambition, vanity, meanness, aristocratic feeling and conscious inferiority; some talent in the chicanery of his profession, ready to discover little flaws, full of large words and trifles, pretending to be a great man, and set down by all the discerning as being rather small. He has held some town office and for his zeal in behalf of an unprincipled faction, which has disgraced our country, he is expecting to have a snug birth next winter at Albany. He will doubtless obtain it, for he is a proper representative of the party to which he is devoted. He had listened to Reformer till his blood began to boil, for though his heart is as cold as a frosty night in January, his blood does sometimes get heated.

Publicus. Mr. Reformer, your remarks betray nothing but a heated fancy and a wild enthusiasm. You are a restless demagogue, laboring to excite the people with bombastic descriptions of imaginary evils. You want an insurrection, you are concocting a conspiracy against our government, you are inflaming the minds of the people, stirring them up to sedition, merely to disorganize the social compact to gratify your own diabolical malignity. You are a dangerous man in community and ought to be lashed by every man who regards the welfare of his country.

Reformer. Ha, Publicus, in what sly corner were you concealed, that I did not discover you? You start too rapid, I'm afraid you will lag before you get to the end of your race. Use a little economy of your strength, it will last the longer. Why, what is the matter? Why does your brow contract, and such venom spit from your eye? Don't shake so. What! Hast a fit of the ague? Little quinine perhaps would be good.

Publicus. Reformer, I am out of all patience. You want to introduce misrule, disorganize everything, involve us in all the evils of anarchy. I can hear it no longer. Love to my country.

Reformer. Love to your country! By my stars, if I am not disposed to be merry. Who ever suspected you of the unnatural crime of loving your country? Heavens! I should as quick suspect the Old Man below turned missionary, and in good faith laboring to convert souls for heaven.

Publicus. Merry or not, just as you please, I tell you, community ought to check your extravagance by the strong arm of the law and let you know their government has power to prevent the promulgation of doctrines fraught with destruction to everything wise or just.

Reformer. Now Publicus you talk like yourself. Would [you] like a fee perhaps for obtaining my conviction of conspiracy in a court of justice? You would make a most eloquent speech! How delightfully you would spit out your words! How amusing it would be to an audience! How the judges would admire your profound views as a statesman! Good, Publicus, can you not stir up some friend to *good order* to commence a prosecution against me?

Publicus. You may spare your sarcasms. If John Adams' Gag Law[1] was only in force, you would get your desserts very soon. But what is it you want? Our country was never more prosperous. We are at war with no nation; internal as well as external tranquility is maintained. Our commerce flourishes; our manufactures are increasing in value and extent; colleges are founded; schools are established—learning encouraged; what more do you want?

Reformer. I want to see the people happy.

Publicus. They are happy—what nation is more so.

Reformer. Perhaps we are less *miserable* than any other nation; but that does not prove that we are happy, or there is no need of improving our condition.

[1][Ed. Brownson is probably referring to the Alien and Sedition Acts of 1798, passed by Congress under President John Adams' term. One of those acts, passed on July 14, imposed severe penalties on those who criticized the government and thereby condemned "any false, scandalous and malicious writing."]

Publicus. To talk of a happy people is mere nonsense. There never was and there never can be, a happy people. There is no misery to speak of, in this country, and I do wish you would cease your babblings. Who wants to hear the eternal croak of the raven or endless hoot of the owl?

Reformer. If certain sounds offend you it might be well to keep out of hearing. You intimate we have little or no misery in this country, and yet call it nonsense to talk of a happy people. Sir, I must admire your consistency. You say there never can be a happy people; I suppose the future lies open to your view, and you know all that can transpire during the undefined ages yet to come. In the time of our revolution, the Tories said we could not gain our independence, that it was folly to contend against the gigantic power of Britain. But Washington, Jefferson and others, did not regard their prophecies. They asked what was right, they fastened their eyes on the desired object; they nerved themselves to the work—they conquered—they triumphed. Had they adhered to the cowardly croakings of the Tories, what were we now? Vassals to a transatlantic tyrant. Had I lived then, I would have been foremost in the battles for liberty, and I shall not cease my exertions in behalf of man because a little attorney says I cannot succeed. You may call me enthusiastic, call me what you please. I believe mankind can become happy, that they can become like a band of brothers, entwined with the cords of fraternal affection, living in peace and mutual felicity. I believe it, and I will labor to accomplish it. If I fail, I fail in a noble cause. If I am condemned by my contemporaries, I will find my reward in the approbation of my heart.

Publicus. You may give your lectures and write as many declamations on the degeneracy of the times as you please. But why meddle with politics? What business have *you* to interfere with the measures of government?

Reformer. Sir, I am a man. I am a citizen of this country. I have an interest in it. Its government declares me equal to any other man—aye, equal to the biggest of you. You, sir, with all your professional dignity, can claim no more from government than I can. If it give you the least iota more than it does me, it departs from its first principles, and commences its march in the road to tyranny. Do you ask why I interfere with politics? Why do *you* interfere? What right have you to meddle with those things in preference to me?

Publicus. Reformer, I am not to be insulted. I shall not state the superior grounds I have for concerning myself with politics. You could not appreciate them, if I should. But what is this mighty wrong in politics, you harp so much about?

Reformer. I want correct public measures adopted. I want men entrusted with the administration of public affairs, who will be the agents of the people, not their masters; who will sanction laws for the good of the whole, not for a few; who will seek the greatest happiness of the greatest number not of a few monopolists. I want the interests of the farmer, of the mechanic, and the workingman protected, instead of building up a monied aristocracy.

Publicus. But their interests are regarded. The farmer, mechanic, and workingman are a majority of the nation, if they have not had their interests protected, the fault is their own.

Reformer. Granted the fault is their own. They have the power to correct it, and I wish to persuade them to do it. Hence one reason why I meddle with politics. The great body of the people have too long trusted such men as you; who, when you want their votes, will call them the "bone and sinew of the land," and a great many other pretty names—promise to protect them, till you get elected, and then—and then, what? Aye, what? You go to the legislative halls, you make long speeches, pass three or four hundred laws, couched in such ambiguous phrase that the most talented among us cannot understand them without a seven years laborious study—you make your session an electioneering campaign, and canvass, in each speech you make, in each measure you support, votes for your re-election, or for the election of some friend you promised to support next year if he would support you this. You forget the people—squander their money—ruin your country, and then say you have worn out your life in the service of your fellow citizens. You ask what do I want. I want the people to tell such men they may stay at home—their services are not wanted. I want they should elect men of plain, practical good sense, who have feelings and interests in common with the great body of their constituents. This they have heretofore neglected. I ask them to neglect it no longer. I press it home upon them. Their own interest forbids them to neglect it longer.

Look, sir, at our legislatures, what law have they passed for years that is not a damage to the country? An intelligent member of the Senate of this State said he would take his oath, he sincerely believed every bill for which he had voted was injurious to his constituents, and he was so fully convinced of the corruption and iniquity practiced by our representatives that he will no longer accept a seat in any of our legislative bodies. The patrimony of this State which, under wise management, would have made us independent for years, has

been squandered, the State is almost bankrupt and our last legislature called for a tax to support the ordinary expenses of government.
Where have gone the State funds? Look at your colleges and schools
for your rich and [man-] made nurseries of aristocracy[2]—look to the
amount squandered for toys and to reward public defaulters. The
reward to Myron Holley[3] is a specimen of the wisdom and faithfulness of our agents. A public defaulter, who had speculated with the
public monies, has granted him the very lands he purchased with
money belonging to the State. There he lives in luxury on the fruit of
his iniquity. How great is the amount for which the credit of the
State stands pledged, to aid monopolists in building canals, etc., I
need not particularize. There is not a single law in our statute books
that is exclusively for the benefit of the poor, while hundreds can be
pointed out for the benefit of the rich. This you call right? The rich,
who are able to protect themselves, must have the aid of the law to do
it more efficiently; while the poor who cannot help themselves; why,
poor devils, they shall find none to help them. Such is the spirit by
which our agents have been actuated—to help those who can live
without it, and neglect those who need help. Half of the session last
winter was spent in chartering banks, and discussing measures for
the benefit of the monied aristocracy, but no time could be found to
repeal the barbarous law for imprisonment for debt.

[2][Ed. Sentence unclear from the original.]
[3][Ed. Holley (1779-1841) practiced law for a short time in upstate New York
and then left the practice and was elected to the New York General Assembly in
1816. He also became involved in purchasing land for the Erie Canal and later
some charged him with mismanagement of state funds for personal gain.]

3.

COMMON SCHOOLS

Genesee Republican and Herald of Reform
1 (August 18, 1830): 1

I must ask my readers to turn back to our last number and note particularly an article on "Juvenile Books," copied from the *Cayuga Patriot*.[1] It will be found to contain some valuable suggestions, stated in the usual clear and forcible manner of the editor of that able, and, in general well-conducted paper. Mr. Doubleday[2] has paid no little attention to the subject of education and his observations are generally correct. I wish for a different system of schools, or rather, I wish our schools organized on a different plan from what they are now, but I am not indifferent to the practical improvements which may be introduced into our present system. Our common schools might be made far more advantageous to children than they are, if a little attention were paid to the development of the intellectual powers and the best methods of instruction adopted.

The first and most obvious error that strikes us in our common schools is the injudicious selection of teachers. The station of schoolmaster is important, much more depends on him than people are aware. To trust our children to the care of a man who has no knowledge but a mere acquaintance with *sounds*—who knows little of the human heart, who knows nothing about the means of kindling the fire of intellect in the young scholar, and giving him a thirst for knowledge—who can do nothing more than repeat to the child the words his master repeated to him—whose moral character is problematical and whose sole desire to be a school teacher is to find an easier employment than to drive through the snows and storms of winter at the usual occupation of farmers or laborers—to trust our children to such a man is not very wise, yet such are the majority of our school teachers. Boys 18 or 20 years old, whose minds have never been developed, who have all the wildness and giddiness of that period, are

---

[1][Ed. See *Cayuga Patriot* 17 (August 4, 1830): 3.]

[2][Ed. Ulysses F. Doubleday was editor of the *Cayuga Patriot* and was the former publisher of the *Gospel Advocate and Impartial Investigator*, which Brownson edited in 1829 and which was united to the *Cayuga Patriot* after Brownson left the paper.]

not calculated to be very good guardians of children nor are they likely to advance them in useful knowledge, yet such we employ, for we can usually employ them *cheap*. This error should be corrected. Persons selected who have experience, who have the knowledge and the faculties to lead children through the paths of science with ease and rapidity. Give sufficient encouragement to such men to make it a business and they will easily be found.

Another error of no small magnitude is the character of the books we put into the hands of our children. Anyone may mark how readily a child listens to a story told in terms he can understand. All children love to learn; they are pleased with novelty and anyone may notice with what animation a child receives a new idea. The great art of teaching is to bring our lessons to the comprehension of the pupils. But when we put into the hands of a child a book he does not understand, from which he can receive no idea, need we wonder he soon loathes the book and prefers the animation of play? The *English Reader*[3] is a book very much used in common schools. It has good lessons, fine language and noble sentiments, but what can a child ten years old understand of it? The same objection is made to most of our school books. They are above the capacity of the learner. The books Mr. D. mentions are in general free from this objection.

There is a great mistake in the mode of teaching usually adopted in our schools. The memory is almost the only faculty exercised, whereas it should be the least. The habit of attention and of reflection is what is most needed and should be most labored by the teacher. The scholars are kept too long on the spelling lessons, when they learn nothing only a mechanical succession of sounds which they forget the moment they find the words in another place and with a different arrangement. But I must [words indecipherable] I [have] to offer on this subject til my next.[4]

[3][Ed. Lindley Murray (1745-1826) edited the *English Reader* (New York: Isaac Collins, 1799, and many subsequent editions).]

[4][Ed. There are no extant copies of the subsequent issues of the *Genesee Republican* that Brownson edited.]

4.

PUBLIC EDUCATION. ESSAY 6

Genesee Republican and Herald of Reform
1 (August 18, 1830): 1

The system of public education, then, which we consider capable, and only capable, of regenerating this nation, and of establishing practical virtue and republican equality among us, is one which provides for all children at all times; receiving them at the earliest age their parents chose to entrust them to the national care, feeding, clothing, and educating them, until the age of majority.

We propose that all the children so adopted should receive the same food; should be dressed in the same simple clothing; should experience the same kind treatment; should be taught (until their professional education commences) the same branches; in a word, that nothing savoring of inequality, nothing reminding them of the pride of riches or the contempt of poverty, should be suffered to enter these republican safeguards of the young nation of equals. We propose that the destitute widow's child or the orphan boy should share the public care equally with the heir to a princely estate; so that all may become not in word but in deed and in feeling free and equal.

Thus may the spirit of democracy, that spirit which Jefferson labored for half a century to plant in our souls, become universal among us; thus may luxury, may pride, may ignorance be banished from among us; and we may become, what fellow citizens ought to be, a nation of brothers.

We propose that the food should be of the simplest kind, both for the sake of economy and of temperance. A Spartan simplicity of regimen is becoming a republic and is best suited to preserve the health and strength unimpaired, even to old age. We suggest the propriety of excluding all distilled or fermented liquors of every description; perhaps, also, foreign luxuries such as tea and coffee might be beneficially dispensed with. These, including wine and spirits, cost the nation at present about *fourteen millions* of dollars annually. Are they worth so much?

Thus might the pest of our land, intemperance, be destroyed—not discouraged, not lessened, not partially cured—but *destroyed*[;]

this modern Cicre[1] that degrades the human race below the beast of the field, that offers her poison [word indecipherable] at every corner of our streets and at every turn of our highways, that sacrifices her tens of thousands of victims yearly in these states, that loads our country with a tax more than sufficient to pay twice over for the virtuous training of all her children—might thus be deposed from the foul sway she exercises over freemen, too proud to yield to a foreign enemy, but not too proud to bow beneath the iron rod of a domestic curse. Is there *any* other method of tearing up this monstrous evil, the scandal of our republic, root and branch?

We propose that the dress should be some plain, convenient, economical uniform. The silliest of all vanities (and one of the most expensive) is the vanity of dress. Children trained to the age of twenty-one without being exposed to it, could not, in after life be taught such a folly. But learnt as it now is, from the earliest infancy, do we find that the most faithful preaching checks or reforms it?

The food and clothing might be chiefly raised and manufactured by the pupils themselves, in the exercise of their several occupations. They would thus acquire a taste for articles produced in their own country, in preference to foreign superfluities.

Under such a system the poorest parents could afford to pay a moderate tax for each child. They could better afford it than they can now to support their children in ignorance and misery, *provided* the tax were less than the lowest rate at which a child can now be maintained at home. For a day school thousands of parents can afford to pay nothing.

We do not propose that anyone should be compelled to send a child to these public schools, if he or she saw fit to have them educated elsewhere. But we propose that the tax should be paid by all parents, whether they send their children or not.

We are convinced, that under such a system, the pupils of the state schools would obtain the various offices of public trust, those of representatives, etc. in preference to any others. If so, public opinion would soon induce the most rich and the most prejudiced to send their children thither; however little they might at first relish the idea of giving them *equal* advantages only with those of the poorest class. *Greater real advantages* they could not give them, if the public schools are conducted as they ought to be.

---

[1] [Ed. Cicre was an enchantress described in the *Odyssey* who detained Odysseus for a year and turned his men into swine.]

We propose that the teachers should be eligible by the people. There is no office of trust in a republic, more honorable or more important, nor any that more immediately influences its destinies, than the office of a teacher. They ought to be chosen—and if we read the signs of the times aright, they *will* be chosen with as much, nay, more care than our representatives. The office of General Superintendent of public schools will be, in our opinion, an office at least as important as that of president.

At present the best talent of the country is devoted to the study of law; because a lawyer has hitherto had the best chance for political honors and preferment. Let the honor of teacher be equally honored and preferred; and men will turn from a trade whose professors live by the quarrels of mankind to an occupation which should teach men for the honor of reform to live without quarreling.

5.

CAYUGA PATRIOT

Genesee Republican and Herald of Reform
1 (August 18, 1830): 2

The editor of the Cayuga Patriot, says we advocate the "abolition of all laws for the collection of debts."[1] We do. Our reasons, more fully than heretofore, will be given in our next. He says we "contend the state ought to maintain and educate all the children." In the unqualified manner he makes the statement he does not give our views correctly. We contend equal education is the right of all, that individual happiness demands it, and the perpetuity of our free institutions, without it, is a dream; that it is the business of the state to see it done, and that the people should instruct their legislatures to establish a system of schools, which shall bring every branch of knowledge equally within the reach of every child, male or female, rich or poor. This is all we ask.

While children are receiving their education, they must be maintained. Many parents are not able to do this. This is not the children's fault, and they ought not to suffer on account of the parent's neglect or inability. They do now; and we wish to devise the means by which it may be prevented. We therefore propose a system of schools, which will receive all the children of the state, furnish all with the means of every branch of useful knowledge. How shall these schools be supported? This will soon be answered. The schools are to provide each child with the requisite instructors, with food, clothing and lodging, during the period they reside at the school. We propose this for two reasons. First economy, second for the sake of equality. A uniform

---

[1][Ed. See *Cayuga Patriot* 17 (August 11, 1830): 3. The editor, Ulysses F. Doubleday, maintained a running commentary on Brownson's editorials in the *Genesee Republican*, opposed his views of educational reform, and, as a National Republican, was not only opposed to the Workingmen's Party but to Brownson's support of the workingmen's cause because he believed Brownson had supported the agrarian and infidel causes associated with the New York City workingmen's more radical segment. Doubleday at least associated Brownson with agrarianism and infidelity, charges that Brownson repeatedly denied. For some of this editorial battle, see the *Cayuga Patriot* 17 (July 7, 1830): 3; (July 14, 1830): 3; (July 21, 1830): 3.]

diet, simple and wholesome, may be provided at a far less expense, not than that of the poorest families, but far less than the average expenditure for victualing children as they now are, and with far more advantage to their health. The same remark applies to the article of clothing. By instituting a uniform dress, all that is now expended for fashion's sake would be avoided. A neat, simple, convenient and durable dress might be substituted for the finery of the rich and the rags of the poor. This would have the most admirable effect in producing equality of feeling, in training up all children with the idea they are equals—a most useful idea for young republicans.

But how shall they *be* supported? This question creates the difficulty. We propose that these schools be schools of industry. That agriculture and the several mechanical branches shall be practiced by the scholars. Nothing is more important to virtue than that children acquire industrious habits. Devoting a part of the time to labor will make the body hardy and robust, and the mind clear and vigorous. These points are so well settled they require no argument. It is ascertained that children, at the age of ten or twelve, will by laboring six hours a day support themselves. This would leave six hours for study, [as] much time as they ought to study, and as is now occupied in our common schools. When the children have arrived at the age of ten or twelve, we may pronounce the schools *self-supporting*. As the scholars grow older they would do more and we believe, eventually it will be found they will do enough to defray the expenses of the younger establishments. But in case they do not, where is the deficiency to be supplied? From two sources, each parent contributing a certain amount for each child, and the rest to be supplied from the state treasury. This is the bare sketch of the system we propose. Mr. Doubleday objects "it takes away the incentives to industry." Mr. D. cannot object stronger to a system that should take away the incentives to industry than we do. He knows we always objected to Owen's Utopian scheme at New Harmony,[2] that it destroyed individual enterprise, would take away all the motives to exertion, and finally sink man into a mere animal that would eat, drink, propagate his species and die. Such we conceive would be the condition of any society, where individual enterprise was destroyed, and motives to industry removed. But we do not perceive how such an objection can bear

[2][Ed. Robert Owen (1771-1858) was a Scottish industrialist-socialist who wrote *A New View of Society* (1813) to expressed his socialist views, emphasizing the environmental influences upon the development of character. In 1825 he set up a utopian community in New Harmony, Indiana, to work out his social philosophy. The experiment failed by the end of 1827.]

against the plan we propose. Industry would be encouraged from the circumstance everyone would be bred to it from infancy; it would be honorable for all would be accustomed equally to it; it would be pleasurable, from the exercise it would require, and from the vigor and activity it would give the mind and body. Just mark that aged man. He has property enough to support him. But he labors constantly—why? Simply because it was the habit of his early life. And labor would be desirable from the ease, independence and respectability it would bestow. This is not all. Children are still to be cared for; the means of paying the tax for this education keeps alive anxiety; their own case and comfort urge on still more, and every motive there is now, to industry, would remain, though we grant that excessive anxiety for children which is now felt, would be moderated. This, so far from being considered objectionable, should be deemed desirable.

Mr. D. objects still farther that it would take the children from the parents, and he makes a very pathetic appeal to the parent's heart against it. We can appreciate the appeal. But we deem it ill-timed. We find the present system of education is liable to the objections he makes against ours. At present the child must be sent to college, not infrequently to the distance of hundreds of miles. Gentlemen in Virginia send their sons to Union College in this state, to the Seminary in Auburn,[3] to Harvard, to Yale and not seldom to Europe. Mr. D. has no sympathy in these cases. He only thinks of the separation between the parent and the child, when the child is in his own neighborhood, under his weekly, daily and hourly inspection. As for destroying the control of the parent, we propose no such thing. We would strengthen the ties between parent and child rather than weaken; we value those ties, and esteem that little heaven created by the mutual love of parents and children, of brothers and sisters. Our plan in our opinion would indeed make it a heaven where none but angel voices should be heard. We have no wish to have children *forced* from their parents, nor do we wish to see the system adopted till the people generally, shall be in favor of it. We deem the system impracticable at present. We are not of a very sanguine nature, and however anxious we may be, to see it adopted, we are willing to wait the progress of opinion. In the meantime we would discuss the subject, induce the people to view it with the importance it deserves. Government

[3][Ed. Union College in Schenectady, New York, had its origins in 1795. The Auburn Theological Seminary was founded in 1818 by New School Presbyterian presbyteries of the Synod of Geneva, New York, for educating candidates for the ministry. The Seminary became a part of Union Theological Seminary (New York City) in 1939.]

cannot and ought not to establish such a system of education until the people are convinced of its utility and clearly demand it. To raise a political party to carry the measure by mere excitement is a thing if we ever did contemplate with a moment's approbation, we are far from approving now. All reforms in this country must be effected by the progress of opinion. If we may judge from the signs of the times, the period has nearly arrived when some great change must take place in the existing plan of education. What plan will be adopted we are unable to say, as one of the people we give what we deem the best. If ours be adopted, of course we shall rejoice; if the people decide otherwise, we assent to the republican maxim, the majority must rule.

We think the only way in which the measure we advocate can be carried into effect is by individual effort, establishing schools on a similar plan, and convincing the people, by actual experiment of their excellence. Or if the legislature would establish what might be called a model school at the expense of the state, and receive into it children from every county; we think the effect would be good. It is worth the experiment. To avoid all difficulty about selecting children, take from each county such and only such, as belong to the poorhouses, or whose parents are supported at public expense. This would support those children as cheaply as they are now; it would be placing them in the road to respectability, and it would test the principle. If found good our people would not be backward in adopting it generally; if found bad, why there would be very little loss.

For ourselves we have no doubt of the *ultimate* practicability and high excellence of our plan, as such we shall continue to advocate it with what zeal and ability we can command, till we see cause to change our mind. We believe it would strike at the root of all our evils, and make us, free, great and happy.

We have been thus explicit in giving our views, that Mr. D. can have no excuse for misrepresenting us. The objections he made seem to us not to bear against our system. He can now see what it is. If he objects, we wish him to state his objections in a calm and candid manner. Such a course will have more weight with us and eventually with the public than mere cant or idle slang. We hold ourselves ready to meet all objections that may be offered and if convinced we are wrong, we have not so far enlisted self-love in defense of our plan that we cannot abandon it. We believe Mr. D. has a real desire to raise the standard of education, and while we are convinced he means well, we can easily pardon him for the uncourteous manner in which he treats us. We wait his reply.

6.

WORKINGMEN'S CONVENTION

Genesee Republican and Herald of Reform
1 (August 18, 1830): 2

Some few places have suggested the holding a State Convention at Salina, and we believe a few delegates are appointed to meet there on the 25th inst[ance]. We do not think there will be anything like a full representation of the people at that place; consequently, whatever nominations it might make would hardly be worthy the confidence of our fellow citizens. We do not see any propriety of getting up a third candidate for governor. The workingmen are not contending for office, but for principle, not for a party, but for measures. Now there is no difficulty. Let the workingmen attend the meetings of the several towns and counties, and use the influence of their numbers in sending such men to the State Convention at Herkimer as will nominate such men for the offices of governor and lieut[enant] governor, as will regard the interests of the people. In this case the workingmen can make their weight of some consequence. But if they separate—attempt to form a *party* by themselves they gain nothing. The workingmen of Genesee are the majority of the inhabitants of the county. Let them then send three delegates to Herkimer or what other place they please who will regard their interests. Let every county do the same and the workingmen will have a majority in the Convention and can nominate a Workingman's candidate, and when they have done they can elect him. This strikes us as the better way. We want reform but we hope for reform through the ranks of the republicans of our country. We impress upon the workingmen, not the importance of forming a new party, which shall be the stepping-stone of a new set of political trimmers, but of attending to their own interest and electing men who will do the same. Who is there to elect a governor besides the farmers, mechanics and workingmen? These classes have suffered themselves to be dictated by a few aspirants. Let them spurn dictation and act themselves, and what does it matter whether the convention which nominates be at Utica, at Salina or at Herkimer?

We have said we advocate the *measures* of the workingmen not their *party*. The term Republican is sufficiently significant for us and we have seen enough of politics to know that the moment that we start a new party there are thousands of desperadoes ready to make it a hobby to carry themselves into office. We see it in the Anti-Masonic Party. Starting from good feelings supported by pure patriots as the world every saw, it has for its leaders men, to say the least, of very questionable republicanism. The Workingmen's Party, advocating measures which will prove the salvation of our country, has among its supporters as a party—men who are enough to damn any cause whatever. The Republican Party is corrupt, it has men for its leaders that should be dropped and we will do all we can to have them dropped. But we need not form a new party to do this, liable to all the objections we make against others. Let every press in favor of the workingmen boldly espouse their interest, do all it can to get good men elected to office and to get correct measures carried. If the thing is not accomplished this year—if the reforms are not now effected, we will keep them agitated, we will keep them before the people till they are, this is the only way we know, to correct the errors into which we have fallen. Such are our views.

7.

PATRICK O'HARA: CHAPTER VI[1]

Philanthropist 1 (July 23, 1831): 141-43.

Religion, strange mysterious word! I have asked the living, I have called upon the dead, I have poured over books, sought through all nature, by day, by night, in sickness, in health, in my hopes and in my fears, in my love, in my hatred, in my forgiveness and my revenge—all, all, have I implored with tears and in every accent of entreaty to unfold to me what thou art.   *New School*

I must now be allowed to advert to my religious history, for the views I entertained of religion and the zeal with which I devoted myself to sacred subjects gave the bias to my mind and determined my future character.

I was born in the land of the Puritans; about the time when modern revivals, as they are termed, were becoming frequent. The staid and drab-colored religion of the Puritans, which consisted in suppressing all emotions and resigning up all intellectual sovereignty, was giving way to a religion of impulse, fanaticism, and mere boisterous rant. My temperament, my situation, my education, all induced seriousness, disposed me to religious reflections, to silent and somber meditation.

The thought of death was awful. When I first learned that I too must die, it seemed as if the springs of my life were broken. The buoyancy of my feelings left me, and for days I did little else than weep at the intelligence. To die, to be laid in the cold ground, to be left alone, to never see anyone again, to never speak—O it was a terrible thought. I asked why I must die? Why I could not live always? They told me God would take my life, I was in his hands, and whenever he chose he would take me away. "Why does God do this?" I asked. They answered not.

"What is God, that he should do this?"

"A spirit, your sovereign."

"But what is a spirit? and why is he my sovereign?"

No reply was given.

[1][Ed. If there were previous chapters, they could not be located in the extant copies of the *Philanthropist*.]

Surely, thought I to myself, God cannot be a very good being to take my life. It can do him no good, and I do not see why he cannot let me live. I was not more than five years old when this occurred. The impression was lasting. I have never escaped its influence. All my studies and nearly all my thoughts were henceforth to be of a religious cast.

I was soon informed that I was totally depraved, that I was born with a nature wholly corrupt; that I was infinitely hateful in the sight of my God; that I was not only born to die, but I was in danger of going to hell where I should be endlessly miserable. This was the unkindest of all their instructions. I could see much that was lovely in nature; I delighted to pluck the opening flower, to inhale its sweets; I delighted to gaze on the everlasting mountains and felt to adore when surrounded by the wild, rugged and romantic scenery amidst which I was reared; but to be told all this delight, all this pleasure, all this awe and devotion, proceeded from a corrupt heart, and could be only abomination to God, struck me dumb. My spirit fell, and inwardly I cursed my fate, cursed my maker for the wretched, the thankless existence he had given me.

I was soon instructed in all the mysteries of the "fall of man," the "incarnation of God," his "death for the elect," his "resurrection from the dead," etc. all of which I understood as well at eight years old as I do now at fifty.[2] These doctrines are perhaps full as well suited to the comprehension of children as of grown people, and the infantile intellect will, perhaps, be full as ready to believe them as any. They however puzzled me a little at first. I could not understand how the eating of an apple by Adam, could make me guilty, but I saw it all plain, soon as I learned that Adam stood *proxy* for all his posterity, and by a very pleasing fiction, like many sanctioned by our laws, God counted him as the whole of the human race that was or ever should be. This had a remarkable beauty in it. It superseded all enquiry into our personal characters. To determine what we were, whether we deserved to be saved or damned, God had only to enquire whether Adam stood or fell. It thus saved a vast deal of labor on the part of God, and made it a matter of perfect indifference to us, whether we did good or evil; for in either case the answer "you deserve endless damnation for what Adam did," was enough. If we did

[2][Ed. Brownson was only twenty-eight when this piece was written. Patrick O'Hara is fictional, but reflects Brownson's experience, as is evident in his diaries, his letter to Edward Turner (July 17, 1834, in Universalist-Unitarian Archives at Andover-Harvard Divinity School), and his autobiography (*Works* 5:1-200).]

well, "original sin" would damn us, if we did bad, it could do no more.

The incarnation of God was a holy mystery, I did not explain it to myself and as I was too young to appreciate the beauties of the "Miraculous Conception," that passed by without much thought. The death of God was quite another thing, but as Watts had said, in one of his hymns,

> Well might the sun in darkness hide
> And shut his glories in,
> When God the Mighty Maker died
> For man the creature's sin.[3]

I concluded it must all be right.

The doctrine of election and reprobation, I objected to in toto; and though they gave me Edwards, and Boston, and I know not how many books of the same stamp, I could not believe.[4] It seemed too much even for a child, eight years old as I then was, to embrace. The Bible had given me to understand God was good to all, better than an earthly parent, and I could not believe that earthly parent very good, who would give all his good things to a small part of his children and starve all the rest to death.

The doctrine of endless misery, I hardly knew what to think of it. My feelings revolted at the thought; all my notions of justice, love and mercy seemed to forbid it. But as the idea of power was most prominent in my notions of God, as I was taught to view him rather as a sovereign, than as a Father, I assented and reluctantly admitted it might be.

Thus stood my mind at eight years old. Thus far I had good Calvinistic training, and in the main was considerably orthodox. The good pious sisters said I should be a great man yet, should be an ornament to the church, etc. I continued to read such religious books as I could find, to think, to reflect more and more upon my condi-

---

[3][Ed. Isaac Watts, *Hymns and Spiritual Songs, 1707-1748*, ed. Selma L. Bishop (London: The Faith Press, 1962), Book 2, Psalm 9, verse 4. Brownson's original text had "man's" for "man."]

[4][Ed. It is not clear which of Jonathan Edwards' works he is referring to here, but we do know from his autobiography that he had read Edwards' *History of Redemption* when he was young, see *Works* 5:4. Reference may be to Thomas Boston (1677-1732), the elder, who was a Scottish minister and author of *Human Nature in its Fourfold Estate* (Edinburgh, 1720). See DNB 2:886-88.]

tion. At thirteen I became really under, what was then termed, concern of mind.[5]

It is worthy of remark that in those days, the art of making saints was by no means brought to the perfection it can boast now. It then took many months, sometimes years, to bring one out. Now it is no trouble at all. The same labor-saving machinery seems introduced into this spiritual factory that there has been in spinning and weaving cotton, and a thousand other things not necessary to mention. It is not singular for a man (or rather a boy) to get up in the morning totally depraved, lying under the curse of God's wrath, and exposed to all the torments of hell for his exceeding sinfulness; at nine o'clock, to attend a prayer meeting, polluted with sin, infinitely hateful to God; at half past nine to be convicted, at ten converted, examined and propounded; in the afternoon to sit with the saints a good Christian. This is rapid work; but what else could we expect from this age of steam and railroads?

We had no such easy times when I was a boy. Full three months I lay on the brink of hell, groaning in spirit, and praying to be born again. It was a long and a weary time I had. Long, long, did I weep over my sins, without being able to recall one thing I had done for which conscience condemned me. I prayed and prayed, but all to no purpose. They told me to give myself up to God. I strove to do it; I felt anxious to do it; I wished the assistance of his holy spirit; sought it with tears, but all in vain. They told me it was all my own stubbornness of will, and that I deserved to be damned for my obstinacy. They told me to go to Jesus. I looked for him; I prayed to him; besought him to come and reign in, and over, me. It availed nothing. There I stood, in my mind's eye, upon the very edge of a mighty precipice, down which it made my brain reel to look. Down there I could see the Devil with his imps, grinning and shaking his grizzly sides, and tossing with his trident poor miserable souls from one pit to another; now fanning the sulphurous flame, and spreading its horrid glare over the pale and sepulchral countenances of the damned. Then he would turn towards me. The waves of fire would seem to rise; he would brandish his trident, as if to take my life. I would recoil, with horror, with my frame trembling and covered with a cold sweat.

Then I would look up to God. There I would see him in heaven, seated upon his great white throne, laughing, *tête à tête* with his Son and the Holy Ghost. The moment his eye caught me, all would

---

[5][Ed. "Concern of mind" was a Methodist term that designated the beginning of a conversion experience. On this, see the introduction to EW, 1:144 n.]

change; frowns would settle upon his countenance; flames dart from his eyes; his hand grasp firmer the awful sword; his voice, as with myriads of thunders, would roar out "Begone!" Thus it was. Hell burned before me; heaven frowned above; all seemed rage, hatred, revenge and torture. Around among my fellow beings, all seemed cold and hateful and I felt lone and friendless in the universe.

It was then I felt the full curse of existence. I loathed all food; I could not sleep; I wasted to a skeleton; but I could not die. I felt I must live—must live eternally; waste and waste away, yet remain; burn and burn forever, yet never die! Must eternally feel the fire in my soul, spreading through all my limbs, my body, swell, and writhe, and burst with the intense heat, yet ever endure. O how I prayed to the mountains to crush me. O worlds would I have given to have been annihilated. All was vain. Life was given, and must remain. No remission, no mitigation. O mockery! I exclaimed, why speak of a God of mercy! I could curse, with all my soul, a being that would confer existence but to increase the sum of misery.

O it was a horrid state of mind. It makes me pale, and feeble, and sick, to recall it. I would roll on the ground, beat my sides and gnaw my tongue for very anguish. I would turn and turn, pray and pray, plead and plead, for mercy, but it seemed there was none. "Thou shalt be damned," rung in my ears, and I gave way to despair; my brain reeled, my eyes swam round-days and weeks passed—I know not how.

It was a dark and stormy night. I had been to a meeting to hear one of the "New Lights," as they were called, several of my own age were *brought out*, and told their experience. I could say nothing. I could not weep. I scorned to beg for mercy after having been so often denied. I went home. I threw myself upon the bed, with an anguish of soul that only few ever feel, and fewer still survive. The night was dark, except when illumined by the fitful streams of lightning. The thunder rolled as if to announce the day of doom. I always loved to hear it thunder. There is something so majestic, so much of lofty grandeur and sublimity in that heavy roll, that I believe to hear it would give me a thrill of delight even in hell.

My case had approached its crisis. The time had come, when nature must sink or triumph. The darkness disappeared; the storm subsided; the thunder hushed his voice; all was silent, calm and bright. I lay entranced. A soft, an inexpressibly sweet sensation pervaded my whole frame. There was a light around to which the day would have seemed as night; yet it was midnight. I could see every part of my room clearly and distinctly, yet I was not startled. All my guilt, all my grief, all my anguish, were gone and I felt as if ushered into a new world, where all was bright and lovely, where the air was perfumed with sweet spices, where soft and thrilling music breathed from every dwelling and warbled from every grove. I could bear no more. The contrast of feeling may be imagined. I broke out so loud that I was heard all over the house:

"I have tasted heaven today, what more can I contain?"

Thus was I born again.

8.

AN ADDRESS
ON THE FIFTY-FIFTH ANNIVERSARY
OF AMERICAN INDEPENDENCE.
DELIVERED AT OVID, SENECA COUNTY,
N.Y., JULY 4, 1831[1]

FRIENDS AND FELLOW-CITIZENS,

Your partiality has called me to perform a duty, which has often been the province of genius, of moral, political and mental worth. The recollections of the day, its powerful and endearing associations, awaken emotions that I may deeply feel, but feebly express.

This is the Birthday of Freedom. Fifty-five years this day, the representatives of a high-spirited, but injured people, threw down the glove to the world's masters in behalf of long-degraded, insulted and enslaved humanity. The noble daring of the deed—the high, uncompromising love of liberty which prompted it—the fears, the hopes—the intense anxiety it excited—the dangers it aroused—the exposure to trial, to want, to distress which it occasioned—the hardy bravery, the stern independence of character, lofty patriotism and generous self-sacrifice it displayed—the victory, the triumph, the peace and prosperity, to which it led—all the sad and the pleasing associations we link with the day conspire to make this the day of days to Americans; to make it too full of memory and hope, too holy and spirit-stirring, to enable us to assemble for its celebration, with a quiet pulse or an unexcited feeling.

We have assembled this day to commemorate the most brilliant epoch in the march of human improvement. We commemorate an event which gave birth to our nation and which shall, in its progressive career, snatch a world from the empire of tyrants and give freedom to the human race. It is a high and holy event. Our minds are not turned to the birth of a future despot, to the achievements of a merely victorious general, nor to the mere martial prowess of conquering armies, no less fatal to the millions by success than defeat.

[1][Ed. Ithaca, N.Y.: S. S. Chatterton, 1831.]

No, my friends, we celebrate the birth of freedom; the victories of justice; the triumphs of the rights of man over the claims of tyrants.

It is with no ordinary feelings that Americans should meet to commemorate the 4th of July, 1776. That was a day of deep import—a day that opened a new era in men's thoughts, and in men's acts. It dawned with good to man. Generations shall be unfolding the events it involved; and it shall accumulate new loveliness and glory through all coming time. With it commenced our national existence; with it is entwined the memory of the great, the good, the sage and the heroic. With it is associated, in our minds, the master spirits of our people; and, in its sacredness, is enshrined the memory of departed worth—such as the world has seldom seen, or will see again. With it are connected all our ideas of national suffering—national heroism—national triumphs; and fastened on it, are all the patriotic lessons of our fathers who have gone. Dear must it be to every American heart! Who would not consecrate it to the memory of noble daring; to high resolve; to deeds that ennobled man; to individuals, whose moral and mental greatness, whose firmness, stern integrity and undying love of country, have spread a halo of glory around the human race? Let it remain then through all time as the nation's jubilee; as the day on which to meet and rekindle our love of liberty—to fan yet brighter the patriot's fire, and extend still farther the philanthropist's hopes.

We meet in peace. The roar of artillery and the martial reveille are but the notes of our rejoicing that peace dwells in our borders. If the distant sounds of war from the old world, from the people struggling with their masters and conspiring to break the chains of their despotism strike on our ears, we can look around on smiling landscapes; our wives and children are secure; no ruthless invader tramples on the hopes of the husbandman, carrying terror before him, and leaving famine, pestilence and death in his rear. Our flocks and herds graze unmolested; the grain waves in homage to him who cultivates the earth; and we can "sit down under our own vine and fig tree, with none to molest or make us afraid" [Mic. 4:4].

The condition of our country is truly flattering to patriotic pride; and its unrivaled prosperity in every part affords an interesting comment on our free institutions. Cold must be the heart, and unworthy the genial sun of freedom, that does not swell with noble emotions on recalling our past history—dwelling on the much we have done, the much we are doing, and the high hopes we have excited for the future. Far and wide we have felled the eternal forests; beautiful and lovely are the cities and villages we have erected where a few years since curled the smoke of the wigwam, or where prowled the beast of prey. We have made the wilderness smile by our industry; and we have peopled it with millions of free and intelligent beings.

But I stand not here to repeat the story of your achievements, nor to inflate your vanity by rounded periods and sounding epithets on your present greatness. I love my country. I glory in having been born an American. I would not seem insensible to the much we have gained, the much we possess when compared to the king- and priest-ridden countries of the old world; but I would also remember our work is only commenced—nobly commenced indeed, yet still only in its infancy.

It is the misfortune of man, in his collective capacity, to imagine when one important point is gained, that the whole work is done; and to conclude when he has taken one step beyond his ancestors that he has reached the end of his journey. Liberty is an old word, but of changeable meaning. A few years since, it had a very limited sense. That nation was supposed to possess liberty that was uncontrolled by any other. In 1776 it took a wider meaning and implied not only national independence, but a right to choose our own form of government and to select our own rulers.

The victory we gained gave us liberty in this sense. This was a giant stride in the march of human emancipation. Man seemed in this mighty leap to have outstripped himself; it seemed he had borrowed the soul of some Divinity that he could accomplish so much; and considering what he had been, what he is now in most countries, it is not strange that his achievements appeared almost incredible. But, by a close inspection, with the eye of the philosopher, of the philanthropist, we shall easily discover we then only gained the starting points—merely opened the lists to human reason and human perfectibility.

Liberty has yet a wider sense—one vastly more important than mere national independence, or the right to choose our own government and rulers. With these man is but half free. There is a more subtle, and a more powerful, tyrant that lurks within and enslaves the soul. Custom, habit, influence of wealth, of some adventitious circumstance, may make, or keep, the many vassals to the few. There is the dark bondage of the mind that may remain. Ignorance, bigotry, superstition, may enter the soul and destroy its native power; the hidden fire of intellect may be smothered for want of courage to fan it to a flame. Man may become afraid of man; may lock up his thoughts in his own bosom and bow to popular prejudice; or worse, the tender shoot may be trampled as it first discloses its concealed beauty; the infant mind may be crippled; its native energy destroyed ere it is developed; and the being bearing human form may grow up ignorant, unthinking, unreasoning; with no ideas but those he may chance to borrow—poor, feeble; worthless, brutalized, dark and desperate, prepared for "treasons, villainies and spoils." Such may indeed,

> deem themselves most free,
> When they within this gross and visible sphere—
> Chain down the wing'd thought, scoffing ascent,
> Proud in their meanness;[2]

but they are the veriest slaves that live. There are no chains like those which fetter the mind, no despotism like that of vice. We may boast of our liberty; we may boast of our zeal, the bravery, the self-sacrifice, the hardy endurance of toil, of danger, of want, the stern patriotism and untiring perseverance, and unrivaled victories of the heroes of our revolution; we may boast of our extended territory, our rapid improvements, our unparalleled industry and enterprise, our universal commerce, our increasing wealth and national greatness; but our boasts are mere wind, if there be not *freedom to the mind*. Liberty— the very soul of liberty, must be enshrined in every human breast. Every thought must be free; every aspiration must be high, holy, unrestrained; or all our pretensions are idle breath; we have no bulwark for freedom, no safeguards for the rich legacy left us by those who fought our battles and gave us national existence.

That our liberty is written on paper, that our rights are recorded in constitutions can avail little if they be not written on the heart. They must sink deep into the soul; the love of liberty must mingle with every breath—must flash from every eye—glow on every cheek— impart its high born air to everyone's manner—to his speech, his walk, to his whole deportment, or valueless are all the proud and spirit-stirring associations of this auspicious day.

Fellow Citizens, there is no true liberty where there is not a high-toned virtue. He only is free, who feels no restraint but the will of God—who yields only to his devotion to truth, and to moral rectitude. It is only this moral and mental liberty that should be the patriot's and the philanthropist's aim. Give but these to the degraded peasantry of Europe, and thrones fall—dynasties are forgotten—the rights of man are recognized and secured. 'Tis the slavery of the mind which

[2][Ed. Samuel Taylor Coleridge, "The Destiny of Nations: A Vision," (1796, *Sibylline Leaves*, 1817), lines 28-30, in *The Poems of Samuel Taylor Coleridge*, ed. Ernest Hartley Coleridge (London: Oxford University Press, 1927), 131-48, quote on 132.]

paves the way to that of the body, and the slavery of individuals which induces that of nations. The timid slave of ignorance, of base passion, of low wants, and groveling vice, may be a vile minion of power, and make his body a footstool for the aspiring demagogue to clamber to a throne; but it belongs not to such as he, to detect, seize and secure, the rights of man.

Friends, bear with me. I am most anxious to impress this all important truth, *that our only hope for the full development and perpetuity of our free institutions is in the moral soundness of the people.* Our rulers are men from our midst; they do and will partake of the prevailing passions of the times. They will be the creatures of the reigning tone—the vice or the virtue, of the people from whom they are selected. In a general corruption of morals and manners, they escape not uncontaminated. They drink at the popular fountain, and will always be affected by the diseases it generates. To the most stupid and least observant, then, it must be evident that in a government like ours, virtue—high, stern, unbending—virtue, must be maintained by all our citizens or else we have not the security desired and needed.

We complain of our public officers, of their want of public spirit, stern integrity, and generous disregard of self, but our complaints are misplaced. Our politicians and public men exhibit only the prevailing spirit of the times; and as it would be hard to find one who would not exhibit the same disregard of the public, the same all-absorbing selfishness, it ill becomes us to complain. True, party spirit rages to an alarming extent, evincing very clearly a diseased state of the public mind; true, all seem scrambling for place to fatten on its rewards; but are only our rulers and prominent politicians to blame? This were a partial view. The demon who sports with our security and threatens our free institutions, possesses not merely a few individuals; he is the reigning spirit of the times; and you all feel his influence, and in a greater or less degree, yield to his unholy dominion.

I know on this day it is customary to extol the deeds of the fathers of our country, to speak in terms of the most exaggerated praise of the patriots, sages and heroes of our revolution. No man venerates that band of worthies more than I. No one feels more deeply the dignity they conferred on human nature. Their names are embalmed in my heart, and silent be my voice and dead my pulse, when I feel no emotion at the mention of a Washington, a Franklin, a Jefferson and their noble compeers. But we are their descendants; are their countrymen; and unworthy were we of their fame if we gave them only cold praise with our lips, while we treasured not up their virtues in our hearts, nor exemplified, or imitated, them in our lives. The best praise, the best monument to their departed worth, is the living practice of their virtues. I know also it is customary, on this day, to boast of our virtue and intelligence. But I cannot flatter. I cannot boast of that we do not possess. I would not wound vanity, nor damp the ardor of hope; but I were betraying the confidence which called me here to refuse to probe the heart where national good requires.

My friends, we are not that enlightened and virtuous people we pretend; compared with other nations we may be eminently so; but compared with what we might and should be, we are not. It were poor praise to our noble institutions, a poor compliment to the blessings of liberty, for us to feel contented with being as good as nations which groan beneath the lash of tyranny. We have advantages which no other nation can imagine and are we not to exhibit corresponding excellences of character? Friends, I fear we have too often neglected this thought. We seem daily departing from first principles; and, instead of aiming at a high, commanding, simple and unaffected republican character, we are enraptured with foreign gewgaws; every day aping the spirit, the manners and the usages of monarchical governments. There is an all-absorbing selfishness which prevails; avarice has become our besetting sin, and its deep brand is being stamped on every heart. It is in this prevailing spirit of the people that the danger lurks; it is in this that originate the vices we charge upon our public men. The moral feeling is bad; and unless we correct it, aye, and correct it in our own hearts, our republic falls and must one day, like Athens or Rome, sigh under the whip of the despot.

Speak I harshly? Charge I my countrymen wrongfully? Would to God I did and that the evils I see were only the dreams of my own disordered imagination. But look at the increasing fondness for show and parade; look at the tide of luxury pouring in; look at the "high life below stairs"[3] which glares upon us from every miserable hut; look at the combustible state of the public mind, the power of faction, the jealousies and maddened zeal of rival parties and rival sects, which have become proverbial, and tell me if what I say is not most lamentably true? There is danger, a lurking evil that menaces destruction, but gladly would I believe it were only in my own fancy that I see it.

Allow me now to advert to the want of independence among our citizens on the subject of religion. We may meet thousands who have one opinion for the public and another for themselves. Man seems afraid to avow his honest convictions, seems to imagine his reputa-

[3][Ed. Unable to identify quotation.]

tion depends on locking up his own thoughts and conforming to popular opinion. He dissembles his own opinions and is to the world what he is not, and would abhor to be, to himself. This embosoms incalculable danger to our free institutions. This habit of appearing what one is not, of professing to believe what he cannot, or of acquiescing in what he abhors, is fatal to all mental energy; it corrupts the secret source of virtue; taints the whole moral character, and paves the way for the commission of deeds that the sun might blush to behold.

Our noble institutions guarantee us freedom of thought and freedom of speech; but a sickly public opinion obtrudes itself as a test law and already the young mechanic, the merchant, the physician and the lawyer, on commencing business, dare not avow what they believe, much less defend their honest convictions, if they chance to be those it is unpopular to express. Is this republicanism? Is he a republican who would control thought and usurp dominion over conscience? Is he a republican who will submit to such unholy tyranny? Thought should be free as the air we breathe. Opinion should be free as the common light of heaven; and where it is not so, there is no true liberty. Were it not so here, our declarations of rights were a solemn mockery, our celebration of this day a mere farce, an insult to the Congress of '76. But thought is controlled here. It is submitted to here. Even here man yields outwardly his most sacred opinions to his brother, and sacrifices truth, honesty, moral feeling upon the altar of hypocrisy. Yet we pretend we are free! enlightened! virtuous!

But I forbear. The evil is told. It is a thankless task to reprove; and I would not check the flow of generous feeling, nor damp the ardor of those pure and philanthropic hopes, which the proud associations of this day excite. Whatever may be our errors, whatever of mischievous tendency we may have encouraged or tolerated, we have a remedy in our own hands. We have conquered the power to improve. We have secured the right, and the ability, to change, to modify, to correct, without violence or danger to our excellent institutions. Our laws and usages are not those of the Medes and Persians. They originate with the people, in their free will; they are designed to effect the greatest good for the greatest possible number; and whenever they fail of the designed end, we can change or suspend their operation, without invoking the genius of revolutions, or departing from the spirit of our present form of government.

But the errors to which I have alluded, are not those of government; they are those of the people. We are prone to charge too much upon government, as well as to exact too much from its exertions.

Government can cure but few of the evils of any community. Its province is mostly negative, to check the encroachments of individual upon individual, and to secure to each the reward of his own industry. The great business of life asks no aid of government. The people, as individuals and social beings, must conduct it as self-interest prompts, and wisdom or ignorance, vice or virtue directs. There can be no bad government where the people, as individuals, are wise, virtuous and independent. There can be no good government where the people are the slaves of ignorance and vice, the victims of crime, or the votaries of luxury and licentiousness. As individuals, as citizens, as patriots, it should then be our grand study to acquire just principles, and form characters noted for honesty, truth, honor and humanity. Each will then possess in his own person an item of that moral and mental freedom, that shall go to make up the whole sum, of national liberty and independence. Let each aim to discharge, promptly and cheerfully, the several private and social virtues, let all aim at pure hearts, benevolent dispositions and unspotted lives, and there will then be an elevated national character; there will be a free and virtuous population; all the blessings of liberty and righteousness will be secured, and transmitted unimpaired to the latest posterity. Turn, I beseech you, turn your attention to your own principles and conduct, to the forming of free, high, commanding characters, as individuals, if you love your country and desire to see it free, great, flourishing, happy. Hope its security and prosperity from individual excellence of character, rather than from legislative enactments, or the resolutions of public meetings. Here, on this principle, you may commence your "internal improvements" in earnest, and fear from the appropriations and exertions you may make no danger to the constitution of your country.

But as true as a high, uncompromising moral virtue is the only sure pledge for national independence and the perpetuity of our free institutions, so true is it that this virtue can never exist without a high mental cultivation. There is no permanence, no worth, no loveliness, in the inspirations of ignorance. There is no hope, no promise of good from the morality of a people over whom hangs an intellectual night, spreading its leaden influence over the faculties, and benumbing all the energies of the human being. It will only be the bursts of base passion, the destructive flashes of barbarous zeal, or the dark workings of envy and revenge. Knowledge is the food for the soul, and the only food that it will relish, or which will develop its strength and preserve its health. Knowledge, correct and universal, must be diffused; the mind must be disciplined; and all its almightiness must be aroused, exerted, to give to virtue its finish and to man his felicity. Education must wake up a day in the soul, and give life, activity and energy to the whole intellectual man, or moral excellence is but a dream. Every son and daughter of our republic, must be enlightened, or all our boasted acquisitions, and possessions, depart and leave us to slavery and barbarism.

The history of the past demonstrates this. Where now are the nations which fill so much of ancient story? Egypt has fallen and long since passed beneath the barbarian's yoke. Yet Egypt was the nursery of the arts and sciences, and by her genial care many of them were brought to a perfection we emulate in vain. Athens has fallen. The Grove, the Portico, the Lyceum, the Garden, no longer echo with the wisdom and refinement of Plato, the moral sublimity of the Stoic, the deep thought, the extensive research of the Stagirite, nor, with the amiable philosophy of the Gargettian.[4] A dark night rests upon the scattered fragments of the earliest and loveliest of republics. But Athens was the seat of learning, the academy of Europe. Her sons were the masters of all that belongs to deep thought, extensive acquaintance with the phenomena of nature; were rich with all the creations of genius, and able to seize, abstract, and body forth, the beautiful, the lovely and the sublime in forms that shall remain models to all coming time. Rome too, once haughty mistress of the world, by her arts and sciences, as well as by her arms, now sits in solitude upon her seven hills, sighing over her fallen grandeur and departed dominion.

Why? Because there were wanting men of enlightened minds? Surely not for the want of philosophers, sages, heroes, statesmen, or orators. No, my friends, the secret of their fall is not in the want of knowledge, correct and extensive in the few; but in that the many were ignorant. A few only were enlightened; a few minds only were cultivated while the mighty mass of intellect remained rude, rioting in the wildness of primeval chaos. It was in that general ignorance, with those millions in worse than Egypt's darkness, that originated the diseases which corrupted the body politic and hurried it on to its ruin. The knowledge of the few was too weak to dispel the surrounding darkness; it gave but a feeble glare, and was soon overpowered by universal night.

[4][Ed. Brownson is probably referring to François Rabelais' (?1494-1553) giant king noted for his enormous physical and intellectual abilities. The peace-loving Gargantua was also the mouthpiece for educational reform and the hero of his satire *Gargantua and Pantagruel*.]

Let the past teach us wisdom. Let us avoid the rock on which were wrecked the hopes of all our predecessors. It is ours to wake up the millions—to pour the celestial rays of knowledge into the whole mass of human beings. There is yet an incalculable amount of mind unimproved. It lies waste, or overgrown with the noxious weeds of error and vice; or it nourishes the *miasma* to spread crime over our beautiful country and destroy all our fond and high built hopes. Let me repeat it, there is no security to virtue independent of a high mental cultivation. Our moral superstructure must rest on mind—must be supported by the understanding, or it will have neither beauty nor permanence. As it is necessary each individual should be virtuous to sustain a free government, so is it necessary that the whole should be enlightened in every branch of useful knowledge, to produce, and sustain, the virtue required. Each individual of this republic, should be instructed in every duty obligatory upon him or his fellows, and should know its importance and the best means of performing it. And unless this be the case, we have no security for individual virtue, nor for national independence. Well does it import us then, to attend to the improvement of our schools. Our highest wisdom, our holiest thoughts and wishes should be turned to multiplying the facilities of giving every branch of useful knowledge to all, of all ranks, sexes or conditions. We have already done much. Our citizens have not been indifferent to education; but they may do much more; and they will not have done their duty till the means of a competent education are within the reach of every son and daughter of this republic.

Permit me to add, our schools not only need extending, but the modes of instruction they adopt are susceptible of much melioration. It is not the mere ability to read and write, it is not mere acquaintance with grammar, logic, and mathematics, that constitute true knowledge. There is a moral and a mental discipline that is too much, and too fatally, neglected. Our schools should teach our children to think, accustom them to reason, to reflect; should impart to the young mind a knowledge of things, not merely of sounds; give it ideas, not merely words. Let our schools become nurseries of intellect, of moral feeling and virtuous habits, and then let them embosom all the children of the land, and we have a bulwark no power can break through—a defense strong as thought can reach, or necessity ever require. Each school becomes a palladium of our safety; each school raises up an army of enlightened patriots that shall fully appreciate, and triumphantly defend, our free institutions.

While we are meeting to resolve on constructing railroads and canals; while we are rapidly extending internal improvements—multiplying and securing the physical resources of the country, we must not, fellow-citizens, forget the intellectual mine. Your railroads and canals, your multiplied facilities for trade and wealth, will only facilitate your enslavement; first to avarice and luxury, and then to the ambitious demagogue, who will seize your base and guilty passions as the means of his own elevation if you do not at the same time cultivate the moral energies and avail yourselves of the resources of mind.

But it is a matter of gratulation that this subject is awakening and fixing the attention of our citizens. There is a new zeal aroused in behalf of education, and it is becoming generally understood that our safety is in the virtue and intelligence of our *whole* population. A new energy has lately been given to the cause of popular instruction by the establishment of lyceums in our populous cities and in many of our villages. The press, that mighty engine, is enlisting on the side of progressive improvement; and though we may find much, at present, to regret, we may look forward with joyful confidence to exertions hereafter to be made. The present is a period of great fervor of mind—of bold and fearless enquiry. Men's minds are aroused from their former quiescent state; all around there is activity, energy and experiment. Old notions are examined; old usages are tested; new projects are formed; a new class of emotions seems waked up; a new language is introduced: and from the wide, and deep, agitation of the public mind, we can but augur good to man, justice for his wrongs, and melioration to his sufferings.

The old world has aroused. Since the last anniversary of the event, we this day commemorate, there have been great and important changes—changes which influence, and will influence, the whole moral and political world. France, a country we can never forget on this auspicious day, our generous ally in "the days that tried men's souls,"[5] has risen to wash out the stain the sad catastrophe of her former revolution cast upon free governments. Her brave and generous population have proved themselves worthy to be free, and they are actually on the march to liberty.[6]

England, the land of our fathers, allied to us by a common language, a common literature, and similarity of institutions, though

[5][Ed. A reference to Thomas Paine's famous "These are the times that try men's souls," in *The American Crisis* 1 (December 19, 1776).]

[6][Ed. Reference here is to the French July Revolution of 1830.]

proud and aristocratic, yet the most free of European nations, has taken up the cause of the millions, and promises to aid them on in the march of reform. Poland, the land of Poniatowski and the immortal Kosciusko,[7] has revolted from the Northern Autocrat, has taken up arms in behalf of herself and of man. Bravely does she struggle. Justice nerves the patriot's arm and fires his soul to conquer. Hope stands tiptoe; and every freeman waits with breathless anxiety the result of the fearful grapple. A revolutionary spirit is abroad; the millions arouse in their own behalf, and ere long free institutions shall be established over the whole civilized world. We rejoice in the spirit of the times, though we rejoice with trembling.

Fifty-five years today and the first free republic ever known was born. For nearly half a century, excepting the feverish excitement of France, we stood alone, the admiration of the new world, the puzzle of the old. Now, nearly our whole hemisphere is free. South America can boast her republican institutions and her Washington too, as well as we. But the Liberator has gone. The abused, the slandered Bolivar,[8] second to none but the Father of our republic, has imprinted his name on the hearts of his countrymen; and free from faction, from intrigue and jealousy, he reposes from his labors, while all the friends of liberty drop, in silence, a tear to his memory!

Our example has waked up the world. The principles which our fathers staked "life, fortune and sacred honor" to maintain, spread; they triumph; and they will yet fully prevail over all the enemies of the human race. Man shall yet be free; shall yet prove himself worthy of his high origin and noble capacities. The thought is big with joy. We rejoice and well we may, for we shall always have the proud prerogative to say, we were the first to prove man is capable of self government.

[7][Ed. Tadeusz Andrze Bonawenture Kosciuszko (1746-1817) was a Polish statesman and general who fought in the American Revolution and led an uprising in Poland for national independence. Jozef Antoni Poniatowski (1763-1813), a prince and nephew of the last Polish king, Stanislaw A. Poniatowski, fought under General Kosciuszko and attempted to liberate Poland from the Tsarist yoke.]

[8][Ed. Simon Bolivar (1783-1830) was a South American soldier and statesman who led the liberation of northern South America from Spanish imperial control.]

9.

UNITARIANISM

Philanthropist 2 (November 5, 1831): 3-5

We have said our paper would aim to defend Unitarian Christianity as we understand it. A paper for this purpose is much needed in this State. No one of right feelings but must be grieved at the bondage in which the general mind is held by Presbyterian influence, and no one but will be equally grieved at the fatal extreme, to which those run who break from popular restraint, and set at defiance the predominant sect. To counteract these evils there has long been wanting a publication that should firmly resist the encroachments of the orthodox on the one hand, and carefully guard against any licentious extreme on the other. There has been wanting a rallying point for the friends of a mild, rational and benevolent religion; that desideratum, in some degree, the *Philanthropist* will labor to supply.

We are frequently asked, "What is Unitarianism?" "Who are Unitarians?" "Do Unitarians believe in the Bible?" "Are they anything but Deists and Atheists in disguise?" One may amuse, or grieve oneself, according to the humor of the moment, with the ignorance which prevails on this subject. Not that a few are not well informed, but the great body of the community are as ignorant of Unitarianism as they are of the great Cham of Tartary.[1] Some have heard there are a few Unitarians "down east," but the mass are unable to decide what the term may mean.

In answer to the question, what is Unitarianism? We reply, it is, in the apprehension of Unitarians, the gospel of Christ, freed from the false notions which ages of ignorance and barbarism substituted for the beautiful morality and simple and sublime theology taught by the Nazarene reformer, the *Son* of God. Its theology is the belief in one living and true God,—the Father of all, to whom we are accountable for all that we are or possess. Its devotion to him is the incense of a grateful heart which delights to dwell on the proofs of

---

[1][Ed. Probably referring here to a prince or medieval sovereign of China, or to a ruler over the Turkish and Tartar and Mongol tribes in parts of Europe and Asia.]

his paternal affection, and fears to disobey him because its love to
him, its reverence for his character makes one abhor the thought of
being capable of acting contrary to his will; because it would be treating him with irreverence and disfiguring his likeness within us. Its
morality is universal benevolence, the practice of justice, the love of
mercy, and efforts to improve, exalt, happify ourselves and the whole
human race; to develop the Divine likeness impressed upon our natures; to give free scope to the mightiness of thought, the sublimity
of moral feeling, to our noble aspirations after holiness; in a word, to
imitate the moral perfection exhibited in the life of Jesus of Nazareth.

In answer to the question, "Who are Unitarians?" We reply, the
whole Christian church was Unitarian till the 4th century, or at least
the doctrine of the Trinity was unknown till the times of Athanasius,[2]
even if as early. When the Roman power was broken, when ignorance and lawless tyranny presided in state and church, the Unitarians were overpowered, and the greater part of them extirpated by
the sanguinary zeal of opponents, who by being the most successful
came to be the orthodox. In modern times to answer the question,
we must name many of the greatest and best men ever known, men
whose intellectual and moral worth have spread a halo of glory around
human nature. We may mention a Milton, who will be remembered
as long as learning or genius shall be regarded—a Locke who opened
the vast storehouse of the human understanding, taught man to turn
his mind within and learn the vast treasure he possessed in the intellectual world; to a Newton whose name will not be forgotten till
science is no more, a Chillingworth, a Priestley, even Dr. Watts in the
latter part of his life, if not the amiable Doddridge.[3] In this country
we might mention some of the brightest ornaments of American literature; some of the most eminent members of the American Pulpit,

[2][Ed. Athanasius (c. 296-373) was bishop of Alexandria in Egypt. He became
an ardent defender of the Nicene definitions against Arianism.]

[3][Ed. William Chillingworth (1602-44) was an Anglican divine who had converted to Catholicism and then returned to the Church of England where he
authored the famous *Religion of Protestants a Safe Way to Salvation* (1638 and many
subsequent editions). Joseph Priestley (1733-1804), a scientist who discovered
Oxygen, a former Presbyterian minister, and a philosopher, held an Arian view of
Christ, rejected the doctrine of the Atonement and inspiration of the Bible, and
helped to found the British Unitarian Society in 1791, prior to his emigration to
the United States in 1794. Isaac Watts was identified in EW, 1:4. Philip Doddridge
(1702-51) was a dissenting divine and hymn writer who opposed Calvinist rigidity
in his *The Rise and Progress of Religion in the Soul* (1745) and was a participant and
supporter of the eighteenth century evangelical revival in England.]

of American lawyers, statesman and orators. So far as great names may go Unitarianism can claim as great, if not greater, than any other denomination.

In Germany, where the literati, as Mr. Dwight[4] observes, "are a hundred years in advance of all others," where for the last fifty years theology and sacred literature have been prosecuted with unparalleled assiduity and success, Unitarianism prevails to a considerable extent. It flourishes in Transylvania; it is the established religion at Geneva,[5] the place where Michael Servetus,[6] by the instigations of Calvin, was burned over a slow fire, made of greenwood, for denying the Trinity. It is predominant among a large portion of the English Dissenters, and has found its way to some extent in the church establishment. In this country, in the New England states it has taken deep root; especially in Massachusetts, particularly in Boston and its vicinity, where its advocates are by far the majority. It spreads to the South and West, and the simple Doctrine of the Unity of God bids fair to be soon the predominant belief of our country. Unitarianism has wealth, learning, talents, character, and piety on its side, which may compare with any denomination in our country. Though we urge not this as a proof of our sentiments, we do adduce it as a reason why every man who wishes for the truth should examine our claims. If this be done it is all we ask. If the mind can after due examination reject our sentiments, we ask it not to believe them.

[4][Ed. It is unclear which Dwight Brownson refers to here.]]
[5][Ed. Unitarianism was not the established religion of Geneva.]
[6][Ed. On Servetus, see EW, 1:78.]

10.

CHURCH AND STATE

Philanthropist 2 (November 5, 1831): 5-8

"Church and State." Start not, gentle reader, at these appalling words. We are not now about to make a set attack on the orthodox. We have heretofore given an exposé of what we deemed the dangerous movements of a certain class of divines and some of their adherents; we now propose to make some observations, which may be worthy the consideration of those who profess to be the advocates of liberal sentiments.

There is need of caution in our charges upon any class of people. Charges of the appalling nature of those which are made against the orthodox should not be thoughtlessly uttered, nor repeated on slight evidence. We gain nothing when we accuse our neighbor of that of which he is not guilty; we gain nothing when we charge him with crimes which cannot be proved; we gain nothing by vague declamation and continual accusation. This is, in some measure, a matter-of-fact age; and we should be careful that we make no charge that is not substantiated by clear and specific proofs.

This is an age of great fermentation; men's minds are too much agitated, and it does not behoove the philanthropist to increase the fearful excitement. Although the age requires facts rather than abstract principles, it yet has a tendency to association—to act by combination, and to approve, or condemn, on mere party grounds. In politics we no longer ask "is he capable? Is he honest?" But, is the proposed candidate for office a firm adherent of our party? In religious and ecclesiastical matters we seldom ask, "is the measure just? Is it likely to be attended by beneficial results?" But, "is it orthodox? Is it the measure of *our* party? Will it advance *our* sect?" This is a bad state of things; but let the professedly liberal, ask, if they are not doing something, as well as the orthodox all, to perpetuate it?

If the orthodox propose a measure, no matter how good, how desirable, and how feasible, it is enough to ensure it opposition from one portion of community, that it has an orthodox origin. Should the liberal party propose a measure of like character, equally just and desirable, it will be decried, by the orthodox as an infidel measure. This is wrong. We should recollect the orthodox are our fellow beings, our fellow citizens, and many of them our fathers, our sons, and our brothers. They are not without good qualities; they have warm hearts and not infrequently clear heads. They deserve from us, at least, respectful treatment; and their measures should be viewed as the measures of brothers: if good, opposed; if bad, lamented; and if of dangerous tendency, approved.[1] We are never to forget they have the same rights that we have, and that it is possible they may suggest some good things as well as we all.

But it may be said "the orthodox oppose us, encroach on our rights and are aiming at a control of all that is dear to us." Be it so. Because the orthodox abuse us, that is no reason why we should abuse them. Their conduct is not the measure of our duty. And if we do by them as they do by us, wherein are we better than they? And why have we any right to call ourselves the liberals? We must treat them justly though they treat us unjustly; we must be kindly affectioned towards them though they misuse, misrepresent and persecute us. It is no reason that we should do wrong because they do. Let us be just, though the world be wrong; and say with the Sage of Monticello, "that it is better to set the world an example of a good action, than to imitate a bad one."[2]

It is to be feared that many who oppose the orthodox, do not enquire carefully enough, what spirit dictates their opposition. We may oppose a bad thing in a wrong spirit, and thus be as blameworthy as though we had opposed a good one. It should be the wish of the liberals to build up what is right, rather than to put down what is wrong. It is no reason why we should oppose the benevolent, or ostensibly benevolent, institutions of the day, because they are supported by the orthodox. If an orthodox man does good, let us be glad; if a heterodox man does good, let us be equally glad.

We have opposed the missionary operations, because we have thought they were doing little, or nothing, for the heathen, and because the missionary society is amassing immense funds, that we fear will give to the party possessing them, an undue influence. So we oppose all those great plans on which we have before commented, not because they are supported by the orthodox; but because, by

[1][Ed. Sentence as in the original. It makes more sense in the context here to say: if good, approved; if bad, lamented; if of dangerous tendency, opposed.]

[2][Ed. Thomas Jefferson to Correa de Serra, 27 December 1814, in *The Writings of Thomas Jefferson*, ed. H. A. Washington, 9 vols. (Washington, D.C.: Taylor and Maury, 1853-1854), 6:405. The actual quotation reads: "I have ever deemed it more honorable and more profitable too, to set a good example than to follow a bad."]

presenting some grand objects which equally enlist the feelings of all denominations, they will amass immense wealth from them all, which is likely to pass under the control of *one* sect, and thus that one obtain an undue ascendancy. This we apprehend is the only ground of opposition which a good Christian can assume.

We oppose the "Sunday School Union," though not Sunday schools. We are perfectly willing the Presbyterians should have them; we only object to their abuse. We object to any one sect's soliciting scholars on the ground no sectarianism is introduced into the schools, and then making it the great object to indoctrinate them into the peculiar notions of the party. Let it be done openly and we have nothing to say. Let each sect stand on its own ground, and boldly acknowledge the object of the Sunday schools is to train up adherents to itself, and then we know where to meet them.

With regard to church and state, it is trusted the writer of this need make no allusion to his own opinions. They have been too often stated to require repeating. We would remark, the constant cry of "Church and State," will do harm to the liberal party. The cry will ere long cease to alarm; and then, if there be a party in favor of a union of church and state, they may move on unmolested, at least, regardless of all our solemn warnings, and strong appeals to the public. We but betray our folly, or our love of faultfinding, when we keep eternally harping upon "the dangerous movements of the orthodox." Where there is error let it be exposed, with charity, but with firmness; where there is an attempt made on our liberties, there let it be met by a bold and manful resistance—meet it with determination, but in good temper. There is no need that liberal papers should be all the time filled with articles on this subject; still less, that every man who can scribble a paragraph, and who calls himself a liberal because he hates the orthodox, should be all the time venting his spleen. If there be a measure of dangerous tendency, let it be faithfully exposed, and then let the matter rest, till something new transpires.

We make these remarks because we deem them called for; and because they define the course we shall for ourselves pursue. It should be the object of those who conduct liberal papers, to liberalize the minds of their readers; to enlighten the understanding; and to promote an elevated tone of moral and religious feeling. It should be their object to discover what is true, rather than to detect what is false; to establish what is useful, rather than to pull down what may be hurtful; and to "unite all hearts, if they cannot reconcile all opinions." Christ prayed for his disciples that "they might all be one" [John 17:21], and if there be one thing more desirable than another in this world, it is that we cultivate unity of heart, and be animated by a fellow feeling. Let us who are arranged with the liberals, strike out some truly liberal ground—let us take our stand, on high and holy ground, above the petty disputes of the day where every sincere lover of true religion, where the wise and the good of all denominations may unite, and labor for the spread of the Redeemer's kingdom and the melioration of the human race.

We do not mean that we are never to enter on debatable ground, but, that whenever we do it is to be done with that elevation of mind, and that liberal tone of feeling, that will ensure the respect of the enlightened portion of community who may differ from us, and retain their friendship though they remain unconvinced. We are all liable to err, and this consideration should teach us mutual forbearance, and admonish us to contend for our peculiar opinions modestly, though we do it firmly. By observing this course controversy may be disarmed of its evils, different opinions may be safely compared, and a good hope indulged that truth will be elicited.

11.

LETTERS TO REV. WM. WISNER[1]

Philanthropist 2 (November 5, 1831): 11-14

Dear Sir,

I find my apology for publicly addressing you in the importance of my subject, in your extensive influence, and in the manner you have spoken of the sentiments I deem it my duty to advocate.

I have been informed that during the late "protracted meeting" in this place, you represented Unitarianism as the "doctrine of the devil," and were careful to admonish your hearers to beware of being ensnared by the "devil's preacher." You have heretofore spoken of the "moral poison" of Cambridge and have frequently denounced what you have termed the "Socinian heresy"[2] in no measured language, and seem to have let no opportunity pass of prejudicing the minds of your adherents against what I deem the pure doctrine of the gospel.

I am not the man, sir, to question your right or your duty to labor to prove your doctrine, or to disprove mine; I would simply remind you that it does not become the Christian to denounce, that there is a mild, courteous, and forbearing temper, which as preachers of the gospel, it should be our study to preserve. I know human nature has its frailties; I know it is not always easy to command one's feelings. I myself have, heretofore, been betrayed into a harshness of expression and a severity of censure that ill became my profession and which I can but deeply regret. The recollection of my own weakness on this point admonishes me not to complain of mere personal allusions, and will, I hope enable me to bear with meekness the appellation "Infidel wretch," which you were so obliging as to bestow upon me.

[1][Ed. Rev. William Wisner (1781-1871) was the late pastor of the First Presbyterian Church in Ithaca, New York. On Wisner, see *The Memoirs of Charles Grandison Finney: The Complete Restored Text*, ed. Garth M. Russell and Richard A. G. Dupuis (Grand Rapids, Mich., 1989), 328, n.3.]

[2][Ed. The heresy was named after Fausto Paolo Sozzini (1539-1604), a native of Siena, who, after leaving Italy, spent some time in Geneva before moving to Poland. He denied the essential divinity of Christ, rejected the natural immortality of man, and advocated a Unitarian view of God. His anti-Trinitarianism was condemned by the Polish masses and by Protestant as well as Catholic church authorities.]

I regret, sir, you should have deemed it your duty to speak of Unitarianism in such unmeasured terms. Your hearers, from your account, could but form very unfavorable, and in my opinion, very erroneous conclusions respecting it. To call it the "devil's doctrine" was the very way to cause your hearers to reject it without examination. Shall I believe, sir, that you would have your friends reject any doctrine, without knowing wherefor? Shall I believe you would check the spread of any sentiment by giving it a bad name? An apostle, exhorted "to prove all things, and hold fast that which is good" [1 Thess 5:21], and the right and the duty to read and interpret the Bible for ourselves is the fundamental principle of Protestantism. Shall I infer that you are opposed to the apostle; that you have departed from the principles of the Reformation? Have I not a right thus to infer, when you prohibit, by your influence, free discussion and prevent your hearers from becoming acquainted with a doctrine by denouncing it to them as damnable?

You, sir, are no ordinary man. You stand high in community. Your influence in your own denomination is great. There are not a few who look to you as their spiritual Father, and who listen to you with all the docility of the child. Yours is therefore a responsible station. Your words drop not idly from your lips. They cherish the truth, or they establish errors. They are powerful in opening or closing mental eyes; in advancing, or retarding, the gospel. This consideration should, and no doubt does, bear with solemn weight on your mind; it should sink deep into your heart, and cause you to weigh well what you say. I hope therefore you duly considered what you said when you called Unitarianism the "devil's doctrine."

I am at some loss to satisfy myself why you chose to denounce the doctrine I advocate. You doubtless believe what you preach is true; you doubtless believe that the evidences of its truth are so numerous, so clear, and so irresistible, that no one who examines them can for a moment doubt. In your estimation your doctrine is based on eternal truth, supported by the voice of Jehovah. To discuss your doctrine then, you must believe will only establish it the firmer. Whence then your fears which led you to denounce mine? If your doctrine be true and mine false, could you have any apprehensions that your hearers would, after examining the claims of both, embrace mine? If not, why seek to deter them from becoming acquainted with Unitarianism? It certainly was no compliment to your hearers, to intimate they might possibly embrace it, or that it was necessary to warn them against it if it were as odious as you represented it. I know not why you should have done so, unless you honestly believed

Unitarianism was the "doctrine of the devil." I can hardly believe you would have thus said had it not been your honest conviction. The deference I would pay to your judgment and my respect for your talents, acquisitions and character would make me hesitate and enquire carefully whether you be not right, did I not reflect that there are names equally great on the other side.

I would not wantonly dissent from Mr. Wisner, but I can hardly admit the whole Christian church during the first two ages, ages of its greatest purity, embraced only a "doctrine of devils," yet during that period the church, as every theologian does, or may, know, was Unitarian. I can hardly believe that the doctrine defended by a Milton, a Locke, a Sir Isaac Newton, a doctrine believed by the pious Watts, and perhaps by the amiable Doddridge, and others scarcely their inferiors in worth and in fame, was the "devil's doctrine." Still it may be worth enquiring. It is possible they were wrong, and perhaps, sir, it is possible you may not be right. I take the liberty of calling your attention to the subject. It is one, sir, of no trifling importance and as we are both fallible men, it is possible we may err notwithstanding the confidence each of us feels that he is right. Each of us should be ready to "buy the truth and sell it not." There is, sir, a cogent reason why we both should attend to this subject. Unitarianism is spreading with great rapidity. It has enlisted on its side, wealth, talents, learning and apparent piety. It is advocated in language that comes living and breathing to the soul. It appeals to refined taste, to enlightened understandings, to liberal minds, to warm hearts and to elevated moral feelings. If it be, as you suppose, a dangerous heresy, it is high time it should be put down if it can be by fair and manly discussion. If it be true, certainly, you must wish to be no longer fighting against it.

Believing that your assertions respecting Unitarianism proceeded from a partial acquaintance with the doctrine; believing also, that were you fully acquainted with it you would become its warm supporter, I take the liberty to present to you in a series of letters, its principal traits and some of its many recommendations. I shall make no attack on your sentiments. I shall attempt to delineate and defend my own. I make no war on my fellow Christians nor on their creeds. I believe many a man's religion is good, though his creed is bad. And I had much rather seek for what I could approve in your views than what you embrace which I could but condemn. I am not disposed in these letters to you to depict the horror of Calvinism, nor to point out its inconsistencies. With these you are, doubtless, far better acquainted than myself; and, as it seems to me they must give you sufficient trouble, I shall not array them before you. I will try to draw your attention from these to something which I deem preferable—to the glorious gospel of Christ.

I shall, in my next, attempt to delineate the doctrine I advocate; that doctrine which you have termed the "doctrine of the devil," and shall labor to prove that so far from being the "devil's doctrine," it is the doctrine of the Bible, the doctrine of God.

Wishing you health, peace, and the enjoyment of the riches of Divine Grace,

NO. 2 (November 19, 1831): 20-24.

Dear Sir: In prosecuting my design, I must be allowed to observe some method. I shall, therefore, present you the several topics of my creed separately, and devote one letter to the discussion of each.

In this letter, I shall give you my view of religious liberty, free discussion and the use of reason.

In my estimation, the very essence of Christianity is moral freedom and enlargement of soul. It imposes no restraint, prohibits no exercise that is not morally wrong. Its aim is to free the soul from sin; to bring it into a holy liberty; and moreover it is satisfied with no forced obedience, with no service that is not cheerfully rendered. All attempts, then, to coerce the mind, to bring it into captivity to any set of articles of faith, or to any formula of worship, must be anti-Christian and mischievous. "The devil," says St. Athanasius, "doth use violence, for he hath a bad cause; but Jesus uses none, for he hath a good cause. He says, 'if any man be my disciple let him come after me.' He forces no man to come, and enters not by violence where he is excluded."[3]

I deem it the right of every individual to choose his own religion—not indeed that he has a right to choose any except the one God has given, but he is at perfect liberty, or should be, to determine which that is. He has the right to read and interpret the Bible for himself. I, nor any body of men, have the right to prohibit you from reading God's word; nor have we the right to require you to adhere to our interpretation of it in preference to those your own judgment may adopt. It is not mine to interpret the Bible and pronounce you a "heretic," an "infidel," "the devil's preacher," because you do not adhere to my construction. I have no right to pronounce you on the

[3][Ed. Not able to identify the exact quotation, but the substance of the message is found in St. Athanasius' (c. 296-373) *History of the Arians*, #33. On this, see *A Select Library of the Nicene and Post-Nicene Fathers of the Christian Church*, volume 4, *St. Athanasius: Select Works and Letters* (1886; reprint Grand Rapids, Mi.: W. R. Eerdmans, 1956, 1969-76), 281. See also *Patrologia Graeca* 25:729D-731A. I am grateful to Michael Fahey, S.J., for locating this text for me.]

road to ruin, your soul in danger of endless perdition, because you interpret the Bible differently from what I do. It belongs not to me to pronounce your honest convictions the "devil's doctrine," because in the exercise of my understanding I have come to different conclusions. The Bible has given you the same rights it has me, the same it has to everyone else; and it has given to none the right to demand acquiescence, much less belief, in their own opinions. As those who would presume to dictate must have exercised the right to decide for themselves what they should dictate, they must allow to you the right to decide what you will receive.

But, what is true of you is true of every other individual. If no one has a right to impose his belief on you, neither have you the right to impose your belief on him. Each individual stands on independent ground. His faith is between him and his God. To his own master he stands or falls. Hence, I am opposed to making the decrees of councils, the decisions of conventions, the votes of presbyteries, synods or general assemblies, the standard of religious character, and the rule of Christian fellowship. Religion is not a matter to be determined by a plurality of voices. It is strictly an individual concern—a matter of conscience—of which no human tribunal can take cognizance, over which, no body of men, however pure their motives, holy their lives, or wise their counsels, can have jurisdiction. It is an inalienable right, which the individual cannot surrender without crime, and of which the majority cannot divest him without stepping between him and his God and becoming in principle as much a pope as the pretended successor of St. Peter.

The right to interpret the Bible must exist somewhere; now, you must have the right to interpret it for yourself; or somebody else must have the right to do it for you. Do you, sir, acknowledge anyone individual, or any body of men, that has the right to say to you what construction you must put upon the word of God? Do you not claim the right to determine whether the construction you are required to put upon it be correct, or incorrect; and do you not feel at liberty to embrace or reject as your own judgment shall decide? If you do not, let me ask if you are not liable to be deceived? Were you to rely on my interpretations, would you be safe? Might I not be deceived? And is it impossible that I might wish to deceive you? As much respect as I have for your honesty and ability, I dare not trust my soul's salvation in your hands. I dare trust a matter of so much importance and delicacy to the management of no one. I fear that it will not be well attended to if I do not do it myself. And, sir, you will pardon me if I suggest what we both well know, that the people can never be safe if they leave all these matters entirely to the clergy. They should feel it their right and their duty to examine for themselves, to form their own opinions, and rely on their own decisions.

I will admit, sir, that in contending that every man has the right to decide for himself and to abide his own decisions, it is everyone's duty to do his best to decide correctly. Voluntary ignorance forms no excuse for error of opinion. Every man should do his best to ascertain the truth; his whole life should be one of enquiry—of patient examination and untiring efforts to obtain it. If on this point you or I neglect our duty, our errors of opinion will rise up in judgment against us. This is a solemn thought! Especially since we assume to be teachers and are doing much to fix the opinions of thousands! If to the criminality of not having searched faithfully for the truth, we add the injury done to others by inculcating falsehood, how great will be our condemnation! I tremble, sir, when I contemplate this subject; and were it not that I am conscious I have done my best to be right—conscious of this from the whole of my past life and that I have borne and still bear no little reproach for my honest and untiring efforts to be right, my pen would drop from my hand and would leave my task where I commenced.

But sir, I not only contend for the right to examine for ourselves, but I contend it is the duty of every man to practice free discussion. We know there have been numerous errors in the church. It is possible some remain, and perhaps some mischievous ones have not yet been detected. We know there is a vast variety of opinions now prevalent, and we know they cannot all be right. Does it not behove us to enquire, to discuss freely, the claims of all? I am firmly of the opinion that there is no little truth in reserve that may yet burst forth to cheer, purify, ennoble, and happify the human race. There has indeed been giant spirits engaged in the search after truth; but they were giants in chains; they were fettered by creeds; tied down by human systems and shorn of their strength. I wish for free discussion. Let no one say to himself, or to the public; "thus far will I go, but no farther." Let no one before he commences his enquiry say what he will prove, by what system he will abide; but, let him go forth in his strength, untrammeled by confessions, prepared to follow truth wherever her light shall lead, though she may compel him to traverse unknown lands, and to bear, what he may have deemed, barbarous names. When men will thus enquire, truth will emit her coruscations, will ere long shine forth in full glory, and the melioration of the human race be effected.

I need not to you, sir, prove that it is right to discuss freely all religious subjects. You have presumed to do it more than once. Neither need I attempt to show we have a right to reason on these subjects. You well know to discuss the claims of any doctrine is to reason. And to you I need not say it is right to use that noblest of our faculties. Were I writing to one who was not aware of this noble energy of his nature, to one who had never felt this "God within," to one who had never contemplated the mighty power of reason, that faculty which unites the present with the past and the future, which links earth to heaven, and man to the Deity—I would labor to show it no crime to reason. As it is, I will only remind you, Paul "*reasoned*" and "disputed" for two years in his "own hired house" [Acts 28:30]. God says to Israel, "come now and let us reason together" [Isa 1:18], and Jesus replied to the Jews, "why judge ye not of yourselves what is right" [Luke 12:57]?

I do not pretend that reason could have discovered all the truths of religion, but revelation can discover them only to our reason. The naked eye discovers not all the phenomena of the heaven presented by the telescope; yet had we no eyes, the telescope were of no use. So of revelation; it assists reason, but without reason it were useless. I use reason to determine whether God has given me a revelation; what that revelation is; what its suitableness to my condition; what are my best means of complying with its demands, etc. I do not determine *a priori* what God should reveal and then infer what he has revealed; but I do exercise my reason in interpreting his word; I own I attempt to explain that word by itself, by the general laws of matter and human experience, and, that still more important revelation in the soul, or that internal light "which lighteth every man coming into the world" [John 1:9].

These, sir, are my views on religious liberty and the exercise of reason. We are made rational beings, and we are wanting in justice to ourselves, and in respect to our God, when we refuse to exercise all, especially our higher powers, on the religion he has revealed. It is important, sir, that we do this. Our devotion to be cheerful, to have worth, or to be abiding, must be rational. The history of the past very clearly admonishes what we are to expect, when the people resign up their consciences to their spiritual guides, and neglect to examine for themselves. You are well aware that during the "dark ages," reason and theology were divorced; the consequences are written in characters too plain, in language too powerful, to be passed carelessly by or to be soon forgotten. I would not those consequences should be again felt; to avoid them we must teach man to feel his strength; to appreciate the nobleness of his nature; to claim his rights, and exercise his higher and better powers. That you may hereafter be able to co-operate with me in waking up the human race to the importance of this, is the sincere wish of . . .

NO. 3 (December 3, 1831): 37-42

Dear Sir: In this letter I shall solicit your attention to my views of the Scriptures and the rules for interpreting them.

It is customary with many—and even you are not free from the charge—to represent Unitarians as infidels, to deny them to be Christians, and to accuse them of denying the Bible, or at least, such parts as do not coincide with their tenets. This charge is one peculiarly aggravated and unjust; for no people read the Bible more attentively, or take more unwearied pains fully to understand it, than do Unitarians.

In the views which I present on this as on all other topics I speak for myself, not for others; though I believe myself to speak the sentiments of Unitarians generally, especially on the Scriptures. I view the Scriptures of the Old and New Testaments, as a revelation from God to man, or, rather I treat them as faithful records of the revelation which God was pleased to make, for our instruction, our improvement and our consolation. I do not view all parts of the Bible equally important; I take my doctrines from the new, rather than from the old dispensation. The Old was the Jewish; and was particularly designed for that people, and that stage of improvement which the Jews had reached. Its authority is determined by the New Testament, which is, in all cases, to be our final appeal.

In studying the sacred volume, I aim to be guided by the spirit rather than by the strict letter. The Bible you are well aware was written by different individuals, in different languages, and in different ages of the world; each writer has his peculiarities; his own way of viewing, and expressing, his sentiments, or the revelations made to him; the language which the writers used was very different from ours—allowed a latitude of expression, and exuberance of metaphor, a richness and variety of costume, which is inadmissible in our colder languages of the north. The usages of the people to whom they wrote, their modes of thinking, the imagery which surrounded them, the various localities, by which they were affected, were all different from ours, and tend to make the strict literal meaning not always the true one.

Again, the Bible was written a great many centuries ago; it has passed through a variety of hands, not always honest ones, and, though it has suffered less than any other book, yet it has suffered much, as every biblical critic well knows. True, it has not suffered so as to impair its credit in the least, but it has enough to make us cautious of resting any important doctrine on a mere verbal rendering. This caution is still more important in reading a translation, and especially our common version. I think much of our common version; it is perhaps as accurate a one as could have been made in the age when it was produced. No translation can give the exact meaning of the original. There are shades of thought the translator cannot catch and express in another language, especially when that is idiomatically different. This is certainly true, when the language to be translated has ceased to be a living language. There are a multitude of expressions which depend for their meaning on the manner they are pronounced, on the current usage, on allusion to some known circumstance, which passes away before the phrase may cease to be used. Much depends on punctuation. How difficult were it to understand a modern writer, if not punctuated? Yet the Bible, you know, was not punctuated at all. To all these, and many more difficulties, which I have not time to enumerate, add the peculiarities of our common version and we may easily perceive, mere verbal meanings are not always safe. The language of our translation is one by itself. Its terms are not those in common use; its style is antiquated, and must frequently convey, to the common reader, sentiments—if any at all—almost the reverse of those intended by the original writers. You well know, few persons, from our version alone, can obtain any accurate, or indeed proximate notion of the Bible.

Said I not right then, when I said we should be guided by the spirit rather than by the strict letter?

I do not advocate a mystical nor an allegorical interpretation. I do not pretend to find a moral in every nail used in Solomon's temple nor a hidden meaning in plain historical narrative. By the spirit I mean the scope and design of the whole—the true, intellectual meaning. When I read that "if a man strike me on the right cheek, I am to turn him the left also" [Matt 5:39, Luke 6:29], I do not understand it to the letter, that I am to allow him to strike, or, as it were, invite him to strike, me on the other; but, that I am to beware of a revengeful disposition, to be always peaceable and forgiving, never returning injury for injury, but contrariwise, good for evil.

When I am told that to be a disciple of Christ, I must "hate father and mother" [Luke 14:26], etc., I do not infer that to be a Christian I must hate my parents; but, that I am to value duty as paramount to every other consideration—that I am to fix my eye on the line of my duty, and to pursue it, without the least deviation, though it be opposed to all that is dear to me, though it require me to leave father, mother, brother and sister, and even to sacrifice my own life, as did Jesus, as did the apostles, in laboring to introduce the gospel and to raise man to his just moral elevation.

When I read he that hath "faith like a grain of mustard seed may say to this mountain, 'be thou removed,' and it shall obey" [Matt 17:20], I do not infer faith can remove a mountain; I only recognize in the expression that to accomplish any important work we must set about it with confidence; that, if we would surmount any striking difficulties or overcome any powerful obstacles, we must attack them with vigor and resolution, fully bent on victory and confident we shall succeed.

These examples, taken at random, will show you what I mean by the spirit. It is what I deem the true and only meaning. I do not contend for a double sense in scripture language. I believe the sacred writers spoke in plain language to those that heard them; and, when we have arrived at the exact meaning they intended to convey, or, if you please, at the meaning a plain common sense man would have obtained from hearing them, we have hit upon the true meaning and may be satisfied that we are safe.

You will perceive, sir, this mode of exegesis, requires a constant exercise of our highest faculties. It is important that the affections be right; for the judgment is greatly biased by the temper of the heart. We must not only have pure feelings but should take up the sacred volume with a sincere desire to be guided only by what it teaches. We must have no favorite theory to defend nor darling tenet to make out. Our wish must be to obtain the truth, and to obey it; whether it flatter our self-love and support our own peculiarities or not. If we take up the book with this state of mind, and for this honest purpose, and exert our reason, follow the illumination of that spirit, a portion of which "is given unto every man to profit withal" [1 Cor 12:7], I feel confident we can ascertain the true, intellectual, meaning of the sacred volume, arrive at its spirit, the reality which the sacred writers designed to communicate, and on that we may safely rely. This is all we want and by due diligence this we may obtain.

I will own to you, I am no advocate for plenary inspiration. I do not believe every word given us as Bible, is inspired. I would not give the infidel such an immense advantage over me. But do not misunderstand me, I do not mean to assert those portions that are uninspired, are not essentially true, I only mean they are portions of the Bible which required no inspiration. We need no other inspiration than common sense and common honesty to record what we see. The memoirs of Christ, by the evangelists, I consider faithful records, but not inspired compositions. The evangelists, in most cases, recorded what they saw, what they heard and felt. This they did as faithful historians, as credible witnesses, and honest men; and I cannot conceive more was required. To grant more would discredit their account. Contend, sir, that the evangelists wrote by the aid of infallible inspiration, and I will not insure you an easy triumph over the infidel. You know, sir, there are discrepancies in the gospel histories—not indeed any to discredit the writers as faithful historians, if you allow them to have written as honest men who saw and heard things as men, and recorded them as they impressed their own minds; but enough to destroy their veracity if you contend for their plenary inspiration. Under this latter supposition, the slightest error in fact, or in judgment, is fatal to their testimony; and you well know that in contending with Deists, all Christians have failed to maintain their cause unless they have conceded what I ask. It is not, sir, that I would weaken confidence in the Bible, that I deny plenary inspiration, but that I may strengthen it. The position for which I contend is the only one conformable to fact and you will not deny that it is very indecent for a Christian to be found contending for that which is not true.

In the Bible I recognize several distinctions. Some of it is historical, some prophetical, some moral, or didactic, some hortatory, some doctrinal. The doctrinal is all that required inspiration, beyond the natural powers of the human mind, and the internal revelation made directly to the soul of every man. I make the enquiry when I take up any particular writer, under which of these divisions, what he has written is to be ranked; I then make a distinction between the point he would illustrate, and the means by which he illustrates it; between the end he would establish and the arguments he brings forward to establish it; between the lesson he would enforce and the particular considerations he urges to enforce it. The first, I conceive, is all that is really important; and that, I believe, is always inspired, infallible, and may be safely followed in all cases. The latter partakes of the peculiarities of the particular writer, is not infrequently *ad hominem*; sometimes partakes of the economical method of reasoning then in vogue; sometimes must be treated as an *obiter dictum*, and sometimes, perhaps, as the error of judgment in the writer himself. The first is for us; the second was such as holy men deemed important for the age and country in which they wrote.

These remarks will enable you to collect my views of the Bible, and of Scripture interpretation. Whatever sentiment is fairly taught by the Bible, whatever can be made out fairly and rationally, to be the sense of the sacred writers, I receive as true, as the voice of God.

How say you, how can anyone say, that I am an infidel? That the class of Christians with whom I am proud to arrange myself are unbelievers in the Bible? We believe, sir, what the Bible in reality teaches; though we do not choose to advocate what men have made it teach, in addition to the intention of the sacred writers, or what they conceived themselves as teaching.

Unitarians are assiduous in acquiring acquaintance with the Bible; they go to the original sources; they bow not to human authority and will not rest till they are satisfied they have ascertained its true meaning. They may not credit all that has been said by commentators, by polemics, and the manufacturers of huge and unintelligible systems of theology. They have learned of Christ to call no man master on earth, for one is their master in heaven. They are willing to be taught of Jesus; it is their pleasure to sit at his feet and receive the words of life as they drop from his lips; but they are not willing to be guided by mere human authority. If this make them infidels, then are they such; if to read the Bible and to be guided by its true sense forfeit the Christian character, then that character is forfeited; if to separate what is human from what is divine, and to contend that the human is fallible, but the divine may be implicitly followed, be to deny the Bible, then do Unitarians deny it; if to call to their aid all the helps of modern science, human literature and human reason to unfold the lessons of divine wisdom, and to recommend and enforce piety, and excite Christian love, be opposed to the gospel, then are Unitarians opposed; otherwise they are not, and you, and all who brand them as infidels, should be rebuked. If this be the way to support the "devil's doctrine," and they are the "devil's preachers" for so doing, I pray you to tell me what are they who are their opponents?

In my next I shall endeavor to prove the unity and exhibit the parental character of God. I beg you to read, meditate, weigh well; if I am wrong reply. If you do not reply, your silence may be construed into assent to the reasoning of

NO. 4 (December 17, 1831): 55-59

Dear Sir: I request your attention in this letter to my views of the Divine Being. I do this the more readily, because my views have been obtained after much examination and doubt and have proved sufficient to rescue me from the abyss of scepticism, and to give me a cheering hope in the doctrine of life and immortality as brought to light in the gospel.

I view God as ETERNAL. He is the great, the universal principle of vitality—existence itself; which had no beginning, and can have no end—unless we are prepared to conceive a total end of all being, that what is now the universe may be an immense void—a mighty blank!

He is INTELLIGENT. Not merely life in the abstract; not a blind necessity—a mysterious energy, that vivifies, that acts without design, labors to no end. He is intelligence itself; an incomprehensible mind, that acts with a plan, and performs because his nature prompts and his wisdom approves. He is the source of all intelligence, and all minds may be considered but as rays from him, the central sun.

He is SPIRITUAL. I cannot define spirit. There is something in my friend that I love—something that I see not, taste not, handle not; yet something which the soul perceives, and with which it communes even when our bodies are apart; something which distance cannot separate, time dissolve, nor death annihilate. What is it? It is nothing which the outward senses can detect, but it is no less real on that account. This, sir, is what I term the spirituality of our nature; that image of God in which we were created, and by the help of which I form my conceptions of the spirituality of the Divine Being. What this spirituality is I know not; it is something too subtle for the external senses, too refined for the grossness of language; but something really present to the soul which holds with it, whenever in its purity, a silent, but inexpressibly sweet, communion.

He is ONE. I need not quote Scripture to prove this. You, sir, are too familiar with the sacred volume to render it necessary for me to repeat its testimony. You are well aware that the leading doctrine of Judaism, was the Divine Unity. Moses and all the prophets assert and re-assert it, time after time; Jesus corroborates it, directly and indirectly: directly, in quoting that declaration, "Hear O Israel, the Lord thy God is ONE—Jehovah" [Deut 6:4]. Indirectly, "there is none good but ONE, that is God" [Matt 19:17]. The apostles unanimously bear testimony to *one* God, "the Father of our Lord Jesus Christ" [Col 1:3]. And even you would contend as strenuously for the oneness of the Divinity against polytheism as the most strict monotheist whatever.

That God is ONE is attested by all antiquity in its sober moments. The ancient Hindoos, Persians, Chinese, Japanese, Egyptians, Arabians, Hebrews, and the intelligent among the Greeks and Romans asserted and defended the unity of God. The polytheism which at times prevailed, was occasioned by the misinterpretation of symbols and visible emblems introduced by the learned as helps to the unlearned; but, by the latter made a source of gross superstition and mischievous error. I will not now labor to prove this. I presume you will not question it; I believe that no intelligent theologian will deny it.

That God is ONE is indicated by the oneness of design and harmony of operation observable in his works. All is apparently under the control of one Almighty and invariable will, and verging to the completion of one great, grand and all harmonious design. It is not easy to conceive this to be the result of different wills. It is just what we should expect from one, and from one independent and unchangeable. Had there been different minds, different wills consulted in its creation, were different minds engaged in its government, should we discover that striking harmony which now excites our admiration and bids us adore the unseen Governor? Might there not have been some jar? some clashing? some sun warring with sun? some globe running afoul of globe? and now and then a universal tumult raging?

That God is ONE may be desired, if not proved, by the necessity of his unity to fix our devotion, and concentrate all the energies of the soul in pious reverence and filial love. Were there a multiplicity of gods our minds were distracted, and our affections baffled, in attempting to choose one on which to fasten, or weakened by being shared by them all. To have a strong, ardent, and abiding piety, our hearts must fasten upon one being, one God, and concentrate all the power of love on him. It needs but a glance at common life to prove this. Let the affections be divided among many and they are weakened. Take one away and grief is soon over. But let the heart collect all its power on one, that one is bound up in its own life—there is then an affection strong and abiding; increasing in power and endearment; gradually swallowing up the whole being and constituting the sole object of existence. Take the loved one away and life is shattered, its cords are broken and the soul withered. The same principle holds good in devotion to God. If there be but one God, it seems tangible to the mind; there is no dividing the affections, no doubt and hesitancy in choosing; the heart grasps at the simple truth and concentrates all its energy, fastens all its deep feeling upon that one and thus has a devotion constant as its own being and stretching beyond the limits of mortality.

But this oneness must be real; be plain, be what it purports; for, if you pretend this oneness exists only in a certain sense, and that in a certain sense, the Divinity is shared by a plurality of persons, be they two or more, the heart has its misgivings; its doubts and hesitancies. It may love the Divinity as one in a sense in which it is many; it may adore it is as many in a sense in which it is only one. It may in meting out its due share of love to each person in the Godhead give to one more than his due portion, withhold from another what belongs to him—all these and many more considerations you can but perceive would tend to perplex the worshiper, to harass his mind and to destroy all the joy of devotion. You, sir, have no doubt, experienced all these difficulties, and have had to check the spirit of devotion till you were assured it should flow to the Father, to the Son, or to the Holy Ghost, or to all three conjointly. Why not then say with the voice of nature, of antiquity and of the Bible, that God is ONE, and mean too, what we say, that he is one in every sense, as much as any individual mind is one? One God is all we need. For if infinite, he is adequate to all the work there is, or can be, for the Divinity to perform; if he is finite, a hundred might be too few.

Waiving, however, all further considerations of his unity, to complete my view of the Divine character, I must tell you that I prefer to contemplate him as a Father. I call him my Father, and I mean something more by this term than that he is my Creator. He created the wood of which my writing desk is made, but it were absurd to pronounce him its Father. But I can approach him as a Father, and am commanded to be a follower of him as a dear child. It is in this view that I discover the worth of the Divine character. Here I discover an intimate connection between the human and the Divine natures. Here God appears not in the dread character of a sovereign; here I see him not as a stern unfeeling tyrant, a vindictive judge; but as MY Father. Devils believe there is a God and tremble; but devils cannot view him as their Father; they only see the Divinity as a nature opposite theirs; they read in his righteousness their own doom; see in his purity their own destruction. Thus they tremble. All, as well as they, must believe and tremble, who view God merely as their dread sovereign, as their stern unfeeling Judge, who believe that he is governed by no law but his own power; and believe too, that is exercised by mere caprice, now choosing one to be his favorite, and now dooming to hell another equally as good—all who thus contemplate the Divine Being must "believe and tremble" [James 2:19]; but they who view him as their Father, their kind and affectionate parent may see him under a milder aspect, may believe and rejoice; may rush to his embrace, recline on his bosom, and seek, from him, security against the storms of the world, the ravages of sin, and the desolations of the evil one.

In a word, sir, I view God as one, as eternal, intelligent, spiritual, the "Father of the spirits of all flesh" [Num 16:22]. In him I have ONE object to love and adore. My mind is not distracted by a mul-

tiplicity of beings claiming my reverence, my adoration; my piety is
not weakened by an enquiry, whether this respect is due the Father or
the Son, whether this homage belongs to the first, or second, or third
person in the Godhead, whether this prayer shall be to God as the
Father, to God as the Son, or to God as the Holy Spirit. No, sir; I
worship God. He alone is the being who has a right to religious homage; and to him alone I am to consecrate my life and devote all my
powers of body, soul, or mind.

In him I see my Father, kind, tender—more watchful than maternal affection; ever present, ever provident, and ever controlling all
events to the good of those that love him. I love to draw near to him,
to hold with him a silent communion; to pour out to him the various feelings which agitate my soul; to resign myself to his keeping
and rely on his parental care, and trust all my concerns to his wise
disposal. When the angry heavens frown, when cold, unfeeling poverty banishes earthly friends, when bigotry persecutes, sectarian wrath
slanders my character, and mistaken zeal blasts my reputation, and
holds me up to public indignation I draw near to my God; pour out
my soul to him, and shield me in his warm embrace. This may be the
"devil's doctrine," if so I preach his doctrine, aye, am proud to preach
it, am happy in its belief.

In my next I shall call your attention to the person of Christ, and
ask you to help me settle the question, "whether he be God, or a
dependent being?"

Wishing you clear perceptions of the truth, and opportunities to
defend, promulgate and enjoy it, I am . . . .

NO. 5 (January 31, 1832): 109-11

Rev. and Dear Sir. Sometime has elapsed since my last, a multiplicity of other engagements is my apology. There is, however, no
harm done for the subject may be discussed at one time as well as
another.

You may conceive me entering on a delicate subject; but it does
not become us as lovers of truth, as bold enquirers, to shrink from
any question however it may shake our preconceived notions. Is Jesus
the Eternal God? This is the question and we owe it to ourselves, we
owe to our friends, we owe it to the Christian church to settle it if we
can.

When I read of Simon the son of Jonas, I seem to recognize two
persons, or beings numerically distinct—Jonas the father and Simon
the son. Should I speak to you of a king, wise, powerful and good;
should I inform you this king's subjects were dissatisfied with his
reign and ignorant of his paternal kindness, and that he, anxious to

reconcile them unto himself, sent his only begotten and well beloved son to them with assurances of his love and tender regard for them; should I represent this son as everywhere speaking of his Father, declaring he came by his Father's authority—came to do, not his own will, but the will of his Father who sent him, would you not distrust my sincerity or my sanity should I add that son and that father are numerically one and the same being? Should I continue, "the Father was pleased with the services of his son, he publicly approved him, and, though his subjects heaped every possible indignity upon the son, the father still approved his course, and finally place him upon his throne at his own right hand"—would you not advise my friends to have a watch over me to keep me out of harm's way, if I should thus talk? Would you even condescend to ask me how the Father and his son could be the same person, or the same being; and would you not smile with incredulity when I spoke of the king's approving himself, and setting down on his own right hand? When I do thus talk I hope my friends will attempt to correct me by physic and good regimen, rather than by logic, or any attempt at reasoning.

Now, this case which I have supposed is similar, though not so strongly drawn, as the one we meet in the New Testament. Jesus usually calls himself the "son of man"; in one or two instances he plainly tells us he is the "son of God"; he declares he came from "heaven not to do his own will but the will of the Father who sent him" [John 6:38], that he is "not alone" [John 8:16; 16:32], "the Father who sent beareth witness of him" [paraphrase John 5:37]; that it was "his meat and his drink to do the work his Father gave him to do" [paraphrase John 4:34]; that of certain events no man knew, "no, not the angels which are in heaven, neither the son but the Father only" [Matt 24:36; Mark 13:32]. What shall I say to him, who in view of these declarations and many more of a like nature, contends that Jesus the son who was sent, and the Father who sent him, are numerically the same being? Who not warped by system can draw such a conclusion?

"God so loved the world that he gave his only begotten son to die" [paraphrase John 3:16]. Do tell me, sir, if I am to believe that the son who was given to die is that same God who gave him to the world for that purpose? If so, why did it not read, "God so loved the world that he gave himself to die?" "God commendeth his love towards us in that Christ died" [paraphrase Rom 5:8]. How much plainer had it read, "God commended his love towards us in that he (God) died for us?" Once more, "This is my beloved son in whom I am well pleased" [Matt 3:17; 17:5; 2 Pet 1:17]. This you know was spoken of Jesus. Why did it not read, "Jesus spake and said, "I am God. I am well beloved by myself. I am well pleased in myself." This would have been plain, but you may perceive the Bible would require a great alteration before it would express clearly that Jesus is the Eternal God, or numerically the same being as his Father.

Again; Stephen, you know, says he saw Jesus "standing on the *right hand* of the Father" [Acts 7:56], the writer to the Hebrews, says Jesus "sat down on the *right hand* of the Majesty on high" [Heb 1:3]. Do, sir, explain to me how an individual may sit or stand at his own right hand; and, if you contend those expressions are figurative, I pray you point out anything they can prefigure, if Jesus and the Father are not as numerically distinct, as you and I? Jesus says, he *came from* the Father, and *goes to* the Father. How do you understand the position, that a being can *go from* himself, or *come to* himself? Jesus prayed to his Father; does a man pray to himself? He says to his Father "not my will but thine be done." How will this read, if we suppose Christ was the same being as his Father? "Not my will, but my will be done" [revision John 6:38]. I hope, sir, you do not believe Jesus was guilty of such quibbling, for a softer name I cannot give it.

But, if Jesus was numerically distinct from the Father, then he was not the Eternal God. I have already proved[4] there is but one God, and I will not insult your understanding by laboring to prove the Father is that one God. If Jesus be separate from the Father, he is dependent on the Father, consequently not God. This comports with the uniform testimony of Scripture. Jesus expressly said, he could "of himself do nothing" [John 5:19], "his work was not his own but the Father's who sent him" [paraphrase John 9:4] and his "Father was greater than he" [John 14:28]. I deem, sir, these considerations enough to settle question; if not more and stronger ones hereafter shall be offered. My limits forbid more in this letter. I must reserve what else I have to say on this part of my subject till my next.

NO. 6 (February 14, 1832): 115-19

Rev. and Dear Sir. I beg you not to misinterpret my object in addressing you this series of letters. It is not mere idle amusement; it is not for mere display; it is not to show how well I can defend the doctrine I profess, nor to exhibit its superiority over yours. No, sir, I have a higher and a holier object. I wish to elicit truth—to engage your well known talents and your high, undying zeal, in the work of fair and manly discussion.

---

[4] See, Letter, NO. 4.

The day of idle contention with me has gone by. The time for me to trifle has passed. I see my fellow beings, divided, torn by contending factions; I see them stirring up unholy strife; I see them making war upon their own interests, withering the heart by their ungodly rage and I weep for them. I see the demons of discord, of sectarian zeal, of wrath, of death, hovering over them, and I burn to avenge their wrongs; banish their enemies, and lead them to the fountains of true pleasure.

I know, sir, I am enthusiastic. It is well I may be. I have not only seen others suffer, but I have suffered myself. I have not escaped the shafts of adversity and I have had my full share of the evils I deplore. On my first setting out in life my wish was for the truth. I could not then believe there was any harm in knowing it, in adhering to it, nor in boldly proclaiming it. I burned to obtain it. I gave my days and my nights to its pursuit: I gave deep and anxious thought. I gave an impartial, an ingenuous mind, but, alas, my success did not equal my efforts. I sought it in books; I sought it in the world around me; I invoked all nature, I called upon the elements, but they heard me not. I sought it in my own heart; I dived into metaphysics, and attempted to fathom the abyss of mind; I prayed—in long and agonizing prayer, to the invisible Being, to Him who fashioned the Universe, and who presides over its destinies. Deep and anxious thought was traced upon my youthful brow, but truth still escaped me. I look back upon that day of solicitude and almost despair with a feeling no language can describe.

Men of your profession told me all was plain, that the wayfaring man, though a fool need not err, yet I saw nothing but dark inexplicable mystery. Wherever, and at whatever I looked, I saw mystery like an evil genius brooding over it. The world was a mystery; the growth of a spire of grass was a mystery; my own existence was a mystery; the moral and political world was a mystery; the doctrines, those of your faith enjoined, were a mystery, and yet I was assured if I did not believe aright the Great God would damn me in an eternal hell! What could I do? I trembled lest I should believe wrong, I searched and searched, I prayed and prayed, for the truth, but dared not say I had found it. Hell seemed to yawn before me. I seemed to see the angry heavens scowl upon me, and He, I was taught to call my Heavenly Father, it seemed to me, was clothed with terror, hung round with implements of torture, now winging the forked lightning to drive me to the blackness of despair forever!

And when I did find what I believed was the truth, when with all the buoyancy of feeling, generous enthusiasm and glowing philanthropy it inspired, I stepped forward to tell the world what I had discovered, how was my lesson received? Sir, the truth should be told. I blush for the reception I met. Had I been listened to with mere incredulity, had I been met with a fair and manly refutation, I could not complain. When I stated what I honestly believed, men in your profession cursed me. Those with whom I was intimate and for whose welfare I would have sacrificed my life, shunned me; nay, pronounced me an emissary of the devil. My motives were impugned, my character traduced; my good name destroyed and all my earthly prospects blasted. Even now, I am alone in the multitude; that very multitude whose welfare is the all-absorbing topic of my thoughts, deem me, as you pronounced me, "a poor infidel wretch." You know not, you cannot imagine, the sacrifice I have made, and am still making, for what I deem the good of yourself and the rest of my fellow beings.

These considerations must pardon me if I am enthusiastic. He who can bear all these and still retain his love for mankind has a right to be enthusiastic, and to call even your attention to the subject of improving the condition of mankind by giving them a religion they can understand and one that will make them happy.

On this subject, sir, I am in earnest. Every wise man loves religion. Every good man possesses it, and all should be religious. But if it be so dark and mysterious, that, none except a favored few can understand it, how deplorable is our condition! This village, this country, this continent is not the whole world. There are millions who never heard your doctrine, and millions who have heard it that neither understand nor believe it. What shall become of them? Has a wise God, a universal Father, given us a religion which only those gifted like yourself can comprehend? Sir, I do not believe this; I dare not so libel the character of Him whose tender mercies are over all. Religion is a matter in which each individual of the human family is deeply interested; all are required to be religious and should not religion be a thing which all can understand?

I tell you, sir, I believe that poor man who is bound to the dust he treads, whose almost every thought is required to obtain the means of subsistence for himself and family, has a soul as precious in the eyes of the Deity as yours or mine. I cannot, in my estimate, leave him out because he is poor, ignorant and sunburnt. To such as he the gospel was preached; for such as he Christ went about doing good. How, then, dare we call that the truth of God which this poor man cannot comprehend, which would require all his time to master! Sir, to preach mysteries to that man, and threaten him with endless punishment, if he does not believe and obey, is cruel as the grave. Do you never think of this when you deal out the dark sayings of your creed? Do you never think your reasonings are above his capacities and that they require a mass of learning he has no time, no opportunity to obtain? O, sir, the clergy will have a heavy debt to answer for in the day of judgment!

If religion be designed for all mankind, it should be plain, simple, adapted to the capacities of all. Whatever requires a mental power not common to all, whatever requires a degree of discrimination and laborious research which every man may not pursue, consistently with his duty to himself, to his family and to society, or whatever must render the many dependent on the few, making it the duty of a privileged class to explain and of the great body of the people to yield a blind assent to their expositions, can make no part of the religion a common parent would give his children, and by those who have any just notions of things, it must be forever rejected.

Religion includes faith, or belief. Faith is the result of evidence or that which the mind deems such. Every man is required to believe; but can he be required to believe that of which he has never heard? And should not the evidences extend to all, be equally within the reach and comprehension of every individual? Man is a creature of numerous wants; these he must labor to satisfy. He must support himself and those dependent on him. This must necessarily include a large portion of his time and prevent him from turning over all the legends of antiquity and of sifting the truth from the falsehood. Can that be the true faith which must require one's whole life to become acquainted with its evidences? This would be charging Providence with negligence or unkindness in adjusting the balance of our duties.

The heathen know nothing of your faith; were you to preach it to them they could not comprehend it. Yet they are as much bound to be religious and to have the correct faith as you are. But yours they cannot have. Shall we say God disregards all his children except those who chance to live in what are called Christian countries? I tell you I believe no such thing. True religion must be within their reach as well as ours, or we may cease to speak of the impartiality of Jehovah. I therefore, conclude true religion is what every man may possess with every varying degree of intellectual development, and in ever clime, whether called Christian, pagan, Jewish or Mahometan. In accordance with this principle I understand the mission of Christ; his religion was for all, is within the reach of all, the comprehension of all, and what all may find sufficient reason for believing. This I shall endeavor to prove. My next will therefore invite your attention to the object of Christ's mission. I shall follow that with another letter on the work he did; and that with another, deducing proofs of his inferiority to the Deity, and that will be followed by another on the office of the Holy Spirit, which will close the series.

NO. 7 (February 28, 1832): 141-44

Rev. and Dear Sir. In this letter I design to show you for what Jesus came into the world, and also to prove, as conclusively as need be, that the object for which he came is perfectly intelligible.

I know men have had strange views of the object of Christ's mission; I know some have talked about an agreement between the Father and Son—have told us, that Jesus came to pay a certain debt contracted by man, and to open a door by which God can justify us without forfeiting his character for veracity; but as I have never been admitted into the secret cabinet of Heaven, you must pardon me for not speaking of its councils or decisions. I am not wise above what is written; nor am I curious to know what mortal man may not know. I shall leave all these supposed legal obstacles in the way of man's salvation, which many have found it necessary to crucify their God to remove and confine myself to a few plain matters of fact.

The whole mystery of our salvation is easily unraveled and the lowest capacity may readily comprehend the whole of it. The whole resolves itself into a few words: "Be just, be good, be holy and God will accept you." All that God ever did, all that he ever will, require of us is that we "do justly, love mercy, walk humbly with our God"— "visit the fatherless and widows in their afflictions, and keep ourselves unspotted from the world," Micah 6:6, 7, 8. James 1:27. This is all God requires, and this is all that is necessary to secure our salvation.

Now, do not interrupt me by alleging man has sinned; for this I admit as well you. But, does the fact, man has sinned, alter, abridge, or extend, the requirements of God? By no means. God's demands remain eternally the same. The sinfulness of man produces no effect on God. His law stands immutable. What shall be done with the sinner? Will God accept him? Certainly, if he does good, obeys the law. But will not his previous transgression be filed in against him? To what end?

It is sometime said God has threatened us with punishment if we sin, and should he pardon us, or, what is the same thing, accept us when we reform, his threat would be unaccomplished, and his word forfeited. I threatened my boy the other day, promised him a whipping if he did a certain act. He did it; he came to me with every mark of penitence; I thought I had acted very foolishly in making the threat, and therefore did not whip him. Think you God ever makes such threats? They do no good. The consequences attached to sin, and which result in God's ordinary providence, are sufficient punishment, and the only punishment I find threatened; that, of course, is not removed; but when the person does good, he is entitled to a different reward. He then receives the consequences of goodness; and the consequences of sin are no longer felt; for this plain reason, he is no longer a sinner. The only good punishment can do is to aid in effecting one's reformation; when reformed, why punish him? You, perhaps recollect the assurance of Ezekiel, that if a wicked man should cease from his wickedness, and do the things which are lawful and right his wickedness "should no more be named"; Ezekiel 18:19, 23—also it is possible the parable of the prodigal son may occur to you. This parable (see Luke 15) teaches a very important lesson. The poor wretch received his portion, went away, and spent it in a very foolish and wicked manner; but when he returned to his father, he was embraced with affection, received as one from the dead, and I believe, was not upbraided with his former prodigality.

This reasoning may convince us that all that is necessary on our part is to be good; and I do not believe God was ever so situated he could not, consistently with his own character and government, accept all who become good. It was always consistent for him to forgive transgression on condition of repentance, and this is one of the most endearing traits in the Divine character; this invites the wicked to forsake his way and the unrighteous man his thoughts, and turn unto the Lord who will have mercy, and to our God who will abundantly pardon, Isaiah 55:7. Now, I do not believe this mercy was ever purchased for us; it is free, rich, flowing spontaneously from the bosom of our God. It wanted no sacrifice to dispose our God to be merciful, nor to clear away the legal fictions to enable him to abundantly pardon? This could not have been the object for which Jesus came. For what then did he come?

"Thou shalt call his name Jesus for he shall save his people *from their sins*." Mt 1:21. "Him hath God raised up to bless you by turning everyone of you away *from your iniquities*" Acts 3:26. His object, then, was a moral one. He came to reform his people. He came to lead them to repentance, to reformation, that "they should walk in newness of life" [Rom 6:4]—"live soberly, righteously, and godly, in this present world" [Titus 2:12]. All that was wanting, was, that we should "cease to do evil, and learn to do well." This was his object. Hence, his first words were; "Repent and believe, or obey, the Gospel" [Mark 1:15]. I will not dwell on this, for I think no one can deny it. He came to seek and to save that which was lost; to heal the morally diseased, to bring us home to God, that we might all "do justly, love mercy, walk humble" [Mic 6:8], "love our neighbors as ourselves" [Lev 19:18; Matt 19:19], and "do by others, as we would they should do by us" [Gal 5:14; James 2:8]. It was a noble object. To reform the world, to make an end of sin, and purify us unto God— O, it was worthy the Great Author of our religion. How he was to effect this shall be the subject of our next.

One consideration more, in this letter, and I close it. This object is a plain one. You can understand it and so can I. It was simply to make men good. No dark mystery envelops it. He who runs may read. The wayfaring man though a fool need not err. "Be good and God will pronounce you just; repent, and break off from your wickedness and God will accept you," is the lesson which it reads to all. This is the language of common sense; it finds an echo in every heart and what fools we must be to cavil about it! It is true that many will start at this, because it is too plain; because it gives to no one a factitious importance. Be it so. All nations may understand this; and all may hope for acceptance, if they do as well as they can; whether they have ever heard of your peculiar notions or not. The power to be good is present to all men, and the wise and good of all ages and of all countries, have been Christians in spirit, if not in letter, and of course accepted with God. Cornelius[5] was accepted while yet a heathen and the heathen may stand as good a chance of heaven as you or I. All that is asked of them they can give; and they know as well what they should do to be good, as any in Christendom.

It is true, this view of the subject may not be very profitable to the clergy. It may put into the heads of the people to believe they can know something of the matter, as well as the clergy all. It may spoil the clerical trade; but if the people are gainers, why should we complain? We should be satisfied. Religion is for all, and all should be able to obtain it without money and without price; and so they will be when it can come to them in its native simplicity. When we have stript it from all the disguises in which it has appeared; when we have presented it, as it came from its author in all its native loveliness, all will know it, love it, obey it, and there will be no longer any need that we should continue to teach every man his brother; for all shall then know the Lord from the least to the greatest. If that time should come the clergy can cultivate the earth, and not be as they are now, dependent on mere charity for the necessaries of life. I hope, sir, you will not take it unkind in me, attempting to strip Christianity of its

[5][Ed. Reference is to Acts 10:1-48.]

mysticism. I really believe I am doing a service to my fellow beings, by making it plain. You and others may curse me for it; but some will rise up to thank me, and I shall have the consciousness of having aimed well and having done what I could for the human race. This reflection will not plant my dying pillow with thorns. Both of us may be glad of the reflection when we come to die. In my next I shall call your attention the works Jesus did.

NO. 8 (June 12, 1832): 228-36

Rev. and Dear Sir. It is sometime since I addressed you my last and I own you have had some reason to think I had forgotten you. But I have not and shall not till I have closed the series I promised. The subject of this letter is the work Jesus did.

I regret that I must, in this, deviate from the affirmative course which I have usually pursued, and detain you for a while on what he did *not* do. Jesus did not appease the anger of God, nor purchase us his favor. I presume you agree with the Apostle that "God is love," and will admit to me that in love there can be neither wrath nor hatred. Will you then contend that God who is love, was ever so angry at man that it was necessary for his own Son to die to appease him? I will not press the question: it is shocking to my feelings and I gladly pass it over.

Nor did he come to purchase the favor of God for us. If I mistake not, Paul has assured us that "God commended his love toward us in that Christ died for us" [Rom 5:8], and Jesus himself said, "God so loved the world, that he gave his only begotten son to die that whosoever should believe on him might not perish, but have everlasting life" [John 3:16]. Now, if God loved us when he gave his son, and if, as Paul reasons, he gave his son to commend that love toward us, then certainly God already loved us, and it was not necessary for his love or favor to be purchased or procured for us.

There is, sir, something peculiarly revolting to my feelings in supposing it was necessary for Jesus to make a sacrifice to induce his Father and our Father to love us. It detracts much from the Divine character to say he was so wroth with us that he would not look kindly on us till soothed with the dying agonies of his well beloved son! It gives me a thrill of horror when I am called to be grateful to a being for his love to me, when that love was bought with blood, and when that being himself is one that delights in blood and is only made gracious by murder! Pardon me, sir, I can worship no such God. He in whom I put my trust always loved me and all his children; always did me good and always did good to all. I knew it not and did not do as I ought, and my grief is, that my gratitude is so cold to him who was always my tender Father, my faithful Friend, my bountiful Benefactor, and my gracious Protector. His love sent his Son to redeem and save me and in that love is my confidence.

Jesus did not suffer vicarious punishment. He did not, he could not, suffer instead of the guilty; he did not bear your punishment and mine. He could not. If, as you suppose, he was God, it was against him we had sinned, and I will not name the idea of God's dying to pay a debt due to himself. If the sinner owed a debt he could not pay, it was to God he owed it, and, if Christ was God, he owed it to Christ. If Christ died to pay that debt, he died to pay himself!

Again, if Christ was God he could not suffer. I presume you will not contend with Watts that

> God, the mighty Maker, died
> For man, the creature's sin.[6]

Divinity cannot suffer; the immortal God could not die, the infinite Jehovah was never laid in the tomb hewn out in a rock by Joseph of Arimathea. God die! Sir, I dare not dwell on the idea. It is as abhorrent to all our pious feelings as it is impossible in itself.

If Christ was not God, he was a created, a finite, being, and of course was as much bound to obey God on his own account as you or I. No matter how high you exalt him, his duties will keep pace with his powers, with his exaltation. Now, he had nothing to give wherewith to pay this debt of man's. He could perform no work of supererogation and you will agree with me that his death could be no satisfaction for sin. It will not help the matter, if you say Jesus was both God and man; the Divinity could not die, and that which died, was only human, and of course was only a human sacrifice; and a human sacrifice, you will admit, would be inadequate to the work you lay out for the Savior to do.

But to pass over this, there is another difficulty. My sins are mine. Now, I am the one who is guilty. You think it would breed disorder in heaven, if I should go unpunished, and you say God has declared I shall be punished. Well, be it so. "God will by no means clear the guilty" [Exod 34:7]. Now, punish Jesus, lay on him the full penalty of my sins, is that punishing me who am the guilty one? Suppose God accepts the sacrifice, and saves me, do not I escape the punishment due my sins? Yes, sir, you have only punished an innocent person to screen the guilty. Turn it which way you will, disguise it as much as you can, and it amounts to this and nothing more. The

---

[6][Ed. Isaac Watts, *Hymns*, Book 2, Psalm 9, verse 4.]

innocent suffer and the guilty go free! You know sir, my sins were not
Christ's sins and could not be, and only I ought to be punished; and
if I am not punished, if another is punished instead of me, then
God's declaration, "the soul that sinneth shall die" [Exod 18:4, 20],
is not true, and if you contend that Christ's death was a substitute for
the death threatened sinners for their sins, I leave you to settle the
controversy with your Maker.

Jesus did not die to make a satisfaction to Divine justice for the
breach of the Divine laws. We have seen he could not, and if he
could have died for the purpose which some suppose, I ask if the
spectacle of his death would be satisfactory to justice? I know it is
said, God vindicated his broken law in the death of his Son. I ask
you, sir, how? Did it vindicate his broken law to punish the innocent
and let the guilty escape? I know it is said God then showed his
hatred of sin and his love of justice. How? Did it show his hatred of
sin when he nailed to the cross his Son whom he loved and who had
never disobeyed him? When he sacrificed him to appease his own
wrath and to enable the wicked to escape punishment? Did this show
God's hatred of sin and the exceeding sinfulness of his creatures?
Pause, sir. It could only show the exceeding cruelty of God towards
his Son and a total disregard to the sinfulness of man. Sir, in the
name of heaven, I beseech you to review your creed and never speak
of justice till you abandon it. Do not allow yourself to be deceived by
words without ideas. Your creed is so familiar, you have so often
repeated its phrases without thinking of their import that you are
not aware of the shocking ideas it conveys to those who have examined it! Pardon me, sir. My feelings betray me. I mean you no disrespect; but, I know your creed cannot seem to you as it does to me, for
if it did, you would abandon it immediately.

Once more, Jesus did not come to open a door of salvation for
sinners or to raise them to a salvable state; for, as I have said, or
intimated before, man was always in a salvable state. It was always
just for God to justify the penitent and of course there was, as I
proved in my last, none of this preliminary work to be done. But
enough of this. I have long since learned it was a very easy thing to
find fault; but to detect error is not to discover truth, and to prove
you are wrong is not to prove that I am right. What then did Jesus
do?

He commended to us the love of God—brought life and immortality to light—disclosed the true character of God, and imaged
forth his moral perfections in his life—taught us clearly our duty,
presented us the true motives to its performance, and assured us by

his own triumph over sin, by his constancy under persecution, and his firmness in death, that human nature is adequate to the demands made of it and that we can fully discharge all the requirements of our God.

But to be more particular. Jesus taught righteousness. This he taught by precept and by example. His precepts deserve attention, both as to their matter and their manner. In manner, they are simple, within the lowest capacity, yet equal to the loftiest genius and affording matter for the sublimest flight of thought. He made no parade of learning, resorted to no dogmatic pomp, nor to metaphysical disquisition. He at once seized the conclusion to which he would have his followers come and he plainly stated it.

In matter, his precepts involve only that which is of universal obligation. There is not one of his maxims that is not applicable to all countries, and, in its spirit, to all ages. These precepts, too, comprise the sum of all moral and religious excellence. They enter into no minuteness of detail, give us no labored commentary on human duty, but they seize at once the all-comprehending principles which, if imbibed and followed out, will invariably lead its possessor right whatever be the age or country in which he lives, whatever be his rank or station in life, the nature of his employment, the party with which he may be associated, or the form of government under which he lives.

Now, sir, I think the bare disclosure of these few all important truths was of immense utility to man. Who before him, or since, have superseded or equaled him? No possible improvement can be made in his moral principles; for they are in fact, the germs of perfection and when cherished and nurtured into life by our love and obedience they lead us to the highest degree of excellence. And it is the flexible character of those precepts—their adaptation to man in every circumstance in which he can be placed, that I would have you notice. This, sir, stamps his religion divine, and proves him who first disclosed it, entitled to the reverence of the whole human race.

Again; he taught us the truth, not only in reference to human duty, but in reference to God and the human soul. You, sir, will not contend it was of little consequence to have the truth taught us in reference to the Divine character; nor will you deny that at the time the Messiah came, there was the most deplorable ignorance of the true God prevailing. Men had formed to themselves gods in their own image and paid them a worship which degraded the human mind, debased the soul and corrupted the hearts, manners and morals of the worshipers. All the world were polytheists with the exception of the Jews, and even they were scarcely better; for they viewed their Jehovah very much in the light of a tutelar Deity. The true knowledge had become lost and the witness within was silenced by the force of prevailing education, habits and manners. Surely it was then of some consequence to have the truth told us respecting the Divinity.

This Jesus did. He taught more clearly his unity than it was before taught, except, perhaps, by Moses, and he disclosed the parental character of the Deity. Previous to him, men viewed God mostly as a being of power; they trembled before a stern and inexorable Judge; they shrunk like slaves from the presence of their tyrannical master. Hence the spring of their obedience was fear and their devotion was servility. There was no sweetness in their piety—no love mingled with their offerings, and no childlike confidence in their resignation. This Jesus corrected, by teaching us to say—not "our Lord," but "our Father." In this he told an affecting and an ennobling truth. By this one disclosure he raised us from earth to heaven and from slaves to be sons of God and joint heirs with himself. This lessened the distance between us and our God and brought us and our Father together, to a purifying communion of soul. This softened the harsh features of religion and rendered our duty to God pleasing and inviting. I know, sir, that too many have labored to cover up this glorious truth which Jesus taught, and I have heard even you preach, when it seemed your whole aim to take from me my Father and set me back in the cold, dark slavery which depressed the soul till Jesus taught us it is a child of God. But, sir, if you will repeat the truth of Jesus, that God is our Father, and that we should be followers of him as dear children, you will find it a more successful method of converting men from sin to holiness than the method now followed by yourself and Mr. Finney.[7] Indeed sir, I do conceive the paternity of God is his most endearing trait, and this alone, if properly presented would lead the whole world to his embrace. This Jesus did present; it was a work of vast importance, and would have effected the regeneration of the world, had not his misguided followers covered it up. He "brought life and immortality to light." He did not originate this doctrine for it was taught before he came. But it had become so obscured as to be of little weight in forming men's characters to virtue. He taught it more clearly and gave it higher sanctions than it had before received, and brought it home more immediately to men's "bosoms and business." This, sir, is an important doctrine. It flows as a natural conse-

[7][Ed. On Charles Grandison Finney, see EW, 1:19 n.]

quence from the truth Jesus disclosed respecting our relationship to God. It has a most important influence in forming our characters, in exalting our conceptions and in stimulating us to moral improvement. I speak of it, not as you teach it, connected with election and reprobation, nor as my quondam Universalist friends maintain it, but as Jesus taught it, a continuation of our present existence, making this state of being the spring time of our life, which will have an immense influence in establishing the degree of happiness or misery we shall here and hereafter receive. I view this doctrine only as connected with the fact we shall all rise from the dead, all live hereafter in a social state, which will be happy or miserable in proportion as we are fitted for each others society and have a just cultivation of the inner man. This view of the doctrine gives it a practical bearing upon our lives—gives to it the weight of eternity in inducing us to be good, to improve our time, employ our faculties and exert all our powers in acquiring elevated and pious characters. Also it holds out encouragement to us in every situation; it not only assures us vice shall be punished, but it assures us, oppressed virtue shall yet raise its drooping head, that truth will ultimately prevail and real worth finally triumph. It assures us our labors are not in vain; that if we sow we shall reap, that the improvement of the spiritual man, here, will be an eternal gain. The theme, sir, is most inviting, but I cannot now pursue it. But I put it to your heart, if Jesus did not confer an immense benefit on you and me, and the whole world, by bringing this doctrine to light, making it plain, convincing, inviting, purifying, and ennobling. Just glance over these points to which I have alluded, you will perceive that they include the whole—not of Calvinistic theology—but of Christianity. Now, was it of no consequence to have Christianity disclosed and established? A system of religion which gives you and me our hopes of immortality, and through which we receive the sweets of piety, and all the luxuries of devotion? Remember, Jesus taught this and by his labors of love, under God, it was established, and surely you will admit this gives him a claim to our reverence and to our warm affection.

Add to this, sir, what he did by his example. His example, sir, was the most quickening miracle in human history. In his example you may see moral perfection; you may see piety and devotion in all their sweetness, constancy, and power. There, sir, you may see a firmness of principle proof against all temptation; a confidence in God superior to all adversity; a love for man stronger than death. Go, sir, read the simple memoirs of his life—mark his eloquence, soft and suasive, warbling through the synagogues of Judea, or now kindling with rebuke, striking terror to the bigoted Scribe and boasting Pharisee; see him, poor, despised, rejected, scorned, persecuted, not having where to lay his head, still going about doing good, visiting the house of sorrow, wiping the tears from the mourner's eyes, or mingling his own with weeping sisters at the grave of their brother; binding up the broken heart—pouring the oil and wine into the wounded spirit, and making the sufferer whole—mark this, see him the poor man's friend, the help of the needy, the hope of the despairing, the solace of the wretched—mark him, sir, being and doing all this amidst scorn and reproach, exposed to persecution, to death, and say if it will not make one "a sadder and a better man?"[8]

In his example we see all the virtues, all the excellences which human nature can reach. We see in him all that power of mind, that firmness of spirit, that singleness and energy of purpose, that undying love of mankind, that unshrinking devotion to God and duty, and that unwavering confidence in Heaven which make up the perfection of the human character. Sir, the very contemplation of such excellence begets a growing likeness of itself. It speaks a language all can understand; it speaks to the heart; it imparts power, energy, purity and strength by its silent but affecting eloquence. Who marks the "man of sorrows" [Isa 53:3], who traces him by the good he did, and the reproach cast upon him, who sees him alone, unaided, except by God and the justness of his cause, bearing up against an opposing world, firm and unbending in principles, baring his breast to the shafts of the enemy, submitting to be treated as a malefactor, meekly bowing his head to the executioner, that he might vindicate truth, establish righteousness, and secure the regeneration of the world—who can see him thus struggle, preferring death to departure from the work given him to finish—who can see the wicked triumph and hear him in the agony of death, holding fast his integrity, pray God to forgive his murderers and not wish to be like him?

His character, sir, is the most quickening power in the universe. No one can read it and not admire; no one can trace his life and not feel his selfishness depart; no one can see what he suffered for truth and human nature and not feel rebuked for his indifference; no one can see his piety, and not kindle with devotion; no one can see him die by wicked hands for oppressed humanity that he might raise us

---

[8][Ed. Quotation may be a paraphrase of a line from Coleridge's *The Rime of the Ancient Mariner*: "He went like one that hath been stunned, And is of sense forlorn; A sadder and a wiser man, He rose the morrow morn." See *The Poems of Samuel Taylor Coleridge*, 209, line 624.]

to our birthright, and not feel his love for man warm and his spirit stir to aid in reforming a world.

Sir, there is power in the cross. In that you may see the perfection of heroic, saintly and godlike virtue. In that you may see the deep depravity of mankind and the mighty sacrifice it required to establish truth and wake them to the love of virtue. And, sir, when in the discharge of duty, troubles and difficulties arise, when dangers beset you, the wicked scoff, the boastingly righteous revile and the bigoted persecute, look at the cross! Jesus endured the same; when you are tempted to yield, to forbear your labors, and leave the world to sin and Satan, look to the cross—Jesus stood firm, no dangers could intimidate, no flatteries beguile, no temptations divert his course; and when discouraged, sin seems to have gained the mastery, wickedness to be triumphant, look to the cross! Jesus faltered not; he gave not back; he gave his life—he conquered in his death. And his spirit lives. It will live through eternity. It is the spirit of truth, the spirit of God; it breathes through his examples, it kindles a saintly and heroic virtue in the good; it will triumph and prove the salvation of God to the ends of the earth. But enough.

12.

FUTURE STATE

Philanthropist 2 (November 19, 1831): 17-19

The doctrine of a future state of conscious being is one that few have disbelieved, and one that still fewer have not wished to embrace as an anchor to the soul. Whatever may be our religious or skeptical notions, we all wish for a fairer and better land into which we may find admittance when we bid adieu to the sorrows of this.

When the world first indulged the hope of another life, if indeed, it be not as old as the human race itself, it is impossible to determine. No historical monument points to an age which had it not; no traveler has visited a country, however barbarous or savage, that has not in some shape a wish, a hope, or a belief in some future existence for their deceased friends. However rude, barbarous or whimsical their notions may be; however wild and fantastical the beings with which they people the regions beyond the grave; all ages and all countries have believed, and do believe, such regions exist, and have a clearer, or less perfect, conviction that they will there live again as sentient beings.

What originated this wish, hope, or belief, it is impossible to ascertain. There have never been wanting individuals who had it not; hence we infer it is not innate. It was not tradition, for tradition can only perpetuate; it has no power to originate. The belief must have existed before tradition could hand it down. It can hardly be said that nature teaches it. True we see transmigration from one state of being to another among some of the insect tribes. The caterpillar winds itself in its cone, and after a few days, bursts its grave, and sails on colored wings, a beautiful butterfly. But because the insect passes from one state of being to another, we cannot with certainty infer the same of man. And should the analogy hold good in all its parts, it would not meet our wants. The butterfly is not immortal. It sports in the sunshine for a few days, and is no more. So man would live but again to die.

Poetry has found in sleep an image of death. But the resemblance is slight. In death the vital functions cease; in sleep they go on. The gloom of winter, the renovation and joy of spring, have been adduced as poetical emblems of death and the resurrection. There is something beautiful in the thought. The autumnal winds sigh lonely through the forests; the cold desolations of winter succeed; and wrap the earth in its winding sheet. The sun gains the vernal equinox; the warm south wind blows; the snows melt; a mild and genial air breathes over the earth, and all start into life. Gladly would we view this emblematical of man's resurrection from the tomb in the spring of immortality. But the dead live not. The plant that had withered, the stalk that was dry, feels no revivifying power. That green blade is from a root that died not, and that beautiful flower is from a seed newly germinated.

Man, as viewed by our senses, seems only born to propagate his species and die. The infant is weak, feeble, in mind as in body. For a few days it grows up; flourishes with promise; reaches its maturity; casts its leaf; withers away to second feebleness—to infancy—to death. The elements which composed the body, return to their native elements, to form new combinations, to constitute parts of plants and animals, again to separate, to be again recombined, and thus on. In this man can read no future conscious being. Nature, so far as we can read her language, reverses not the decree, "death is an eternal sleep." Whence, then, the universality of man's belief in a future state? Is it the result of imagination? Is it a mere dream? We would not, if we could, answer this in the affirmative. We would not disbelieve. Without the hope of another, this were indeed, a wretched world. We would believe, even if in error; for if we err, we secure the bliss of believing, and can never feel the pang of disappointment.

Where ignorance is bliss, 'tis folly to be wise.[1]

There is something curdling to our blood in the thought we are to be no more. There is something too painful to be described, almost to be endured, to stand by the newly made grave and see let down into the cold earth, the one we have loved, whose soul was commingled with our own, and to feel that it is the final end—to feel that there lies the form we have often clasped in transport; there are closed the eyes which shone with intellect; there are mute the lips that discoursed so often music to our ears; there is stilled the heart that beats to warmest and kindest feeling. All, as the clods rattle upon the coffin, vanish, and we stand lone and withered beings. It is as if the life spring was broken. A somber hue comes over the whole of

[1][Ed. Thomas Gray (1716-71), *On a Distant Prospect of Eton College* (1742), st. 10.]

nature. The soul is dark. Not a ray beams out to pierce the dark cloud that hangs over it. I have thus stood by the grave of my friend; I have thus looked upon his dissolution as the end of all that I loved. It is enough. I would not stand there again. Wisdom may assert we die to live no more. But

> Oh let her read nor loudly, nor elate
> The doom that bars us from a better fate;
> But sad as angels for the good man's sin,
> Weep to record, and blush to give it in.[2]

The soul shrinks from the thought of annihilation, and it would seem that shrinking back—that horror at non-entity—indicates that death cannot be the end of our being. Perhaps it is not unreasonable to infer a future state from the capacities of the soul itself. Few who have contemplated the soul, its mighty powers, its sublimity of feeling, its moral grandeur, its continual aspirations after something it has not, its wish to stretch beyond the narrow circumference of the earth, beyond the stars, beyond the farthest limits of space, to rise and hold communion with the Mysterious Power it feels but sees not. Few have taken this view of the human soul, and have not deemed it destined to survive the frail tenement of clay in which it is lodged. Who can believe a being of such varied and extensive powers, so high, so noble, and often so godlike in its aspirations and achievements, is born but for an hour? No it cannot be.

> ——— I can feel, that though a clod
> Of the dark vale, there is a *sense*
> Of better things—the fit abode
> Of *something* tending up to God—
> A germ of pure intelligence.
> I know not how the Eternal hand
> Has molded man—but this I know,
> That while 'midst earth's strange scenes I stand,
> Bring visions of a better land
> Go with me still, where'er I go.[3]

[2][Ed. Thomas Campbell (1777-1844), *Pleasures of Hope* (1799), pt. II, l. 356-57.]

[3][Ed. Not able to identify quotation.]

13.

JUSTIFICATION

Philanthropist 2 (December 3, 1831): 35-37

Trinitarians would have us contend for the Deity of Christ because a being less than God could not have atoned for the sins of the world; and without an atonement they tell us we can have no hope of justification in the sight of God.

There is an important principle involved in this. What is justification? Does God justify us for what we are? Or for what some other being has done?

There is no mystery in justification. God is truth. It is impossible for God to lie. When he pronounces a man just that man must be just; for God will not, he cannot, call him so when he is not. God speaks the truth; he will never pronounce me a just man while I am a sinner; he will not justify me and receive me as holy till I am so. The matter is plain then. Let man be just and God will justify him.

The second question is answered. God justifies us for what we are or because we are just, not for what some other being has done. Where then is the argument for the Deity of Christ?

But has Christ done nothing? Made he no atonement? What atonement was needed? Who needed it? God did not. He is unchangeable. His nature is love. He is, always was, and always will be, gracious. When he made his creatures he loved them, pronounced them very good. He loves them now. That love is undying. It is higher than the heavens, broader than the earth, deeper than hell, many waters cannot quench it, all the floods cannot drown it. He needed nothing to make him gracious to man. He needed no precious holocaust to make him look with compassion on man—no dying groans, no spectacle of bleeding innocence and suffering gods to prompt him to our rescue. It was always just for him to pardon the penitent and justify the just, to accept the holy. There was, then, no legal obstacle to remove, no divine wrath to appease, no love from God to man to purchase. God was always right—he wanted no atonement. Did Christ make none?

Did man need one? What did he need? God was right, but man was wrong. God was gracious but man was not; God loved man, but man loved not God. There was the difficulty. God required man to be just before he would justify him. But such man was not. Such it was necessary he should be before he could be happy. Whatever Christ did was done for man—done to remove, no legal fiction—no obstacle on the part of God, but the difficulties which existed on the part of man. We, not God, received the atonement, which was not a satisfaction paid to divine justice but a commendation of our Father's love to us. "God commendeth his love towards us in that while we were yet sinners Christ died for us" [Rom 5:8].

But we dislike the term atonement. As that word is now used it detracts from the goodness of God, destroys the freeness of his grace, and places us under obligation only to the son who purchased the divine love, not to the Father who sold it. We prefer the term *reconciliation*, as being more congenial with the original term and more expressive of the real objects of Christ. Man was not reconciled to God, was not just, was not in conformity to the truth, was not holy, it makes no difference which term you use—while such, he could not enjoy the Divine Goodness, he could not appreciate his Father's love, nor enjoy the bounties of Providence, consequently must be miserable. Christ came to remove this difficulty. He came a messenger from the throne of love; he bore in his right hand the green Olive Branch, emblem of peace from God to the world, with his left he pointed to the volume of moral righteousness; he bade man read, obey, and be happy.

We are indeed justified through the merits of Christ; not that his obedience is imputed to us, and that his sufferings atone literally for our sins; but, because what he did, taught, exemplified, and suffered, become the moving cause of our righteousness—tend to kindle the love of moral excellence in our hearts, to lead us to just views, just feelings and just practice; thus making us *personally* holy, which is the only ground on which we can be accepted by our heavenly Father. Christ has done much, but had he been God he could have done nothing that we needed. We wanted to see the moral perfection of human nature exemplified. Jesus being made like unto us did set us a perfect example. That we may safely follow. But had he been God, what would his example availed us? It would not have proved to what excellence we as human beings might rise. It was an example for gods, not for man. All the beauty of his character vanishes when you call him God; all that was endearing in his life, all that awakened our sympathies and fired our souls with the love of virtue, has gone, and the gospel has no worth.

14.

ESSAY ON REFORM

Philanthropist 2 (December 17, 1831): 51-55

That is a wrong view of religion which supposes it to deal with only one class of affections. Religion is for man; it embosoms whatever belongs to his well-being through all stages of his existence and in all his relations, whether of time, or eternity; whether to his God or to his fellow; to himself or to his race. The gospel is but another term for those great and all comprehending principles which are necessary to perfect the human character, to make all feel and act as they should, to produce the greatest sum of human happiness. It comprises moral and political as well as theological science; and is able to direct us in the affairs of this world as well as in those of another.

It is to be deeply regretted that the power of the gospel to wake up human excellence, to draw forth human virtue, and to give us just social feelings and social institutions has been so often passed over or so little valued. The morals of public and private life should be the same; and the gospel requires us to act sincerely, conscientiously, wisely, under a sense of our individual responsibility, in all cases; whether it be in our own domestic circle, in the temple of worship, at the ballot box, in the magistrate's chair, or in the halls of legislation.

I design in the following Essay on Reform to examine how far we follow the gospel in our social feelings and institutions; to point out the gross inconsistencies between our practices and our professions; exhibit some of the evils which we endure, their causes, and the means of their removal. Some portions of the Essay were written and published while I was the editor of another paper;[1] the design is now enlarged; what was then published is remodeled, and the whole, I hope will now be presented my readers. I shall proceed leisurely, may be at times somewhat desultory, but hope to preserve something like regularity, and be able to reach the conclusion in our present volume—perhaps not till another.

---

[1][Ed. Brownson may be referring to the *Genesee Republican and Herald of Reform*, which he edited from July to November of 1830. It was a short-lived paper in favor of the New York Workingmen's Party.]

There has been enough of idle and mischievous contention; enough of barren speculation, and bitter controversy on mere topical theology. It is time we take a higher and a holier aim—time that we seek to ascertain whether human virtue and human happiness be a dream; whether man must always devour man, and brother study to supplant brother; or whether, after so many ages of wrongs and outrages, he may not learn wisdom, appreciate the dignity of his nature, act as becomes his high origin, and finally avail himself of his vast, almost illimitable, resources. That he is a sufferer is but too certain—that he is the author of his own misery few can doubt. Why not then enquire if the means to enjoy existence are not within his reach.

I shall be led into an important enquiry—be engaged in a discussion of all others the most intimately connected with the principles of human action. I address myself not to the gay and frivolous crowd who are ever averse from the exercise of thought, not to the herd of superficial readers who are enamored of what by a strange perversion of taste is called "polite literature," consisting of lovesick romances and tales of fiction as destitute of probability as they are of genius—but, to those who are accustomed to investigate, to those who prize the stores of intellect, and who hope by cultivating the mental world to meliorate the condition of man. I appeal, to the philosopher, to the philanthropist, and to the Christian. By the criticism of these and these alone will I estimate the worth of my enquiries and determine the value of my propositions.

The mode in which the Essay is presented may detract something from its merits. Newspapers have become so common in this country that their influence is in a great measure lost. They have been so much engrossed with mere party politics and so completely subservient to contending partisans that any elaborate discussions of first principles that do not have an immediate bearing upon the success or defeat of rival individuals or of rival parties are little read, and less regarded. An Essay, which, a few years back, would have immortalized the writer, is now deemed but common place, and, given to the public in the columns of a newspaper, it is thrown aside as matter of no consequence. It is pronounced mere newspaper trash, written to fill up the space in its columns, and probably designed simply for sectarian or party effect. Though I shall bestow no little labor on the series of Essays I now commence, though I shall discuss subjects of infinite importance to human society, few will read my numbers and still fewer will appreciate their subject matter. Yet, perhaps, I may reach some minds and quicken into action some friend to mankind.

The position I must occupy is one not very desirable. One can but have an awkward feeling in commencing reformer. It is an invidious character. It assumes much and seems to say to the world that he who assumes it is wiser or better than those who have gone before him. It provokes some home questions; and almost invariably attracts attention from what is proposed, to the qualifications, the acquisitions and claims, of the proposer. The man is examined with no little disposition to find him deficient. He is censured with no excess of charity, but with a secret exultation at every fault which can be laid to his charge. Those whose vices he may expose and those whose consciences he may probe are gratified to discover any fault or defect in his life, and are never ashamed to indulge a malicious pleasure in making him appear criminal or ridiculous.

There are few persons whose characters will bear a close and malicious examination; and there are few sentiments which may not be caricatured and made the laughingstock of the idle and the unreflecting; or that may not be perverted, so as to appear mischievous to the bigoted and to the ill-natured. But for myself, I think, truth would be no less truth if proclaimed by his satanic majesty of the lower regions than if spoken by the Archangel Michael of the celestial abode. The character of him who proposes a valuable reform makes up no part of the reform, and need not be a subject of enquiry. The maxim, "do by others as you would they should do by you," is equally authoritative, whether falling from the lips of Confucius, of Jesus, or of Simon Magus. It addresses itself to the reason of man, and derives its authority, not from him who gives it, but from its own excellence in promoting the welfare of human society. A contrary maxim, one producing evil, and whose general adoption would introduce confusion, crime and misery, would be without authority, would be unbinding upon rational beings, let who would pronounce it.

The world has long labored under a mistake. The *ipse dixit*[2] of a revered character has been deemed sufficient evidence of the truth of his assertion; and the sanction of a great name has been considered authority enough for a principle of action, however detrimental it might be to the welfare of human beings. The world has thus bowed to precedent and feared to think for itself. It has imagined a state of perfection in the past and dared not depart from what was then approved. Why is this so? Had men more giant intellects in days of yore than now? Was nature then more clearly perceived—were her operations marked with keener senses and pronounced upon with sounder

2[Ed. Latin for "he himself said it," i.e., a dogmatic statement or assertion.]

judgments? Had our fathers any better opportunity of discovering moral or physical truth than we? Are not the moderns born with the same senses as were the ancients? Is not nature as open to our inspection as to theirs? Why then feel this servility to those who have gone before us? The ages which have passed away have left us many good things; but they are none the better nor are they any more authoritative because they come from antiquity.

One generation has no right to make laws or adopt institutions for another. The idea, so long prevalent, that one generation has the power to bind its successors is fallacious as well as mischievous. The world belongs to its possessors and is at the disposal of each generation only for itself. We have a right to dispose of the world as we will, to impose what laws, restrictions or obligations, we please, upon ourselves, but the generation to come is not bound by our doings. Why then shall we feel that one generation has the right to control the opinions of another? Why feel ourselves bound to submit to the *dicta* of other times or of other men? Have I not the same right to decide for myself that my father had for himself? As I have no right to dictate to my child what opinions he shall embrace, no right to force my opinions upon him, how can it be admitted my father had any right to dictate my opinions or to force *his* opinions upon *me*?

Each individual stands on independent ground. Each, endowed by the law of his being with the same rights as the other, is not subjected to another, nor can he exercise authority over him. Each then has the supreme control of his own actions and a right to embrace, uncensured, and uninterrogated, the conclusions to which his own mind arrives. It therefore follows that we are not authorized to exercise any control over each other, except what may be exerted by the simple force of truth. It will also follow that no one is bound to submit to any other authority. The enquiry should be "what is truth?" No matter where it is found, no matter who discovers it, or what the character of him who proclaims it. Truth is immutable; it vacillates not with the character of its defenders; is the same, is equally authoritative, falling from the lips of the profligate as from the sober; from the young as the old; the foolish as the wise. It is eternally the same. No adventitious circumstances can alter its character; wealth cannot adorn it, nor poverty tarnish its luster. Virtue, in its friends, cannot make it more true—vice cannot sully its purity. We may then dismiss all enquiry respecting the date of the disclosure, whether the measures advocated are ancient or modern; all enquiry respecting the person who proposes reform, be he young or old, wise or foolish, good or bad. The only subject of investigation with us is, "are his propositions important? Are they just? Are they practicable?"

NO. 2 (January 14, 1832): 81-85

I wish it were in my power to make my readers perceive that religion is no mysterious affair. It is, in fact, nothing more nor less than the right exercise of all our faculties. It is nothing above, foreign to, nor different from, our ordinary powers and what we may every day feel, know and perform.

It matters not to me which term, religion or morality, is used; either term, I consider, comprehends the whole of man's duty, whether it branch out to his God or to his fellow. All that is required is a right state of the affections and the performance of just actions. When the heart is right there is felt love and gratitude to God. But this is not different from that state of the affections required to love our friend and to be grateful to our benefactor though he be a human being. The same springs of the heart are moved in one case as in the other; and the same class of emotions are awakened, though differently directed.

We should analyze our feelings and ascertain what it is we really mean by love to God. The human mind cannot take in the whole of the Divinity at once. It is compelled from its limited capacity to view the Deity as an assemblage of qualities, as separate attributes, combined and operating together. When I view God as my Father, it is the qualities I recognize in a father that I love; and this is the same state of the affections, of which I am conscious, when I love an earthly parent. When I view God as good and love him for his goodness, it is the same exercise of the soul as it is to love goodness in a human being. It is the same when I view him as merciful, as forgiving, as kind and benevolent, in his character. Love for him in view of any of these characteristics is the same as the love I have for them wherever, and whenever, I may see them displayed. In fact, to cultivate love to God is only cultivating those affections and acquiring those principles which are requisite for me to discharge promptly, cheerfully, and perseveringly my duty to my fellow beings.

Want of love to God is a breach of morality, because it argues an immoral state of the heart. He who does not love God has a bad tone of feeling, is impure in his affections. He is, indeed, one who does not love goodness, benevolence, wisdom, justice, mercy, etc., for to love God is only to love these; and no one will pretend he who does not love these is a moral man.

It is plain then our duty to God is but a branch of our general duty; and equally plain too, that it *is* a branch of morality. He, therefore, who in discussing morals, forgets piety to God will but ill perform his task. So, on the other hand, he who in delineating our duty to God should pass over morals as belonging to another subject, would greatly err. There is no separation in the case. Piety and social duty are streams from the same fountain, only taking different directions; and they do, in fact, end in the same spot—the promotion of human happiness. Either, and both ask, and it is all they ask, that we should so cultivate the heart and the understanding, and that we so conduct that we can live pleased with ourselves and in love with our fellow beings.

Religion, or, if you please, morality, does not stop with merely regulating our affections towards our God nor in fixing the private virtues. It embosoms political science. Political science is only man's duty to man in his associated capacity. We bear various relations in life. We are related to God; we are related to our fellow beings, as individuals, as neighbors, as members of the community, and as citizens of the government. Now, the perfection of our characters consists in the proper discharge of all the duties implied in these several relations. These relations do not belong to different individuals but one and the same individual bears them all; and it is important that he be faithful in observing them all, as it is he should observe anyone. He should, too, be governed by the same principles in the one case as in the other. They are not different duties, they are only parts of man's whole duty. Political science differs from private morality only as to the scene on which it is displayed, and the particular class of actions it regulates. Private morality differs from piety towards God only in the particular direction given to the actions and the turn taken by the affections.

In this view of the case, it is requisite the politician, the statesman, the public officer, should be a religious man, as it is that anyone should; and though I do not say we should have a Christian party in politics, I do say we should be as religious in political affairs as in anything else. I would have no theological test, but I would have a religious test for every office—not prescribed by law but by public opinion. Do not let me be misunderstood. I do not ask a man to be a member of any sect; I only wish him a man of right feelings, whose heart is rightly cultivated and capable of feeling the full weight of his whole duty. He, who neglects his duty in one case, may in another; he who has no love for the goodness of God, no reverence for his wisdom and no respect for his providence, may fail to regard the same qualities in his fellow man. I do not couple religion with any creed nor with any form of worship. It is the principle of the heart and where that principle is wanting, I certainly cannot place full confidence.

I deem this subject important. I tremble for my country when I see her councils guided by men of no principle, who feel no accountability to a higher power. In choosing a friend, I would always choose one of whose integrity I had no doubt: one whom I believed to be guided by principle and who felt, in all its hearings, his whole duty; and who had the firmness, to discharge its particular branches, and act in view of the whole of it, wherever he should be placed. I should demand the same qualities, in one, I should select to manage my private affairs; and why not in choosing one to officiate for me in public? Every man should feel his relationship and accountability to his God as much when acting in a political capacity as when engaged in the temple consecrated to piety.

It is matter of deep regret that men do not feel the importance of being conscientious in all they do, and of being governed by the same just principles in all cases and at all times. I know not how a man can make a distinction between religious and political principle, nor can I conceive how a man can be conscientious in the one part of his duty who contemns the other. Duty is duty. It should at all times be seen in its full extent and should be at all times felt as indispensable; and he should be deemed as immoral, who in any instance knowingly and voluntarily departs from it.

There is much said of a union of church and state. Much, too, to no manner of purpose. For my part, I only dread a separation of church and state. That is, a separation of religious principle from what is deemed political science. I want no act of a civil nor of any ecclesiastical government to regulate my religious belief or to establish a form of worship for me to observe. I allow no civil, no ecclesiastical, tribunal to usurp control over my conscience and to meddle with that branch of my duty which is obligatory on me or can be discharged by me only as an individual. Still I dread a separation of that religious principle, which we are all bound to cherish in private life, from our councils of state and our halls of legislation. I wish that holy principle, that fear of God, that admiration of his wisdom, that love of his goodness, that aspiration after his perfection, which quicken the heart and awaken its nobler and better feelings, should pervade public life and shed their hallowed influence over all our public men and all their public acts. Such a union of church and state as this, I wish; and such a union as this, I think every good Christian must also wish.

Let me be understood. In this union of church and state I contemplate no power in the state to regulate our pious affections. Law has nothing to do with these; law cannot reach them; I only wish the man who makes and he who executes as well as he who obeys the laws should be possessed of right feelings and governed by just principles. And this, it strikes me, every wise man must wish. And I may add, till this devotion and steady adherence to correct principle be deemed indispensable in all the affairs of life, there will be little of private and still less of public virtue among us.

From the above reasoning it may be seen that in my view of the case, notwithstanding mine is a religious paper, I do not conceive myself as forfeiting its character, should I touch occasionally on political science. My business is with man, in all his relations, whether to his God, to himself, to his brother or to society. As I contemplate viewing him in all these relations in my Essay on Reform, for reform in reference to all these is needed, I have devoted this number to vindicating my right to do it, without forfeiting the character I bear before the public. In prosecuting my design I shall rapidly sketch the errors into which we have fallen in reference to our duty to our God, in our political transactions, in our private feelings; secondly exhibit what should be observed in relation to them all; and lastly suggest the means by which we may avoid the former and secure the later.

NO. 3 (February 14, 1832): 113-15

The design of my Essay requires me to glance at our errors, in reference to that part of our duty, which relates to our God.

These errors have reference to the method of proof which we usually adopt; the character of the Divine Being; the obligation and nature of his demands, together with our means of complying with them.

In this age of reckless enquiry, of fearful agitation and severe trial, it is not only necessary that we should contend for the truth, but, that we contend for it on just grounds and by sound arguments. There is nothing more fundamentally necessary to the healthy and vigorous state of the moral constitution than the firm unwavering belief in one God, the moral governor and spiritual Father of the universe; yet this belief may be lost, or not produced, if we attempt to prove there is a God by arguments which are not sound, or by a method of reasoning which is essentially defective.

I can read Clark, Tillotson, Locke, Paley, and other giant spirits of other days, and still doubt the being of a God.[3] To me they all seem to have failed to meet the difficulties in the case and to have taken for granted the very points they should have proved. All I ever read on this subject but increased my doubts and plunged me deeper and deeper in scepticism.

My own experience must count for something to myself. Theology has been to me something more than mere speculation. It engrossed my infant mind. It is connected with all I remember of my early visions and entwined with all the endearing associations of childhood and youth. When reason first awoke, while thought was unfledged, it was to me a subject of deep and cherished feeling. In the early dawn of youth, there was nothing I so much dreaded as that which should divert my thoughts from the Deity, and interrupt my silent, but blissful intercourse of soul with the "Father of our spirits." I loved the night, for it seemed to shadow him forth and to give him a local habitation. I frequented the deep solitude of the forest; I climbed the cragged mountain, stood upon its huge cliffs; I gazed with rapture on nature in her wildest and most fitful moods; for in the lone, wild, grand, sublime scenery around me, I seemed to trace His work, and to feel his spirit reigning, in silent, but not unacknowledged majesty. I was never alone. I felt the Deity was with me. I loved his presence. A consciousness of it created my joy and waked my holier and better feelings. Those were hallowed days! Their memory is deep graven on my heart. As I view them mellowed by time and distance, it is with emotion I say to myself, "They are gone!"

Such was the state of my young affections; such the religious feelings of my childhood and youth. They were not learned from

[3][Ed. Samuel Clarke (1675-1729) was a British philosopher and theologian, considered by orthodox theologians to be a deist or an Arian, who authored, among other works, the *Scripture Doctrine of the Trinity* (1712). Archbishop John Tillotson (1630-94) of Canterbury was a latitudinarian who wanted to include all Protestants, except Unitarians, in the Church of England. He gave reason a predominant role in his understanding of the Bible and the Christian tradition. John Locke (1632-1704) was a British empiricist philosopher who fostered, among other issues, an evidentiary approach to understanding Christianity, as was clear in his *Reasonableness of Christianity as Delivered in the Scriptures* (1695). William Paley (1743-1805), rector of Musgrave, Westmorland (1776-82) and archdeacon of Carlisle (1782-1805), was author of the famous *View of the Evidences of Christianity* (1794). *Natural Theology* (1802), which was very popular as an apologetical text in many nineteenth-century American colleges, was Paley's last published work and covered in more thorough fashion the same groundwork as *Evidences*, emphasizing the evidentiary approach to Christian apologetics. On Paley, see DNB 43 (1895), 101-07.]

books; they were not produced by human teachers. They were the simple feelings of nature—the child led by instinct to seek the embrace of its parent. But soon as I entered the school of theology, and began to take my religion from books, I began to doubt. The more I read the stronger grew my scepticism. Inclination, interest, early habit, and even a lively sensibility to devotion, struggled against it in vain. I stood upon the precipice. I looked down the abyss of atheism, ready to take the awful plunge; aye, I . . . . [4]

I look back with startling horror upon that eclipse of the soul, that midnight of reason, from which I am but just recovered. Still my doubts were first awakened by reading Paley's Natural Theology.

The appeal to the light, order, harmony, and mechanism of nature *may* confirm him who already believes in an Almighty Architect, but will never convert the atheist. He will ask you to prove what you call design is the work of a designer. He will not ask you to prove the world did not come by chance; he would rather you should show the things to which you refer him were produced, and before you accuse him of ascribing the world to chance, he would wish you to convince him it ever came at all. Whatever is *made*, necessarily implies a maker, but the difficulty is to obtain proof the world ever was made. I will not pursue this argument, lest I weaken the faith of some who have no different evidence from that usually presented on which to depend.

There is in my opinion, need that we meet the atheist on different ground. At some future day I hope to give, in full, the considerations which produced my own conversion from scepticism to an unwavering and joyful belief in one God—my Father.[5] I am anxious to do this because my conversion was as unexpected to myself as it was to my friends; and, because it was so sudden, that there were few to believe it genuine. For the present, I can only add, the atheist who looks only at external nature for proofs of a God will probably look in vain; but, if he will turn his mind inward, and converse with his own spiritual nature, he will hear the still, small, but clear and convincing, voice of God speaking to his soul. My own faith rests on this internal revelation from God to the inner man. I have thus a witness

---

[4][Ed. Ellipsis, as in original.]

[5][Ed. Brownson wrote a number of times about his own conversion from skepticism. See in particular his letter to Edward Turner, July 17, 1834 (located in the Andover-Harvard Archives), his "Letters to an Unbeliever," *Christian Register* 12 (October 5, 19, 27; November 9, 16, 23, 30; December 7, 14, 1833)—also republished in this volume, and *Charles Elwood: or, The Infidel Converted* (Boston: Charles C. Little and James Brown, 1840).]

within; and, having this witness, I can find its testimony corroborated by the whole of external nature. I forgot the spirit, looked only at the flesh, and this witness was unheeded. It was therefore I doubted. I turned my thoughts inward. I heard the voice of God, I believed—felt myself again locked in the embrace of my Father.

NO. 4 (February 28, 1832): 129-35

In my last No. I alluded to the defective testimony usually adduced to prove there is a God; in this I shall animadvert on the ordinary methods of proving Christianity.

Before we set out to prove Christianity, we should clearly perceive, and distinctly comprehend, what are the propositions requiring proof and what kind of testimony we have to allege. This has not been duly regarded. The parties at issue have not always understood themselves—they have frequently fought in the dark and each has done about as much injury to his friends as to his opponents.

What is it we should prove in order to prove Christianity true? That the Scriptures of the Old and New Testament are genuine and authentic? How are we to prove this? The nature of the case admits only historical testimony so far as external facts are concerned. This, it is well known, is not the most certain kind of testimony. There is room for much doubt and hesitancy. How much is said of Alexander the Great. Yet it has been seriously doubted whether there ever was such a man. Homer has immortalized the city and siege of Troy or Ilium, yet it is even now a question whether there ever was such a city, and if there was, where it stood.[6] Now this same uncertainty runs through the whole of ancient history. The Bible is not free from it. And further, the historians may have been honest but deceived themselves; they may have been dishonest and have deceived others; the records may not have come down to us in their original purity; they may have been interpolated or corrupted by fraud, or altered by the carelessness, or the misreading of transcribers. These circumstances necessarily reduce the testimony of ancient history, in all cases, from absolute certainty to, at least, nothing more than very high probability. This is as far as we can go in cases best attested. Higher proof than this, the Bible cannot receive from external testimony. No sensible man has ever felt so certain that it was true, that he did not wish for more convincing testimony.[7]

----

[6][Ed. The site of Troy, an ancient city in northwestern Asia Minor, was discovered by Heinrich Schliemann and excavated by him from 1870 to 1890.]

[7] I beg the reader not to misinterpret this passage. I do not design to weaken, in the least, confidence in the Bible. I only mean that we can never fully prove it by external testimony. I believe I yield as hearty an assent to the Scriptures, to their

But admit the Bible is, in the main, a genuine and authentic work—and this I verily believe—what have we gained of evidence to Christianity? "The Scriptures are a genuine and faithful record," is one proposition; "Christianity is true," is another, and in some minds, a very different, proposition. The Scriptures are not Christianity, they are only a record of it. The record may be genuine, that is written by those to whom it is ascribed; it may be authentic, that is, a faithful and true narrative of what did actually transpire, and yet the doctrine, or opinions, recorded may be false.

The Bible is a record of matters of fact, and matters of opinion. The truth of the record involves the truth of the matters of fact, but not of the opinions, or doctrines recorded. Moses may actually have seen the "burning bush," he may have been addressed in the manner related; all this is matter of fact. But that it was Jehovah who addressed him, could have been only a matter of belief to Moses, and though the history faithfully records that opinion or belief, it can be no voucher for its truth.

Now, Christianity is not a series of facts, but of doctrinal propositions and moral principles. The truth of these propositions, and the correctness of these principles are what we want proved. But the genuineness and faithfulness of history can never do this. Therefore when we have proved what is generally attempted in reference to the external, or written, word, the main question, in my apprehension, is left untouched. As mere belief in the Scriptures is not Christianity, so proving them faithful and genuine is not full proof of the religion of Jesus.[8]

I ask again, what is it we should prove, in order to prove Christianity? That Christ actually performed the miracles recorded of him in the New Testament? What is a miracle? It is defined, "something done contrary to the laws of nature." How am I to know when a thing is, or is not, a miracle? To him who is ignorant of the laws of nature, many things appear as miracles which to the philosopher are easily solved on natural principles. How can I pronounce a thing contrary to nature unless I am acquainted with the whole of nature

general fidelity and genuineness, as most men; but, my confidence is inspired by a different process of reasoning from that usually adopted.

[8] This will be obvious to those who can distinguish between a matter of fact, and a theological or moral doctrine. Were we wishing to prove there was such a person as Jesus, that he actually did what is recorded of him, I admit we should labor to prove the authenticity of the record. But, these facts, to wit, there was such a person as Jesus, and he performed the miracles ascribed to him, do not constitute Christianity. Therefore proof of these is not proof of what Jesus taught.

and know exactly all its powers? I know no being of less knowledge than Omniscience who can tell whether a thing is or is not a miracle. But admitting there are real miracles, how am I to know it, unless I see them? The miracles recorded in the New Testament, may have been performed; but I have only human testimony of the fact. That testimony may err. The original spectators may have been deceived; they may have exaggerated them; and passing through a multitude of hands, how am I to know the miracles have not swollen to something very different from the circumstances which first astonished the beholders? All these are circumstances which tend to lessen confidence in the historical account, and to weaken my belief in the fact that they were performed. No man can be *certain* the miracles were actually wrought; the most which the very nature of the case will admit is a high degree of probability.

But admitting they were performed—and certainly I am ready to make the admission—have we admitted anything which involves the truth of Christianity? Suppose we have proved the miracles or the works called miraculous were done, have we proved Christianity? I think not. These miracles are not Christianity; the most strenuous advocate for them will not, upon due thought, pronounce them anything more than evidences of what Christ taught. They are a series of facts entirely distinct, and depending on facts of a very different order for their proof. Why then shall I labor to prove them? They cannot prove what Christ taught. Christ's teachings were moral propositions, but these are only displays of physical power. How then can they be proofs of Christianity? Can a display of physical power prove a moral or religious doctrine? I beg you to inform me by what process of reasoning you prove there is a future state of existence, from the fact that he who asserts it, opens the eyes of the blind and unstops the ears of the deaf? This has not been duly considered. Volume after volume has been written to prove the miraculous account given us in the Bible, and I verily believe, when we have proved that, we have proved nothing essential to the doctrines and morals of Christ. There has been so much labor lost. The miracles are isolated facts; they might have served to fix attention on what Jesus said. But when we have proved they were performed, we may still ask is that which Jesus taught concerning God, the human soul, a future state, and human duty, true?[9]

[9] This is in opposition to nearly the whole Christian world, and probably may bring no little obloquy upon the author. Be it so. What is liberty of thought worth if we are denied the right to communicate our views to our fellow men? I do not question the history recording these miracles. I do not question that they were

The proof of miracles is not proof of Christianity. What then must we prove? That Jesus was the Messiah? I know nearly all Christians deem this necessary, but I do not believe it indispensable. The Messiah was a personage expected by the Jews; from whom they anticipated much, and to whom they had been exhorted to yield a cheerful obedience. Now, we never had that expectation. We are not Jews; no Messiah has ever been promised to us. It might have been expedient to convince, or persuade, the Jews that Jesus was the Messiah, or promised prince, but if he was a teacher of the truth, and if he set an example of moral perfection, what does it matter [to] me, whether he was that precise personage or not?

There is room to doubt, whether Jesus of Nazareth was the personage described, predicted, by the Jewish prophets and hoped for by the Jewish people. I have read the prophets with no little attention, and—though I lay no claim to unmatched abilities, I believe I possess as much discernment and as much ingenuousness as the common class of mankind—I cannot say I have found a single prediction, so clear and definite, that it was certain it could be applied to no other person. The assertion may be a bold one, but it is a fact. Do we not weaken confidence in Jesus, by contending he was what the Jewish people were expecting? Would it not be better to view him simply a "man approved of God"—"a teacher of the truth"—"a worker of righteousness," without any regard to the peculiar notions of Jews or Gentiles?[10]

But, were we to prove clearly, beyond the possibility of doubt, that Jesus was the Messiah, we should not, even then, prove Christianity. *That which Jesus taught is Christianity*, and it is that we want proved. What Jesus was is one thing; what he taught is another, and in the minds of some a very different, thing. What he taught us of God, of our own natures, and of our duty, is his religion: and this is all we are interested in having proved; and this is what we must prove true, in order to establish the truth of Christianity. We may prove all

---

performed for wise and benevolent purposes; I do not question, that they fixed attention on Jesus, and disposed his hearers to listen with a favorable state of mind to believe what he taught; but I must be pardoned if I cannot see in the extraordinary display of physical power, proofs of the immortality of the human soul, and of what is man's duty to his God and to his brother.

[10] Here again, I beg not to be misinterpreted. That Jesus was the person, the gross, literal interpretation of the Jewish prophets would lead one to expect, I do not believe; but, that he was the teacher from God capable of fulfilling the spirit of the Jewish law, and thus in a spiritual sense answering to the Jewish predictions I believe.

the other things and leave this untouched. This is all that we want. If we believe this we have the Christian faith, whether we believe the other things or not. But how shall we prove this?

This is the question. We can prove it by no historical records. But we have the witness within us of its truth. Men in all ages have had the witness: "The grace of God which bringeth salvation, hath appeared unto all men" [Titus 2:11]. The "sound is gone out unto all the world" [Ps 19:4], and the wise and good of all ages and of all climes have borne witness to its truth.

What we term Christianity is no new doctrine; it was not original with Jesus; it was older than Moses and more widely spread than that lawgiver's name. The life and immortality were not created by the gospel, they were "brought to light" by it. The apostle to the Gentiles did not conceive the doctrine he preached was original with Jesus. He says it was "preached aforetime unto Abraham" Gal. 3:8, and the whole drift of his argument to the Jews was designed to prove the religion he was inculcating was nothing more than the ancient religion of the Patriarchs, of the sages, and holy men of old. This is the view I take of his religion. I find traces of it among all nations and in the earliest historical notices which have reached us. That noble precept of Christ, "whatsoever ye would others should do unto you, do ye even the same unto them" [Matt 7:12], Sir William Jones[11] says he had seen verbatim in the original of Confucius, a Chinese philosopher who lived, at least, five hundred years before Jesus.

Still farther, I am not willing to believe God's will was never known except to that petty tribe of semi-barbarians inhabiting the mountains of Palestine; and that even they knew it not until as it were a few days ago. God is the God of the whole earth. All are his children; all needed his revelation, and we are assured by the Apostle Paul that a "portion of his spirit is given unto every man to profit withal" [l Cor 12:7]. If I cannot know my duty, and learn my Father's love without a revelation, I must forever remain ignorant of it, unless I have the revelation made to my own soul. A revelation to my neighbor is none to me. God may speak to him; but it is man that speaks, when that revelation is reported to me. I believe then, in an *internal*

[11][Ed. Brownson is referring to Sir William Jones (1746-94), greatest of the early British Orientalists, who after 1783 as a judge in India translated from Sanskrit into English the laws of Manu and the Hitopadesa, both of which, according to Arthur Versluis, *American Transcendentalism and Asian Religions* (New York: Oxford University Press, 1993), 18, were "influential on the [American] Transcendentalists."]

revelation from God to the human soul—a revelation old as the human race, extended to every individual, and continued through every generation. This is the word of God, which was with him "in the beginning," which is "gone out into all the earth" [Ps 19:4], which is "the true light which lighteneth every man" [John 1:9]—aye, it is God in the soul, speaking in a still small, but clear and distinct voice. This is the living witness. All men have had it. "Holy men of old spake as they were moved by it" [2 Pet 1:21], and the sacred books of the Jews are a record of the views which wise and good men of that nation had of it. The sacred books of the Chinese, Japanese, Hindoos, Persians, etc. contain records of this revelation, as viewed by the ancient and admired sages of those countries.

Now, this inward revelation, this breathing of God into the human soul, beareth witness to the truth of what Jesus taught and this is the way to prove Christianity. We do not prove it from books; we do not prove it by historical testimony; we prove it by the witness of God within us. Now, if instead of reading the external word as the revelation of God, man would read the word in the soul, listen to the living teacher within, "who speaketh unto every man in his own tongue, wherein he was born" [paraphrase of Acts 2:8], he would readily learn what Christianity is and also the facts which prove it true.

I cannot enlarge on this subject. I believe the proofs of our holy religion are within our own bosoms and I can but regret that we have so long been poring over the letter, losing our faith, and starving for the want of spiritual bread. Let the gifted advocates of our religion, cease their immoderate contentions about ancient records. God is ever present. He speaks in all ages, in all languages, to all hearts. Let all listen and obey. Religion will then be established. Christianity will be embraced by every mind, and the spirit, or disposition of Jesus, reign in every heart.[12]

NO. 5 (March 13, 1832): 145-50

That is an interesting study which relates to the Divine character, and none would have been more profitable, had it been pursued with singleness of purpose, and with a just sense of the powers of the enquirer.

To acquire a knowledge of the Divinity, we must study carefully the records transmitted us from holy men of old, the world round

---

[12] I do not mean to underrate the written word. My views of it are given in Letter No. 3, to Rev. Mr. Wisner. I do mean however, that this inward teacher must be its interpreter and this living witness corroborate its truth.

and about us, and the world within us. The records give us the views taken by wise and good men in different ages of the world, and in different parts of the earth. They are highly useful, but not alone sufficient. If they were, there would be no work left for new minds; thought would be superseded; and our duty would be to bow to authority and acquiesce implicitly in what others have said.

The world around us—the material universe, in itself considered, is silent. It is matter—matter in motion, indeed, but cold, dull, thoughtless matter, incapable of demonstrating the existence, much less, the character of a Deity. Matter must have a mind, must be imbued with a soul, before it can speak. We must conceive the magnificent idea of a God, must be assured that the universe was made, and that he made it, before we can trace him in all we see, hear, and feel. Men, indeed, speak of design, treat of the mechanism of nature, and thence infer there is an Almighty Architect; their arguments are subtle, are learned, are plausible; but we believed before we heard them; whole nations have admitted there is a God and have adored him, while unable to appreciate them; and he who doubts, is never convinced by them.

The world within us is that which must disclose the Divinity, and shed the light by which we may read the external universe. He who would be convinced there is a God, must look into the human soul, the only thing on earth which can image forth the Deity. In the nature and capacities of soul, we learn all we can learn of the nature of God, of his power and Godhead. In our own spirituality we form our conceptions of his, and the soul, by its restlessness, its longing after what it has not, by its constant efforts to burst its bounds and soar beyond the farthest flight of thought, by its multiplied creations, and its ceaseless actions, leads us to the Great Fountain of life, the Eternal Mind, the Father of our spirits. The image of the Deity is instamped on human nature; we feel there is a God; we bear that about with us that constantly reminds us of his being and silences the rising doubt. All this is anterior to any reasoning on the subject, independent of any argument, and of any human instruction. We need not labor to prove there is a God. If there be anyone who doubts, we leave him to the workings of his own soul. If he finds not within himself proofs of a Deity, there is no argument to convince him.

The question now is not, whether there be a God; that point is conceded; but, what is he? What his character? What he is, as to his own nature, we know not, we need not ask; but, what is he to us? The common answer would pronounce him a King, the Lord, our Sovereign. Man, though allied to Heaven, still clings to the earth.

His thoughts that would rise, are pulled down by the dull clay he drags in his train. He mingles too much of earth in his conceptions of the Deity, and the follies of men shadow forth his God. He seizes upon all the powerful, the commanding, the stern, and terrific images found on earth, upon all the creations of his own dark and impetuous passions, and names them—God.

I view not Deity as a sovereign. I may be the first to say thus, and care not if I am. I dislike the image. To my ears there is harshness in that word, sovereign. It calls up visions of despotism—of the tyrant in state, of the cowering, cringing herd, bearing human forms, but not human souls, trembling before him, and falling prostrate at his nod. I dislike the image. It chills the blood; it freezes the heart; it curbs the free thought. I look not upon Deity as a king. That word, king, has a strange sound in republican ears; and a form of government, I cannot uphold on earth, I will not adore in heaven.

The character of God, as usually presented, is borrowed from an oriental despot. He is seated upon his lofty throne, before whom angels kneel with trembling awe, before the dazzling splendor of whose majesty the cherubim veil their faces; clothed with power, he holds the scepter of command and rules the nations with his rod. Men are his subjects—aye, his *slaves*, approaching his presence with downcast looks and souls cowering in the dust. I worship no such being; I love no despot; I hold sympathy with no soul that submits to his rule.

Yet such is the God we are commanded to love with all our hearts; such is the God who has a temple in almost every land, and such the God who is preached in almost every church, by almost every minister of religion. He is a fitting God for tyrants who would ride on the backs of their brothers; his were a fitting worship, to enslave, to make the degraded serf submissive to the burthen of his master; but such is no God for a free spirit; no worship for a mind swelling with free thoughts, disdaining to bow to aught, save superior excellence. Man, conscious of the dignity of his nature, the nobleness of his birth, his lofty endowments, and his high destination, will never worship mere power; his devotion must be kindled at a holier shrine, and his homage must be enforced by a higher appeal than to his weakness.

The philosopher may be amused, and the Christian grieved, at the influence this view of God has had on genuine piety and sound morals. To what horrid doctrines has it not given birth? Following out the figure of the oriental despot, God has been painted a lawless tyrant and been supposed to govern by mere caprice. Hence, came that ignoble scheme of election and reprobation—a scheme which could have originated only in a servile mind, bowing to a tyrant-

God. I will not dwell on its extreme partiality and shocking cruelty; it is enough to add the words of its friend, John Calvin: "*Hoc decretum, quidem, est horribile, fateor.*"[13] No man of just views and feelings can love such a God as Calvin's; every higher feeling, every nobler attribute of the soul rises indignant at the command to worship him; and they said well, who enjoined a radical change of nature to enable us to obey him. Nature must indeed be changed before we can worship such a God.

This same mistake, viewing God, simply as king, as sovereign, tyrant, is that which gave rise to those dark, mysterious, and cruel rites which have cast such a deep and somber gloom over the whole of religion. The temples were dedicated to power, and the incense offered, was of fear and servility. The blood chills, the heart freezes, at the worship which has been offered. There was no mind in it: there were none of the breathings of a lofty spirit, none of the workings of a free soul. Recall the deep gloom of the Black Forest where the Druid invoked his God, the human blood reeking upon the altars of Wodin and Thor![14] Jupiter with his thunderbolts! The shrieks of human victims, sacrificed to Molock, the Sidonian and Carthaginian God![15] The thick darkness, the stern and awful grandeur of Jehovah Adonai, the God of the Jews! How awe-inspiring! Before these gods man shrinks to nothing; he crawls on the ground; he wraps himself in sackcloth and ashes; he cries out: "Have pity on thy slave!" Such gods destroy all man's nobleness; they bind him down to the earth, compel him to lick dust with the serpent.

This notion of God as a tyrant, must be corrected, or his worship will only nurture a race of slaves. Men must cease to represent their heavenly Father, by the mere emblems of power, or their souls will be strangers to the high thoughts and noble aspirations of free spirits. They must not interpret too literally, the Scriptures which liken the believer to a *sheep*. A sheepish disposition is not that most befitting a freeman. It may do for a degraded peasant, may do for the

---

[13] I confess this is, indeed, a horrible decree. [Ed. Calvin's *Institutes of the Christian Religion*, 3.23.7.]

[14] [Ed. Wodin or Odin was the greatest of gods in Norse mythology; Thor was the god of thunder, bringer of rain, provider of abundant crops, and protector of peasants and farmers in Norse mythology.]

[15] [Ed. In the Old Testament Moloch was a god of the Ammonites and Phoenicians to whom human sacrifice was offered. Moloch meant king among many ancient Semitic peoples, and some authorities have evidence of the title on Carthaginian inscriptions. Brownson is probably referring to the biblical prohibition in Lev. 18:21: "You shall not give any of your children to devote them by fire to Moloch, and so profane the name of your God."]

subject of a Russian Autocrat; but not for a child of God. The docility, and quietness which it implies were well enough, were proper for the inhabitants of oriental climes, where liberty was unheard, and her soul-reviving power unfelt. It was designed to express the highest degree of excellence, for that condition; it can only mean that we should have the highest degree of excellence admitted by the condition in which we are placed. We want a different race of beings: we want free minds, bold spirits; and such the gospel was designed to nurture; but long as we paint its author a mere being of power such a race will not be found.

It does seem to me we usually present our God with a character very much like that ascribed to the tyrant Gesler.[16] That foolish tyrant is said to have erected on the great square before his palace, a post, to have placed upon it a hat and commanded his subjects in passing, to bow before it as a test of their obedience and fidelity to him. That stern Patriot Tell, refused to obey the wantonness of the tyrant, and we all bow to that high sense of independence, that noble daring which set the tyrant at defiance. If God acts on the same principles, if he commands in mere wantonness, would not a just estimation of freedom, a due respect for the natures we possess, lead us to feel towards him, as felt the peasant Tell towards the tyrant Gesler?

True, in one sense, God may be viewed as a sovereign. Not that the well instructed Christian ever worships mere power; he recognizes in God only the sovereignty of mind; he ascribes to him empire, but it is the empire of a free mind over minds equally free, albeit inferior. You may see an assembly; heavy responsibilities rest upon their deliberations; an awful crisis has occurred; their decisions are big with the fate of millions. All are free; each may offer his own opinion and follow his own determination. A giant mind discloses itself, a mind of a greater stretch of thought, of clearer comprehension, bolder in conception, more prudent in counsel, and firm in resolve. He speaks; his words fasten conviction; every judgment approves his proposition; all rally around him; lean on his advice and decide with his wisdom. It is then the sovereignty of mind stands confest [sic]; inferior minds own his superiority and obey his directions. This is a faint image of the sovereignty of God. The power that

[16][Ed. Gessler von Bruneck, the legendary tyrannical Austrian bailiff of the Swiss Canton of Uri, supposedly forced William Tell, another legendary figure and hero of the Swiss struggle for freedom from Austrian domination during the early part of the fourteenth century, to shoot an apple off the head of his son because Tell had refused to pay homage to Austria. The legendary story was retold many times in Switzerland and Germany.]

he wields is not merely physical; it is not mere brute force; it is mind ruling mind by fastening convictions of its own superiority and fitness to guide.

The Christian bows to God, not because he feels bound, not because he dreads his power; it is because he feels and owns his moral superiority. He bows not because God is able to crush him with his Omnipotence. He never does, he never will—no, not for hopes of heaven—bow to mere physical power. It may crush him; may chain him to the wheel; may bid the vultures feed on his liver; but his mind will be free, and the homage he yields will be the free, unbought suffrage of his heart. He bows to his God, but not as a slave, not through compulsion; it is because he sees and feels his moral excellence deserves it. He yields to mind, same—on the same principle, as he would bow to the superior wisdom, knowledge, and goodness of his brother.

Men have sought to glorify God by lessening the worth of human nature; and to exalt him by depressing themselves. This has passed for humility. It is mock humility. He will most clearly perceive and most readily acknowledge God's superiority, who has the most exalted views of his own nature. I know we should be humble—but only under a sense of our sinfulness. We should worship God; but the worship he requires is the voluntary offering of a free mind; not that fulsome flattery of the slave crouching to his master, extorted by fear of his rod or by hope of reward, not because he is fully convinced his master is worthy of praise. That which usually passes for Divine worship must be as degrading to the character of God as it is depressing to the free spirit and paralyzing to the noble energy of our souls. What must be his view of God who believes him pleased with the vile offerings of servility, and the fulsome praise of a mercenary spirit—aye, who believes he commands it, on pain of endless damnation? It is time we rise above such folly; time for us to learn, God does not exact worship as a sovereign, that he forces no one to praise him, and that he is pleased with no incense that is not the free will offering of a free soul cheerfully bowing to moral worth.

"Our Father" is the endearing appellation by which we are taught to address the Great Spirit. This is an image and a reality. God is our father and we should be followers of him as dear children. This is an appellation big with meaning. "Our Father," what tender associations does not this call up? What visions of fondness, of untiring love, of careful provision and anxious watchfulness! Men have not yet learned what the appellation means. The time is coming when they shall learn; when all shall adore God as their Father, and trust to

his parental care; then will be paid him a worship of reverence, gratitude and filial love. This appellation softens the Divine character,
makes it cease to be a source of fear, of appalling dread; and, instead
of prostrating us in the dust, it draws us to a fond embrace, and
encourages a silent, but glorious, and cheering and purifying intercourse of soul with the Great Being who made us. Let men look
upon God as their Father, and they will love him; the dark and mysterious worship paid him, the cruel and bloody rites adopted to pro-
pitiate his favor, will be as if they had not been. The heart will be
drawn out in affection, worship will be pure, honorable to God and
ennobling to us.

NO. 6 (June 12, 1832): 225-28

The most important question which, as religious beings, we can
ask, is, what does the Deity demand of us? No abstruse speculations
into the nature or even character of the Divinity can be of any avail,
further than they present the true object of worship and teach us
clearly and satisfactorily what worship is demanded.

To ascertain what worship God demands, we must have due reference to his character, far as known, and to our nature and capabilities. The reasoning of my last essay represented God as our Father,
and that under this relation, not merely that of a Sovereign or of a
governor, we are to worship him. I may proceed yet further. He can
require nothing of us on his own account. He is perfect; he can experience no want; he can receive no injury; he can partake no benefit.
His happiness is complete; arising from the perfection of his own
nature; it can neither be augmented nor diminished. He does not
hunger, nor can he thirst; he cannot be weary, nor does he faint.
What can he want? What can he receive? If he did hunger he would
not ask us to feed him, did he thirst he would not ask us to give him
drink; "for, the earth is his and the fullness thereof" [Ps 24:1].

Now, what can such a being demand of us? Praise? What is praise?
An idle hymn, filled with fulsome adulation? It cannot be reasonably
supposed that mere sweet sounds, or mere expressions of admiration
for his greatness, goodness, wisdom and tender providence, are of
any account to Him. They cannot increase his consciousness of his
own perfection. He knows himself, his power, his immensity, his
omni-benignity and his unfailing mercy, far better than we do;
and all the universe combined, cannot make him more sensible of
what he is, or more self-complacent; and wherefore then will he
demand it?

There is great need of care, lest we ascribe to the Deity that vanity, that love of praise which we perceive common to ourselves. He is

above all such littleness. Even man is degraded by vanity and often rendered ridiculous by his love of praise; shall we presume to think God can be exalted by that which lessens a mortal? I fear men have too often so thought and I see much in the religious world which I can ascribe to no other origin. We must elevate our views and think more highly of infinite excellence.

God is our Father; can he then demand anything of us which is not good? A good Father loves his children and seeks to make them great, wise, good and happy. Why may we not believe our heavenly Father is as good as an earthly one? He then can consistently demand nothing of us which shall not tend to exalt, purify and make happy his children. We are not then to suppose he requires anything of us inconsistent with the improvement of our natures and the increase of our happiness. He does not ask us to make painful sacrifices, to resign up our faculties and to forego our happiness. A good father could never make such demands of his children and God will not of his. He does not ask us to come before him, "with burnt offerings and with calves a year old. He will not be pleased with thousands of rams, nor with ten thousands of rivers of oil" [Mic 6:6-7]. He does not ask me to "give my firstborn for my transgression, the fruit of my body for the sin of my soul" [Mic 6:7]. These are not ours to give, and if they were, he does not want them. The shock of feeling in surrendering a child, acts which would make us miserable, or which were cruel to others, are not demanded by him, and would be no worship to him if they were. What then does he demand?

"He hath showed thee, O man, what is good; and what doth the Lord require of thee, but to do justly, love mercy, and walk humbly with thy God?" [Mic 6:8] This is a clear and a most rational answer. As he needs nothing for himself, as he seeks in his requirements not his but our good, the prophet answered wisely. From this answer, I infer, all the worship God requires of us is the improvement and exaltation of ourselves; and this is all the worship that I can conceive it in our power to render him.

This may be startling to some; I beg them to pause, before they condemn. How does a child honor its parent? When is a parent best pleased with his child? The parent's delight is in his child's welfare. He feels most honored when he sees his child pursuing a course of honorable action, when he sees him developing his mind, acquiring principles of probity, honor, and respect for goodness, laboring to perform an elevated and useful part in the drama of life. God is a father too, and what must be that course which he will most approve in his children? The same. He requires them to develop, and improve the natures which he has given them, to use for wise and just ends the noble faculties which he has bestowed on them. He asks them to understand themselves, to know the powers he has conferred, the use to which these should be applied, and that they exert all their faculties in that manner which shall most exalt them and show forth the greatness, the wisdom, the goodness, the tender providence of him their creator and Father. We honor God, by showing ourselves great and good; for then we show a great and good being made us; we praise him when we study his perfections, aspire after his excellence, and shape our affections and our actions after the pattern set us in his example. We worship him by being like him, "perfect as he is perfect" [paraphrase of Matt 5:48]; and in drawing near to him by a kindred excellence, we show our confidence in him and our real love and devotion to him.

I wish to impress this truth, that to worship God, we must be like him, and that we praise him not by what we say, but by copying, far as our finite natures will permit his moral perfections. That son shows he thinks of his father, studies his character, and approves it, admires it, when he copies it, and does as near like his father as he can. So do we show forth our love for God, our approbation, and our admiration of his character, when we imitate it far as we can. These is a delicacy in this kind of praise, which might be illustrated by a thousand examples. But it is not necessary. All can perceive that the highest tribute of respect which we can pay to any man is to imitate his good deeds, and to show him we are so taken with his character that we are anxious to make it our own. The principle holds good when applied to the question we are discussing.

If this be true, the most acceptable praise to God, is perfecting ourselves. The Divine character contains all we can conceive of greatness, wisdom and goodness. To approach that character must be to elevate ourselves, to improve in wisdom, to increase in goodness, and to become more truly great. This is a worship that is tangible to our understandings and one that will exalt us and honor our Creator.

NO. 7 (June 26, 1832): 241-46

In my last number I labored to show the only real worship to God in our power to give is the exaltation of our spiritual natures. To worship God we must study to be great, wise, good, merciful and pure in heart. We must copy in our feelings and in our lives, the moral perfections of our heavenly Father, as displayed in his word and works. This furnishes us with a criterion by which to test the fitness and utility of external service, which I shall now proceed to examine.

External service to God, in Christian countries, may be termed prayer, praise, preaching, attendance at church, Baptism and the Lord's Supper. Are these necessary? Any, or all? Wherefore?

I do not enquire whether any or all of them are enjoined in Scripture. I am discussing first principles and am desirous to assign a philosophical reason for everything I recommend as a part of religion. The religious world must come to this, and no matter how soon. I begin with Prayer. Is it necessary? Wherefore? Does it alter the plans of Jehovah? No: but it leads us to contemplate the perfections of God, to dwell on his Providence and his relations to us and has a tendency to beget in us a growing likeness to that excellence to which we address ourselves. It draws not God to us, but us to him, and thus enables our souls to gather purity and strength by communion with our heavenly Father. If it be thus, it is proper; if it be not thus, it is no part of religious worship.

Some object to prayer because God is unchangeable, and, of course, it cannot alter his purposes. I once so thought and treated prayer rather as a matter of custom than as something proper, defensible by any sound reasoning; but my opinion has changed. God is unchangeable, I admit. He gives us food, he causes the earth to yield fruits for the sustenance of life; but who would thence infer that it is improper to cultivate the field, to sow the seed, and watch and cherish its growth, as the means of procuring a harvest? In the world around us, there are appointed means for us to use to obtain temporal blessings, and why should it be any more unreasonable to believe that there is an appointed medium for the reception of spiritual good? The world is a system of means adapted to the accomplishment of ends, and I know no good that can be obtained without complying with the established law of means. Prayer may be a means of preserving the health of the soul, and of increasing its power.

We should not usually pray for worldly blessings—there are other means we must use to obtain them. If we meet with difficulties, we are not to call upon Hercules, but to put our shoulders to the wheel, with full assurance that when we have done our duty God will not suffer us to go unrewarded. It is only for spiritual blessings that we should pray. We should pray for inward power, for freedom and energy of soul, for calm and serene passions, pure and pious affections, and for kind and benevolent feelings; we should pray to be made good, to be prepared for what may await us, that we may acquit ourselves with firmness and honor in the discharge of the duties assigned us. For these I think we may reasonably pray; and I see not why prayer is not the proper medium for their reception.

There is here a necessary caution to be offered. Prayer should never be made to work upon the feelings of those who may hear us; it is perverted when it inflames the passions and kindles the fanatic zeal of the weak, the timid and the credulous. That only is prayer which is breathed from the heart to God. It is a sincere desire, a fervent aspiration after spiritual good. The words of Christ seem to confine it to the closet and to make it a matter solely between the individual and his God. The closet, where all worldly cares are shut out, where all is still and silent, seems the most fitting place for man to hold intercourse with the Deity and to prefer his petitions for spiritual strength, purity, comfort and guidance.

There may be some doubts as to the propriety of public prayer, at least some whose piety is not to be questioned have so thought. But it is sanctioned—not by the example of Jesus, for he went apart to pray—but by the example of the apostles and of the church in every age. It certainly is improper as it is frequently performed. One needs but a slight acquaintance with modern revivals and with fanaticism in any age to be convinced of this. It is now made the medium of stirring up men's passions, of denouncing Divine wrath and of frightening women and children out of their senses. But, if it be calm, sober, dignified, yet simple and fervent, such as it ever should be, and always will be with him whose devotion is kindled at the altar of true wisdom, it is an agreeable, may be a useful, and, in the opinion of wiser and better men than the writer of this, is a highly proper and necessary exercise. I would correct its abuses, but I know not that I could consistently with my own feelings dispense with it as a part of public worship.

Of the propriety of family prayer, there can be little doubt. The Scriptures, indeed, have not enjoined it, but each man whose heart is right, will be drawn to it. In the bosom of his family, retired from the world, where all disguise is thrown off, where thought may meet thought, and heart meet heart, it seems very fitting that the man should bear the united aspirations to the throne of his Father and his God. There is something touching, something endearing to the heart in seeing the family surround, in love, the domestic altar, and pay their morning and evening devotions to the Great Spirit of the Universe, beseeching his favor, entreating his guidance, and cheerfully committing themselves to his paternal protection. But in all cases prayer must be tested by the rule laid down. It is proper only as it draws us nearer to God, enlivens our devotions, invigorates, purifies and exalts our spiritual nature, makes us better, holier, more like the great Being whose perfections we adore.

Praise is a term often used to designate that part of external service performed by singing. The propriety of this must be tested by the effect it has on the performers and on the listeners. The power of music to soothe the passions and excite pleasing emotions has been noticed in all ages. There is a reforming power in sweet sounds, which the sober moralist may emulate in vain. The influence of good music to refine the feelings, to correct the taste, to harmonize the passions and inspire one with noble thoughts and urge him on to noble deeds is so obvious that it need not be labored. In this view praise, if in no other, is a part of real worship.

Preaching is, or is not, a part of Divine worship, as it is, or is not, fitted to have a kindly influence on those who listen. Preachers should be viewed simply as instructors, and if their instructions task the mind, kindle the love of excellence in the heart, arrest the wicked, arm conscience in defense of justice, and win the erring back to the paths of virtue, they are valuable, highly so. But preaching, merely because it is preaching, is of no value. Because we have listened to a sermon in the church it does not follow that we have performed any part of divine worship. If the sermon has left the heart untouched and cold, if it have imparted no strength to the mind, vigor to the resolution, constancy to the will, or kindled no holy aspiration, it has been listened to in vain, and we have no reason to flatter ourselves that we have participated in Divine worship.

Attendance at church comes under the same rule. The meeting together once a week to pray, to sing, to listen to valuable instruction, to mingle our social feelings, to brighten our social affections, by meeting our friends and neighbors and interchanging our kind salutations and enquiries is well calculated to cultivate our better feelings, to soften the harsh points in our characters, to refine our manners and our tempers, and promote good neighborhoods, and friendly and profitable intercourse. It is of the highest utility and because it is so it is a part of the worship of God. Let this be observed.

Of Baptism I have not much to say. The rule is laid down by which it may be tested. A formal pledge may at times be useful; it may encourage and invigorate the weak, it may induce a greater watchfulness over ourselves, and prompt higher exertions to be what we have pledged we will be, than we should otherwise have made. In this case it is instrumental in aiding the spiritual development and moral improvement required, and is so far a branch of divine worship and is proper. Still I do not believe much benefit results from it. It is of too positive and artificial a cast to comport well with a purely spiritual religion. It will breed superstition in weak minds, and be very apt to beget irreverence in minds of greater strength.

The Lord's Supper is somewhat different in character. It is of no use unless understandingly partaken. He who sits down to the table and discerns nothing but the bread and the wine, or who fancies he is better and holier, merely because he has partaken, will derive no benefit from the ceremony. The act should be deemed commemorative of exalted worth, and the pledge of common brotherhood and mutual friendship; and when thus viewed it becomes a source of rational joy and strong encouragement. Why do we keep in remembrance the birthday, or the death, of great benefactors of the human race? Why do we celebrate the day of our independence, and make it a day to commemorate noble deeds, and on which to form high resolves and re-swear to be free? The same principle in human nature, that leads to these, should lead us to commemorate the sufferings and death of him whose love for man was so great, whose devotion to truth and human salvation was so strong that he chose rather to die than to turn from the glorious work in which he was engaged. It is fitting we commemorate this act for it leads us to contemplate a character which embodies all of moral perfection. In commemorating the death of Jesus we pay a tribute to exalted worth, to moral purity, to greatness of soul, firmness and energy of spirit, to warm benevolence, to undying philanthropy, and to unfaltering devotion to duty. In doing this, we may catch some of that excellence we celebrate. In doing this, we are led to recount the labors of love it cost to establish truth, to vindicate the cause of justice and place man in the path of spiritual improvement; we are led to reflect on the feebleness of the band which first attacked the world's prejudices, which raised the voice in behalf of reform; and we are induced, too, to go over, in our minds, the dangers to which the master was exposed, the persecutions he met from the stubborn religionists of his time; the efforts made to strangle his cause in its cradle, the firmness with which he bore up against a world, the courage and the meekness and resignation with which he met the appalling death of the cross; the subsequent trials of his followers; the attacks upon the infant religion and the cruel persecution of its friends when they were few and powerless in the world's eye; and also, we view its triumph, its comparative prevalence, its increasing power, and the ease and security we enjoy under its shadow, contrasted with those who first struggled to nurture it into life. One can hardly go over the various topics of reflection this view would present without being a wiser and a better man.

Taking this view of the Lord's Supper, and which is the correct view, it is highly proper, and it were well for us all at suitable times to celebrate it. But it is proper to remark all that I have touched upon, as external service, in itself is not religion, and is of value only as it aids us in the moral and spiritual exaltation of ourselves, as it fits us the better to fulfill the great purposes of our existence. Under this view external service becomes our duty, and it will be deemed our privilege; it will be adopted as the pleasing means to help us forward in the march of improvement. We shall then resort to the sanctuary or assemble around the table of our master to gather strength; we shall listen to preaching to have our minds stirred up and our good resolutions confirmed; we shall retire to the closet to unbosom ourselves to our Father and to invoke his presence to be our comfort and our guide.

15.

PROTRACTED MEETINGS

Philanthropist 2 (December 17, 1831): 62-63

These meetings, which, for the last eighteen months, have swept our country like the tremendous simoom of the desert, are, so far as we can learn, subsiding, and the frightened traveler is beginning to rise and shake himself from the dust. It may be well to look around and enquire their effects.

That they have been in most instances encouraged by good wishes and sustained by a zeal for God, and ardent love for immortal souls, we doubt not; that they have done some good, it were blindness to deny; still we must pronounce the ruin, involved in their progress, tremendous.

They have produced a feverish and sickly religious taste. Sound reasoning, sober sense, calm and rational enquiry are become dull, insipid, uninviting to the religious world. The mind has been intoxicated, sustained so much by artificial stimuli that it has received the same shocks and become subject to equal debility with the body of the drunkard. It has no longer any strength of its own; but wastes in a dull and torpid state till artificially excited.

They have produced false notions of religion. Instead of conceiving it the sober exercise of all our faculties, the direction of all our powers to the accomplishment of wise and just ends, they make it a mere thing of feeling, mere phrensy—something out of the ordinary course of things produced by means wholly unnatural and to be sustained by means wholly artificial. The young convert is made to place piety in a class of affections wholly foreign to our nature. He has a feverish excitement, a singular feeling, produced by causes he has not analyzed and he fancies himself born again; the cause of the excitement ceases; he sinks below the natural tone of his feelings; has doubts and misgivings; loses his hope; fears he has sinned away the day of grace, is in despair, or cold to any new religious impression. To keep him anywhere within the range of piety, or supposed piety, violent, and overstrained exertions are required on his part and on the part of his spiritual associates. There is then an end to sober preaching and to enforcing the moral duties and the social virtues. Hence it is no preacher can be popular unless he addresses himself entirely to the feelings and be able always to inflame the passions. Community will one day regret this. The individual, when he sees the ruin of his piety by such means, will deeply deplore it.

They produce uncharitableness. Instead of making religion a source of love and good feeling, they make it an occasion of spiritual pride, arrogance, self-conceit, and bitter contempt of all those who come not up to the tone of feeling they produce, and who join not the church by which they are encouraged. It is painful to think of the confusion these meetings produce; the mischief they do to good neighborhood; the kind feelings they blast; the strong and endearing affections they wither; the domestic discord they produce! Almost every day we learn some new instance of their mischief. We hear of families broken up, or filled with endless broils and heart-burnings. Husbands tell us that by these meetings the affections of their wives have been estranged; that they are scorned by their tender companions, through the instructions of well meaning, but misguided, clergy; fathers and mothers tell us that in these meetings their children have learned to insult their gray hairs; or mock their affectionate counsels; and even to tell them they are going to hell, that they deserved to be damned! Oh, can we look with calmness on the scene which turns the milk of human kindness into wormwood and gall; that deadens all the tender sympathies of the female bosom towards the husband of her love and the father of her children; that destroys all confidence between husband and wife, between parent and child, destroys filial piety, and sunders the tenderest ties of our nature! We exult not. We grieve that such has been their fruit.

(March 13, 1832): 154-55

Another objection to protracted meetings, and to the machinery adopted in them, is, that they lead to insanity. It is a painful thought that any should so preach the gospel of peace as to make it the means of depriving people of their reason; yet the fact is notorious that these meetings do have an awful effect that way. We were informed not long since, of two individuals in this village, raving maniacs through the influence of revival meetings. In a late visit to Elmira, Tioga Co., an old friend of ours, related with tears in his eyes, the distraction of his niece, a most amiable and excellent woman. He requested us to publish her name and the circumstances but we cannot. We would not harrow up the feelings of her distressed husband; nor record the case to wound her heart should she chance to recover. More than a hundred cases have been reported to us within a year; some of them most distressing in their character and painful and mortifying in their results. The husband has taken the life of his wife, the mother of her innocent babes, all through the influence of religious mania. Surely it is time to pause, to weep over the infatuation which prevails.

There is nothing in the gospel which requires this. We do not recollect that any instances of insanity are recorded as resulting from the ministration of the apostles, nor are we willing to believe any measures which are attended with such horrid consequences, can be blessed of God. A case has lately occurred in Elbridge, Onondaga Co. which makes one's heart ache. A pious old lady, an excellent woman, one we had long known to be such, was drawn within the vortex, induced to run constantly to these protracted meetings, became deranged, and in a few days was hurried out of the world; and her minister said, at her funeral, he "hoped when he died, he should die in a like condition." Is there to be no end to this? We beg of our orthodox friends to pause, and ask if "God has not sent then a strong delusion, that they may believe a lie and be damned?" Surely they are verifying the old maxim, "Whom the Gods resolve to destroy, they first make mad." Let them continue a little longer to practice upon credulity and weak nerves, and they will have raised a storm of indignation, they will not easily escape. This people will not much longer submit to be deprived of reason; they will not sustain a misguided clergy in the adoption of means, which make our wives and daughters maniacs, and mothers the murderers of their children. There is a point beyond which human nature will not be crowded. Let him who rives the Oak beware of its rebound. There is many a man who has looked on, in silence it may be, but with a gathering indignation. When such a man awakes, when he does speak, and ere long thousands such will speak, the offenders may well fear their day is come, and their doom settled. *To be Continued.*[1]

---

[1][Ed. This essay was never continued.]

16.

A SERMON ON SELF-DENIAL[1]

Philanthropist 2 (December 31, 1831): 65-75

"If any man will come after me, let him deny himself, and take up his cross and follow me" Mt. 16:24.

There is nothing more painful to the benevolent heart than the many gross perversions of the religion of Jesus. The plainest precepts of the Nazarene Reformer have been enveloped in gloomy mystery; and the holiest and most sublime system of religion ever communicated to man has been converted into a mere engine of sectarian craft and sectarian folly.

The passage just read in your hearing, my friends, plain and consistent in itself, conveying a most useful moral lesson, has been adduced in support of a doctrine as much at war with Christianity, as it is with the dictates of reason and the interests of mankind. It has been supposed to countenance that cold and forbidding character, which morose tempers, gloomy imaginations and ignorant zeal, have been fond of ascribing to our holy religion, and which has made it the bugbear of the young and warm hearted, and the butt of ridicule to the infidel and licentious wit.

The doctrine of self-denial rationally explained is as much an injunction of sound philosophy as of religion; but when construed, as it too often has been, to mean a denial to ourselves of all the rational pleasures of life, of all the innocent enjoyments, good things and amusements, offered us here, by a wise and munificent Providence, for fear our Heavenly Father will not love us unless we make ourselves miserable, it becomes as dishonorable to God as it is degrading and mischievous to man. It is a false principle of religion to suppose that Deity is displeased with our endeavors to make ourselves happy, or that he will hate us if we dare once think of aught save self-mortification and self-abasement. The past history of the church affords us too many, and too lamentable proofs of the mischievous consequences of this false principle. The gloomy cells of the monastery, the undue abstemiousness, the penance, the self-mortifications, the self-inflicted

[1][Ed. This was a sermon that was delivered at Ithaca, on the First Sabbath in February, 1831.]

flagellations, and numerous lacerations of the body for the good of the soul, so highly esteemed by the religionists of by-gone ages—the bitterness which the stricter sect of professed Christians even now exhibit towards all play of the warmer feelings of the heart, and to the indulgence of any innocent amusement—the severity with which they condemn all buoyancy of spirit and youthful hilarity, all satisfaction felt in the possession of anything appertaining to the world, may seem to justify the sneers cast upon our religion, and to pardon the conclusion some have drawn, that "Christianity teaches us to gain heaven by the sacrifice of everything dear on earth."

This has done great injury to mankind, as well as discredit to religion among the more enlightened, and especially among the young and warm hearted part of mankind. Whoever will look at the volume of the Creator's works, cannot fail to read, on every page, a refutation of this gloomy and unsocial dogma. How beautiful is this world! How full of life and love! How kindly has Heaven poured forth a profusion of beauty and ornament, beneficial to our wants and pleasing to our sight! He has everywhere, apparently, studied to awaken the pleasure of the beholder. Art never decorated a palace with half its splendor, nor imitated it in the richness and variety of its luxuries. How splendid, how numerous and variegated the costume of the flowers and herbage! How gay the dress, how sweet the song, of the feathered tribes! Surely, had the taste of one of these sour, gloomy and morose interpreters of religion, been consulted at the creation—if we may use the words of a prescribed writer, "not a flower would have bloomed nor a bird been permitted to sing!"[2]

We look at ourselves, mark our susceptibilities, the warm emotions of love, the rich pleasure of indulging our social feelings, and interchanging kind offices with our friends, the keen relish we have for the riches, which Deity bestows, and the zest with which we can feed on his bounties—the gratitude they inspire to the Giver, and the kind feelings they awake from one to another—these, all these forbid us to think our God envies us our enjoyments here, or that he is more averse to our happiness in this world than in another.

Neither the Christian nor the philosopher will condemn the pleasures life can give. The language of Deity, of reason, or of desire, while addressing man is, "Go, my son, partake freely of my bounties; enjoy my gifts. I am pleased, I am satisfied, when thou art happy." It is but mistaken folly, or the fears of a morbid temper that can imagine one entitles himself to Divine favor by slighting the Creator's

---

[2][Ed. Not able to identify quotation.]

goodness—turning from every solace life may give, and neglecting every opportunity of awakening the softer and better feelings of the heart, and of promoting the pleasures of the warm and generous emotions, of kind and endearing affection.

But, shall we call in question the truth of our text, and insinuate its lesson is false, is mischievous? By no means. The text is true. I have remarked, self-denial rationally explained is an injunction of sound philosophy as well as of religion. It will now become our duty to present our text in its true light, to exhibit the true doctrine of self-denial, and calmly, but earnestly, bring its lesson home to ourselves.

The text was spoken in consequence of what Peter had replied to a remark made by our Savior. Jesus had told his disciples that he should go up to Jerusalem, and that there he would be persecuted and crucified by the Jews. Peter, who was not infrequently the spokesman for the disciples, rebuked him and told him "far be this thing from thee, Lord" [Matt 16:22]. It may be, pure affection prompted this rebuke; but, from the sharp reply of Jesus, one would think it was not love for his master but ambition that made Peter thus forward.

It is evident from the gospel history that previous to the crucifixion the disciples viewed Jesus as a temporal prince; as a lineal descendant from the house of David, they conceived it his object to restore the kingdom of Israel, then a Roman province, to the rank and dignity of an independent nation, that he would reign king over the Jews, and become the most potent of earthly monarchs. As they were the first to recognize his claims and as they followed him in the days of his obscurity and humiliation, they thought they might look forward with confidence to some important posts near his person in his exaltation, or when he should come into his kingdom. That Jesus did anticipate a political, as well as a moral revolution, has been thought by some and perhaps is not improbable. But it needed no superhuman observation to assure him his countrymen were too debased to be entrusted with the government of themselves, and that they were too much divided, too much distracted by petty jealousies and petty interests to make any vigorous efforts for their political independence. Whether he ever did anticipate anything of the kind, it is evident that at the period of his history which we are now examining, he entertained no such thought. Still, the disciples entertained it, and they could not avoid foreseeing that his death would blast all their prospects of temporal aggrandizement and that they would probably have to shrink back to their fishing boats with all the chagrin and vexation of disappointed ambition.

It was, probably, this consideration that induced Peter to attempt to dissuade Jesus from going up to Jerusalem. He plainly perceived that if at that time, Jesus should be crucified, all for which they were contending would be lost. Hence, the sharp rebuke from Jesus, who told Peter, he "savored the things which be of man, not those of God" [Matt 16:23]. Intimating that their dreams of human aggrandizement, were inconsistent with his design, and that they must deny themselves of all such fleeting visions and be able like him to bear the cross to the place of execution and yield their lives as martyrs to the moral renovation he was laboring to effect.

The disciples labored under a mistake. The objects of Jesus were of a different character from what they imagined. His was to be a moral, not a political, revolution. He had come to evangelize the world; to establish a new order of things; to build up a system of righteousness that should send joy, peace and love throughout the world. This was his object. The disciples dreamed of human glory, of wealth and honors. These they desired. But while thus earthly in their feelings, while dazzled with visions of stars and coronets, they could be no useful assistants in the work of the moral Reformer. Hence, the importance of self-denial. Hence, Jesus well said, "if any man will come after me, let him deny himself, take up his cross and follow me." It was simply saying, "if any man will engage with me, in the arduous task of reforming the world, he must deny himself of all dreams of earthly glory, all desires of human greatness, and mere worldly wealth; he must be prepared to meet with the loss of all these; he must have that disregard of self, that firmness of purpose, that steadiness of resolve, and that undying devotion to duty which will enable him to face danger, unintimidated, and even death unappalled."

You will at once, my friends, perceive the propriety of this, if you will go back, in your minds, to the time when our text was spoken. Jesus was engaged in an unpopular work. His doctrine was an innovation upon long established and deep rooted prejudices. His pure morality was a standing rebuke of the ignorance and barbarity of his countrymen. All he did, all he taught, all he enjoined, was at war with existing usages and approved modes of thinking. It awakened the indignation of the priesthood and aroused the fears of a despotic and easily exasperated government. What then could he promise his followers to flatter their ambition, or to feed their love of wealth? Their cause was derided and their master treated with contempt. The great would stand aloof. Their cause was proscribed and the ministers of vengeance hunted their master. The rich would not hazard their wealth; for those who espoused the cause might, at any moment, be stripped of what they possessed, and deem themselves fortunate if life itself were spared. How easy then to see the importance of their denying themselves and acquiring even a contempt for riches and honors. If they did not thus they could be no firm adherents; in the hour of adversity they would waver; when danger threatened they would shrink from their posts and leave their master to stand alone.

This was an important consideration. Jesus could promise no ease, no security to his followers. His cause required no little exertion and active engagedness. There were mighty obstacles to surmount; powerful enemies to combat; extensive countries to traverse, exposed to dangers on every hand—from the elements and from men. The cause presented his followers only a scene of action, danger and privation. Was he not right, then, to inculcate self-denial? How soon without it would his disciples have despaired and shrunk from their noble enterprise!

They must take up their cross. This is easily understood. Criminals were compelled to bear the cross on which they were to be crucified from the hall of judgment to the place of execution. Thus Jesus carried the cross, or wood, on which he was crucified, till he fainted and the executioners compelled one Simon of Cyrene to assist him. In our text it pointed to the mode by which Jesus would suffer, and admonished the disciples what they must be prepared to meet, and that, unless they were thus prepared, they were no true disciples, they were no useful coadjutors in reforming the world. For, with what benefit to the noble cause could they labor if afraid of persecution, afraid of death, and only anxious about temporal concerns? Their cause exposed them and would expose them to the envenomed shafts of persecution. Not only their property and reputations but even their lives were uncertain. They must be prepared to stake everything for the noble work of regenerating a world. Hence, they were to count all earthly things as dross and to hold their lives of no consequence. Then, and only then, could they go forward with a firm step, a quiet pulse, a steady adherence to the grand cause, and with hopes of ultimate success.

Such I conceive the true doctrine of my text. Still it may be used in a larger sense—be accommodated to the general doctrine of self-denial.

Life is a complex scene. All the objects which surround us are of a mixed nature. Our actions are so involved in the actions of each other; the conduct of one is so modified, overruled, or changed, by the conduct of another that the immediate results are often very different from the more remote. Experience daily proves some things and some actions produce a momentary pleasure but entail lasting pain. We often find a path at its entrance, adorned on either hand with flowers that charm with their rich and variegated hues and regale the sense with their sweet fragrance. The birds warble their soft notes from the overhanging groves. We enter with joyous heart and bounding step—fancy we have found the path which leads to the fountain of exhaustless pleasure. Soon, however, the grove darkens; the carpet of flowers disappears; the music of the morning songsters is succeeded by the howling of the beasts of prey; the open champaign, or the landscape variegated with hill and dale, of cultivated fields, grazing herds, and laughing and joyous man, we had pictured, proves to be a measureless wild, inhabited only by the prowling wolf or the ferocious tiger. We soon lose ourselves by the endless windings of our path, exhausted sink down by the cataract's roar, and wish, but too often vainly wish, to retrace our steps and deny ourselves the pleasure promised by the alluring invitations of the path at its entrance.[3]

It is the misfortune of mankind that the greater part never reflect on these deceitful appearances. They seize the momentary gratification, short lived pleasure, which is "all a fleeting show," regardless of the consequences or general result of their pursuits. They scorn the least self-denial and while in the pursuit of pleasure ruin their constitution, and lay the foundation for heaviness of heart and lasting regret.

It is thus individuals hope for pleasure from mere animal gratification—grasp at everything which can awaken or answer desire; and thus, too, is it we see the sensualist, after he has run his whole routine of sensual delights, returning with disgust, draining the intoxicating bowl to stifle the compunctions of conscience and blunt the pangs of disappointment; and thus it is, we hear him in the bitterness of soul, feeling his own ruin, and the inanity of all his pursuits, exclaim, "all is vanity and vexation of spirit" [Eccles 1:14, passim].

A glass of wine may exhilarate the spirits; if this were all, it were harmless. But another leads to intoxication, and the pleasing sensation passes to beastliness, to pain, to the keen pang of remorse. A

---

[3] I am indebted to Johnson's tale of Obidah, or the Journey of a Day. [Ed. Reference here is to Samuel Johnson's *Rambler* article, number 65. On this, see *The Rambler* in the *Yale Edition of the Works of Samuel Johnson*, vol. 3, ed. W. J. Bate and Albrecht B. Strauss (New Haven and London: Yale University Press, 1969), 344-49.]

deep depression follows the exhilaration; the health is impaired; the taste vitiated; the capacity for receiving and retaining pleasure weakened, and the man unfitted for his own or others' society. Wisdom, even the love of pleasure itself, admonishes that, if the indulgence of appetite lead to this painful result, we should refrain, deny ourselves the momentary pleasure that we may avoid the lasting evil. But, alas! we find those who mock at this rational self-denial, deaf to the voice of wisdom, pass on, sip at every flower, regardless of the poison which may be mingled with the fancied nectar!

There is another class, smaller though still numerous, who, deeply impressed with the consequences of unrestrained appetite and passion, at the extremes of indulgence, condemn everything and stamp a curse on our most innocent amusements. Even the smiles of irrational nature offend them. They would even shroud the heavens in mourning and dress the earth in sackcloth! The child that laughs and prattles, the youth who gives way to the buoyancy of his feelings and the full flow of his sportive spirits, the man who can be pleased with a play, or with the lively exhibitions of mirth—wished by all and in which the coldest may at times warm—each is, by too many of the professed guardians of religion and morals, considered as in the broad road to ruin, and unless everything of the kind be denied, will sink to endless perdition!

Perhaps, it will be so; but I hope not. This is a world in which there is much to endure. All have their share of suffering and God forbid that we should becloud the few sunny spots that may lie in our path. Let us not my friends aggravate the miseries of life; let us not impose voluntary sufferings on ourselves or fear that Deity would frown upon us were he to look down from his dwelling of love, and see every face clothed with the cheerful smile of content, and every heart pleased and buoyant with the full enjoyment of the riches of his providence.

I have not time nor have I the inclination to pursue the doctrine of self-denial through all the minuteness of detail. Your own reflections must do this. The rule is given, may it be your pleasure to learn its application. Think not, however, it is a trifling task. It is of the highest importance to be done; and it will require years of strict discipline, if not your whole lives, to master it.

The ruling passion of our countrymen is desire of gain. From this flow most of our virtues, our prosperity, and most of our vices; and is that which embosoms the seeds of our ruin. It is this which creates our enterprise, and gives the spring to our commerce; which whitens every sea with our sails and fills every port with our ships. It is this which clears away our forests and speaks into existence our thousands of smiling and lovely villages. A long catalogue of evils flows also from the same source. But I am not now in the humor to point them out. No man who understands and regards his own words will speak against wealth. Its acquisition is proper and desirable when regulated by justice and moderation. But, when allowed to engross all our faculties and to absorb every moment of our lives, it is apt to contract the understanding, to vitiate the moral sense, and to render us inattentive to the means we adopt. Here is room for self-denial, for here the pleasure ends and the evil begins.

The man who loves happiness will not wish for an upbraiding conscience—will not be anxious to have his brain haunted by the appalling images of widows robbed of their mites, and orphans despoiled of their portions. No matter how vast a man's possessions, how extensive his houses and lands, if he cannot look with a quiet conscience on the means by which he acquired them. If the poor upbraid him for his oppression, if he see the multitude he has wronged hear their demands for justice—hear their blasting curses upon him for rioting on what they may claim, it will afford him little pleasure. It kindles a deep and burning hell in his bosom; all his wealth will be unable to save him from the misery of his own reflections; to cheer his lonely hours; to support him in the melancholy of old age, and to smooth the path for his tottering steps to the grave.

It will be well for each to reflect on this, to be careful no love of gain, no thirst for riches, induce him to sacrifice his integrity; that no momentary pleasure of acquiring wealth betray him into any act of oppression, of fraud, of injustice. The plain principle to be observed, in this and in all other cases is, to deny our selves what may be a momentary pleasure, that we may avoid what would be lasting pain to ourselves or to others; submit to temporary pain that we may secure lasting enjoyment.

Such, my friends, is the true doctrine of self-denial. How applicable to us and to all human beings! It requires nothing of us that it is not for our interest to give. It allows everything which it is not injurious to keep. Have we observed the rule? Let each commune with his own heart, let each when coolly reviewing his conduct by himself ask, if his conscience does not upbraid; if he have not been too intent on a momentary gratification; if he have not overlooked consequences and acquired habits of thinking and acting which he will one day regret?

But there is another view in which I would apply this subject. We, my friends, are placed in circumstances not very dissimilar to those which surrounded the primitive disciples; we, as well as they, came forward as reformers. We attack long existing and long venerated practices. We take up the challenge in behalf of rational religion and common sense; we have seen the darkness which covers the land and the gross darkness which covers the people; we have heard the cry of oppression, we have wept over "man's inhumanity to man"; we enlist on the side of humanity; we wish in some measure to effect a new order of things; we wish to dispel the cold and heartless night of ignorance and bigotry which hangs over the moral world; to brush away the clouds which intercept the rays of the sun of truth; we would reach the heart, soften the affections, destroy the selfish spirit which sports with our happiness, and throw around each a bright and sunny heaven of benevolence; we aim to beat down the walls of partition, to let the human race flow together, and make each man sensible, that man wherever seen is his brother, woman wherever found is his sister, that all are fellow beings and should be bound to each by a fellow feeling.

Such are our objects. To accomplish them we strike at deep rooted prejudices, and have to expose ourselves to the contempt of the ignorant, the abhorrence of the fanatic and to the persecution of the bigoted and designing: we acquire nothing in wealth; nothing in honors; for, our cause is unpopular, proscribed, nothing for which people usually labor is promised us; nothing to gratify the selfishness so common to us all. See ye not then, if ye will be reformers, what ye must deny yourselves? Would ye be true soldiers, would ye be resolved on victory or death, see ye not ye must nerve yourselves to the work? Discouraging circumstances must not change your high resolves; nor danger, nor death, make you turn from the enemy, desert your post, shrink from your duty and leave the important reform unaccomplished.

True we are not compelled to make those heavy sacrifices, as were the apostles; we are not called to resist unto blood. Thanks to the spirit-stirring Genius of Improvement, the "fist of wickedness that would, is bound that it cannot smite."[4] The opponents of a just reform, of a mild and rational religion, cannot take from us our citizenship; they cannot deprive us of liberty; but they can, and will, study to derange our business and to blast our reputations. They will exhaust magazines of wrath; they will heap mountains of reproach

---

[4][Ed. Isa 58:4, and John Milton in *Tetrachordon*. See John Milton, *Complete Prose Works*, vol. 2, ed. Don M. Wolfe (New Haven: Yale University Press, 1959), 581, line 34.]

upon us; but what then? Have we put our hands to the plough to look back? We have taken our stand; and shall we not nerve ourselves to the task before us?

We must study self-denial; we must acquire a command over ourselves, obtain that invincible moral courage, which will enable us to set at naught the foul aspersions that may be cast upon us, and to meet unmoved whatever opposition may be excited against us. We must be calm but determined; moderate but in earnest; mild and charitable but fearless and faithful. No threats of maddened zealots must have power to move us; no flatteries of the sycophants of popularity must induce us to pause, much less shrink from our duty. We must fix our eyes on the great work to be done, to be done in ourselves, and for long degraded humanity, and, steady as the sun in his course, must we pursue our object. Unless such be our strength of mind, such our firmness of resolve, such our steadiness of purpose, such our undaunted moral courage, our labors will be unavailing; our own hearts will be unreformed, our own characters will be unperfected, and the great and noble cause in which we have engaged with so much apparent zeal will evaporate in sound, and our inflated professions die away on the wind.

But, though ours be a state of trial and of self-denial it is not one which yields us no reward. There is something in its very nature that captivates the soul. Its noble daring, its high resolve, its mental energy, its very self-denial, fill the bosom with emotions at once pleasing and sublime. We mark the renovation required and the necessity there is that it should be effected, the grandeur of the work itself, the thought that we may do something to hasten it forward, that we may give it an additional impetus, together with the internal consciousness that Heaven approves our course will give efficacy to our exertions and crown them with immortal and universal triumph—O, there is that in it which makes ample amends for all sacrifices imposed, for the loss of wealth, of friends and even of life.

My friends, be not discouraged; ye see what ye must do, what ye must endure. Let the example of Jesus and of the primitive disciples, give you firmness of purpose, and the promises of Heaven cheer your drooping spirits, fire you with courage, and impel you to a faithful performance of your duty, and give you full confidence, that the religion of Jesus will yet triumph, sin be finished, everlasting righteousness be established, and man everywhere free, great, noble, raise the song of gratitude to his God, and feel his heart expand with kindest affection to his brother. Which may God in mercy vouchsafe. Amen.

17.

A SERMON ON RIGHTEOUSNESS[1]

Philanthropist 2 (January 14, 1832): 85-94

"I have preached righteousness in the great congregation" Ps. 40:9.

The duty of a preacher is seldom understood and, perhaps, less often performed. But it was not to be expected that in the midst of an ignorant and corrupt world, anyone class of men should be perfect in wisdom and in goodness. That the clergy should sometimes have neglected to ascertain their duty, and at others have been seduced from its performance need excite no surprise. The clergy are but men, subject to the same passions as are others, affected by the same causes, governed by the same motives and exposed to the same, if not even greater, temptations; it does not, then, become us as lovers of impartial justice to vent any peculiar spleen at them or to treat them as more depraved than the rest of mankind. You should give them credit for all the good they have done, lament all the evil they may have occasioned, and pass it by with the assurance,

"To err is human; to forgive, divine."[2]

I make these remarks because I am well aware, while one portion of my fellow beings are worshiping, as it were, the clergy, ascribing to them undeserved excellence, giving them credit for virtues they do not possess, and for benefits they have never conferred; another part look up to them as monsters in wickedness, and deem the term clergyman, but another name for all that is base and detestable among mortals. Either is wrong; either has a wrong temper, and acting under the influence of that temper will be mischievous to the human race. I wish you, therefore, my hearers, to lay aside whatever prejudices you may have on this subject. If, in what I now, or at any future time may say, you may discover anything which may redound to the honor of the clergy, I pray you receive it, if it be true; or if I shall offer

[1][Ed. This sermon was preached in February of 1831 and was published to demonstrate that Brownson was not becoming exclusively orthodox or Presbyterian, as some were charging. On this, see *Philanthropist* 2 (January 24, 1832): 85.]

[2][Ed. Alexander Pope, *An Essay on Criticism*, in *The Works of Alexander Pope*, volume 2 (New York: Gordian Press, 1967), 66, line 525.]

anything which seems to lessen their worth, I would that you receive it, if it be not false.

My object at this time is to call your attention to what I conceive it the duty of a preacher to labor to effect; and also to give you a criterion by which you may hereafter judge of my consistency or inconsistency with myself.

The Psalmist declares in our text that he had "preached righteousness in the great congregation." I conceive the only legitimate object of any preacher is the production of righteousness. This should be his polar star, towards which, as the magnet of the soul, he should point all his powers. To this he should shape his doctrines, his reproofs, and his exhortations. Nothing is of any use that does not tend towards it, and my usefulness, as your preacher, will depend on the success I may have in producing it.

Before, however, I attempt to point out what righteousness is, I will ask your indulgence, while I notice some few things which, sometimes, pass for it, but which are either opposed, or unnecessary, to it.

All, or nearly all, who have preached to you as well as to others, have attached themselves to some party, and devoted themselves to the defense of some creed; too often acting as if they identified the progress of goodness with the prosperity and aggrandizement of their own sect. I belong to no party. I disclaim all sectarian names. You have called me a Universalist. I disown the name, though I may not oppose what an enlightened Universalist would wish to effect. I do not wish to be called a Universalist. Should I assume the name of any party, it should be Unitarian, as that denomination approximates nearer, in my estimation, to the spirit of Christianity than any other. Unitarian discourses are mostly practical; their lessons inculcate charity, a refined moral feeling, and universal benevolence. They teach us God is our Father, that all men are brethren, and that we should cultivate mutual good will, and imbibe a liberal and manly feeling towards all men. Unitarian preaching, in general, I approve; but I discover no necessity of assuming any name that can become the rallying point of a sect. You will therefore forbear to associate my name with any party, either orthodox or heterodox. I am an independent preacher, accountable to my God, to truth, to my country, to the people of my charge, but to no other tribunal.

In this respect I differ from most other preachers. But in this I discover no disadvantage. Truth is the property of no one sect, righteousness is the exclusive boast of no one denomination. All have some truth, all have some errors. To join anyone you must support its falsehoods as well as its truths, or they will cast you out of the synagogue. You must study to conceal the faults of your party and often be compelled to suffer reproach from the misconduct of your associates.

If you have a party to which you attach yourselves, you will most likely have certain sentiments which you will feel bound to support, and which, in most cases, your associates will induce you to maintain through fear of losing your reputation, if not your means of subsistence. The party may at first be good; it may be organized for the noblest purposes; the first adherents may be men of enlarged and liberal minds, of benevolent hearts; they may have an eye single to the support of the dearest interests of mankind; but, it can hardly happen that none of more selfish purposes will at length assume the lead, or that, in the progress of events, the majority may not become more intent on building themselves up as a mere party, than on discovering and promulgating truth.

No man, who has attended to the subject, can doubt that the first Christian churches were founded by the best feelings of the human heart, and for the noblest purposes of philanthropy. But, how soon were they perverted to other ends, made subservient to the aggrandizement of a few, and the consequent depression of the many. Each sect, in its origin, has aimed well, and has had some really good things; but each in its progress, deeming itself bound by the perfection it boasted in its commencement, binding its adherents back to the starting point, prohibiting them on pain of excommunication, and often of death, from any innovation or departure from what its projector enjoined has destroyed its utility and involved a long catalogue of evils too numerous to be named and too painful to be dwelt upon.

At present, soon as one thinks of being religious, soon as he feels serious and desires to understand religion and enjoy its consolations, he immediately unites with some sect. This too often proves an end to his progress. The church has its creed, its rules, and its usage, which it not infrequently holds dearer than truth. These the young convert must embrace and zealously support not only while he has the belief and feelings he has on uniting, but through all after life, let his future convictions be what they may.

Now, who is there that does not perceive the ill consequences of these misplaced and mistimed demands? Who so foolish as to pretend that a child twelve or fourteen years old has mastered the whole subject and learned so much that nothing remains to be learned? The fact is, the child, or the youth, usually unites with the church and declares what he will always believe soon as he commences learning, while the whole field of religious science is before him, as yet untraversed. For him, at this moment, to assume to know all that can be known or to know so much as to know he shall never see cause to change his opinion, is most egregious folly, and those, who encourage him to do thus, are doing him and the world incalculable injury. The opinions he now adopts he may soon discover to be erroneous; those he now condemns farther and closer investigation may discover to be true. Ought he not to be free to renounce the one set and to embrace the other without injury to his character? Can he do this, without disgrace, if he be a member of any of our churches? The laws of our churches are like those of the Medes and Persians, they change not; aye, they allow no change. If he, who has unfortunately acknowledged their sway, presume to reason beyond the limits they prescribe, he is called a heretic, his standing in the church is lost, and he is turned out into the world with the damning brand of heresy on his forehead, an object of scorn to all who deem it a virtue never to doubt.

I do not speak at random, my friends. I speak from experience. I was a Universalist, a Universalist preacher. I was so unfortunate in the prosecution of my studies as to have doubts; I withdrew myself from the denomination to which I belonged, and ceased to preach. What was the consequence? Approbation for my honesty? No, they excommunicated me and published me from one end of the country to the other as a rejector of Christianity, as an unprincipled villain![3] This is the principle by which all sects are governed. What encouragement has one to enquire after truth or to aspire to any growth in knowledge after he has united with a sect? Will it not be his wisest course to sit down with the remark, "my church is right, at least I will not enquire, lest haply I find it in the wrong?"

The fact is, nearly all churches, as now organized, are unfriendly to the full development of religious or mental excellence. They are like the Philistine's chains which bound Sampson when shorn of his strength, and those, who come within their enclosures, can do little else than grind in their prison houses. I know of no real advantage they offer to the world. The only bond of union I approve is that which spontaneously springs from similar sentiments, similar feelings and the pursuit of similar objects. The sympathy of a like faith, of common objects, and common feelings, will bind us sufficiently close to each other.

[3][Ed. On Brownson's official excommunication or letter of dismissal, see Introduction to EW, 1:28-29.]

To preach righteousness, then, I do not conceive it necessary to urge you to join a church. I wish you to observe all the good there is in any, or all of our churches, to ascertain all they have of truth, and make it your own; but if you will be wise, you will beware how you receive their fetters, and place yourselves in a situation by which you must father their faults as well as their virtues.

I think it has not failed to strike you that much of what passes for righteousness, with those who assume the direction of our consciences, is, to say the least, of doubtful utility.

I have observed the mass of mankind are not afflicted with any very deep thought; nor do they discriminate very clearly between what is important and what is unimportant. That which is the most noisy or which makes the most show almost invariably attracts the most attention. Hence it is, the ceremonies of religion are much more scrupulously observed than religion itself; and men frequently seem more attached to the *form,* than to the *power* of godliness. Yet, of what consequence is the form without the power? He were a simpleton indeed, who should deem the shadow of more value than the substance. There is, however, great fear many are in pursuit of only the shadow, and that while in pursuit of that they lose the substance.

The Christian world has at times been wholly bent on external worship. It now enjoins a variety of rites and ceremonies and vague duties, which at best are only the lumber of religion. Take joining the church. This just now is all the rage. Is there anything in the mere act itself that makes the heart better? May not a man be equally as grateful to his God and as benevolent to his brother, out, as in, the church? If so, what is the utility of joining? And, do we not often see many of those who join puffed up with a spiritual pride, imagining themselves a great deal better because they have done this act? Do not our churches tend to introduce artificial distinctions? Is there not a perpetual hostility between church members and those denominated the world? Does not the church indulge in the severity of invective against those who do not belong to it? And do not those called the world delight to make the churches the butt of their ridicule? Surely no reasonable man will pronounce this state of things favorable to virtue; and every good man every genuinely religious man will do all he can to correct it.

Take also Baptism and the Lord's Supper. It is well known Baptism cannot purge the conscience from dead works to the life of virtue. A man may receive the rite, while murder is rankling in his heart and while his hands are red with crime. It cannot, therefore, be considered as a purifying ordinance, and to suppose our God will love us any the better for being put all over under water is not very rational. God looks at the heart, requires justice and mercy rather than burnt offerings or any external rite whatever. The same may be said of the sacramental supper. In itself it is of no use. A man can be as good without it as with it. All these things are—useless? May I not say, often worse—mischievous? They draw off our attention from things important; they substitute, in the minds of the unenlightened, the form for the power of goodness, and often flatter them they can secure heaven without any practical usefulness to their fellow beings.

They often lay the axe at the root of the tree of morality, strangle our virtues in the cradle and spread a feverish and sickly superstition over the moral world. True, we are told, they are only symbolical, admirably calculated to refresh our minds and remind us of what we should be and of what Christ has done for us; but, alas! symbols may do very well for the enlightened, for the discerning, but, they are always mischievous to those who cannot, or will not, look at what they are designed to prefigure. I make no war upon them. Education, habit, may have endeared them, and communion seasons may often be peculiarly precious to the Christian. Still, I think it would be advantageous to the moral world to pay no great attention to them. I think it were better to inform the people that rites and ceremonies are superannuated; that these counterfeits of goodness do not pass current with our heavenly Father; that he requires us to worship him in "spirit and in truth" [John 4:24]; that in the days of our ignorance he winked at this mystical worship, but now commands all men everywhere to repent; that is, break off from their sins, "cease to do evil and learn to do well" [Isa 1:16-17].[4]

---

[4]My objections are to churches as they usually exist. I want no other church than the parish; then all may be considered members and made to feel, soon as they come to years of discretion that they are bound to perform all the duties that belong to Christians. My objections to Baptism and the Lord's Supper are against the popular views of those institutions. I am willing Baptism as a simple initiatory rite should be observed, though I consider it not particularly enjoined upon us in the Scriptures. Whatever may be the meaning of Jesus to his disciples to baptize, one thing is certain, no intimation is anywhere given it was to be observed through all stages of the church. To the Eucharist, if viewed simply as a mere token of respect to the Great Founder of our religion, and as a mark of our fraternal love and mutual fidelity I have no objections. On any other view of it, my conscience would not allow me to approach the communion table. [Ed. Brownson's distinction between the church and the parish refers to the general Puritan view that only the converted belonged to the church and therefore had access to the Eucharist. Parish members were all who belonged to a particular territorial parish.]

These remarks bring me to consider what it is to preach righteousness. In illustrating this, I must be allowed to draw the picture of a righteous man, and in portraying his character I hope to be able to exhibit clearly my views of righteousness. I may be entering upon a difficult task. The world is almost a stranger to what I would describe. I seem to myself to be on untrodden ground—compelled to draw from the imagination. But I hope there is more than one who might sit for the likeness.

The righteous man has a lively sense of gratitude to God. I place this first, because, in my opinion, he who has no mind to admire the wisdom and order of the universe, no heart to adore the love and goodness everywhere displayed in the Creator's works, can lay no claim to correctness of thought, much less to goodness of heart. He who notes of what he is made susceptible, who marks the rich provision made for his wants, the vast variety of objects contrived to awaken his pleasure and gladden his heart, must be a cold, unfeeling wretch, if no gratitude glow to the munificent Author of the whole.

He does not attempt to scan the Deity, for that is useless. He does not pry into his will nor attempt to ascertain the secret decrees of God, for these are not revealed, and he is not aware of any good purpose that could be answered by his knowing them. He is satisfied God is love, he knows he is good, for his goodness is manifest in fitting up this world as a splendid palace for us to dwell in by spreading a luxurious banquet of which all are urged to partake with grateful hearts. The good man is content with this; confides in his Father's love, and studies to be thankful for what he enjoys.

Towards his fellow beings, the righteous man cultivates kindness and good will. He looks upon them all as his brothers and his sisters with whom his heart should be entwined with fraternal love.

He is sincere. Whatever he says to them is in good faith. He will not praise them for virtues they cannot claim, nor will he censure them for faults of which they are not guilty. He speaks to them kindly, but candidly. He is cautious that he drop no word which may be to them an occasion of deception. He will never preach doctrines he does not believe true, nor will he ask them to support that which he deems false or mischievous.

He is honest. He gives to everyone his dues. This he does from principle, not through the compulsion of the law. Laws are not for the honest man—they are for rogues. Honest men do not require laws to compel them to do right. They do it from principle, and they may be trusted alone, in the dark as well as in the light surrounded by a multitude of witnesses. For such men laws are useless, and if all were such, laws might be dispensed with. He is, therefore, careful to take nothing which does not belong to him and never to withhold what belongs to another.

He is charitable. He is well aware all are imperfect beings and says to himself, "it is hardly possible that, in the progress of events, no one should injure me. Towards him who does, I must be kindly affectioned. He may have wronged me inadvertently, through some misunderstanding; some unforeseen and uncontrollable event may have compelled him to do it. It may have been through his misfortune, and should excite my compassion, rather than my anger. Moreover, my kind affection towards him will be the most effectual means of convincing him of his mistake, and of converting him from his error and of making him my friend. I would also treat him thus because I may myself do wrong and need forgiveness in return; and it is but just I give to others what I wish them to give to me."

He is merciful. He is tender of the feelings of his brethren. He is ready to pour the oil and wine into the wounded heart, to bind up the broken spirit and to make the sufferer whole. It is his study to lessen the miseries, the misfortunes and wretchedness of his fellow beings, to "light up a smile in the aspect of woe,"[5] and to convert the mourner's tears into streams of consolation. In a word, it is his study to diffuse truth, and kind feeling, to endear the members of society, to bind them more closely to each other, to create peace and joy in every heart, and make all his fellow creatures happy.

In public life, he studies for public spirit that he may be interested in the duties of his station, for integrity that the confidence of his fellow citizens may not be misplaced, for knowledge that he may discharge promptly and accurately the duties which may devolve upon him. In private life, he is prudent, studies frugality, industry and sobriety. Each of these is necessary to him as a man, much more, if he stand in the relation of a husband, a father, a child or a brother. To all these he aims to add gentleness of manners and amiableness of disposition.

Thus far is the righteous man towards his God and towards his fellow beings. Towards himself he is temperate and industrious, as both of these are requisite to preserve his health and to develop his moral and mental vigor. He is not puffed up with pride, nor is he ever self-debased. He endeavors to form a just estimate of himself—to learn his strength, to know his weakness, and to think neither more highly nor more lowly of himself than truth will warrant. In his

[5][Ed. Unable to identify quotation.]

morals he is unbending, never in a single instance departing from the line of duty. Yet, he is not rigid except where principle is at stake. He studies to store his mind with useful knowledge, fortifies his heart with the precepts of sound philosophy that he may not sink in the hour of adversity nor be elated above measure in the day of prosperity.

Such I deem the righteous man, such I have aimed to be; and should my preaching make each of you what I have represented the righteous man, I too, like the Psalmist, may hereafter say, "I have preached righteousness in the great congregation."

Righteousness is gratitude to God, a lively sense of our account-ability and relationship to him. This is nothing more than will be felt by everyone who will read attentively the volume of nature, and care-fully listen to the voice of the Divinity within his own soul. It in-cludes love to our fellow beings—not merely to our own family and friends, or to our own party; but, to the world, to all, for "God hath made of one blood all the nations of the earth" [Acts 17:26]. Our love to them will make us sincere, honest, forgiving, gentle and mer-ciful, in our intercourse with them. It will teach us to rejoice with those who rejoice and to weep with those who weep.

It is no trifling task to be a righteous man. It is a character that cannot be acquired in a few minutes, amid the turbulence of the mob, the turmoil of the crowd and by the aid of excited and in-flamed passions. It requires good sense, good feeling, and sound judg-ment. It sanctions no fiery zeal, no ignorant enthusiasm. Its zeal is kindled at the altar of wisdom and its flame is guided by just knowl-edge. The head must be clear, the affections pure, and the hands must be active. This character is seldom met but it is never passed by unnoticed. It is a valuable character. It is one that well repays the labor of procuring. That serenity of soul, that tranquility of the pas-sions, that vigor of mind, and that health of body which ever attend it amply reward us for all the exertions which may be exacted to obtain it. There is something in the practice of virtue that endears it to the heart. I will not attempt to describe it but *be* virtuous and you shall know for yourselves what it is.

Such, my friends, are the outlines of righteousness—shall I say of Christianity? I will, for Christianity consists not in *believing* as the world has unfortunately supposed, but in *doing*. Its founder was con-stantly employed in acts of benevolence. He went about doing good even when derided, despised, rejected; not having, even where to lay his head, he was engaged in relieving the miseries of his brethren, and gladdening their hearts with the gracious tidings he proclaimed, O let us imitate him. That will at least give us practical Christianity.

I wish to be a good man myself and to persuade each of you, male or female, to be good. If I can do this, I shall accomplish my object. If I can persuade you to set an example of a people determined to receive truth wherever they can find it, practice virtue at all times, in all places, and towards all persons, if I can wake the love of excellence in your hearts, and kindle a flame of benevolence in you all, my object will be attained, and humbly submitting to my God, I will say with the Psalmist "I have preached righteousness."

18.

AN ADDRESS
PREPARED AT THE REQUEST OF GUY C. CLARK,
WITH THE INTENTION OF HAVING IT DELIVERED
TO THE ASSEMBLY ON THE DAY
OF HIS EXECUTION, FEBRUARY 3, 1832[1]

"And the Lord hath given me knowledge of it, and I knew it not. But I was like a lamb or an ox, that is brought to the slaughter; and I knew not they had devised devices against me, saying, Let us destroy the tree, with the fruit thereof, and let us cut him off from the land of the living that his name may be no more remembered. But O, Lord of hosts, that judgest righteously, that triest the reins and the heart, let me see thy vengeance on them for unto them, have I revealed my cause." Jer. 11:18, 19, 20.

Friends and Fellow Beings—I stand here to address you amid circumstances which excite deep emotion. Beside me is a human being, bearing the image of the Deity—a man—a brother, whom you have congregated to see sent prematurely to his God.

I have stood by the bedside of the sick and dying; I have visited the house of sorrow; I have mingled my tears with the mourner, by the side of the newly opened grave. But then I saw only the ordinary, though mysterious, Providence of God, and I could labor to arm the departing with fortitude, and to open the fountains of consolation to the bereaved. But now, I find my emotions as new as they are painful, and demanding language I am ill able to supply.

Death at any time is a solemn thought. To the stoutest heart in its most engaging dress, it comes with appalling dread and if it do not conquer the nerves it at least tries the man. Who can look on a fellow being, see the life-spring break, the soul wing its flight, and be unmoved? Who views with composure the last struggle—the last gasp

[1][Ed. Ithaca, New York: S. S. Chatterton, 1832. Brownson prefaced his published pamphlet with the following: "I do not vouch for the accuracy of the view presented of Clark's case in the following pages; it is the view Clark himself took and in my opinion is not far from the truth. For the general train of thought and the moral lesson of the Address I hold myself responsible. It inculcates a lesson I wish all men to learn, and to practice. Till such shall be the case, our criminal code will continue a disgrace to a Christian community."]

for breath? Who weeps not at death's doings, who averts not his eyes from death's triumphs, though achieved by his usual methods, amid the soothing kindness of sorrowing friends? There is then sympathy for the parting pang; there are, then, tears for the anguish; there is forgetfulness of faults; there is remembrance of virtues; but all these fail to disrobe the tyrant of his startling terror.

How then is it now? Ye have come to gaze on him ye paint a moral monster; ye have come to see a fellow being writhe beneath the agony of a wounded heart and be crushed by his brother. Ye have not come to sympathize; ye have not come to soothe his last moments, and kindly close his eyes as he sleeps in death; ye have not come to remember his good deeds, and to cast the mantle of charity over his errors—no, ye have come to exult over the unfortunate; ye have come to sate your idle curiosity, by seeing the law do its strange work—and can ye look on with a quiet pulse and an unmoistened eye—can ye see unmoved this brother of yours hurried————where?

I say ye have come to see the law do its strange work. Strange indeed! That law which was made to protect character, property, and life is now to prove itself a minister of death. Here stands a fellow being, made like the rest of us, with a common nature—susceptible of all the warm and generous emotions—capable of filling a respectable, a useful station in life, who is now, by that very law pledged to his protection, about to be sent with all your curses on his head to the eternal world!

I beg you to pause—forget, for one moment this man is a murderer; suppress your indignation at his deeds; the horror you feel, and which you too often misname love of justice, and remember he is still a man—that he still bears the "human face divine," and ask, what is it ye have come to see done? Strip this question of its borrowed luster, of the disguise it too often wears, look at it in its simple nakedness, and what is it? The law is about to take the life of a human being!

I blame not the executioner; he but discharges his imperious, though painful duty. Laws should and must be executed. No good citizen will see them violated with impunity. But surely it is time to ask, by *what right* we take the life of a fellow being. Ye condemn this man for taking human life; ye now take his and what do ye, but the very act for which ye condemn him. True, he killed, in a moment of phrensy, the wife of his bosom, and made those children, he loves with all a father's fondness, orphans, but what does the law? It coolly and deliberately kills him.

Ask ye, does this act restore the mother to her children? The wife to her husband? Does it wipe away the wrong done and make society whole? No, it does not. It takes blood for blood and doubles the number of deaths. But, I will only add, vengeance belongs to God, and not to man. We are not God's viceregents; we are not entrusted with the right to take the life of his subjects. We may defend ourselves; we may guard our own security; but we are bound to do it with the least possible injury to the offender.

Say not he should be punished for example; say not he should be hung to deter others from crime. Go, teach your children virtue; go, imbue them with a love of goodness; "train them up in the way they should go" [Prov 22:6]; set them examples *worthy* to be followed; by your kindness, your gentleness, your piety, your usefulness, arm them against crime, and fix their habits on the side of moral excellence. This, this, is the way to deter them from crime, not by hanging your brother by the neck till he is dead!

But, I will not now discuss the propriety of that law which sternly demands blood for blood; I will not now contrast the *lex talionis*, of which this law is a relic, with the mild and forgiving nature of the gospel. This law is a law of our country; while it is such, it must be obeyed, or its penalty inflicted if broken. He, by whose request I now speak, complains not of the law. To its sentence he submits and is ready to answer its demands with his blood; but he is not willing to leave his memory charged with the crime of *willful* murder. He leaves behind him, children still dear to his heart; he would not have them, whenever they think of their father, curse him in their hearts as a willful murderer.

The heart of man is open only to himself and to his God. No other being can trace the secret springs which move him you condemn as the blackest criminal; no other one can tell how much of misfortune, how much of moral turpitude falls to his lot. Ye too often look only upon the deed; ye enquire not its cause. Ye seldom reflect on that war of the passions; that burning hell within; that wild, furious desperation, which prompted the will, and nerved the arm of the murderer to take the life of his brother or his sister.

Could the heart be laid open to your view; could you see all the workings of the mind; could you feel that deep and galling sense of injury under which it labors; that struggle of resolution—the effort to forego the awful deed; now a determination to rise above it; now the fire within is kindled, and he burns to avenge his wrongs; now, his purpose falters; another insult and all the hell of passion is in flame. Now it dies away and he applauds himself that he has mastered his evil spirit; again, he burns, his brain sears, made with his damning purpose, on he rushes—oh, could you trace that tumult of soul; mark each passion; feel each pang "keen as darts to inflict immortal pains, dipt in the blood of damned souls,"[2] ye would relent in your feelings; ye would melt in compassion for the unfortunate homicide.

Think ye any man, coolly, deliberately, maliciously, with no real, or imagined, cause ever worked himself up to that pitch of villainy, that plunged the fatal steel into the bosom of his wife and the mother of his children? O little then are ye read in the human heart! Little know ye of human nature! There was endured the agony of a thousand deaths ere the deed was done!

Thus is it with the most hardened wretch, with him who proceeds most deliberately to his work of death. It is not without an effort, it is not without a deep and desperate struggle, that man can rise up and take the life of his fellow man. Man is never that monster in villainy ye suppose him. There lives not the man who can, coolly, calmly, without a deep and powerful spell upon him, proceed to the crime of murder. All traces of the Divinity are never effaced. There are still some sparks of a holier nature, slumbering beneath the grossest depravity.

Have ye asked, then, what mean these deafening exclamations of "Horrid act," "Daring atrocity," "Hang the wretch, he deserves to die," "Hanging is too good for him," which meet our ears from almost every voice in community? Have ye asked, are these exclamations the result of sober thought, calm reflection, and chastened love of justice; or, are they not the bursts of inflamed passion and unchristian indignation? Ye profess to be Christians; I pray you to exhibit in your feelings that amiable and forgiving temper which your Master enjoined. Weep with the unfortunate; regret what they endure; exult not in their fall; but be able to forgive the offences of your brother "till seventy times seven" [Matt 18:22].

The passage of Scripture which I pronounced in your hearing, and which was selected for me by him at whose request I speak, may tell his feelings, and declare his view of his own case.

It demands that you enquire if there are not reasons to believe the deed for which he suffers, appears to him in a far more favorable light than it does to his accusers. He asks no mitigation of the rigors of the law; but he does ask you not to believe him the most abandoned; if the most unhappy of mortals.

[2][Ed. Not able to identify quotation.]

He views himself a persecuted man. He labored and he still labors under a deep sense of injury. On that point he cannot reason. He dwelt upon it; he brooded over it day and night; it became the all absorbing topic of his thoughts; the more he thought of it, the deeper was he stung; his feelings became worked up to a high pitch of phrensy, till on the subject of his supposed wrongs he became incapable of sane thought or rational action.

It matters not that he overrated his wrongs, that he exaggerated his injuries, that he mistook their origin—it matters not that he believed on too slight a foundation that he was persecuted, and that his wife was really bent on his destruction—the impression was real, and equally powerful in determining his conduct.

Do not misunderstand me. I stand not here to palliate guilt nor to encourage the wicked. In this place, surrounded by the terrors of the law, with the broad expanse of heaven above me, under the very eye of Omniscience, before assembled thousands, I dare not do it, if I would. But as God is my witness and is to be my final Judge, I dare not refuse to vindicate him ye punish as a murderer from unjust accusation, and to place even his character in what I believe its true light. I owe it to him, I owe it to you, I owe it to my own conscience, I owe it to my God, as I hope one day to be forgiven myself.

Each heart knoweth its own bitterness. How difficult it is from a few detached circumstances to form a just estimate of any man's character! There are in those the world brands the most hardened, some redeeming traits; and there are circumstances connected, which, if known, would materially change our notions of their moral turpitude. But can a few casual hints disclose them? Can a few half informed, half prejudiced, witnesses do them justice? I put it to each of you, whom would you trust to delineate your characters and state all the secret springs of your conduct? What man can read your hearts and say, "this proceeded from purity of motive, *this* from thoroughgoing depravity!" How different would be your own view of your characters from that drawn by your best friends, not to say that drawn by your enemies or those willing to see you cut off?

I beg you to look at the case before you. This man felt himself injured by his wife—deeply injured; he did not dream her conduct proceeded from good motives; he knew not she was urged on by certain prudential counselors; hence, his feelings were embittered only against her. He was as a "lamb or an ox" led on, blind, and unthinking of the real cause, till he had slaughtered her he had best loved.

I pray you reflect for one moment. Picture to yourselves a young couple in the hey-day of their most ardent love—high feeling and

romantic—go with them to the bridal altar—hear them exchange
vows of eternal fidelity—follow them to a home of industry, enjoyment and affection. How lovely is the picture! After awhile you may
see the man leaving his own fireside, seizing any amusement, that
can beguile his thoughts and make him forget himself—what is the
cause? Think ye that home is still a home of enjoyment, that it is still
pleasing and attracting to his heart? How often it is we see a man
leaving the woman he has loved, a woman whom the world honors,
and who is able to make a heaven of earth to any man suited to her
taste and temper—how often it is we see him leaving such a woman
and seeking to lose himself and blunt the pain of memory in the
draught of intoxication!

But, the world marks that man, it brands him villain, and bestows all its sympathy upon the wife. She is praised above her merits,
and he is sunk as far below his real worth. Yet *his* heart may be suffering an agony untold. There may be to him a fatal poison in every
draught. He may laugh, but the scorpion stings his soul. No one
heeds his sufferings. The world mocks; he leaves it for his own fireside, but not to be met with smiles, and to find amends for the cold
scorn of the world; but to be met with coldness, to have his feelings
harrowed up, not only by his own misery, but by the wretchedness he
is bringing upon the wife he loves, and the children which share his
affection. Let him thus do, let him thus suffer, and if he be not more
than ordinary man, how long will he bear up beneath the load? Alas!
his case is hopeless! He is in the vortex, every whirl carries him deeper
and deeper to his ruin!

Will a man thus situated reason calmly? Are not allowances to be
made? Let the evil increase; let the wife, urged on by her counselors,
but as [he] believes, by her own determination to destroy him, proceed against him, have him confined in prison, thus ruining his character and blasting his hopes forever, and think ye he may not honestly believe himself wronged, deeply wronged? Will he be likely to
act the part of a rational man? Need I say, no?

He who will in a few minutes be no more, was thus treated—was
thus treated by his wife; and, as he then believed, with the intention
of destroying him forever. Is it strange that his feelings towards her
should have been of fearful power? That he should have dreamed of
a revenge too awful to be mentioned? Yet you may easily believe his
threats were half unmeaning; that, though he talked hard it was rather
to give vent to his feelings, to the bitterness of his soul than to express
any settled purpose of action. To regain his liberty from a prison, he
consented to leave his wife. While absent he brooded over a sense of

wrong—the deep disgrace, the irreparable injury, he had suffered; at times the pang of these sent reason from her seat. But his good genius prevailed. His mind, his heart, again turned to the companion of his holier and happier moments, and he returned to ascertain if they might not yet live together in peace and mutual love. He was repulsed. Absence had not altered the purpose of his wife. He conceals as well as he can, the wound in his heart,—conquers his rising passion, and, at her request, resolves he will depart. He shakes her kindly by the hand—bids her an affectionate farewell, takes a last adieu of his children, and prepares to leave all that was dear to his heart. He leaves, but returns to take one more look—perhaps, to ascertain if the pain of parting had not softened her purpose; he is upbraided because he is not gone; he is assured he must leave, or be sent to prison, assured this too by her to whom he was bound by the most sacred ties. Then, then, it was the smothered hell burst forth. Stung to the heart, phrensied by his anguish of soul, on, on, he rushed—the deed was done!

He felt, he honestly believed it was all her fault, that she had sworn in her heart to ruin him. "The Lord has given knowledge, but he knew it not." "He was as the lamb or the ox that is brought to the slaughter" [Jer 11:18-19]. He knew not then, there were others who had devised devices against him, and thus it was his vengeance lighted on her. Thus it was two were prematurely hurried from the world, as he now believes, by the unkind interference of others.

His eyes are now open, he regrets the deed, but makes his confession only to his God, with whom he will leave it to avenge him on them who urged on his wife to his destruction, and on those who may have mistaken facts in their testimony against him. For to God, to him who judgest righteously, has he revealed his cause.

As lovers of justice, ye should not overlook these circumstances, at which I have rapidly glanced. These do not indeed prove him innocent; they do not justify his act; they may not exonerate him in the eyes of the law from the charge of willful murder; but they must in the eyes of all good men, of men who are willing to be just even to the wicked, and who can judge what human nature is, and make due allowance for its weakness.

Am I wrong? Read your own hearts—respond they not my conclusion? Am I wrong to ask for a mitigation of his sentence—not of that sentence which the law has passed—but of that which from vague report, uncertain rumor, and your justifiable horror at crime, ye may have pronounced in your own hearts. He took the life of a human being; the law has had its course; it has sentenced him to pay his forfeited life; he dies to suffer that penalty he was believed to have incurred. Here the law stops, here its vengeance is staid; and *here* stay yours, fellow beings.

He asks not to live. Life to him were a living hell—a lingering death. It were his bitterest curse. Alas! for that man whose best hope is in death! Alas! for that man to whom life is an intolerable burden; for whom day succeeds day but to lengthen out his misery, and night succeeds night, but to darken his soul and deepen the curse of existence! What is life to him, who if he lives, must live an outcast, shunned—abhorred—stung by a sense of his wrongs and the still deeper sense of his guilt!

Ah! wrong, wrong are they who dream there is no hell this side the grave! Wrong are they who dream they may sin with impunity! What are the terrors of the law, what are the tortures of the body, compared with the inward stings of conscience? The law may do its worst, it may tear limb from limb, the flesh to pieces by inches, it is but as dust in the balance compared with that lash of remorse which the mind inflicts on itself—with that inward horror—that mental agony—that burning hell in the soul of the guilty, which cling to him by day, by night, in the deep solitude, in the peopled city, and most of all when thought turns to that great Being before whose bar conscience stands self-condemned! O ye were not human beings, could ye wish worse to the most hardened of the human race, to the most depraved that wear the human form! Forbear, then, to follow him with your curses to the eternal world; and where the law ceases to punish, there end your reproach.

O my fellow beings, could the heart of this man be laid open to your inspection, could you trace all his secret motives, all his internal anguish; could you feel the fever of his brain, the fire which consumes his soul, my life on it, ye would find more to commiserate and forgive, than to condemn and punish. Ye would exchange your horror at his deed, to regret for his misfortune, and half transfer your curses from him to that combination of circumstances of which he is but the victim.

Ye boast of your social state—boast of its perfection, but it is that very social state which forms such characters as this. Thousands have fallen its victims; thousands will fall victims to it, and ye will continue to boast its perfection, and breathe forth the withering curse upon him who bids you REFORM.

Do I misread your hearts? The curse may be now on your tongues, to blast me because I dare lay that to your social state, which ye charge upon individual malice; because I dare speak in behalf of the unfortunate, and labor to convince you he ye condemn is not as guilty as ye had supposed. Be it so. I heed it not. I have been and conversed with this man in his prison; I have listened to his story, and I believe him less depraved than unfortunate. Under this conviction I have spoken. If I have erred, I have erred on "virtue's side." I cannot justify his deed; the thought of it fills my soul with horror; but I have dared look for its cause, and have labored to turn your indignation, from him the victim, to that which produced it. If I have failed I regret it. If I have succeeded, I shall expect to see you making efforts, to correct the evils which prevail among us, and to present the recurrence of that combination of circumstances which we this day see so clearly and so painfully illustrated.

I pray you to be just, and after ye have sated your curiosity and seen your brother crushed, I pray you to forget the iniquity of this man, and labor to prevent another from incurring his doom, or suffering his fate. I pray you turn your thoughts to the means of eradicating crime by striking at its root, destroying its cause. Above all, do ye learn to be lenient, is better than to be severe, and be ye always more ready, more anxious, to forgive than to punish.

We have been led to reflect on a painful case. She who was hurried out of the world had her wrongs; he who now stands between two worlds has had his wrongs; he has had his injuries; he has honestly believed himself persecuted, plotted against, ruined, by her whose love should have been sacred to him. If he erred as to the magnitude of those wrongs, their origin and the motives which prompted them, remember, "to err is human; to forgive is divine."[3] Let us stay our curses, and deplore the circumstances which have produced the awful catastrophe. Above all, let us who think we stand, take heed lest we also fall. May the example before us teach us wisdom, prompt to watchfulness, and lead us to forgive.

Time passes. A few moments more and a fellow being is ushered into the eternal world; drop a tear for his untimely fate; breathe a prayer for his forgiveness; swear to protect his orphan children and never to visit upon them the memory of their father's wrongs.

Time passes. The executioner waits. We leave the wretched man alone with his God in the indulgence of that charity which "believeth all things; hopeth all things" [1 Cor 13:7].

[3][Ed. Alexander Pope, *An Essay on Criticism*, line 525.]

19.

THE WORKINGMEN

Philanthropist 2 (March 13, 1832): 156

We perceive that our friends the workingmen are still active. In New England they have lately had a convention,[1] which we think must be attended with beneficial results. The laboring classes have not received their due weight, and, while they have born all the burthens of government, they have not shared in its blessings. By a system of legislation, well meant it may be, but unjust in its result, the laboring man, the poor man, is deprived of more than one half of his earnings. Indeed, everything he eats, drinks or wears, is taxed. Our humble self, not worth a cent in the world, paid not less than forty dollars tax the last year for the support of government. Now, this is too bad.

But this is only one item. The whole weight of our laws is against the poor man. Law is an instrument of oppression in the hands of the rich; very seldom of defense in the hands of the poor. As things now are, honesty, high moral virtue are no passports to distinction beyond our own fire side. The most successful over-reacher is the better man, and he who can cheat with the least blush and make it appear most like honesty is the greatest man. We hope this will not always be so. There must be something sounder; there must be firmer moral health or our political constitution will soon be but so much waste paper.

The workingmen have put forward some good doctrines. We have nothing to do with them as the doctrines of a party; but we do view them as the only doctrines which can fully realize the wishes of the fathers of our republic. Did we live in a country where all men are equal and where a man is not disfranchised because he wears a black coat, we should occasionally lend the workingmen what aid our pen could give them. But, we must be silent, or the cry of "church

---

[1][Ed. Brownson may be referring to the meeting of the New England Association of Farmers, Mechanics and Other Working Men held in Boston in February of 1832. On this see, *Columbian Centinel* (February 16, 1832) and Edward Pessen, *Most Uncommon Jacksonians: The Radical Leaders of the Early Labor Movement* (New York: State University of New York Press, 1967), 90.]

and state" will be raised against us, and then what would become of us, the Lord only knows. Still, we have not deserted the political doctrines we advanced while editor of the *Herald of Reform*, nor have we despaired of the reform we then attempted.[2] The cause we then espoused—and which cost us what little reputation we had, has now many and able advocates. It progresses with sufficient rapidity. A new era is at hand. God speed it.

[2][Ed. Brownson edited the *Genesee Republican and Herald of Reform* from July to November of 1830, as extant copies seem to indicate. On this, see the Introduction to this volume.]

20.

POVERTY

Philanthropist 2 (March 27, 1832): 161-63

We stated in our last,[1] that we must dissent from a remark in the *Christian Examiner* respecting poverty. The following is the objectionable passage: "Poverty is the appointment, the beneficent appointment of God. We cannot *cure* poverty therefore, and it will be well for all classes when the idea of this is given up."[2]

We always find in the *Christian Examiner* something to admire, much to approve, and seldom anything to condemn. The above extract is the most objectionable of anything we have ever seen in its columns, and we think it unworthy the liberal tone and practical good sense which usually characterize the work. We say not this with a hostile spirit; we feel ourselves much indebted to the editors of this periodical; we have had our hearts warmed and our minds enlightened by the richness and general excellence of its pages.[3]

Poverty is *not* the "appointment of God." It proceeds from the folly and injustice of man. It proceeds from oppression, fraud, idleness, ignorance, weakness, intemperance, prodigality. Now, unless these vices are the appointment of God, poverty is not. If no man had more than his share, none would be poor; shall we say God has ordained one man to sow, and another to reap? That he has appointed the few to grasp the whole earth and to keep all the means of gain in their own hands? Shall we say it is God that has appointed that poor mother to weep over her naked, freezing and starving children, and to endure the agony of a thousand deaths, as she sees them die by inches—drop piece-meal into the grave? Is it God that ordains the few to hoard up all the productions of the earth, while the many are exposed to all the temptations of poverty, and driven to crimes of

---

[1][Ed. *Philanthropist* 2 (March 13, 1832).]

[2][Ed. The article referred to here was "Mr. Tuckerman's Eighth Semi-Annual Report of his Service as a Minister at Large in Boston (1831)," *Christian Examiner* 12 (March 1832): 116-25, see page 124 for quote. On Joseph Tuckerman (1786-1840), see the Introduction, 25.]

[3][Ed. James Walker (1794-1874) was editor of the *Christian Examiner* from 1831 to 1839.]

blackest dye, by the keen pangs of want? O say it not. 'Tis man, 'tis lordly man, that thus ruins himself and damns his brother.

Much less is poverty the "*beneficent* appointment of God." Poverty a *beneficent* appointment! Great God! What then is bad? Poverty a *beneficent* appointment! Go, thou man of wealth, go visit the abodes of poverty, go scan the squalid wretchedness which it entails, the coarseness, the vulgarity, the ignorance, the vice, the crime by which it is marked, and say if you would participate [in] *such* beneficence? Go ask him who is kicked from good society because he wears a thread-bare coat, and a sun-burnt countenance, who is made the common drudge, who must bear all the burdens of society, minister to the wants of the rich, and be despised and trampled upon for it— go ask him if poverty be a *beneficent* appointment. But, it "may help prepare him for another world." We dare not trust ourselves to speak of a sentiment like this. He whose every thought is racked to devise means to obtain subsistence for the human animal, must be well situated to attend to the wants of the soul! More, the notion is the very one which has destroyed the utility of religion in all ages, and checked all useful improvements. Did the poor man complain of poverty, the priest said, "Happy is the poor man, for though poor and miserable here, he is sure of heaven hereafter"; and the poor man became quiet, the tyrant sat secure on his throne and the priest pocketed his tithe. We pray the writer of the article under review, to re-examine this subject. We *know* more about poverty than he does. We are speaking of that which has been our companion from our birth to the present moment; and we know poverty is a curse, though wealth may be no blessing.

Nor do we believe poverty is incurable. Man has brought the curse upon himself, and he can remove it, not always by individual effort; in his collective capacity he creates the evil, in his collective capacity he must cure it. Let the poor co-operate, let them secure to themselves their whole earnings and the evil will be removed.

Providence nor nature is against us. God is good unto all; nature is bounteous to all who court her liberal hand; but man in his ignorance, in his folly, in his cupidity has so constructed society that the evils of poverty are produced. Let him to work—undo the wrong, supplant his anti-social institutions by social ones, and such as shall operate for the good of all and poverty will not be incurable. By no means let him give up the idea that poverty can be cured. Let him take courage, and instead of palliating, alleviating, strike boldly at the root of the evil. It can be done; it must be done; it will be done, and then the glorious sun of the millennium shall burst upon the

world, and "every man will sit under his own vine, and his own fig
tree" [Mic 4:4].

Look on yonder earth!

The golden harvests spring; the unfading sun
Sheds light and life; the fruits, the flowers, the trees
Arise in due succession; all things speak
Peace, harmony and love. The universe,
In nature's silent eloquence, declares
That all fulfil the works of love and joy,—
All but the out-cast man. He fabricates
The sword which stabs his peace; he cherisheth
The snakes that gnaw his heart; he raiseth up
The tyrant, whose delight is in his woe.
Whose sport is in his agony. Yon sun,
Lights it the great alone? Yon silvery beams,
Sleep they less sweetly on the cottage thatch,
Than on the dome of kings? Is mother earth,
A step-dame to her numerous sons, who earn
Her unshared gifts with unremitting toil,
A mother only to those puling babes
Who, nursed in ease and luxury, make men
The playthings of their babyhood, and mar,
In self-important childishness, that peace
Which men alone appreciate![4]

[4][Ed. Percy Bysshe Shelley (1792-1822), *Queen Mab*, canto 3, lines 193-213,
in *The Complete Poetical Works of Percy Bysshe Shelley*, vol. 1, *1802-1813*, ed. Neville
Rogers (Oxford: Clarendon, 1972), 252-53.]

21.

UNITARIANS NOT DEISTS

Philanthropist 2 (May 15, 1832): 193-95

There are those professing to be Christians who seem extremely desirous to identify Unitarians with deists. The editor of this paper has more than once been charged with being a deist. We repel the charge, not so much because we are unfriendly to deists, as because it is not true.

In the first place, deists deny all revelation from God to man, except such as may be gathered from the general order, harmony, and laws of nature. They neither admit an external revelation, as that recorded in the Bible, nor an internal, to wit, God speaking by his spirit to the human soul. Now Unitarians admit both. We know not a single Unitarian that does not believe the Bible contains a record of a revelation made from God to man. Though they may not regard the mere verbal reading of the written word of such binding authority as some other sects profess to do, yet we believe all Unitarians without a single exception do regard as the truth of God, whatever can be fairly made out to be the real teachings of the Bible.

All Unitarians, so far as we have any knowledge, do believe in an internal communication of the soul with its Father—in an inward light, an inward teacher, nor merely reason or conscience, but that which illumines conscience itself, and gives to it all its power. Now, it may be, some value this internal light more than they do the external word but all admit both to be true—from God. So far as we can judge, here is a material difference between the deist and the Unitarian, and we should deem it idle to reason with that obtuseness of intellect which could not perceive it.

In the second place, there is a more important difference still—the deist denies the particular providence of God. The deist seems to believe that Deity in making the world, fixed the laws by which it was always to be governed, set the vast machine in motion, and now has little or no concern in its management. Every Unitarian believes God superintends and governs the world and all its concerns by his immediate presence and power. The laws by which the universe is governed exist not in the universe but in the nature of the Deity. We know not how the Divinity acts on matter, but the religious man can in no instance separate in his mind the all pervading presence and superintendence of the Deity from the material universe. That order, that uniformity we discover in the motions of the universe, and in what we term the operations of nature, exist in God, and are only displayed in his government.

The deist supposes nature has a sort of independence of God, but the Unitarian believes no such thing. He believes God governs with a steady unerring hand, swayed by no caprice, by no love of change, but by a wisdom that saw from the first what was the best. Hence, it is, we see order, uniformity, a regularity, lasting through all time, and from the past, enabling us in some measure to predict the future. The deist views this result as the laws of nature, not the will of the Deity, but laws instamped on matter and left to their own operation. This is an important distinction. It is essential to the very nature of piety that we feel the presence and the agency of the Divinity are everywhere; that the heavens declare his glory and that the firmament showeth Him forth, that he lives and breathes, and exerts his controlling power through all nature. But to suppose he has abandoned the government of the world to certain imaginary laws impressed on matter is so far as the pious affections are concerned the same as supposing there is no God at all. We want to see God everywhere, to feel him at all times, and to read him in all events, and in all things.

Yet, it is proper to remark, that though Deity governs all things, that he governs by means adapted to the natures which he has seen proper to confer. Gravitation, attraction, electricity, and the like are the agents of his power and his ministers in controlling the material world. He governs mind by different agents, and he exerts no power over the human soul except in accordance with that freedom he has made a necessary part of it. Still he is present with it; has a particular regard for each soul he has made, and shields it by a particular providence. This, we are satisfied is the belief of every Unitarian. It is ours. Take away the idea of God's particular providence, a providence that has a respect to each individual however lowly or highly exalted, and there is nothing left that we can conceive of piety or in religious worship deserving a moment's regard.

Here is an essential difference between the deist and the Unitarian, a difference involving the very essence of pious affection. The deist doubts the propriety of prayer. His God is seated at his ease in the distant heavens regardless of the transactions on earth. Prayer cannot move him, prayer cannot reach him, it is useless. The Unitarian views prayer as the soul's highest privilege. He believes his God is ever present, ever ready to hear; and he deems it as natural for the soul to express its wants to him, as for the child to its earthly parent; and he as readily presses to the bosom of his God when in danger, or in need of aid, as the child to the bosom of its mother.

In the last place, very few deists of our day believe in a future state of existence. This is man's only sphere; man's beginning and his end. The Unitarian believes in a resurrection from the dead, in life immortal and in a future state of righteous retribution. Is this no difference? Are those who call us deists ignorant? Or are they willful slanderers?

22.

PRIEST AND INFIDEL

Philanthropist 2 (May 29, 1832): 209-21

Some years since, I journeyed to the western and northwestern sections of our country.[1] The character of the backwoodsman, rude, coarse, strong, hardy, but not destitute of kindheartedness, offered me an interesting study. The Indian, with his patriarchal simplicity, with the free step, lofty fire, and proud dignity of his native forest, interested me yet more, made my stay much longer than at first intended, and taught me some of the most valuable lessons I have ever yet learned.

During my stay in a distant settlement, where more of the savage than the civilized manners prevailed, I became acquainted with an old man of marked appearance, and of a most interesting character. He wore the Indian dress, spoke the Indian language, and at times affected to be a son of the forest. But his speech betrayed him; and the gleams of learning and cultivation which would now and then break out, proved him not only of the "pale faces," but one who had seen, and perhaps had suffered, much of civilized life. He was old; his head was white; his form was bent; but his eye still burned with the fire of youth; his step was firm and elastic; his motions vigorous, easy, and unconstrained. He was usually reserved, but there were times when the reminiscences of the old man made him talkative.

I was much with him, for I had an instinctive reverence for age, and an insatiable thirst for knowledge. There was too, an air of mystery about him—something hidden and dark. I was certain he was not what he seemed, and young curiosity was eager to ascertain the secrets of his earlier life. There were times, too, when he seemed to read my wish, and when he appeared half inclined to gratify it. But he seldom gave me anything more than detached sketches, which fed, without satisfying, my wish to know who and what he was and had been.

We were sitting one evening, in that season when Spring flings her flowers into the lap of Summer, before the door of a rude hut,

[1][Ed. Brownson may be referring to his 1824-25 trip to Detroit. On this trip, see the Introduction to EW, 1:8-10.]

constructed as a temporary shelter for some new emigrant. Around us was joy, life and beauty. A little clearing lay before us to the banks of a noble river which bore on its pride to the "Father of Water"; back of us lay the eternal forest, in all its wild and solemn grandeur, untrodden by civilized foot. The sun was just sinking behind the trees, and gilding their branches with its gold. The wild notes of the woods sounded the evening hymn, and Nature smiled as the soft breath of the evening Zephyr fanned her bosom. I was sad, though serene. The passions were unruffled, the feelings had received no blight, and the heart had endured no chill. My hopes were ardent, and life before me, unequal but not rugged. It was the eve of my departure. I must leave the wild freedom in which I had reveled, the coarse but warm and affectionate friends I had won to myself during my short stay amidst the scenes of nature, and wend my way back to civilized man, and submit again to the bondage of civilized life. I turned to the old man, just as he had closed an interesting descant on the loveliness of nature, and had passed from nature to its great Original; I turned towards him, and remarked, the time of my stay had expired; that active duties called me away, and in the morning I must set forward on my journey. "But," added I, "my father, give me your blessing, and let the parting counsels of age be a lamp to my feet and a light to my path through the journey of life."

He seemed moved. He turned his keen but benevolent eye upon me, half swimming in its own moisture: "Young man, must you go? I dismiss you with regret. I am old. I am a blighted trunk. My branches have withered, and moldered at my feet. I am alone. The generation that knew me has gone. Your presence has been to me a light from the scenes of my youth. You have brought the warm blood into my veins; laughing countenances, joyous hearts, sportive spirits have surrounded me, and I have felt half young again. Must you go? Hear me. I see just now—I know it is fancy—but there comes to me now, the youth I best loved. He shows a fine, open, unsuspecting countenance, with a smiling, half humorous eye, which conceals a thoughtful and serious mind. It is Robert Dumain. The vision vanishes, but he is pictured on my heart.

"Listen. Robert Dumain was my most intimate friend. His was an ardent temper, a heart generous and confiding. All the world was before him, and he was resolved to enjoy his share of it. He was poor—was an orphan—but it grieved him not. Others had made their way through the world, carved their own fortunes, and left a name to admiring posterity. He felt that what others had done, he might do. We had been associates from infancy. We had lodged together; we had eaten together; we had sported together; we had pursued our studies together, and were as brothers, until by the advice of our village parson, he left our neighborhood to prepare for taking orders, as a servant of the church.

"Young man, listen. I am not what I was. I was—well, let it pass. That sapling is tall, straight, vigorous and healthy. It promises to be the pride of the forest. Its sap may be drained, its leaf will fade, its branch wither. I had an early blight of feeling—I had a barrenness of soul. The passions had raged, burned and seared the heart. I could not love; I could not hate. I became cold and lifeless; nothing could make me feel. I was as the ocean when the tide is stilled—when the long and fatal calm rests upon its stagnant bosom. Many years did I travel, in hopes to travel from myself; change of scene brought no change to me.

"Years wore away, and I continued the same withered and desolate being. I was the mere wreck of humanity, rotting on life's tideless ocean. I continued to travel—where, I cared not—wherefore, I asked not. One evening, one like this, after having wended my solitary way through a dark and hideous forest, I suddenly burst upon one of the loveliest villages which I had ever seen. It lay along the margin of a small but beautiful river, which glided along in a serpentine course under a fringe of willow, and flowering herbage, far as the eye could reach. The village stood partly on elevated ground, commanding a fine prospect of the plains which spread out upon the opposite side of the river, for some three or four miles, skirted by hills, now gradually with a gentle slope, and now abruptly, rising into mountains, at length losing themselves in the clouds. The village might contain some three or four hundred houses, built mostly after the same model. All bore the marks of neatness, convenience, but none of extravagance. The terraced gardens, rising one above another, the shrubbery adorning the approach to each house, the trees for shade or fruit, liberally, though it may be irregularly, distributed in all directions, now in their richest dress, gave to the whole somewhat of a picturesque appearance, and pointed it out to the traveler, as the residence of rural refinement, competence, equality, content. At a short distance, on an eminence which overlooked most of the village, half buried by a grove of young pines, near a fine waterfall, where nature seemed to have collected the beautiful, the wild, the grand, and the solemn, stood the village church, with its tall steeple pointing to a fairer and better world for the good.

"The bell chimed to vespers, as I came in sight of the little paradise which lay spread out in loveliness before me. Perhaps it was long since I had heard the bell of a village church. The home of my fathers, the scenes of my childhood, the pew in which I had so often sat and listened to the gracious words of our parish minister, came to my heart, and I know not but a sigh escaped me, though I had foresworn to feel.

"In my early life, I was of a religious turn. Every Sunday unless prevented by sickness, after I was old enough, to accompany my mother to the place of worship, had I listened to the words of the holy man. There was something about him to interest. He was rather under the medium height of men, his figure, somewhat *embonpoint*;[2] his countenance, was mild, frank, good humored, with here and there a trace of dignity. His eye was keen, cheerful, social, usually soft, but capable of lighting up with the fire of genius. The old man was always familiar with his parishioners, and loved now and then a good joke with them. He was of a social turn, and at times, might seem as much of a sportsman as a student. He had been familiar with books, but he seemed to treat them somewhat lightly, was not often in his study, and apparently paid more attention to the world round about, and within him, than to even the sacred books of his profession."

"He was never known to speak a harsh word; he loved his fellow beings, and labored to win the erring back to the paths of virtue. He seldom played with Jove's thunderbolts. He seemed to delight only in recommending the paternal goodness and undying love of the Great Spirit. What was his peculiar belief no one knew—no one thought of asking. He taught us that the best disquisition on faith, was the example of a holy life; and that we should call that man brother, embrace him as such, whose walk was adorned by the practice of goodness. He discouraged contentions about words, and strife about unintelligible dogmas, which might indeed ruffle the temper and impair our mutual love, but could not very well secure peace on earth, or win heaven for our souls hereafter. His sermons were usually off-hand performances, but they were warm with benevolence; they glowed with a holy temper, and fitted us for heaven, as much by what they made us feel, as by what they taught us to believe. Indeed he seldom touched upon mere belief; he always avoided controverted points, and steered so clear of metaphysics, and mystery that the child heard him with interest.

"While he lived we had no quarrel respecting religious faith or connection. He assured us that the Christian had a mild temper, benevolent feelings, and was anxious to embrace every man as a

---

[2][Ed. French for "obese" or "stout."]

brother, every woman as a sister: he told us our common Father loved all his children, that he was pleased to see them all love each other, to see them all good, interchanging the kindest feelings and best offices of social life, studying to endear the hearts of all to each other, and to melt all into one great family, where no discordant note shall be heard. He has long since paid the debt of nature—I wept over his grave. I cannot believe he is lost. True, his successor said he was a heretic, and offered to prove him so by more than five hundred passages of Scripture—but, to me his memory is sacred. I hope he is in heaven. While he was our pastor, it is true we did not boast of our piety and humility; we said little about the topics which sectarians discuss; but we were peaceful, we loved each other, and blessed the Great Spirit for his tender care of us.

"Another minister came, not like the one we had lost. This was a dark looking man—a tall, spare, half a skeleton like being. He condemned the preaching which had made our village happy for more than half a century; he assured us the good man for whom our tears were yet fresh was an instrument of Satan to lull men asleep, to prepare them for the everlasting fire of hell. The truth, we were assured, was now preached. We had stirring discourses; the terrors, the thunders of Almighty wrath came thick and heavy; men's hearts trembled; we became alarmed; we anxiously enquired how we might escape the awful vengeance suspended over our heads. The true religious faith, we were told, now prevailed; but times were sadly changed. For peace we had war; for good will, we had angry dispute; for happiness, we had sectarian jealousies. We talked a great deal more about religion but we seemed less friendly and less contented. As we increased in orthodoxy, we became ill tempered and quarrelsome as we made our calling and election sure. I grieved, for the pleasant times were gone. We had meetings every evening in the week. Our women became so zealous for God, that they forgot the duties of wives and mothers. Men did little else than wrangle and anathematize each other. Well, all was a mystery to me; I became disgusted, loathed the name of religion, and from that time, when I was about twenty years of age, till approaching the village before me, I had not entered a church.

"The chime to vespers—it recalled happier days and holier feelings. The scene before me—the aged matron, the village maiden, the grandsire on his crutch—man in his prime—the youth with buoyant feelings and bounding step—the child with its sweet smile and guileless heart—all wending their way to offer up the evening thanksgiving to the great Father of all—it waked my cold and calloused heart, and made me hasten my steps to join the devotions of the happy villagers. I reached the church but did not enter. There is something of superstition which clings to the boldest infidel, and the scoffer quails where the believer passes unawed. I reached the door, started back, I knew not why. Sight, hearing, all sense left me—how long, I know not.

"When I recovered my consciousness, I was lying on a bed in a plain but neatly furnished room. The curtains were partly withdrawn, and a man who might be past middle age, was bending with a calm but tender look over me. I had seen that face before. The crowding shadows of years flitted past me ere I could recollect when, or where. But it was the clergyman of the parish, my youthful associate, Robert Dumain. It was the light and graceful youth, ripened into the grave and thoughtful priest. Though a little my senior, his brow was smooth, and his form showed the pressure of time had been light. He did not recognize me. Time had made sad waste with my young appearance. My face was furrowed, my form was bent, my hair was white, and my voice at times trembled with premature old age: I soon told him who I was, and half envied him his pleasure in meeting me.

"I was not long confined to my bed; I had learned to keep the body under, and to make the dull clay yield to the mastery of mind. Soon as I was sufficiently recovered to bear conversation, Robert commenced an anxious but delicate enquiry respecting my travels. He had lost track of me and supposed me long since dead. He was glad to meet me. He hoped my journeying was over, and that I would be persuaded to rest me in his pleasant village. He hinted at my infidelity and modestly enquired if I had seen any cause to change my opinion. He put the question with some anxiety and my first emotion was displeasure at his intermeddling with my opinions.

"Robert," said I, "your profession I respect. I would not wound your feelings, nor do violence to your prejudices. Accident has thrown us together, and for a moment I have half forgotten myself, and felt as I did when we were fellow students. I cannot think with you on the subject of religion. Let us have no topic to embitter our meeting."

"He was not satisfied; he seemed resolved to press the subject, and I began to feel a gathering scorn, when he replied: "You mistake me, my friend. I am governed by no improper feeling. I would step between no man and his God. We were youthful associates; we were as brothers—almost as one soul. We took different courses. Years have elapsed since we met. You have traveled without religion. I have aimed to travel with it; let us compare notes, and by combining experience learn wisdom."

"Robert you upbraid me with my misfortunes. You have been fortunate; you flourish "as the tree by the rivers of water" [Ps 1:3]. I was early blighted, the lightnings of heaven have scathed me more than once; you see I am unhappy, and you would lay my misfortunes to my infidelity, and thus draw an argument in favor of what you call religion."

"No, I do not. I love you too much to wish to aggravate your feelings, or to wound your pride. I know you have doubted religion. I too may have had my doubts on some points, and I would profit by experience. I wish to know your thoughts after twenty years of close observation. I never contend with my fellow beings; I leave them to enjoy their opinions; but I am not too old to correct my own, if I have erred."

"Look on my broken form, my wrinkled brow, my head whitened, not with age, but with the fever of my brain!"

"Nay, that is not sufficient. You have had enough to break a manly frame, independent of your scepticism."

"Robert, listen. Years have passed since I communicated with my fellow beings on the subject of religion; but I have thought, observed, reflected. You know my youth was serious, that my seat was seldom vacant at church. I loved our good minister. He dandled me on his knee when I was an infant; he first opened to me the book of knowledge, and taught me to love my brother. I loved, when I grew up, to visit him, to spend hours with him, and listen to his instructions. I loved him as I did my father. While he lived, I was religious, after the fashion of his religion. I knew no unbelief. Death called him away, another minister came, who called him a child of Satan, and assured me I should go to hell if I believed as he did, and only practiced as he enjoined. Troubles, quarrels came; our church was soon divided; three or four new ones established which did nothing but fight each other. Then I became cold—doubted—aye, abjured religion."

"Have you never seen cause to regret that abjuration?"

"Hear me. I have been a traveler. You know the cause which made me a lone wretch, condemned to roam, and still to roam, and still to find 'no spot of this wide world my own.' I have looked on man; I have studied human society, and human manners. I have marked the effect of what men call religion. I have seen man shut the door in his brother's face, for a mere difference of opinion; I have seen the father disown his son for an honest expression of his religious faith; I have seen the milk of human kindness soured in the mother's breast towards her child, because that child chose not the maternal church; and seeing this, could I wish for religion?"

"But you mistake. This was not religion; it was the abuse of religion."

"I have heard the same remark at London, at Rome, at Constantinople, at Pekin, and from the boasted sons of Brahma. Still wherever I have been, I have seen the same abuses. Superstition breaks man's spirit, and makes him crouch like the camel to receive his burden. Superstition pollutes the fountains of love, dries up human sympathy, and gives to man the ferocity of the tiger and the greediness of the wolf. I have heard the muezzin call to prayer from the minarets of Constantinople, I have heard the vesper bell in the Eternal City, 'the sole monument of the world,' I have heard the Brahmin, the worshiper of Lama, the Buddhist, the Pagan, the Moslem, the Catholic, the Protestant priest, each proclaim his creed, extol the purity of his faith, the loveliness of his religion, and wherever I have been, I have seen man warring with man—man, vulture like, feeding on man; wherever I have been, I have seen the priest leagued with the despot, and the fetters of heaven forged to give new strength to those of earth; wherever I have been, I have seen the mind chained down by the priest and the body bound by the civil tyrant. Free thought is curbed, the soul is 'cabined, cribbed, confined,'[3] to suit the will of some fellow lordling who might have to live by the sweat of his brow were it permitted to breath the pure air of heaven and to exert freely its own omnipotence."

"Nay, my friend, you are too severe; you merely declaim."

"Robert, I love you. It is a long time since I have pronounced these words. I love you not as a priest, but as the companion of my early life, the partner of my juvenile rambles, the confidant of my youthful hopes and fears. I speak to you not as you now are, but as you are pictured to my heart, in all the free and generous confidence of unsuspecting youth, when I would unbosom my thoughts to you, as I would to myself. I but speak as I believe. I know your excuse. I know you grieve over these evils as well as I. I know your heart revolts at such things. But what shall I say? They everywhere prevail; call them abuses of religion, where is the good done by what men call religion to overbalance them? Point to the church where we were reared? To the one over which you are pastor? I feel the argument, but it recoils on your own head; our old pastor by keeping theology out of sight, by keeping it veiled and confined within the walls of the

---

[3][Ed. Shakespeare, *Macbeth*, III, iv, 24.]

sanctuary, as much as does the Turk his wife within the walls of the Harem, he was able to keep peace in his church. You follow his example. But none of the good done by him, or by you results from your theological teachings. It is the holy example, the moral lesson, the benevolent advice, the warm and affectionate love to the church, that produce the good you would ascribe to religion. A good man, avoiding all disputed topics, dwelling solely on moral goodness, studious only to promote the moral virtues, may be a blessing to society. Let him take one step beyond, let him once broach theological dogmas, and the history of the world stamps the priest a curse to man."

"But, my friend, what has been your support? You have derived no aid from religion; how have you borne up under the load of adversity heaped upon you?"

"I have nerved my soul to it. Wrapping myself up in scorn of the world, I have disdained to bend."

"You did not always scorn mankind."

"Aye, that I did not. I had my dreams. They were blissful dreams. I dreamed of benevolence, humanity, greatness of soul, energy of spirit, and I stepped forward the champion of my race."

"That you did. There were great hopes of you then. But you have disappointed both your friends and enemies."

"Myself, more than anyone else. Men are determined to be beasts of burden. They curse the mind that dares resolve their freedom, and cut off the hand that presumes to unloose their fetters. I attempted the work, and gave it over in scorn, and have since had no fellowship with my race."

"But you could not be inactive; what did you after this?"

"Read the Book of Knowledge."

"Did that give you happiness? Did it satisfy the inward thirst of the soul?"

"Satisfy! Does the ocean overflow? Are the rays of light exhausted? Expect one or the other as soon as that the soul should be satisfied. The acquisition of knowledge may cease to charm, but the soul will never say it has enough."

"Was the enquiry after knowledge always pleasant? Had its pleasure no alloy of pain?"

"Ask ye that? The desire of knowledge is the fabled vulture feeding on the entrails of the damned. Is it pleasant? Aye, if it be pleasant to rack the soul, and work the whole being up into thought till thought itself is dizzy—aye, if to search with feverish sense, to survey heaven, air, ocean, earth, to crowd all nature within the brain, and to feel that all is emptiness—aye, if to grasp for years with the insatiable thirst of the miser, and to feel that nothing is gained, that worlds on worlds remain to be explored—and then, to sink with the humility of knowing how little can be known—to wither away with the knowledge that all things are vanity, that there is nothing worth knowing—worth a wish—a thought—a passing turn of the eye—if that be pleasure, go read the book of knowledge. If to feel the body give way, the temper sour, the nervous irritability increase, if to feel the damning assurance that you have no fellow, that your sympathy is dead, that you are not as ordinary clay, that you are to have no communion with beings around you, that you must lock up your treasures in your own bosom, while that bosom throbs with anguish, the brain sears, and reason is on the verge of insanity—if this be pleasure, go expect it from the pursuit, the burning pursuit of knowledge."

"What did you, when you learned this?"

"Plunged into dissipation—sought from the animal what the soul denied; feasted on beauty till it was a drug, indulged appetite, till I found it increase, as the ability to enjoy passed away—sought the gambling 'Hell'—excitement in ruin—drained the inebriating bowl till I rolled in the ditch."

"What then?"

"Chased the meteor ambition, the *ignis fatuus*,[4] fame—entered the field of battle—laughed at thousands slain—sought posts of honor—gained them—was huzzaed—disgraced."

"What then?"

"Turned miser, counted over my gold—filled my coffers, heaped thousands on thousands—grew mad that I could not eat my gold, could not wear my gold, could not drink my gold—had no one to enjoy it with me."

"What then?"

"Nothing. I had run through the world; tried all it could give; pronounced it vanity; myself vanity; cursed myself—the world—everything, ceased to feel, and stood alone, unmoved by love or hate, by joy or grief, by pleasure or pain. I felt all was tried and ceased to act."

"*And is this the substitute you would give us for religion?*"

"Mock me not. I did not make the world. I have tried it. I have told you what it is. It is a bad world, it is a bad world, it makes one's heart sick to look around on it. He is a fool that dreams of happiness."

"Did you try genuine affection?"

---

[4][Ed. Latin idiom for something illusory or unreal. The term often refers to a light seen at night moving over swamps, believed to be caused by the combustion of gases arising from rotting organic matter.]

"I sought it with tears, and spurned it as soon as gained. The heart was empty. The world had nothing to fill it. We have nothing to do but to wrap ourselves up in ourselves and bear what comes."

"It is late my friend, will you listen to our devotions?"

"I can listen."

"Robert then called in his wife, and three lovely daughters—the eldest might be thirteen, the youngest, perhaps seven. They were the very pictures of health, of innocence—I had three such sisters, they died of broken hearts. One of them read a simple hymn, which the whole family joined in singing. No—I did not weep, but my heart swelled, my throat was full. The husband, the father, the priest, offered a short prayer, which was more the expression of thanks than the preferring of a petition; his voice was deep toned, but sweet, his devotion seemed warm, from the heart. I half envied my friend as I looked upon him and his family before the domestic altar. Long forgotten emotions were awakened, and I felt a change was coming over me.

"The devotions closed, each of the children kissed their parents and bade them good night and retired. It was too much. I wept. Yes, I who for years had forsworn to feel, wept, at sight of filial affection sweetened by early piety! My friend conducted me to my bedroom, we parted in silence. I did not sleep that night. My friend had told me nothing new, had offered me no new deduction of reason; but he had set me an example, he showed me *a happy family*, convinced me there was happiness on earth. I felt I had missed my way and that my friend had found it.

"I stayed some days longer with my friend. Each member of his family had a regular employment, which was lightened by the good nature and grace with which it was borne. He was contented and happy in his devotions, in his domestic and social relations. I became acquainted with a number of families in the village, equally contented, equally happy. One evening, the one before I left him (it was the last time I ever saw him), I asked Robert to disclose to me the secret of his enjoyment. "You see," he said, "how I live. I have no secret. Would you be happy, look not too far. I trust my God, love my family and my fellow beings, keep within my own sphere, and in that aim to do all the good I can."

"But tell me how you get along with all these crude notions of religion?" said I.

"Let them alone. Religion's office is to cherish, purify, and strengthen the kind affections. It is not a set of articles to be believed, but a series of holy principles to be cultivated in the heart. Cultivate gratitude to God, aspire after his excellence, cherish love and charity towards your fellow beings, fill the vacuum in your heart with kind feeling and endearing affection, and you shall be happy. There is no secret, no mysterious nostrum. Recall your young affections, and all shall be well."

Thus far the old man related his adventures with a firm voice; but I perceived the struggle with his feelings had been too great, a change came over him; but after something of a pause, he continued: "Old as I was this lesson was not thrown away. It made me a new man. The withered affections were restored. I found one—she is gone. I shall meet her in heaven. I am ready for the grave. I have lived more than fourscore years and ten. I am alone. There are none to weep for me. Well, be it so. I feel life is departing. A strange feeling comes over me. Where are you, young man? All things fade—give me your hand—this is kind. Go, return to your fathers, young man. Take the blessing of a dying old man. Remember, be good. Cultivate piety towards God—benevolence towards mankind. Indulge kind, social affections—trust in God—you shall be happy."

His voice ceased, but his face brightened up, his eye for a moment shone with unearthly luster; gradually all settled down to a quiet state, and he calmly breathed his last. I watched by his corpse that night. I postponed my return to pay the last offices of an earthly friend to the departed. We laid him in a grave in the forest; the Indian maidens strewed it with evergreens, and sung his requiem. His soul is in heaven; his last words are engraven on my heart.

Reader, thou mayest call the above a fiction. I will not dispute thee. The sober moralist will call it the lesson of truth. If its gossamer drapery of fiction, borrowed from the literature of the day, will entice the novelist to read it, and if its moral aid in checking a gloomy theology on the one hand, and a dark and withering scepticism on the other, the most fastidious it is hoped will pardon its disguise. The writer knows full well the evil effects of both extremes. He has grown dark and desperate under the influence of Calvinism and felt his affections wither and his sympathy die, under the dread dominion of scepticism.

23.

CALVANISM[1] AND INFIDELITY

Philanthropist 2 (May 29, 1832): 221-22

If there be anyone truth on which we can depend, it is that Calvinism leads to infidelity. The gloomy and morose picture it presents of God is revolting to all the finer and better feelings of the heart. It chills the devotion, deadens the affections and in the end makes us disgusted with all religion. To a reasonable man it will at times seem more honorable to God to deny his existence than to present his character in the harsh and terrific light in which it is presented by the followers of the Genevan reformer.

There is, in spite of all aspersions, a native benevolence in the human heart, a natural relish for virtue, and it is shocked at any manifest violation of justice and humanity. We read with horror of a Cataline, of a Nero and a Caligula.[2] Deeds of darkness, of cruelty and blood, of wanton sport with the fortunes, reputation and lives of our fellow beings awake our indignation, and call forth the fullness of our disapprobation. We shun the monster; we instinctively shrink from his presence. Now, we cannot ascribe that horrid character to God; we cannot paint him a being of terror, shrouded in the lightning, hung round with implements of torture, looking down with scorn on his children, delighting in their agony, or riding forth in triumph over prostrate millions, and pausing but amid a ruined and devastated world—we cannot ascribe such a character to God and retain any love or reverence for his divinity. The heart rises in rebellion against him; all the better feelings, all its love of justice, its admiration of wisdom, all its veneration for goodness, all its fondness for sympathy and compassion rise up against such a God, pronounce him the focus of cruelty, and a million times worse than no God at all.

[1][Ed. Periodically Brownson misspells Calvinism. It has been corrected in all places, except in titles like the present one.]

[2][Ed. Catiline (i.e., Lucius Sergius Catilina, c.108-62 B.C.) was a Roman conspirator denounced by Cicero. Claudius Nero (A.D. 37-68) was a Roman Emperor (54-68) who persecuted Christians during the time of Saints Peter and Paul. Caligula (i.e., Gaius Caesar Germanicus, 12-41 A.D.) was Roman Emperor from 37 to 41.]

Disguise Calvinism as you may, it does paint its God as this horrid monster; it trembles before a stern despot; it bows to power without justice and worships eternal and omnipotent cruelty. Now is it strange that when such views of God, views which outrage all the native benevolence of the heart—is it strange that when such views prevail, and are pronounced orthodox, that men of strong common sense but not of extensive research should abjure religion, and close in with infidelity? This is the true secret of the spread of infidelity among us. Calvinism must answer for it.

This is evident from the fact that all the objections, which unbelievers urge, are urged against the Calvinistic theology which prevails. They take their views from Christianity as it prevails, and against those they point their argument, wit, and ribaldry. Powerful argument this—why liberal Christians should exert themselves, why they should labor more and yet more, to disseminate a rational religion, one which shall meet the wants of the age, coincide with the religious sentiment natural to man, and not be exposed to the philosophical and moral objections which are raised against the popular theology of the day. We entreat our friends to think of this.

24.

TREATMENT OF UNBELIEVERS

Christian Register 11-12 (December 8, 1832): 194

Mr. Editor. As it is a well known fact that there are many in our community who either disbelieve Christianity or have doubts of its truth, it has occurred to me that some suggestions relative to the course we should pursue towards unbelievers might be both useful and agreeable to your readers. These suggestions will have reference to the manner in which we should treat their persons, their objections and doubts, and to the kind of arguments we should urge for their conviction.

It is hard for one who has never doubted the truth of revelation to appreciate the exact state of the unbeliever's mind. Christians are too apt to imagine everyone's unbelief flows either from some obtuseness of intellect or from some obliquity of the moral sense. They cannot conceive that anyone can find any real difficulty in the way of embracing the gospel. To them Christianity is full of light and love; they see in it everything to engage the heart, to awaken and fix all the sweeter and holier affections of our nature, and to give free scope to all the higher and nobler exertions of mind; and consequently, they cannot conceive of any cause for rejecting it but the most consummate ignorance or the most willful depravity. They are, therefore, very liable to treat the unbeliever with a severity that ill befits themselves and wholly ruins him.

Christians have been misled on this subject. It has been thought an offence to doubt Christianity—[an offence] of such magnitude against the well-being of society that any means which could make unbelievers odious and deter others from doubting were justifiable. It is a gross mistake. It is unchristian to treat any man with contempt or with unkindness. The Christian spirit is manly, firm, but it is also meek, gentle, courteous and charitable. He is no Christian who has a different spirit. As Christians, then, we should treat all men courteously, charitably, with gentleness, and kindness. We have no right to be harsh, bitter, overbearing or censorious. When we are so against unbelievers, we forget our religion and wound our Savior in the house of his friends without doing any good to them.

There is no necessity for us to treat unbelievers otherwise than kindly. Christianity is founded upon a rock. It cannot be overthrown. The waves may dash at its base, the winds and the storms may rage from above, but it shall survive their fury and abide the ravages of time. We have no need to resort to any improper methods to sustain it. When we do, we provoke attack rather than ward off threatened blows. We, as Christians, have the truth, the truth of heaven on our side; we can afford to be just, we can do more, we can be generous. We *must* be fair, candid and generous, if we would gain the love of the unbeliever and win back the alienated.

Charitable and generous treatment to unbelievers is the best policy. It is a bad way to convert one to our faith, to begin by telling him he is either a fool or grossly depraved. The road to the understanding lies through the affections. If you cannot make a man think favorably of you as a man, you will not have much success in converting him to your faith as a Christian. Unbelievers are men, men of discernment, men of feelings, often of acute sensibility, and they never can be won to Christianity by a morose countenance and a harsh voice. They will dislike the man who censures them and if he be the advocate on religion, they will scorn religion out of despite to the advocate.

Our first study should be to convince unbelievers that belief in the gospel has a favorable effect upon our own character, that it makes us really more polite, amiable and winning, in our behavior. No argument will be able to convince them of the truth or desirableness of the gospel, if they receive nothing but contempt, neglect, or censures from those who believe it. They read the language of the eye, of the carriage, and of the tone of the voice. If this be forbidding, if it speak a cold heart and a censorious disposition, they will have no wish to become believers.

We should be anxious so to treat them that our conversation shall interest them, and that they will feel themselves more pleased with us as associates than they can with unbelievers. I apprehend an unbeliever seldom converses with one who calls himself a Christian without having his feelings wounded. Indeed it is too common to think it is no matter how much a Christian scoffs at an unbeliever, or how often, or how deeply he wounds his feelings. Sorry am I to say this; but it is too true. We do sometimes treat unbelievers as though they were out of the pale of humanity. Whether they deserve to be so treated or not, is no question with me; is it wise so to treat them? Certainly not, if we would win them to the fold of Christ and give them the cheering and purifying hopes of the gospel.

I can readily conceive much of the unkind treatment unbelievers receive, is really undesigned and even unsuspected on the part of those who give it. It is so difficult to enter fully into their feelings, and to comprehend the real nature of their troubles that those who have never doubted may be pardoned much of the pain they occasion; yet it is of great importance that we study to gain their good will and win their love for Christianity, if we do not convince them of its truth. Our own general conduct and our treatment of them will effect this object sooner than any reasoning we can adopt. But, enough till my next.

NO. 2 (January 12, 1833): 6

It is important that clergymen should be attentive to visit frequently those who doubt. Unbelievers complain that Christians neglect them, and this sours their minds against us. This can be remedied. Clergymen need not fear contamination. Jesus ate[1] with sinners. If unbelievers are vicious they are the one[s] who demand the services of the clergyman. He should be anxious to reform them. Also by visiting them he will be able to ascertain their real difficulties. That they are unbelievers is no reason why he should neglect them; he should be anxious to convert them. But this he cannot do unless he visits them—learns and answers their objections.

The objections of unbelievers, though often trivial and sometimes shocking to believers, should be heard with patience and replied to with seriousness and candor. What is to us trivial seems of great consequence to them; and what we may deem shocking, possesses a very different character in their estimation. It is not everyone who has been over the whole ground of controversy. There is many a one who stumbles for the want of additional light. But, if when he ask for it he be denied, or be upbraided, he will only be driven further from the true faith. There is too much reason for giving this caution. I could relate hundreds of instances, where men have become violent opponents of religion, merely because clergymen abused them for doubting.

It will be found of great consequence to concede that doubts may proceed from other causes than depravity of heart, or enmity to Christianity. We must concede the fact that a man may doubt the dogmatical part of Christianity and still be honest. Christians can scarcely admit this. They contend that love of vice, opposition to the purity of the gospel, and dread of the punishment it threatens, are the principal causes of unbelief. This is a mistake. Abate those who in

---

[1][Ed. Original text had "eat."]

the western country support the Orthodox, and unbelievers are not to be distinguished from the rest of the community in the virtues of private and social life, so far as my knowledge extends. They no more love vice than professed Christians. And so far as we can discover, it is not the purity of the gospel, but the supposed absurdity of it, to which they object. They generally admit the excellence of its morality, and object only to its dogmas.

Allow unbelievers to be honest, and you disarm them of hostility. You can then meet them on fair grounds. Their angry feelings will be suppressed; their boisterous passions silenced. The reason and judgment will be awakened, and when men will reason carefully and judge candidly, religion will have nothing to fear. But we shall find ourselves unable to convince unbelievers of the worth, much less of the charity, of our religion, as long as we hold out to them, what they will term, the abusive notion that they are unbelievers because they are wicked. We should never begin to convert a man to our opinion, by assuring him he differs from us only because he is in love with vice. He feels he is as good as we, and he will not wish to unite with those who charge him falsely.

We ought also to concede to the unbeliever his right to be an unbeliever. I fear there are few who will not think there is a degree of wickedness in proposing this concession. But I know it important and I believe it just. It is frequently asked why should any but a wicked man wish to destroy the Christian faith, and the true answer is not always imagined by believers. The active opposition of unbelievers is not because they believe Christianity false, but because they think they are denied the moral right to oppose it. Concede them the right and very few of them would wish to exercise it. They complain that if they express their honest convictions that the dogmatical part of religion is not true, they are slandered, their families and friends are *pitied* and neglected. This they allege is paying a premium for hypocrisy, and virtually denying to them the right to enjoy, and freely express, their own opinions. Hence in opposing Christianity, they seem to themselves to be contending for the freedom of opinion, for mental independence, and for the sacred rights of conscience. Admit that they have the same right to oppose, that we have to advocate, Christianity, and their opposition will cease. I mean the right, as long as they honestly disbelieve it, and are governed by pure motives.

Now, can we make this concession? Why not? Either man is accountable to his brother for his religious faith, or he is not. If we contend that he is, had we not better go back at once to mother church? If he is not accountable to his brother, then has no one a right to interrogate or censure him, let his faith be what it will. Have my brother and I equal rights? How comes it to pass then, that I have any more right to censure him for not believing, than he has me for believing? "But his want of faith may be prejudicial to the community." So he may think is my faith. If the question is to turn on this point, the Catholic will seem to himself to have a good plea against the Protestant, and in his own estimation the Calvinist against the Unitarian.

Men's minds are bursting their fetters, and the spirit of the times demands unlimited freedom of opinion. The right to believe or disbelieve is demanded, and the sooner it is conceded the better. "But the unbeliever will be free then to seduce with his sophistry, the young and thoughtless. He will destroy all religion." His freedom we have no right to destroy. Besides by conceding him the right, we deprive him of his most effectual argument in seducing the young. He tells them Christianity is opposed to freedom of inquiry, that it holds lightly the sacredness of conscience, and that those who dare question it, are persecuted. This excites their indignation, and the prospect of persecution awakes their love of adventure, and enlists their sympathy with the unbeliever because they believe him a sufferer.

This is not all. As soon as this is conceded, the whole controversy is simplified. The simple question is then, "is Christianity true?" Now the question is, "Have I a right to disbelieve Christianity?" Unbelievers take it for granted that Christians deny them this right, consequently make the question as much as possible, one of right. They contend for their rights; in this they seem to have the better of the argument, and because they are right in this instance, too many with a fatal precipitancy, conclude they are right in every other. Let us treat them with respect, concede them honesty, concede that they have so far as men are concerned the full right to express their unbelief, and nearly all the real causes of their opposition will be removed. We shall then be prepared to argue with success. The kind of arguments which will be the most useful, I shall state in my next.

NO. 3 (February 2, 1833): 18

I beg not to be misinterpreted in the remarks I am about to make on the kind of arguments that we should urge for the conversion of unbelievers. I give the result of my experience. I state that which will have weight with unbelievers without meaning to decide on the correctness or incorrectness of those arguments usually urged, which I may pass over.

The greatest difficulty in the mind of the unbeliever, the hardest to be removed, is the authoritative character of Christianity. Many an unbeliever would embrace Christianity with great readiness, if it were presented to him simply as a system of truth, not as one of authority. I do not know that I express what I mean. The believer supposes himself called upon to believe Christianity not because it is true, not because it is founded in the nature of things and is adapted to man's moral nature, but because it is a system of authority, of positive legislation.

Now I think this difficulty may be obviated. What is the authority of Christianity? Is it authoritative because it is found in a particular book? Because it comes from a particular person? It is not authoritative because it is true? Were it false, would it be deserving our attention? Certainly not. Its truth, then, is its authority. Truth is always authoritative. Every man is bound to obey the truth. And truth is truth, let it come from what source it may, and be supported by whom it may.

But how shall we determine whether it be true or not? I answer in the words of Jesus to the Jews, "Why, even of yourselves judge ye not what is right" [Luke 12:57]? We have in ourselves the means of determining whether Christianity be true or false. When I propose Christianity to an unbeliever, I refer him to the workings of his own soul, to what passes in his own mind, for proofs of its truth. When I bring the evidences of a matter of fact to a man's senses, I suppose my labor of proof is done; so when I bring the proofs of a moral or religious proposition home to man's own consciousness, I suppose I have done all that can be asked of me.

If Christianity be a system of positive legislation, I own I cannot in this way prove its authority. Still I can prove what is of more consequence, I can prove the principles are true, and if true, I think I shall have no difficulty in proving that they are binding, binding if not from the extraneous authority of legislation, at least from the intrinsic authority of truth. And when I have induced the unbeliever to admit so much, I am satisfied; for it will not be long before he will admit all else that is necessary.

I would not then present Christianity to an unbeliever as a system of positive legislation, but as a system of truth. I would make a distinction between the doctrine or principles of Christianity and the facts of Christianity. I would present the simple moral and religious propositions of the gospel unencumbered by everything extraneous. I would prove them not by appeals to ancient records, to ancient transactions, but by showing that their foundation is in our own moral nature, that we have that within us which bears witness to their truth.

Unbelievers do not pay much regard to ancient records. They are opposed to being sent back two thousand years for the truth; they think truth is as obvious now as it ever was; and they contend that what is of universal concernment should be within the reach of every individual, and that a proposition, in the truth of which, all are equally interested should be equally evident to all. This is not my reasoning, it is the unbeliever's. But if we can meet his wishes without injury to Christianity, it is better than to arouse his prejudices, by assuring him his demands are unreasonable.

Those evidences of Christianity which are universal, which may be found at all times, in all places, and by all persons of common sense, are those which are the most proper to convince the unbeliever. I would begin, not with the facts of Christianity, not with the genuineness and authenticity of the Scriptures, but with the excellence of the moral precepts; from this, I would proceed to the reasonableness, then to the desirableness, and then to the truth of the doctrinal propositions. The morality of the gospel must be admitted by all to be excellent. Those pure and practical precepts which are scattered through the discourses of Jesus, can be read by no unbeliever without being admired. The doctrinal propositions of the gospel are such as approve themselves to every man's unbiased judgement, and such as commend themselves to every unperverted heart, that is, when presented in their true character, not connected with some other things, which are not absolutely essential to them. But we must present the true doctrines of Christ, for we are not able to prove Christianity as a system without stating to the unbeliever, clearly, the several parts of which it is made up. We must prove it in detail, not by wholesale. We are not very wise in setting out to prove Christianity when we do not know what Christianity is, and we shall gain nothing from the unbeliever, till we allow him to understand distinctly what are the doctrinal propositions which in our estimation make up that system we call Christianity. When we do this, and present them in the simple form that Jesus did, we need be under no apprehension that they will be rejected.

When I had succeeded in establishing the conviction of the reasonableness, desirableness, and probable truth of the doctrinal propositions of the gospel, I would present the Bible, not as an inspired book, but as a remarkable one, worthy of examination. My first object would be to assist him to a correct understanding of what it does in reality teach. To this end, I would insist upon a correct mode of interpretation, inform him that he is to regard not its verbal statements but the spirit of its teachings. After this, I would examine with him the proofs of its inspiration, its genuineness, and authenticity.

NO. 4 (February 23, 1833): 30

I am aware that I may seem too prolix but I cannot dismiss this subject without some further remarks. Kind treatment, strong, over-powering argument, will not be sufficient to convert the unbeliever. Something more, vastly more important, is wanting. Christians must give him, in their lives, a practical demonstration of the truth and excellence of the religion they would have him embrace.

To check infidelity we must soften our feelings towards each other and abate something of the violence of our sectarian disputes. I would not have truth surrendered, I would not have a man acquiesce in false or mischievous propositions for the sake of avoiding contro-versy; but I would have everyone show that he has a greater regard for human happiness than he has for the maintenance of a particular form of worship, or even an unmeaning dogma. While Christians are quarreling among themselves and anathematizing each other for differences of opinions, "scarcely visible to the nicest theological eye," the unbeliever only looks on with a smile of contempt or blesses his stars that he is not of their number. With what face can we ask him to be a Christian while doctors equally eminent for learning and piety, dispute with a savage zeal, what Christianity is?

I confess I have at times felt half ashamed to ask the intelligent sceptic to become a believer. I have felt the force of his reply: "Let Christians agree among themselves what Christianity is, and then I will examine its claims." I hardly know what answer to give to such a withering remark. It half disarms me and I weep to lose the victory through the dissensions of my own army. Christians must be united or they will only empower the unbeliever to triumph. We cannot meet him successfully while we are persecuting each other with as much virulence as the spirit of the age will allow; we cannot ward off his blows while we make our religion a perpetual source of discord in families and of hate and unholy rage in the community. Long as we continue to pervert the gospel to mere sectarian purposes, we shall find it almost impossible to correct the philanthropic unbeliever. He may find his logic silenced, he may become enamored of the beauti-ful theory we present him, he may at first even sigh to possess it; but when he marks its practical result, when he sees it perverting the native benevolence of the human heart, dividing the community into petty factions and arming each with wrath to the other, he will turn from it in pity for man or learn with a benevolent zeal to destroy it.

In these remarks, I merely state what will be the effects of our harsh sectarian disputes on the unbeliever, without intending his justification. Our quarrels about the truth do not exonerate him from his obligations to discover, embrace and obey it. But he may believe they do, and we thus become guilty of his loss. It is our duty to remove the block of stumbling from his path. It is our duty so to adorn our religion by our good works, and to let our light so shine, that the unbeliever may be drawn into our number, to unite his voice with ours in glorifying God.

I know of nothing which does more to make men infidels than do our animosities, our party squabbles, our frivolous disputes, and our sectarian denunciations. They impair men's confidence in religion. They embitter them against it and seem to give the holy sanction of philanthropy to their opposition to it. They cherish the conviction that nothing is certain in religion, that nothing is fixed, and that there is no criterion for determining what is true or false in it. It is even a standing remark in some parts of the community, that "the Bible is like a musical instrument on which a skillful performer may play any tune he pleases." I have heard hundreds of good Christians, when hard pressed, excuse their adherence to notions they could not maintain, and their not yielding to those which were clearly proved to be Scripture doctrines, by repeating this common saying. Can we succeed against infidelity when our friends manifest this want of confidence in our cause, and do little more than furnish the means of our defeat?

There is no need of violent contention—no necessity for party animosity. Let Christians rise above the littleness of sectarian jealousies, above sectarian invectives. Let Christians elevate their conceptions and learn that Christianity is something more than a mere detail of abstruse dogmas and modes of worship. They must learn to view it as a system of holy and all-comprehending principles to be cultivated in the heart and obeyed in the life, not a set of articles to be merely assented to by the understanding. Jesus came not to make able polemics, but to quicken the heart, to breathe new life into the soul, and to enlist all its power in the great work of being and doing good. He judges us by what we are in ourselves and by what we do, not by what we believe. He values the high and holy resolve, the warm aspiration of the heart after virtue, more than the longest creed, or the ablest body of metaphysical divinity ever produced. When Christians learn this, they may dispense with their disputes, and instead of wasting their energies in worrying and devouring each other,

214 THE EARLY WORKS OF ORESTES A. BROWNSON: VOLUME II

they may unite for the promotion of peace and love. They may then become of "one heart," and may present an unbroken phalanx to an opposing world.

It is a lamentable fact that religion's worst enemies have been among its professed friends. They have made it cold and artificial—a system of barren technicalities, of barbarous phraseology and unmeaning dogmas. Instead of looking after the "spirit that giveth life," they have too often rested in the "letter which killeth." Instead of permitting religion to appear in a pleasing form, clad in her own simplicity and adorned by her own loveliness, they have compressed her shape, distorted her features, and tricked her out in robes as unbecoming as they were worthless. They have permitted her to come to us no being of light and love, but a melancholy sprite wreathed with the death shade and chanting the groans of despair. Youth fled in horror at her approach. Light and joyous feelings were exchanged for heavy sighs in her presence. It is time to correct this mistake. It is time that we receive religion as the daughter of heaven and the power of God unto salvation. It is time that the emotions her presence produces be no longer painful, such as all who can look on the bright and sunny side of things dread to have and shudder to recall. It is time that she be permitted to speak to the soul in tones of surpassing sweetness and power, to give a holy calm to the passions, strength to the good affections, and energy to the whole inner man. Then religion will stir all the depth of human love, men will become better, loftier beings. Infidelity will vanish, and all Christians will unite with one heart and voice, to praise Him who is forever and ever.

25.

CHANNING'S DISCOURSES

Christian Register 12 (January 19, 1833): 10

Messrs. Editors: Allow me, through your columns, to express my thanks to Dr. Channing for the very great pleasure I have received from his volume of *Discourses* lately published in your city.[1] These Discourses commend themselves to all admirers of fine writing, and more especially to all who love the pure and rational religion of Jesus. They are adapted to the wants of the age and will be of vast utility not only in proving religion to be true, but in giving correct notions of what religion is. I welcome their publication and sincerely thank their author for this public benefit.

These Discourses are principally designed to meet the objections of a certain class of sceptics, and to exhibit in a clear, condensed form the evidences of Christianity. This is an object worthy the most gifted mind. Infidelity is secretly spreading and is openly expressed to an alarming extent. It is of the last consequence that it be met, and successfully met. It is true, there have been defenses of Christianity published, which have not been and cannot be answered; but they do little to check unbelief.

The writings of those divines who labored so successfully to refute the sceptics of the 18th century are not suited to the wants of this age. Then Christianity was defended for scholars. The mass of the people had no share in the controversy. That mass dreamed not of disbelieving, and as little of having any belief, not *borrowed* from their teachers, and held at the mercy of its owners. It is different now. The many begin to feel that this is a question in which they have a personal interest. They begin to feel the struggles of thought. They are breaking from their leading strings and daring to trust themselves to their own guidance. They have good sense but not profound erudition. Their doubts are excited not so much by the objections which were formerly urged as by what passes in their own poorly developed minds. They distrust antiquity. They have little regard for history or miracle. They distrust the usual witnesses introduced to prove the

---

[1][Ed. On this, see William Ellery Channing, *Discourses, Reviews, and Miscellanies* (Boston: Carter and Hendee, 1830).]

gospel as much as they do the gospel itself. Those truly elaborate and unanswerable works which were called forth in a former age against the cavils of unbelievers do not meet their wants. They feel not their force and cannot judge of their suitableness.

Men now ask for living witnesses, to be pointed to something which they can see and feel is a proof of the truth of the gospel. They have not the patience to follow a Lardner,[2] nor even to examine the shorter but equally convincing work of Paley. They want their own spiritual natures revealed to them, to be made to perceive and to feel the grandeur of the human soul, its august powers, its deep wants, and its yearnings after a higher good than earth can give. That which does this will soonest bring them to the cross, make them lovers of Jesus, and worshipers of God.

Of this Dr. Channing seems to have been well aware. He has surpassed all other writers with whom I am acquainted in revealing the unbeliever to himself, and in making him feel he has a lofty and deathless nature. He wakes up the higher and holier principles of the soul; he calms the passions, conciliates the affections, and prepares the understanding to decide correctly. Here is his chief power and to me his chief excellence as a defender of Christianity. All that anyone needs to become a firm believer in the gospel is to read himself, to read the law of his own heart. He who persuades the unbeliever to do this will be the most successful in removing his unbelief.

The first discourse in this volume is deserving the attention of all unbelievers. The introductory remarks are bold, but liberal, just, conciliating. The answers to objections usually urged against revelation are happy and generally conclusive. The argument deduced from the deep wants of the soul is of itself enough. It was the consciousness of this want, this thirst for something I had not, for something earth could not give, that led me to the gospel; and the conviction that the gospel could satisfy this want, led to the conviction of its truth.

The historical, or external evidence, is clearly set forth, with far less of exaggeration than usual. This kind of evidence is better to guard the believer than to convince the unbeliever. The argument drawn from the origin of Christianity is not the one best adapted to unbelievers. There are good Christians who believe the gospel is no new revelation, but the *republication* of that which God made by his

---

[2][Ed. Brownson may be referring to the independent British minister, Nathaniel Lardner (1684-1768), a non-conformist apologist, whose most famous work was the fourteen-volume *The Credibility of the Gospel History* (1727-57), which tried to reconcile the discrepancies in the biblical narratives.]

spirit to the sages and patriarchs of old. The objections to miracles are clearly obviated, and leave one nothing to wish, but that it had been proved that miracles are a proof of the doctrines of Christianity. The arguments from the character of Jesus, and from the reasonableness of Christianity are full of power, and I wish every unbeliever would examine them. Those portions of the *Discourses* not designed for unbelievers will be not less efficient in working their conviction than the rest. After all, the free, the lofty, the benevolent spirit which pervades all the *Discourses* will do more than all the facts and reasonings in the book to make men Christians.

I did not intend, on commencing this article, this strain of observation. I wished to recommend these *Discourses* to unbelievers, not to criticize them. Were they even faulty, I could not censure them—I owe too much to Dr. Channing. To *his* writings, and to the conversation of *one* who deserves to be more extensively known—one who has sustained rational Christianity for seventeen years in the midst of every opposition, removed from nearly all sympathy with his brethren, and at the sacrifice of nearly every comfort except a calm temper, an active mind, and a warm heart[3]—am I indebted for my escape from infidelity. I shall not soon fail to have a lively sense of gratitude to both. But enough of this. I know from experience that scepticism is not incurable. I do therefore anxiously entreat my skeptical friends to read these *Discourses*. I can recommend them to unbelievers, if not as wholly able to convince them, at least as able to awaken a train of reflection which will end in conviction. I know many unbelievers weep for their want of faith. Let them read these Discourses and they will find them able to sweeten the temper, to calm the passions, to give energy to the mind, and health to the whole soul.

[3][Ed. It is unclear to whom Brownson is referring. He had been married for seventeen years at this point, but he is not referring to his wife here, though she, too, was a major influence upon his return to belief.]

26.

AN ADDRESS ON INTEMPERANCE, DELIVERED IN WALPOLE, N.H.

February 26, 1833[1]

Friends and Fellow-Citizens,

We are met this day for the suppression of intemperance. I invite your attention to the causes which lead to it, to its effects, and to the means of preventing it.

Intemperance is the immoderate indulgence of any of our propensities. It may attach to eating, to sleeping, to our passion for dress, or for society, as well as to drinking. The glutton is intemperate as well as the drunkard. We confine ourselves to the consideration of the immoderate use of ardent spirits, not because this is the only kind of intemperance, but because it is the most prominent and the most pernicious.

In speaking against this species of intemperance much severity of invective has been indulged. I abhor drunkenness as much as any man can abhor it; but it is not always that I abhor the drunkard. His drunkenness is his misfortune, as often as it is his crime; and I find myself oftener inclined to pity and forgive than I do to censure him. The friends of temperance gain nothing by *intemperate* language. Our weapons are spiritual, not carnal—weapons of love, not of wrath; and our business is to protect the unsuspicious and win back the erring, not to pronounce concerning the guilt of a fellow-being.

In those temperance addresses and temperance papers which have fallen under my notice, little is said of the *causes* of intemperance. The criminality of the drunkard and the effects of his drunkenness are dwelt upon with a painful minuteness, and reiterated till they cease to interest or prompt exertion. It were well to avoid this. Too much even of a good thing is good for nothing; what must it then be to have a bad thing constantly ringing in one's ears? It is of more importance to ascertain the causes of intemperance, than it is to be always harping upon its effects; for a knowledge of the causes which produce it may pave the way to its cure.

[1][Ed. Keene, NH: J. & J. W. Prentiss, 1833]

The most prominent causes of intemperance in the use of ardent spirit, are idleness, debt, melancholy, example.

Men do not become drunkards without some cause, or causes, and IDLENESS is obviously one. By idleness, I mean inactivity of mind as well as of body. The man of a well cultivated mind is never idle. His hands may be still, his body may not move, but his mind is employed; he is busy with his thoughts; they keep him company, afford him amusement, and lessen his temptation to excessive drinking. Persons like him can meet together, fill up their time with rational conversation, and be satisfied with "the feast of reason and the flow of soul."[2]

But the majority of mankind have little mental cultivation. Their minds are vacant, dull, inactive. The lower faculties, those which are common to man and animals, are the most strongly developed, and have the greatest influence in determining their conduct. While, however, they have employment, plenty of labor to perform, they may be interested, may be so engrossed that they will not feel obliged to resort to the bottle to fill up their lonely hours.

But, soon as they are idle, they become dull, listless, half dead with *ennui*. Time hangs heavy. They may crack a joke with this one and with that, but all does not do. They soon exhaust their wit and all the topics on which they can feel any interest. Their resort is the dram. This sends a greater quantity of blood to the brain, excites its actions, and exhilarates his whole system. Still idle, surrounded by idle companions, the dram is repeated—today, tomorrow, next day, and—the idler is a drunkard. To prevent this, it is necessary to give all employment. What promotes industry and mental cultivation will tend to lessen the number of drunkards made by idleness.

The second cause I mentioned is DEBT. I know people are often in debt because they are intemperate. I know, also, that many, whose poverty is charged upon their hard drinking were embarrassed in their affairs before they left the walks of sobriety. A man is no man when he is in debt; that is when he is so involved that he despairs of being able to extricate himself. He is half a slave to his creditor—is unwilling to meet him; his movements are embarrassed; his mind is vexed, is soured, and he becomes mad—mad with himself, mad with everybody. He dreads to reflect on the state of his affairs, lets everything fall into confusion—takes a dram and is richer, another and is richer yet, another and he has found forgetfulness, another, and his ruin is complete.

---

[2][Ed. Alexander Pope, *Imitations of Horace* (1733-38), satire 1, book 2, 1.127.]

The remedy in this case is to check as far as practicable the credit system which so extensively prevails. To give a man credit is often the worst injury you can do him. Compel him to earn and pay for the article he buys, before he consumes it, and he may live free from debt, free from embarrassment, free from intemperance. Would all our merchants insist on being paid at the time of selling an article, it would be better for them and, in the long run, 50 percent better for community. The more free you can keep community from debt, the more free will you keep it from intemperance.

The third cause I notice is MELANCHOLY. I use this word, melancholy, in a broad sense. I have seen many a man become a drunkard, ruining the character, fortune and hopes of a most lovely wife; but I never saw one do thus, that was happy with his wife at home, by his own fireside. I know man at times is awfully depraved; I shut my eyes on none of his wickedness, but he is never that wretch which can voluntarily ruin the woman he loves and with whom he is happy, with no other temptation than the pleasure of killing himself by rum drinking.

"Every heart knoweth its own bitterness" [Prov 14:10]. He who seems to us to have no cause of uneasiness may have many a grief, concealed from the world, which drives him to the intoxicating bowl. The loss of a companion, of property, of some dear friend; unrequited affection, disappointment in the worth of one we had loved; disappointed ambition; a disordered nervous system, a constitutional gloom—these, singly or combined, create melancholy, make life apparently insupportable, and drive the weak and unthinking to the bottle. They drink—get drunk—today to drown the shame for having been drunk yesterday, and tomorrow for the same reasons which affect them today.

I cannot speak harshly to these. It is not every man that can command his feelings and make himself superior to circumstances. It is not every man that can be reformed by appeals to conscience. The more you make some feel, the more irretrievable is their ruin. Some require to be soothed. They feel too acutely. The reproaches of conscience may be already too severe. These melancholy persons should be taken by the hand, should be made to forget the losses over which they grieve and assured that all is not yet gone; that they may yet regain their standing in community. They should be led to some bright and sunny spot in life's pathway, where they may forget their unpleasant feelings and learn to joy with a smiling world around them.

The last cause to which I now invite your attention is EXAMPLE. Under this head I include the example of parents and of society generally. Intemperate parents, not always, but generally, have intemperate children. This is owing to example; and something, perhaps, to hereditary transmission of constitution. A good deal depends on innate propensity. Some children, however exposed, will never become intemperate; not because they have a stronger moral sense than those which do, but because they have no inclination to excessive drinking. There is no doubt that the constitution which nature gives has great power in determining whether the child shall grow up a sober or a drunken man. This constitution may be transmitted from parent to child. But, though this does much it does not all. He who has a strong propensity to drink is not necessarily a drunkard. That propensity, if not strengthened by exercise, may be overcome. But in children of intemperate parents it is exercised. It is made powerful by early practice, and its empire is confirmed by habit. This, too, is done before the child is aware of the consequences; before the higher faculties are sufficiently developed to become a restraint. I entreat drunken fathers to reflect on this. They are training up their children to be nuisances to society and a curse to themselves.

The example of associates has its influence. Many a one has become a drunkard through the influence of dissipated associates. One takes a glass, not because he wants it, but because he would not appear singular. From one he proceeds to another; and, having constantly around him a set of idle, drinking fellows, whom he has not courage to shake off, he soon becomes as bad as any.

The example of society generally, or fashion, makes its full share of drunkards. Fashion is all but omnipotent. It will make men do all that man can do. It will make them submit to, even approve, what they would abhor, were it not fashionable. That pert dandy, done up in stays, sporting his cane and whiskers, brainless and selfish as he is, might have some semblance to a human being, were it not his ambition to be foremost among the devotees at the shrine of fashion. And were it not for the same reason so many of the young and beautiful would not find a premature grave by unwholesome practices of dress which it is supposed fashion enjoins.

But he is a fool who preaches against fashion. The Tartars conquered China, but they could not make the Chinese cease to wear long hair. Parents may entreat, physicians may warn, Divines may declaim, and God himself may speak by his messengers, disease and death, and it is all useless. "Ephraim is joined to his idols, let him alone" [Hos 4:17]. The most anyone may hope is to change fashion to the side of health and good morals.

Fashion has made its share of drunkards. It *was* customary with those who gave a tone to society to treat their friends, with rum, brandy, gin or wine, or all together. It was pleasant to take a social glass with a friend, to drink to his good health and good luck. But if this was pleasant to the rich and polite, it was no less pleasant to the poor and vulgar. If it be pleasant to drink above stairs, no one can assign a reason why it is not as pleasant to drink below. If the rich man may treat his friend from the stores which he keeps constantly on hand, I know not why the poor man who cannot keep ardent spirit in his house may not take his friend to the tavern or grocery and treat him to a glass of whiskey. If one might take his gin before his wine with and after his dinner, and perhaps end with a "grace cup" of brandy, I know not why another might not just as well take his morning *bitters*. It is true the drunkard in broadcloth, might be deemed more of a *gentleman* than the one in homespun, he in the new suit than he in rags, but after all, the poor man was only imitating his betters as well as he could. It is true it seems less vulgar for a party to assemble in a splendidly furnished room to sit and drink claret, Burgundy or Champagne, delightful Champagne, than it is to hear of a company of laborers getting together in a dirty grocery, to drink whiskey, but I do not know as the more fashionable set have any right to complain of their coarser followers. And if those in high life, the fashionable part of society, might possibly govern themselves so as not to become drunkards, the same could not always be affirmed of their imitators. Those who aped their habits were pretty sure to overact them. We need no proof of this. Many a man *drank* with his friends, not because he wanted ardent spirit, but because it *was* fashionable, and became fond of the practice, became a drunkard, merely by complying with what he supposed were the rules of good breeding and the marks of hospitality and good feeling. But enough of this.

The *effects* of intemperance next claim our attention. Here I might enlarge, here I might present scenes over which humanity should weep with bleeding heart. But I speak not to passion. My appeal is to sober sense.

Ardent spirit is composed of alcohol and water, combined in about equal quantities. Alcohol is composed of hydrogen, carbon and oxygen, in proportions of about 14, 52, 34, parts to the hundred. In itself it is a poison. When taken in any quantities it deranges healthy action, in large quantities suddenly destroys life. When mixed with water, as in ardent spirit, its effects are modified but by no means prevented.

Ardent spirit, when taken in small quantities, stimulates the whole system, gives energy to all its active powers and for a moment produces an exuberance of life, by no means unpleasant. For a moment the beggar forgets his rags, the blind his loss of sight, the aged the departure of his youth, and the sorrowful his grief. For a moment—aye, for a moment; the pleasure is barely sipped before it turns to pain. There was poison in that fancied nectar.

There is a just medium in the human system that should be maintained. That constitution lasts longest, moves on easiest and performs its functions best which is exposed to neither too great nor too little action. If you stimulate, raise the system above its natural level, give it an excess of action, you derange and weaken its powers. A moderate glass excites our active powers, raises us above ourselves; but we ought to remember that our systems are too delicate to bear for a great length of time this unnatural excitement. We soon sink as much below ourselves as we were raised above. We now become dull, listless, dissatisfied with ourselves and with everybody else. There is a dryness in the throat, a burning in the stomach; there is a feebleness, a general languor that comes over us. We cannot remain in this situation. We must raise the tone. We drink again. But it takes more to raise us to the same ecstasy today than it did yesterday; and hence it is, the oftener we stimulate ourselves with ardent spirit, the oftener we shall want to do it, and the oftener we do it, the greater the quantity which will be required.

But this is not all. The constitution will not long bear this exciting and this sinking away. A friend of mine, relates that he found one winter two black snakes, in a completely torpid state. He brought them to his house, laid them down before the fire, and soon perceived the warmth gave them life. Soon they became quite active. He then threw them into a snow bank and soon they were torpid again. He repeated this process of freezing and thawing, and for four or five times with the same results. Placed before the fire they were alive and active, in the snow they were apparently dead; but on the fifth or sixth time, the experiment failed. The fire produced no signs of returning life, the vital spark was extinguished, the snakes were dead. Such is the effect of ardent spirit. For a few times a man may stimulate himself, but after a while the unnatural elevation and equally unnatural depression wear out the system, the vital energy fails, the man is dead. Your physicians will tell wherefore.

But, my friends, to perceive the ruinous effects of ardent spirit, you need but call to mind that young man you so highly esteemed, and of whom you predicted so much. I seem to see him now just entering upon manhood. I see his fine, open, manly countenance; his mildly beaming eye; his fascinating smile; his engaging address. His mind is well cultivated; his person is prepossessing; a father's heart beats proudly as he marks him; a mother recalls with pleasure the care with which she watched over his infancy and childhood. Society hails him as her brightest ornament and opens to him the path to eminence and fame. The bar welcomes him; the pulpit is ready to receive him. He leads to the altar one of the fairest and loveliest of our daughters; wealth brings his offerings and health weaves her garlands of flowers.

What see I now? Gone is that roseate hue of health, gone is the mild luster of that eye, gone is that fascinating smile, gone is he who might have adorned senates and added glory to his country and to man, and there is before me now, only the tottering frame, with squalid aspect, swollen eyes, bloated countenance, and ruined mind. A poor, worthless, disgusting drunkard is all I see of that noble young man whose morning sun shone so bright with rich promise. Who of us has not seen this young man in his pride, who of us has not gazed with horror on his awful ruins? He is seen everywhere, every town, village, neighborhood has seen him and mourned over his dark and melancholy end.

Take one view more. Enter the house where lately dwelt youth, beauty, and all the pleasures of life. Look at that half famished female, brooding in silence over her ruined fortunes, and her blasted hopes; at her half naked and half famished children, calling in vain for a father's care. That wife has seen better days. It was a bright sun that rose on her bridal morn. Her heart beat high as she pronounced her marriage vows. There she sits in sorrow, waiting the return of him who should have cherished her with an affection which slumbers not. Yet he comes not.

> She has "watched the moon go down,
> But yet he comes not. Once it was not so.
> He thinks not how her bitter tears do flow
> The while he holds his riot in the town."[3]

She sits patient, meek; but she feels that keen anguish which only woman can feel; she feels the loss of lover, husband, friend. She looks upon her children as worse than fatherless; upon herself as worse than widowed. All that can kindle a smile is gone; the heart is broken, a rude hand has snapped its cords, she is a lone, withered thing.

---

[3][Ed. Not able to identify quotation.]

Mark her well, young man, and dash the poisoned chalice from thy lips.

I need not pursue the picture, you have all seen the one from whom I drew it. We have all seen the wife ruined by the drunken husband; and, not infrequently, by his cruelty, brought to an untimely grave. We have seen her die, and leave her helpless offspring to—I will not proceed. I know too well to what are left the children of drunkards. I know too well that the father's sins are visited upon his innocent but wretched offspring.[4]

Is there no way to prevent the immoderate use of ardent spirits? This is the question which now most interests us. Time has been when I should have answered this question differently from what I now shall. Some years since, I was ready to engage in any plan which promised any extensive reformation of society. Then I never doubted success. Then I did not dream that the cause of truth and humanity must quail before haughty vice. Much of my young enthusiasm has left me; and though I abate nothing in my good wishes, repeated disappointments have taught me to expect little. He who labors to reform mankind, labors in a noble cause, but in one from which he will receive few thanks. "Mankind," says the Spanish proverb, "is an ass, that kicks the one who attempts to take off his panniers." No matter. We should not cease to do good because our labors are not as successful as we could wish. I am bound to say I do not believe it possible, at once, to check the immoderate use of ardent spirit. Drunkenness will survive this generation. Individuals, much less nations, cannot change their habits at once. We cannot command the concurrence of all the necessary causes. Physical obstacles may be overcome, while moral ones remain. The moral strength of our countrymen, I fear, is too weak to effect the reform needed. Still we may do much and if we cannot now prevent intemperance entirely, we may put into operation a set of causes, which will finally prove sufficient.

But allow me to say that if we mean to do anything we must act. Mere talk will not do away intemperance. We must act; we must put our shoulder to the wheel if we would recover it from the rut.

But what shall we do? What *can* we do? We cannot cure all drunkards for many of them are past cure. We cannot do a great deal even for the adult portion of our present population. Our labors must be

[4][Ed. This reference is an echo of Exod 34:7, " . . . visiting the iniquity of the fathers upon the children . . . ." Brownson may also be referring to his own father here. He rarely, almost never, mentions his father in his numerous autobiographical allusions in his writings.]

prospective. But if we will act we may do much to prevent the rising generation from becoming drunkards.

How? By the force of public opinion. I have spoken of the power of fashion. We must direct that power against the use of ardent spirit. We must make everyone feel that, in taking a glass of rum, he is as much out of the fashion as a lady would be who should put on the high heeled shoes of our great grandmothers. Fashion will accomplish more than all the admonitions of the physician, the solemn warnings from the pulpit, than the affectionate counsels and entreaties of parents and friend. Bring fashion to bear on those who resort to the bottle, and, though at first some few may bid defiance, it will soon prove all powerful.

But how shall we thus direct fashion, how bring public opinion to bear directly on this point? Public opinion is now too weak on this point—how shall we strengthen it? By association, by joining, if you please, a temperance society. There is no other effectual way to call out and direct public opinion. When you join a temperance society you give your names, your characters, your influence, to make up and direct that public opinion you wish. Let nine-tenths of the people of this town join, and think you the other tenth would not be ashamed to take its glass? Would not this shame form a sufficient restraint in a great majority of cases? We make it disreputable to use ardent spirits, and we prevent its use by all who regard public opinion.

But some have objections to temperance societies.[5] They think they should degrade themselves should they sign a pledge. They can keep sober without binding themselves not to drink. This is a wrong view. We believe men have something of benevolence, and we ask them to come forward, not to aid those who can, but those who cannot, govern themselves. We know there are those who cannot govern themselves, and we appeal to the benevolent that they join with us, that we all unite to dart moral energy into the weak, and empower them to keep their resolutions to abstain. The intemperate should join that they may have an additional motive to become temperate, and the temperate should join that they may give their aid and the full force of their example to the intemperate.

But some do not like the manner in which temperance societies are conducted. I own I have been one of this number. But I have seen

---

[5][Ed. Later in his life Brownson vigorously opposed temperance societies because they tried to use legislation to prohibit intemperance. He saw their tactics as a form of "social despotism." On this, see "Liberalism and Socialism" (April, 1855) in *Works* 10:542, and "The Church and the Republic" (July, 1856) in ibid., 12:10-12.]

the good that they have done. I have traveled over a large portion of our country both before and since the establishment of temperance societies, and I am constrained to admit that with all their objections, they have done much for society. This admission is extorted from me, for I am opposed to self-created societies in general. I do not like the machinery put into operation by this wonder working age. We have too many wheels within wheels, too many governments within governments. The age tends too much to association; people are beginning to act only in crowds, and the individual is fast being lost in the mass.

Still the present is an extreme case and after some years' hesitation, and extensive observation, I have resolved to give to the temperance society my full and cordial support. The case is urgent; something must be done; nothing better has been devised; I am unable to devise anything better, and I feel bound by all my duties as a father, a neighbor, a Christian, a patriot and a man to do all I can in aid of societies pledged to total abstinence.

Besides, in joining a temperance society, we become responsible only for the one we join. We join the Walpole Temperance Society. It is in our own town, its operations are under our own control, subject to no foreign dominion. All parties support it, and really I see nothing to fear from it. Divided as we are in religious belief, in political and other interests, it is refreshing to have one topic on which we can unite, to find one spot, where we can meet on common ground, and unite, heart and hand, in a good cause. We keep too far apart. We should love each other better would we meet oftener, and we should find a better spirit within us, would we oftener find a point of union and more frequently act together.

Some, perhaps, would readily join could they obtain the hired help they need without furnishing ardent spirit. To these, I wish to put a few plain questions: Do you believe it is of any real advantage to your hired man to drink ardent spirit? Do you think that it promotes his health, makes him more faithful to himself, really more happy? Have you not known many a young man become a drunkard from the habit acquired in the haying or harvest field? Is it not your deliberate opinion that your hired men would be far better off so far as themselves are concerned were they to practice on the principle of total abstinence? How then can you reconcile it to your consciences to furnish that to your hired men which does them no good, and which may do them great, irretrievable injury?

Again, are those hired men who use ardent spirits really the best workmen? I would ask our farmers if they usually find them more moral, more upright, more industrious than those who do not use them? Would you deem a bottle of rum in your meadow, a good security that your hay would be well made, well secured, and without waste? I believe the experience of our farmers is the reverse of this supposition. Then you gain nothing by furnishing your hired men with ardent spirit; they gain nothing and why furnish it? From my observation, it is an injury to the employer, and I know it is an injury to those employed, and I know not how a good Christian man can reconcile himself to the practice.

But I am told, "we cannot get help, unless we furnish ardent spirit." With your leave, my friends, I do not believe this, and even if true, have you a right for the sake of money to do that which shall corrupt, or be the occasion of corrupting the morals of your fellow beings? I have heard many a man make this objection before, but, although I have conversed with hundreds of wealthy farmers, I never knew one to make the objection, after he had fairly tried the experiment. Just try it, try it faithfully, one year, and if you cannot get along without rum, go back to your old practice, if conscience will allow. I put it to the good sense and to the good feelings of our farmers, if they should not make the trial and I have too high an opinion of their love of temperance, and of their regard for the well being of their hired men, to believe that they will not. I put it to their patriotism, I put it, if need be, to their generosity.

Some will still object to *total* abstinence. On this I have little to say. We know intemperance is a horrid monster; we know that a large number have no power to govern themselves, and it really seems to me it is due from us, who call ourselves temperate, to abstain entirely for the benefit of those who cannot control their appetite. The temperate drinker is the germ of the drunkard, for no one commences with being a drunkard at first. He who drinks no ardent spirit is safe; therefore, let us "taste not, touch not, handle not."

What, permit me in conclusion to ask, remains for us, but to act? And why do we hesitate? Are we called to undertake some hazardous enterprise, to expose our lives, our characters, or our property? Nothing of this. We are required only to abstain from that which can do us no good, and may do us immense injury. We are called upon barely to write our names, and to write them where it can do us no harm, but where it may be of immense good to us and to our fellow-beings, for time and for eternity.

Fathers! Look on your sons. Do your hearts beat proudly as you see yourselves living anew in them, and do you raise your prayers to heaven for their prosperity? Do then all in your power to remove the temptations they have to become drunkards. Mothers! Look on your daughters. Would you that they become wedded to drunken husbands, be compelled to pine in secret, to wither, and die, unfriended and unwept, while they who should shield them from every blast, by an affection never failing, quaff ruin and death in the tavern or grocery? O, lend us then your influence.

I appeal to the Christian, whose first duty is self-denial; I ask him while he prays that he may not be "led into temptation," to beware how he places a temptation to sin before his brother.

I appeal to the patriot, to him who loves his country, and who knows that without virtue liberty is but a dream; I entreat him to give his name and his influence to arrest the vice which corrupts even the body politic. I appeal to the philanthropist. I appeal to you all, I entreat you by all that is sacred in religion; by all that is binding in human duty; by all your love for your children; by all your desires for human happiness; by all your regard for your country; by your hopes of heaven and by your fears of hell, that you engage in this great cause with earnestness, and that you give to it your names, your influence, and your whole hearts.

27.

FAITH AND WORKS

Christian Register 12 (May 11, 1833): 73

"Not of works lest any man should boast" Paul [Eph 2:9]. "Ye see then how a man is justified by works, and not by faith only" James [2:24].

I have brought these two passages, one from Paul and the other from James together, because they are apparently contradictory and because the subject they involve requires elucidation.

Whatever tends to throw light upon the Scriptures, to obviate objections which may be urged against their lessons and to exhibit the true grounds of salvation can never be uninteresting to the Christian, to the philosopher, or to the moralist.

The passage from Paul seems to teach that works are no ground of acceptance with God; the one from James plainly asserts that works are the main, if not the only, grounds on which we can rest for justification. Two difficulties occur: one, the intrinsic objections to the doctrine usually ascribed to Paul; the other, the apparent collision between two inspired apostles.

The doctrine usually ascribed to Paul, is at war with the holiness of God, with the freedom of man, and with sound morals.

If God be holy, he must be pleased with holiness, and must demand it in his creatures. He can never approve my conduct unless it be good, nor justify me unless I am holy. Holiness is the soul in action, directing all its powers to accomplish wise and noble ends. To be holy, we must exert ourselves, we must employ all the faculties given us. This *we* must do. God cannot do it for us. Should he direct all our faculties aright and make us the passive instruments of performing all the works which holiness demands, he would perform those works, not we; and the holiness would attach to him, not to us. He cannot make us holy without the concurrence of our own wills. Should he disregard our actions and accept us while we were not practically good, he would accept the unholy, and thus show he does not demand holiness in his creatures, which would argue a want of holiness in himself.

Were the Deity, supposing it possible, to make us holy, by some sovereign display of his Almighty power, it would be destroying our freedom and converting us into mere machines. I will not plunge my readers into abstract reasoning, nor bewilder them in the mazes of metaphysics. Still I may add that I view with suspicion every doctrine which destroys man's free agency. Every man feels that he has a certain degree of natural liberty, that he may do whatever he please, when not prevented by some physical obstruction or by some foreign power. And I am sure the Scriptures, recognize this freedom, as plainly as they recognize anything whatever.

If Scripture have any truth, and man's conscience be deserving any confidence, we are accountable beings, and must, soon or late, render to God an account for all we have thought, said, or done, and receive according to our deeds; if good, justification; if bad, condemnation. But, if man be a mere machine that moves but as the sovereign power of the Deity moves it, passive at all times and in all places, where is the ground of accountability? Obedience in such case, is but the regular motion of the sun, and disobedience, no more deserving punishment than the earthquake, or an eruption of Ætna or Vesuvius.

If man be endowed with the liberty of choosing and acting for himself, the Deity must leave him to determine for himself, whether he will obey and be happy, or whether he will disobey and be miserable. If his will be controlled, his natural liberty destroyed, and he forced into holiness, his constitution is violated, and he is, in effect, annihilated. The Deity, then, must justify him while he is unholy, or he must annihilate him, or he must leave him to his own freedom to repent and be accepted, or to continue his wickedness and be punished. This last is the only course consistent with man's freedom, notwithstanding it may be contrary to the passage quoted from Paul.

But admitting that works are not necessary to our salvation, that man is passive not active in the reception of holiness, the doctrine can never be reconciled to sound morals. Every man should feel that he is responsible for his conduct, or he will not be very scrupulous as to what he does. It will hardly arrest the vicious, or check the flow of crime, to teach that all things and all actions are of Divine appointment; still less will it advance the cause of just morals to allege on the authority of revelation that our works have nothing to do with our happiness or misery hereafter, that God saves or condemns without any reference to character. It will hardly aid the moralist to allege that God will save the vile, the criminal, the abandoned, as soon as he will the pure in heart or the just in life. He who thus alleges opens the flood-gates to iniquity.

I know that it is said that "we are saved by grace," "through faith," "not of ourselves," by the "gift of God" [Eph 2:8], that "by the deeds of the law shall no flesh be justified" [Rom 3:20], that "Christ is the end of the law to everyone that believeth" [Rom 10:4]. It is true that these passages and many others, detached from their connection, do seem to indicate that the wicked as well as the righteous, may hope for heaven; but who does not know that such a doctrine must fall like a paralytic shock upon man's powers and make him believe that it matters not what he does?

There have been in all ages of the church those who have drawn this doctrine from the writings of Paul; we have them now, contending for unconditional election and reprobation; and those, too, who aiming at a more[1] human[2] scheme, extend the election to the whole human family, and bid us all hope for happiness as soon as we enter the resurrection world, whatever be our moral character here, alleging that eternal felicity is the gift of God, made sure to all by the death of Jesus Christ. The first class are rapidly receding before the lights of science and humanity, whilst the latter are rising into notice and boldly challenging consideration. In this case, the language of James is appropriate, "What doth it profit, my brethren, that a man say he have faith and not works, can faith save him" [James 2:14]? "Ye see, then, how a man is justified by works, and not by faith only" [James 2:24]. James, by no means, allows a man to hope for salvation without works. He requires us to be "doers," as well as "hearers" of the law, and he plainly teaches us that Abraham and all the ancient worthies were justified by their works. Are James and Paul at issue?

NO. 2 (May 25, 1833): 82

I ended my last with the question, are Paul and James at issue? I answer, by no means. Paul condemns works, but not works of righteousness, not works of charity, justice and humanity; but works of the old Hebrew law, its washings, penances, oblations of fruits; its sin offerings, its peace offerings—its long and fatiguing rites and ceremonies.

It is matter of regret that people do not read the Bible with more attention. It is necessary that they advert to the connection of a passage, ascertain the occasion on which it was written, to whom written, and with what design. Most of the writings of Paul, were controversial, drawn forth by the disputes which agitated the primitive be-

[1][Ed. Originally "mere." Brownson corrected to "more" in *Christian Register* 12 (May 25, 1833): 82.]
[2][Ed. Originally "humane." Brownson corrected to "human" in *Christian Register* 12 (May 25, 1833): 82.]

lievers. The most prominent, as well as the earliest, of these disputes, was that which raged between the Judaizing converts and their more spiritual opponents.

The apostles did not obtain a complete view of the gospel system at once. Their knowledge of it was progressive. At first, they supposed it confined to the Jewish nation; and in the commencement of their labors, they did not dream of departing from the Jewish law, much less of making converts from the Gentile world. This is evident from Peter's hesitation to visit Cornelius; and still more from the treatment he received from the rest of the apostles, till he related, at large, the circumstances, which induced him to visit and baptize that centurion and his family. It was not till these circumstances transpired, that the apostles learned that God would receive the Gentiles as well as the Jews; and it was not till then that any of them could say, "Of a truth I perceive God is no respecter of persons; but, in every nation he that feareth God and worketh righteousness, is accepted with him" [Acts 10:34-35].

After this the gospel was preached to the Gentiles and principally by Paul, a recent convert, and his associates. As Gentile converts multiplied, it became a question, whether they were bound to obey the Jewish law. The question was submitted to the council of apostles at Jerusalem and decided in the negative. Still, the Jewish converts were not satisfied. They gave the Gentile believers much trouble; and, in several instances, drew them away from Paul who maintained the nullity of the Jewish law.

To silence the objections of the Judaizing Christians and to win over others of his countrymen, Paul made use of three different arguments: 1. the sufficiency of the gospel; 2. its priority, and 3. the inadequacy of the Mosaic law.

1. The whole law, that is the moral law, the spirit of the Mosaic law, or the thing really intended by it, was fulfilled by one word, love, and as the gospel most assuredly enjoined love, it was sufficient. But the Jew was not satisfied with this. He could not look from the letter of his law to its spirit. His notions of religion were, in general, very different from ours. He understood by religion the worship of God and by the worship of God the observance of the mosaic ritual. He either did not know or did not believe that God would pardon the sinner on the simple condition of his ceasing to sin. If one sinned, he supposed God would ask something besides reformation, that he would require a sin offering, the sacrifice of a lamb or a goat, to make satisfaction for the offence and to smooth the way for future acceptance.

Paul, if I understand his reasoning, does not affirm or deny this belief of the Jew. He adapts the economical method of argument, and concedes to him for the time being all but the single point he was laboring to make out. He asserts as does also the writer of the Epistle to the Hebrews, that whatever atonement was needed for sin, the same had been obtained by the death of Jesus: and that, if, as it was then believed, "there is no remission of sins without the shedding of blood" [Heb 9:22], the blood of Jesus had been shed and that is enough. He pursues his argument; if as they supposed, through the offence of one, Adam, the many be dead, then, through the obedience of one, the Christ, the many are made alive; if, as they supposed, judgement had come upon all men unto condemnation, so had the free gift come upon all men unto justification of life; that is, through the gospel, all who are just may be justified, notwithstanding the damage it was supposed Adam's transgression had done, which damage it was supposed could be done away only by sacrifice and offering.

Hence in whatever light the gospel was viewed, it was sufficient. It enjoined love, that is real goodness, spiritual perfection, and this was enough to fulfil the whole law. If sacrifice and offering were requisite, Christ had been offered up, his blood had been shed, whatever difficulties were in the way, or supposed to be in the way, they were removed by what Jesus had done, and the Jew might rest assured that he who should possess the religion of Jesus would be accepted, though not an observer of the Jewish ceremonial law.

2. Paul took high ground, and declared "Christ is the end of the law to everyone that believeth" [Rom 10:4]—end of the Jewish ceremonial law. He assumes the gospel to be prior to the law and that it places man back in the condition Abraham was in before the law was given. The Christian is not justified with Moses, but with Abraham, and the patriarchs who lived before the giving of the law from Mount Sinai. In a word, he taught that the gospel was but a renewal of God's covenant with Abraham, or more intelligibly, but the revival of the same religion which was embraced by Abraham. Now, as this religion was confirmed, by the oath of Jehovah, in which it was impossible for God to lie, and as the promise was to Abraham and his seed forever, the Apostle contends that the introduction of the Mosaic law, four hundred and thirty years after could not make it void or of none effect.

This religion which Paul was preaching and which the Gentiles believed was not the Mosaic law, was not a new religion but the same as that held by Abraham and the patriarchs of old. "For" Paul alleges, "the Scriptures foreseeing that God would justify the heathen through faith (or by *the* faith, that is in accordance with principles of Christianity) preached before or aforetime, the Gospel unto Abraham" Gal. 3:8. "You Jews," Paul would say, "impose upon us your law, and tell us that without keeping all its precepts and observing all its ceremonies, we cannot be justified in the sight of God; but you are wrong; by embracing the religion of Jesus we come into the covenant, or religion, of Abraham, and stand on the same ground we should, had your law never been given. By believing in Christ or by embracing Christianity, we are translated from your kingdom of darkness into the kingdom of God's dear Son, and are therefore free from your law. Those of us who were born Jews were bound to obey your law while we continued unbelievers simply because we were Jews; but your law is annulled in everyone that believes and as we believe we are not bound to keep it. The Gentiles, as having never been of the congregation of Jacob, and only becoming Christians they come into the religion of Abraham, not under the law of Moses, of course were not bound to observe it."[3] This argument rests on the supposed difference between the law and the gospel. The gospel is only another name for that religion which was embraced by Abraham. This was prior to the law and being prior to the distinctions in mankind made by the law, the Jew must necessarily admit it equally binding upon all men. This was in fact a natural religion; of course equally obligatory in all ages, in all climes and upon all individuals. The law was a positive institution, founded on arbitrary distinctions, and was in its very nature of limited extent. To make the law superior to the gospel and binding upon Christians were as incorrect as it would be to deprive a son of his inheritance, and to give it to a slave or the son of a bond-woman. The gospel was the elder religion, was that which had a natural right to men's homage; the law from Sinai, was only a servant, the son of a bond-woman, and must give place to the rightful heir. But enough till my next.

NO. 3 (June 1, 1833): 85-86

3. The law was inadequate. The blood of bulls, of rams, and of goats, was unable to wash away sin. The most punctilious observance of the ceremonial worship, enjoined by the Mosaic law, could not make atonement for transgression—could not make "the comers thereunto perfect" [Heb 10:1]. God demanded holiness of life, purity of heart, and a spiritual worship. But these the law could not

---

[3][Ed. Quotation mark inserted here. In original the quotation marks were not closed.]

give. It was powerless as pertained to the affections and the conscience. Therefore "God condemned sin in the flesh, through Christ" [Rom 8:3], that is condemned or abolished the sin of breaking that fleshly or outward law—the sin of neglecting a sensual, external, carnal ritual by abrogating the law which enjoined it.

We cannot now mistake Paul's reasoning. As the Jewish law was so inadequate, as its observance was so inefficacious in perfecting the human character, as he proved it to be, it was evident that by "its deeds could no flesh be justified" [Rom 3:20]. God will justify no man till he is just. The observance of all the external duties enjoined by the law did not constitute one just, therefore it was useless to depend for justification in the sight of God on the righteousness which was by the law enjoining only an outward sanctuary and only outward worship.

By the "deeds of the law," and by the "works" against which Paul reasons, we are to understand the ceremonial worship enjoined by the old Hebrew law. Now, the performance of this worship did not, could not, constitute a man righteous. Righteousness implies purity of heart, and usefulness of life; but a man could do all this Mosaic law enjoined, and still be a wicked man. He could offer a lamb, or a goat, he could observe[4] the appointed fasts, and feasts; he could perform[5] all the acts of worship made obligatory while murder was rankling in his heart, and his hands were red with his brother's blood. The righteousness of the law, then was too low; it was wholly external and might be possessed by the greatest sinner. It was, therefore, philosophically as well as religiously, true, that "by the deeds of the law no flesh could be justified."

The question between Paul and the Jews was a question between an inward, spiritual worship, and the mere external worship established by the law of Moses. He does not question the propriety of the law itself in its proper place, and when duly restricted in its operations, but he teaches something more than that external round of duties is required; that the heart should be right, and that no sacrifice and offering, no attendance upon an outward sanctuary, no punctilious observance of set forms and set days, and set ceremonies, can render one acceptable to God unless he has the spiritual religion of Jesus; and if one have that spiritual religion, he contends it is enough, without having the righteousness which is by that ceremonial law.

---

[4][Ed. Brownson replaced "abuse" with "observe." See *Christian Register* 12 (June 15, 1833): 93.]

[5][Ed. Brownson replaced "profane" with "perform." See ibid.]

Common sense may teach us Paul was correct in principle. When the Reformation commenced in Germany, the Reformers declaimed against the "dead works" of the Roman Catholics, not against their deeds of benevolence, justice and mercy, but against the rites and ceremonies of the church. When the Society of Friends commenced their labors to reform even the reformers, they bore testimony against external worship as they found it among Protestants, and declared for a purely spiritual worship in opposition to it. No great and good minister of the church has ever failed to warn people against forms and external ordinances. Why? Because the *form* is very different from the *power* of godliness; because attention to the externals of religion is often mistaken for religion itself; because the wise and the good, the spiritually minded value only that which is real, and are willing to spend no time in wedding people to that which is not in itself good, and the observance of which does not necessarily make the observer better.

I mean not to condemn external worship; but I do mean to say he who expects heaven merely because he has joined the church, because he prays, sings psalms, goes to meeting and is strict to observe all the forms of religion, leans upon a broken staff, and encourages vain hopes. The greatest sinner in the community may join the church; the worst villain that preys upon society may profess to be religious, may go through with all the forms of prayer and religious worship, and remain a villain as he began. He only can go to heaven, or rather possess heaven, who is in his heart pure and benevolent, and in his conduct just and useful. God is not deceived; no professions, no pretenses, no forms, no substitutes will pass with him for the real possession of goodness. He will dispense heaven to none who are not practically holy.

This was Paul's doctrine. This was the great, the leading principle of the gospel. This distinguished Christianity from all other religion which had ever been proclaimed. The Jew fancied he had in the "dead works" enjoined by his law a substitute for real holiness; or rather he had no higher ideas of righteousness than the observance of his long fatiguing ritual. In this he and Paul were at issue. Paul required him to be spiritually minded, to value things according to their real worth, and to consider himself acceptable to God, not for the multitude of his sacrifices and offerings, but because he was good in himself and because he did good. This is a great truth, and one, obvious as it is, which was then, and is too often even now overlooked. The Jews were gross, sensual, in their conceptions of religion, making it entirely an external thing. Not a few subject themselves to the same charge even now. People, in a religious point of view, deem him who neglects a prayer far more remiss in his duty than he is who forgets to "visit the fatherless and the widows in their afflictions" [James 1:27], and him who cannot relate a marvelous experience than he who fails to "do justly, to love mercy, and to walk humbly" [Mic 6:8]. We are still sensual, still looking for substitutes for religion, and building our hopes of heaven on something besides the possession of moral goodness. If we, at this comparatively enlightened age of the world are guilty of this charge what must it have been with the bigoted Jew? It was absolutely necessary, if he would have him embrace a spiritual religion, for Paul to rebuke him often and severely for depending on his idolized retreat for salvation. It was no easy matter to correct his mistake; no easy matter to induce him to look to the spirit, and become spiritual in his conceptions of religion, and spiritual in the worship he rendered to his God. Thence the frequency with which Paul alludes to this subject, the pointed manner in which he condemns those outward works on which the Jew then depended, and the earnestness with which he urges the spirituality of religion. "To be carnally minded," that is, to have the mind wholly bent on the gross external worship enjoined by the law, "is death": "to be spiritually minded is life" [Rom 6:8]. "The letter killeth" [2 Cor 3:6]. He who depended entirely on that outward worship could have no life. The worship itself was deadening to the soul, repressing every pious aspiration. "The spirit giveth life" [2 Cor 3:6]. He who can look through the letter to the spirit, who can see what the law really intends, and what is that inward perfection God demands, finds something quickening, something which kindles the flame of devotion and imparts real life to the soul.

It was, then, that long fatiguing ritual, that "hand writing of ordinances" [Col 2:14], that "letter" which drew off the mind from the spirit and the life of virtue, that disposition to rely on external instead of internal worship of God which Paul condemned. This was declared to be in itself of no use, and the Jewish converts were rebuked for valuing themselves as better than others, because they performed the outward services here implied and admonished not to impose them upon the gentile believers.

If I am right thus far, good works instead of being condemned by the gospel are by it declared to be the only ground of our acceptance with God. Is this true? If so, why is the gospel called the faith? And why is faith said to be the procuring cause of our salvation?

NO. 4 (June 15, 1833): 93-94

If the reasoning of my last two numbers be correct, the gospel knows no other ground of acceptance with God than good works, or in other words, real moral goodness. On this point the language of Scripture is express. "When the Son of man shall come in his glory, then shall he reward every man according to his *works*" [Matt 16:27]. "We must all appear before the judgement seat of Christ, and receive according to the *deeds* done in the body" [2 Cor 5:10]. "They that have *done* good shall come forth to the resurrection of life; they that have *done* evil shall come forth to the resurrection of condemnation" [John 5:29]. "Then shall the King say unto those on his right hand, Come ye blessed of my Father" [Matt 25:34]. Why? Because they had clothed the naked, fed the hungry, given drink to the thirsty, visited the sick, and relieved the prisoner. "Then shall he say unto them on his left hand, Depart ye cursed" [Matt 25:41]—Why? Because they had done good works? No, because they had not done them. What mean these passages if they do not mean that men are judged by their works, accepted if their works are good, rejected if they are bad. "If thou doest well, shalt not be accepted; And if thou doest not well, sin lieth at the door" [Gen 4:7]. "Say ye to the righteous that it shall be well with them, for they shall eat the fruits of their doings. Woe unto the wicked! It shall be ill with him, for the reward of his hands shall be given him" [Isa 3:11].

Jesus was predicted under the character of a reformer. He was sent to "set judgement (justice) in the earth," he was to be a "Prince of peace" [Isa 9:6], a "Prince to reign in *righteousness*" [Isa 32:1], he was spoken of under the figure of the sun, the "Sun of righteousness" [Mal 4:2]; his very name, Jesus, was given him because he should save his people from their *sins*, and "him God raised up that he might bless mankind," "by turning them away from their *iniquities*" [Acts 3:26]. He came the model and the producer of righteousness. He preached, suffered, submitted to the cross, that he "might bring us to God" [1 Pet 3:18], that is, make us morally good. The "Grace of God" which was manifested by him, "which bringeth salvation," and "which hath appeared unto all men" [Titus 2:12], teaches us, as the ground of that salvation, that we should "deny ourselves of all ungodliness and worldly lust, and live soberly, righteously and godly in this present world." Indeed, "What doth the Lord require of us, but to do justly, to love mercy, and to walk humbly with our God" [Mic 6:8]? And if this be what he requires of us, and if, as Jesus says, the whole law and the prophets be comprised in loving God with all the heart and our neighbor as we do ourselves, who will say that really good works are not sufficient to procure us salvation?

I know it is said that we are saved by the merits of Christ, but I also know, that however great may be the merits of Christ, the Scriptures promise no salvation to him who is not personally holy. "Without holiness shall no man see the Lord" [Heb 12:14]. I own we are saved by the merits of Christ. I own that we are saved by his righteousness; but how? Will the fact that Jesus had merits save me, if I have no merits of my own? Certainly not. Will the fact that Jesus was righteous save me, if I am not righteous? Will God impute the righteousness of Jesus to me, and treat me as though that righteousness were mine, while in my own character I am a sinner? God is a God of truth. He cannot call me righteous when I am not righteous, without speaking falsely. The fact that Jesus was righteous does not make me righteous, and I dare not charge Heaven with the false logic of inferring from that fact that I am.

Jesus was righteous. His righteousness was of the true spiritual kind. It was not the righteousness which came by obedience to a ceremonial law, but by obedience to the law of right which was from the beginning, the law anterior to all other laws, the law of eternal justice, which as Marcus Antoninus hath well observed, "binds both God and men."[6]

Now, this righteousness, this which Jesus had, and which constituted him the spiritual Son of God, exceeded the righteousness of the Scribes and Pharisees. It was of the true sort; no man who did not possess it, could be righteous in the sight of God. All other kinds of righteousness, such as obedience to positive institutions, as the observance of arbitrary rites, the adherence to an outward sanctuary like that of Moses, were not genuine, were not such as God would own. Hence it was strictly, religiously and philosophically true that no one could be saved, except by the righteousness of Christ, that is, without possessing in himself, that same sort of righteousness, which Jesus possessed in himself, and of which he gave us an example in his life.

As Christ enjoined this righteousness, as he exhibited it in his life, it was called *his*, and as no one could be saved without possessing it, it came to be said "we are saved by the righteousness, or the mer-

[6][Ed. Brownson is probably referring to Marcus Aurelius Antoninus (121-80), Roman Emperor from 161. The quotation appears to be a paraphrase of *The Meditations*, 8.2: "What more do I seek, if what I am now doing is work of an intelligent living being, and a social being, and one who is under the same law with God?"]

its, of Christ" [Titus 3:5]. We must indeed have those merits, they must be ours, or we can have no rational hope of salvation. This is what is meant by having that mind in us which was in him, by having "the spirit of Christ" [Rom 8:9], without which we are none of his, and with which there can be to us no condemnation. We are to become Christ-like, to imitate him, to be "perfect as he was perfect" [Matt 5:8], to "be sons of God, and joint heirs with him" [Rom 8:17]. No one can doubt that when we become Christ-like, we become sure of salvation. Jesus "went about doing good" [Acts 10:38], and how except in the possession of a holy spirit and in the performance of good works, can we be like him? It is true the righteousness of Christ is that which saves; but it saves us only as we possess it, become righteous in the same sense in which he was. And as nobody can deny that his righteousness consisted in good works, why may I not say good works are a ground, are the only ground, of our acceptance with God? "Ye see then, brethren, how that a man is justified by works and not by faith only" [James 2:24].

But if this be true, why was the Gospel called the *faith*, why were people exhorted to *believe* it, and why were the primitive disciples called *believers*? I answer this in my next.

NO. 5 (June 29, 1833): 101-2

I think I have sufficiently proved that the gospel is not a system of belief but a system of moral or spiritual righteousness, and that we are saved by good works, not merely by just belief. But it is evident that Christianity is spoken of in Scripture as "the faith," those who embrace it are called "believers," the just are said to live by "faith," and all are called upon to "repent and *believe* the Gospel" [Mark 1:15]. Is it not then true that the gospel was something to be believed?

The limits to which a newspaper essay necessarily confines me, prevent me from giving as full an answer to this question as it deserves. I own Christ and the apostles did call upon the Jews and the gentiles to believe the gospel; but did they call upon them to believe the gospel itself was a system of belief? Did they call upon them to believe that the gospel was composed of a series of articles of faith, the belief in which was essential to salvation?

Let us begin with what Jesus required those to whom he preached should believe. "He that believeth on the Son hath everlasting life; and he that believeth not the Son shall not see life" [John 3:36]. It is certain that the Jews were required to believe on Jesus, to believe in the Son; but shall we stop here? What was meant by believing on the Son? What was meant, or should be meant, by belief in Jesus? "That he was the Messiah," answers one. What Messiah? The Jewish Messiah, the one the Jewish people expected? That were a false belief, for he was not that Messiah. The Jews expected a temporal prince, a king, one who would redeem them from vassalage, restore them to national independence, and raise their kingdom to the highest pitch of human glory. Now he was not that Messiah, and consequently he could not require them to believe that he was. What Messiah then? The one predicted by the Jewish prophets? In one sense, no. The literal interpretation of the Jewish prophets promises such a Messiah as the Jewish people expected. I am aware that I touch a delicate subject; but it must be touched, not with a rash, but a fearless hand. If I am wrong, Scripture and reason are free to correct me, and truth has nothing to fear from falsehood in an open field and fair encounter.

I say, then, the literal interpretation of the Jewish Scriptures authorized the expectation of a temporal prince. The passages usually alleged as predictions of Jesus seem to me to describe a very different personage from him, the unostentatious Nazarene, the humble preacher of righteousness. I therefore do not believe that Jesus was the Messiah in the sense in which it is commonly supposed he was, and of course I cannot admit that he required the people of his times so to believe.

But, let no one be alarmed; my heterodoxy *may* become Orthodox, certainly will, when it becomes uppermost. It cannot fail to strike those who study the Scriptures carefully, who are able to look from the "letter" to the "spirit," that what is affirmed of Jesus, of "the Son," of "the Christ," is not to be understood as if it was affirmed of the literal man, the man Jesus after the flesh, but of the spirit which was in him, of the moral excellence, the spiritual worth, the divinity, which he manifested. Now, no man, who knows anything about the nature of moral goodness, and the operations of the mind in the simple act of believing, can for one moment, suppose, that merely believing Jesus was the Messiah, or the Son of God, can give one spiritual life, or that one should be deprived of life because he does not so believe.

Consider the phrases "Son of God," "the Christ," as designating the spirit of Jesus, the moral perfections which he exhibited, and we can easily ascertain what the Jews of his day were called upon to believe. One idea of "Son" is likeness to the "Father." This likeness may be physical, or it may be moral, that is, spiritual. In this latter sense only can we understand any created being as bearing a likeness to God. The sonship of Jesus, then, was moral, spiritual, consisting in his possessing those same moral perfections which belong to God.

He had the spirit of God, was led by that spirit, and we know "as many as are led by the spirit of God, are the sons of God" [Rom 8:14]. So far as we are led by that spirit, we are the sons of God in the same sense he was, and in the language of Paul were "joint heirs with him" [Rom 8:17].

Now, what were these moral, or spiritual excellencies which Jesus possessed, which constituted his sonship or spiritual likeness to God? The story of his life will answer. They were purity, benevolence, moral firmness, expressed in one word, holiness. God is love; Jesus manifested the same perfection. God is good; he delights to communicate goodness; that same may be affirmed of Jesus. God seeks the happiness of all his children so far as that happiness is compatible with the constitution he has given them; Jesus labored for the good, for the happiness of those same children, the offspring of God, preached, suffered and died, that he might effect their salvation. In a word, there was between him and God a oneness of principle, a harmony of design, a will to effect the same benevolent results.

What did he teach? That no one could be acceptable to God, no one could be saved from sin, who did not possess this same moral likeness to God, this same spiritual worth, who had not a heart to love what God loves, and inward firmness enough to resolve and to labor to effect what he knows is in accordance with the will of God; and furthermore, he taught that whoever had this inward firmness, and this spiritual righteousness, this moral likeness to God, was saved from sin, was a son of God, and might hope for happiness, whether Jew or gentile, whether he conformed to those systems of righteousness then predominant or not. This spiritual perfection constituted an internal sonship, was an "unction" an inward "anointing from the Holy One," was "the Christ formed within, the hope of glory" [Col 1:27]. I say this was what Jesus taught, though I own I have borrowed in some instances from the language of his apostles; but this can be no objection, for his teaching and theirs is supposed to be in perfect harmony.

This internal, ethical sonship, this inward Christ, this moral perfection, this spiritual righteousness which was one with the righteousness of the Father, was the Messiah in which they were called to believe, was what they were called upon to possess, and they were called upon to believe that it was necessary for them to possess this and only this in order to be saved. I do not find that Jesus ever pretended to any other Messiahship than the one here implied, nor that his apostles after his resurrection, after they had given up their notions of a Jewish Messiah, a temporal prince, ever claim anything more for him, nor that they enjoin any other belief than the one here stated.

But, how did Jesus maintain, or support his claims to this Messiahship? By his own works and by an appeal to the Jewish Scriptures. "If I do not the works of my Father believe me not" [John 10:38]. That is, if I do not such works as show the likeness of that righteousness I require you to possess, to the righteousness of the Father, believe me, trust me not. He appealed to their own sense of right. "Why even of yourselves judge ye not what is right" [Luke 12:57]. Even of yourselves you may perceive this kind of righteousness, this spiritual perfection which I enjoin, has a likeness to the perfection of God. Look around you, look within you, mark what you may see, feel and know of God's moral attributes, and tell me if this righteousness which I require of you, and which I manifest in my own example, be not that which will give you an inward likeness to those attributes. Do the works I command, and you shall know by the works themselves whether they give you true spiritual righteousness.

He appealed to their own Scriptures; he contended that his teaching and the spirit of those Scriptures were the same. "Whatsoever ye would that men do unto you, do ye the same unto them, for this is the law and the Prophets" [Matt 7:12], that is the spirit, sum or real intent of their teaching, that which they desired to effect. "Thou shalt love the Lord thy God with all thy heart, with all they soul, and with all thy mind. This is the first and great commandment. And the second is like unto it, thou shalt love thy neighbor as thyself. On these two commandments hang all the law and the prophets" [Matt 22:37-40]; that is, all the teachings of the law and the prophets harmonize with these two commandments. And we may add, these two commandments comprise the whole of the teachings of Jesus, present us the principles of all real religion and of all righteousness. The righteousness he enjoined in these two commands was the true righteousness, that without which no pretensions to piety and virtue could avail anything, and with which no man could be in any danger of exclusion from the rewards of the good.

This he taught, and to prove this to the Jews, he appealed to their own Scriptures. "Ye[7] search the Scriptures, for in them ye think ye have eternal life, and they are [that] which do testify of me; or for me" [John 5:39]; that is, bear witness to the same truths, and place the holiness of one's character in the possession of the same prin-

---

[7] I have cited this passage in the indicative rather than in the imperative form because I think it the true one. The common reading, however, would not affect my argument.

ciples and in the performance of the same works that I do. Was Jesus justified in this appeal? Was the spirit of the law and the Prophets what he alleged it was? We may read for ourselves.

Read Deut. 6:5. "And thou shalt love the Lord thy God with all thine heart, and with all thy soul, and with all thy might." Also Leviticus 19:18. "Thou shalt not avenge nor bear any grudge against the children of thy people, but thou shalt love thy neighbor as thyself." See Psalm 50:7-15. "Hear, O my people, and I will speak; O Israel, and I will testify against thee: I am God, even thy God. I will not reprove thee for thy sacrifices or thy burnt offerings, to have been continually before me. I will take no bullock out of thy house, nor he-goats out of thy folds. For every beast of the forest is mine and the cattle upon a thousand hills. I know all the fowls of the mountains and the wild beasts of the field are mine. If I were hungry, I would not tell thee: for the world is mine, and the fullness thereof. Will I eat the flesh of bulls, or drink the blood of goats? Offer unto God thanksgiving; and pay thy vows unto the Most High; And call upon me in the day of trouble: I will deliver thee, and thou shalt glorify me." Isaiah 1:13-17. "Bring no more vain oblations; incense is an abomination unto me; the new moons and Sabbaths, the calling of assemblies, I cannot away with; it is iniquity, even the solemn meeting. Your new moons and your appointed feasts my soul hateth; they are a trouble unto me; I am weary to bear them. And, when ye spread forth your hands, I will hide mine eyes from you; yea when ye make many prayers I will not hear; your hands are full of blood. Wash ye, make you clean, put away the evil of your doings from before mine eyes; cease to do evil; learn to do well; seek judgement, relieve the oppressed, judge the fatherless, plead for the widow." Micah 6:6-8. "Wherewith shall I come before the Lord, and bow myself before the high God? Shall I come before him with burnt offerings, with calves of a year old? Will the Lord be pleased with thousands of rams, or with the thousands of rivers of oil? Shall I give my first-born for my transgression, the fruit of my body for the sin of my soul. He hath showed thee, O man, what is good; and what doth the Lord require of thee, but to do justly, and to love mercy, and to walk humbly with thy God?"

Now do not these as well as many other passages, which I need not quote, fully justify the assertion and the appeal of Jesus? Had the Jews understood their own Scriptures, had they perceived the spirit of their teaching, they would have recognized in the righteousness of Jesus that same kind of righteousness which their own law and prophets enjoined. And had they seen themselves as they were they would also have perceived that it was a moral reformer, a spiritual Redeemer, or Messiah, that they needed, and that none other could justify the spirit of the predictions on which they relied. But their minds had waxed gross, their views were outward; they imagined that they had all needed truth, and all needed virtue, they saw no necessity, they wished for no deliverer but a political one, for no salvation but a national one.

In this last sense Jesus was not the Messiah; in the first he was. He, that is his righteousness, the system of moral righteousness, which he enjoined, was the only deliverer. There was, there could be, in the very nature and constitution of things, "none other name given under heaven, whereby men must be saved" [Acts 4:12]. No man can be saved from sin without leaving off sinning and becoming a good man. This Jesus taught and he also disclosed in what goodness consisted, the goodness which was from the beginning, the only real goodness in the universe. This goodness must be possessed or salvation was impossible.

We now see what Jesus taught, and what it was necessary to believe; to wit, that there was no real righteousness except that kind which Jesus disclosed and that without possessing that no man could be saved. This belief was necessary because people did not then receive that spiritual righteousness. They depended on other things, and made use of means which could never make "the comers thereto perfect, nor purge the conscience from dead works to serve the living God" [Heb 10:1-2]. It was necessary to make people believe the righteousness which came by observing the traditions of the elders, and their ceremonial laws, was an imperfect righteousness, and that the righteousness of Christ was perfect. This was a very important consideration. For this the apostles had to labor long, and this truth is not fully acknowledged even yet. As this was the first step to be taken, as this belief lay at the threshold, it was much insisted upon, and finally became the mark of distinction between the disciples of Jesus, and the adherents to the law of Moses in its outward character.

The gospel itself was a system of moral righteousness; that means of salvation it pointed out were personal holiness. But before people would rely on it, before they would give up their outward sanctuary, and contend only for this inward worth, for this "Christ within," they must be made to believe this was the true kind of righteousness and that it was all sufficient. It is easy then to perceive why people were exhorted to believe, why the gospel was called "the faith" or thing believed, and why adherents to it were called "believers." He that possesseth this righteousness hath everlasting life. It is not the belief that gives the life, it is having the righteousness within us. The belief so far as it leads to the possession of the thing itself is useful as a means. The possession of the righteousness pointed out will suffice, and if one has that, we need not trouble ourselves about what he believes or disbelieves.

Please forgive me, Messrs. editors, my undue prolixity, and trust me that hereafter I will try to be within more reasonable bounds.

NO. 6 (August 3, 1833): 121-24

It is generally contended that faith originated in our feelings and is the moving cause of our conduct. The great object of the religious world has, therefore, been to ascertain what must be believed in order to produce right feelings and ensure the performance of right actions.

Each party has decided in favor of itself. The Catholic has declared for his own creed, so has the Calvinist, the Arminian, the Universalist, and "the thousand and one" sects into which Christendom is divided. Some of these sects must evidently be wrong, for many stand in direct opposition to each other; but each answers for itself, "It is not I. It is not I."

What shall be done? If it be necessary to have a correct faith, in order to have a correct practice who shall tell us which that faith is?

For eighteen hundred years the Christian world has disputed and settled nothing. The question is as much open for debate as ever. There is no standard which presents itself like to all by which all will consent to be measured. If we appeal to the Bible, each interprets it so as to support his own pretensions. If we appeal to character, we find it good and bad under every variety of faith. If we allege the bad conduct of some as proof of the falsity of their belief, we are told we must not condemn a doctrine because the conduct of its adherents is bad. If we adduce the good conduct of some as proof of the excellency of their belief, we are told that they are good *in spite* of it. What shall be done?

It strikes me, that the notion, which pronounces just feelings and just actions the fruits of a just belief, is itself wrong. They are the fruits of a right spirit and not of a right belief. Men's feelings and actions do not vary in exact proportion as their belief varies. Their hearts are sometimes nearer together than their heads, and sometimes their heads than their hearts.

Belief is an intellectual act, but who does not know that the feelings do not always depend on the intellect? It is not seldom that we see a man with just knowledge, and who can describe the charms of goodness in rich and fervid eloquence, while he is base in his feelings, and vicious or criminal in his actions. One may know what righteousness is, may believe the truth, be able to defend it by arguments of irresistible beauty and strength, but it does not follow from this, as a matter of course, that he obeys the truth and is righteous. He may know what it is to love his neighbor, may believe that he ought to love him, but who would infer from this that he does love him? The drunkard knows he ought not to get drunk, he well knows the ruin he brings upon himself and his family, he resolves and re-resolves that he will be temperate, but continues to indulge his cups. Indeed we must after all acknowledge with the apostle, "the good that I would I do not, but the evil that I would not that I do" [Rom 7:19].

The fact is moral feelings and moral conduct do not bear that invariable relation to intellectual development and religious belief as some would have us suppose. We are not such reasoning beings as we pretend. We do not first reason, take a full view of the case, *infer* what is the proper conduct and then act. It were better if we did so but we do not. The feelings exist independent of the intellect, and they urge us on by their impetuosity, sometimes blindly, but often in defiance of the understanding. The understanding, the intellect, may inform us what are right feelings and right conduct, but it cannot produce them. We may, we do see the good, desire it, resolve to gain it, and pursue the evil. "When we would do good evil is present with us; we find a law in our members warring against the law of our minds and bringing us into captivity to the law of sin and death" [Rom 8:21, 23].

"But is it of no consequence what one believes? Does it matter nothing what one's principles are?" These are two questions, which are sometimes considered synonymous; but they are widely different. It is of the last consequence that one's principles be correct; but it does not follow from this that a correct belief is indispensable.

Love to one's neighbor is a principle. It may be one step in the process of inducing one to love his neighbor to first produce the conviction that he ought to love him; but this conviction does not necessarily, nor even commonly produce the feeling in question. The principle, that which induces the feeling, is what is wanted, and all that is wanted, and if this exists it is no manner of consequence, whether the person believes he ought to love his neighbor or not. He does love him and that is enough.

But, can we produce this love, without first inducing the belief? Most assuredly. Doubtless many a man loved his neighbor as he did himself, before Christian morality declared it his duty to do so.

Aristides[8] was just before Socrates defined justice; and many a man has practiced the most exalted virtue without knowing what the Christian law enjoins or prohibits. To make one love his neighbor we should appeal directly to the sentiment of benevolence, keep the heart open to all generous and kind impulses—give constant exercise to benevolence, and love to his neighbor will exist. Say nothing about what one ought to love, do not undertake to reason him into love, but awaken and direct the sentiment itself.

It should be one part, and that not the least part of education, to exercise and discipline the feelings, to keep children pleased with each other, ready to aid each other, to interchange kind offices, to exchange presents, to weep when one is unfortunate, and to rejoice when he is happy. There are chances enough for the display of these good feelings in every school, and they may there be so developed and strengthened as to remain through all after life in full vigor and activity.

Love to God is a principle. It is one thing to love God, and another and a very different thing to believe that we ought to love him. To love him is indispensable to a good life, but the belief that we ought to love him is of no manner of use, further than it leads us to cultivate the feeling of love. Some may think this is a great deal, but a moment's reflection will convince them it is but little. Love belongs not to the intellect but to the feelings. To produce it, the shortest way is to come directly to the feelings, and not through the circuitous and uncertain route of the intellect.

Suppose we wish to make one love God. Then let us appeal directly to the religious sentiment, and make the heart feel that God is good. We must study to make the heart relish whatever is beautiful and lovely in nature, whatever is benevolent and merciful in the dispensations of Providence. Indeed, let one know the luxury of doing good, and his heart will be opened with love to God. When, as it sometimes has been my lot to do it, I have wiped the tear from the eye of woe, brightened the afflictions of a fellow being and made a brother or a sister happy, I have not only loved my race better, but I have loved God more. I could not then stop to inquire whether I ought to love him or not; I loved him; and while the religious sentiment was as active as it was then, no power in heaven or in earth could prevent me from loving him.

[8][Ed. Aristides, called the just, was an Athenian military and political leader of the fifth century B.C.]

If I wished to make children love God, I would say nothing to them about loving him. I would take them abroad with me to survey this beautiful world, all radiant with the love of God; I would bid them listen to the sweet notes of the forest songster, observe the opening flower, and inhale its rich fragrance; I would take them to the house of sorrow and let them weep with the afflicted; I would let them attempt to soothe the distressed and taste the pleasure of trying to relieve; I would have them enjoy the love of parents, of brothers and sisters, of friends and neighbors; and then I would say to them, "There is a great and good Being who makes all these things so beautiful and lovely who loves those afflicted ones with whom you mingled your tears, who makes you wish to relieve them, who gives you your parents, your brothers and sisters, friends and neighbors, who makes them capable of loving you, and you of loving them." I would do this and leave it to their young hearts to love him or not.

Now, both love to God and man can exist, can be produced, without saying one word about what people ought to believe; and surely if it be essential to believe anything, it is that we should love God with all our hearts and our neighbors as ourselves. If even here, where, if ever, belief is necessary, it be not indispensable, what shall we say of those various articles about which theologians mainly contend?

I would not say that faith is of no use, especially when it relates to practical duties, and to great principles which are to be cultivated in the heart and obeyed in the life. Convince a man what his duty is and you have done much to make him strive to do it. When he sees clearly his duty he may wish to do it and this wish may have an influence in calling into action those feelings which will prompt its performance, which may urge him on and not permit him to rest till he has done it.

That class of opinions which relates to human duty, which necessarily involves action, I most certainly deem of great consequence. I wish these opinions correct. It is for this I labor both as a preacher and a writer. We should know what our duty is and have just opinions respecting its importance. It is the want of just opinions on this point or a just *belief* respecting duty, which has done so much mischief in the world. Had men known their duty and *believed* if they performed it that nothing more would or could be rationally required of them, there had not been so much of bitter controversy and sectarian strife to sadden the hearts of the righteous and to make the licentious scoff. All had then preserved or aimed to preserve, the unity of the spirit in the bonds of peace! All inquiries had then been directed to ascertaining what is proper to be done, and all energies had been employed in doing it, instead of being wasted in fruitless efforts to bring all to a uniform faith. In speaking against the importance of faith, I would not, then, be understood as undervaluing correct opinions of duty of human action, or of those great principles which constitute the good man and the holy life.

But, there is a class of opinions, which are only opinions of opinions, a belief which is only a belief in a belief. It is for this sectarians mainly contend, about this theologians chiefly wrangle and set the community by the ears. It is this belief, or this class of opinions, which I consider as wholly disconnected with human virtue and the salvation of our souls.

The religious sentiment which involves the existence of God, the immortality of the soul, and our accountability, I do not call a belief. It is a sentiment. It is not left to the uncertainty of weak man's logic. The Deity hath himself engraved it upon the heart and incorporated it into our very natures. He who denies the existence of God, a future life and man's accountability is not a denier of the true faith, but a denier of a part of his nature. I would not censure him for not believing the truth, but for not knowing himself, for obscuring to his own vision and for denying the religious sentiment which is as natural to him as is the appetite of hunger or thirst.

This sentiment I would have always strong and active, no means should be spared to make it so; for it is the noblest sentiment of our natures and gives employment to our sweetest and strongest affections. It should lie at the foundation of all our systems of morality, and all duty should be modified in reference to it. But all opinions which are not essential to the existence, to the free, full and right action of this sentiment, which men call "Bodies of Divinity," "Systems of Theology," "Creeds," or "Confessions," are only speculative, only opinions of opinions, can never be essential to salvation, and should never be urged as at all necessary. Of this description is almost the whole class of notions which occupy the attention of theologians, less now than formerly I own: but still too much now, and the sooner this is seen and admitted the better.

The great and only legitimate object of the wise and good is to produce right feeling and right acting. To accomplish this object our whole natures must be exercised. Merely believing a right will do little of itself; but as far as it leads people to cultivate the moral and religious affections and to do their duty, it is useful as a means. It is never to be sought as an end, nor valued for itself. I am willing it should have its place and go for what it is worth; but I do not believe that believing right, or a right faith in a theological sense has much to do with our feelings or actions, except as they relate to ecclesiastical affairs.

Belief that the righteousness of Christ, that which he manifested, is the true kind of righteousness, that we cannot be justified without it, and that there is no condemnation to them that have it, is a necessary belief. But this is in no sense different from believing that certain principles, or a certain designated scheme of human duty, is man's real duty, and that if one do his duty he shall be justified, if he do it not he shall be condemned. Still the belief that the righteousness of Christ is the true kind of righteousness, is essential to salvation, for it is a belief which involves action. It saved the Jew who had it from his devotion to an imperfect righteousness, from a fatiguing ceremonial law, which could not "make the comers thereto perfect" [Heb 10:1], and turned his attention to that which was true, and which if possessed would secure his eternal salvation. It saved the gentile who had it from idolatry, from the impurities of the religious service to which he was accustomed. It saves us who have it, from futile notions of righteousness, and points out to us what we should seek to gain. This is a faith in Christ, and as it produces this effect it may be called a saving faith, and those who have it are well said to be saved by faith.

But the salvation here spoken of is only a salvation from a certain kind of ignorance, and from false and impure systems of religion. It was not a salvation from sin; it was not the salvation for which we most earnestly pray. Those who had it were still exhorted to "work out their own salvation" [Phil 2:12], to make their "calling and election sure" [2 Pet 1:10]. Thus plainly intimating that besides the salvation which came by believing in Christ, another was to be sought by their own works. The belief in Christ only saved them from ignorance, it merely pointed them to the true righteousness, and it was still necessary to possess this righteousness in order to secure eternal salvation. The belief in Christ saved them from not knowing their duty, but did not do their duty for them. This was still to be done. This is all that ever was to be done, and it is the doing of this that secures us justification. To do this is to work and we may "see then how we are justified by works and not by faith only" [James 2:24]. I conclude with the remark that faith is useful only as it saves us from false notions and directs us to the proper work to be done. But all this is nothing if the work be neglected. The end is to perform the right works, and if we do them we are and shall be saved. All we have to do with faith is simply so far as it will aid us to a clear understanding of our duty. But the faith which does this is obvious and contested by no one. We all know our duty; we all know what God requires us to do, and be it ours to do it.

Messrs. editors, my essay is done. I thank you for giving it a place in your useful paper. What your readers think I know not, ask not; but I think I have touched upon some important topics. I have not done them justice; I have done little more than to throw out some disconnected hints, but if they shall have any influence in setting any mind in motion towards the acquisition of truth, I shall be satisfied. Yours respectfully.

28.

LETTERS TO AN UNBELIEVER[1]

Christian Register 12 (October 5, 1833): 158

My Dear Friend. Your last has given me no little pain. It has recalled a period and awakened recollections, I would gladly forget. You remind me that it was once my misfortune to be skeptical in matters of religion and that my former writings and conversation have had an influence in making you the same. This is doubly painful, I regret that you have become a sceptic, and still more, if possible, that you have become one through my agency.

You tell me that since I am the "cause of your scepticism, I ought to help you remove it, or not censure you for it." You are right as well as severe. But I am not sure that I can assist you. It is easier to plunge a man into difficulty than it is to pull him out. Still, since I am satisfied that you sincerely desire the truth, and that you have none of that false pride which makes one ashamed, even when convinced, to disavow what he had once avowed, I will do my best.

The tone of your letter pleases me. It proves that you have an ingenuous mind and an honest heart; that you have no bitterness towards Christians and that you would willingly embrace Christianity if you were convinced of its truth.

---

[1][Ed. Brownson introduced this series of letters with the following note to the editors: "SCEPTICISM. MESSRS EDITORS. I send you for publication in your useful paper, a series of letters addressed to an unbeliever and designed to obviate some of the objections which have been raised against religion. The objections noticed are those which troubled my own mind and the answers given are those which relieved it.

When I wrote these letters, I designed to publish them in a different form from the one I now adopt; but on examining them, I do not deem them worthy to be exalted into a book, though they may deserve the passing attention usually given to newspaper essays. If you think them consistent with the design of your paper, you will oblige me, by giving them to the public." Brownson's manuscript text, "Letters to an Unbeliever in Answer to Some Objections to Religion," which he originally intended to publish as a book, is located in the microfilm edition of the "Orestes Augustus Brownson Papers," Roll # 10. Brownson began to write that 184 page text, as its preface indicates, in November or December of 1832. The substance of those unpublished letters are published in the *Christian Register*.]

This is as it should be. If I judge rightly, you are an unbeliever not from choice but from what you deem necessity. I like the temper of mind and state of feeling you exhibit, not merely because they furnish me the pledge of a candid hearing, but because they are proper in themselves and such as every rational man delights to cultivate.

You ask me, "Why it is criminal to doubt? It is not criminal. I respect your doubts. They prove that you have some mental activity. I have no sympathy with that sleepy state of the soul which is never disturbed by a single doubt, and which applauds itself for its own stupidity. No man can enter the Temple of wisdom but through the portals of doubt." My religion allows—encourages, you to doubt, at least till you are rationally convinced. It asks—it admits—no blind acquiescence. It appeals to mind and must be in accordance with reason, or it is no religion for reasonable beings. We honor no being by resigning our reason, and I cannot for myself embrace, and I will not ask my friends to embrace, a religion that requires us to do it, and thus become idiots or madmen.

There is however a remark in reference to doubt that deserves to be made. Doubts excited by pride, by prejudice, or by a partial investigation, where a full investigation is possible, are not to be respected, for their origin is not honorable. But even then, the error lies not in the doubt, but in the pride, the prejudice which prevented us from judging candidly or impartially, and in the neglect which prevented us from obtaining, when we might, the means of deciding correctly. There is a caution implied here which all would do well to observe, and all who observe it, should have their doubts respected.

You ask me again how I can "embrace a religion which prohibits free inquiry?" I embrace no such religion. From what I have just said you may infer that I do not. I wish everyone to inquire freely, fearlessly, but faithfully and candidly. My religion allows me to investigate all subjects, sacred or profane, ancient or modern, moral, spiritual or physical. It commands me to "prove all things and hold fast that which is good" [1 Thess 5:21]. That which trammels the mind, curbs free thought and breathes forth its withering curse upon free inquiry, is not religion, it is an infamous pretender, exposed at first sight to the abhorrence of the good and the contempt of the wise.

But do not misunderstand me. It is really free inquiry that I approve. We must inquire honestly, with an eye single to the discovery of truth. We must be aware that there is a logic of the heart as well as of the head. The affections have great power over the decisions of the judgement. We must be careful that they do not lead where truth cannot follow. Were you unfriendly to me you would not place half the confidence in me that you do now; and were you to get a dislike to a doctrine, that dislike would half unfit you to judge of its correctness. Every inquirer after truth, should be aware of this, and avoid the danger it involves.

It is of great consequence that the heart be preserved pure. Only the pure in heart can clearly see moral truth. A heart in love with vice or bent on vicious indulgence, always, in a greater or less degree, impairs the judgement. One must be on his guard. He must keep the moral principle sound, and the conscience "tremblingly alive" to the first approach of evil. All one's motives should be just and pure, and then he is preserved in the right state to inquire. The affections themselves will then greatly aid him by becoming a sort of gauge to truth.

We must inquire, not assume; observe, not take for granted. Real knowledge makes us humble. It is ignorance that makes one self-conceited. The true disciples of knowledge are modest. They inquire simply for what is and for what good use may be made of what they ascertain. They have no preconceived notions which they are ambitious to maintain. They receive with submission every fact they discover and quietly give it a place in their catalogue without any anxiety about its establishing or overthrowing their own or others' theories. They know facts will be facts whether they own them or not; and, however humbling it may be, they conclude, that so far as they have systems, it is best to make them bend to facts, since they cannot, if they would, make facts bend to systems.

We must enquire patiently. Truth is not always easy to be discovered. Falsehood too often assumes her shape and counterfeits her language. We must look closely, look far, examine, reexamine with scrupulous care, that we be deceived by no appearances and fail by no neglect. We must submit to fatigue with a good grace, and quietly suspend opinion till all the facts in the case are collated. We must not too hastily conclude our work is done. One has not worshiped in the temple merely because he has entered the vestibule. We must enter the temple itself and sit down at the foot of the altar attentively to hear, patiently to examine, and coolly to judge, before we can claim to have paid our devotions. We must go forth into the fields of nature with our eyes and ears open, with all our senses awake, prepared to observe, to reason, to reflect. We must enter the world within, the world of thought and feeling, and learn what we are, what are the deep wants of the soul, what are our powers, what we may attempt, and what we should let alone. If we fail in one instance, we must try again and always keep up an indomitable resolution to persevere.

It is this kind of free inquiry, my dear friend, inquiry thus guarded, or if you please, thus aided, that I approve, that I believe religion sanctions and commands everyone to pursue. It must be free, thorough, long continued, and as extensive as time, place and ability will permit. No one is bound to achieve impossibilities; but everyone is required to do all he can. It is not, then, the free inquirer who is guilty, but he who does not or will not or dares not inquire as fully and as extensively as he can.

I fear that some of my skeptical friends, great advocates as they are for free inquiry, would not object to having this exchanged for a shorter and a less laborious task. And indeed, as to that matter, the same may possibly be said of some who think themselves very good Christians. It need not be denied that professed Christians have been slow to imbibe the free spirit of the gospel, and have not been very prompt to "stand fast in the liberty wherewith Christ makes free" [Gal 5:1]. But, in spite of all that has been or may be said, you will find that religion is the soul of freedom. It makes one free indeed, and imposes no restraint, that is not necessary to prevent him from injuring his neighbor or himself. Go then, inquire into all subjects freely, honestly, faithfully and extensively as you can, and fear not to abide the result.

But enough for the present; your other objections will be taken up in the order you stated them.

NO. 2 (October 19, 1833): 165-66

You allege, my dear friend, that the conduct of religionists has in many cases been intolerant and fanatical. This is no doubt true, and much that you say on this point does you credit as a man of kind and benevolent feelings.

It is, indeed, unpleasant to gaze on that picture of bigotry and superstition, which is hung up in almost every temple. There is something on which I dread to think in the history of the "dark ages"—a history written in blood, by the funeral torch which lighted to their graves the victims of unchastened zeal and priestly rage. When I recall the mischiefs which in every age have been caused by ignorance, pride, craft and misdirected energy, under the sanction of religion, I weep for man and half wish to blot his past history from the tablets of human memory. But it is in vain. The history is written. The sepulchral witnesses stand arrayed against him; and the best he can do is to admit their testimony and throw himself upon the mercy of his judges.

I might offer some apology but I will not. Man's conduct in every age in reference to religion has grieved the wise and made the merciful doubt, and I concede you the full force of the argument his errors and his crimes furnish you against the truth of his belief. In defending religion I do not justify bigotry, fanaticism, craft, or intolerance. I dislike them as much as you do or can. I have no sympathy with him who would injure a brother for that pardonable offence, a dissimilarity of belief; certainly not with him who would burn a brother because his creed is longer or shorter than his own. It is man's foulest act that he has so done—his most damning sin that he has dared justify the doing of it.

No, whatever you may imagine, I have no apology for him who would usurp dominion over the mind. If there be in the world anyone thing which a man may call his own, and of which he may claim the sovereign disposal, it is his opinion, his religious belief. If I believe that opinion wrong, I may labor to confute it—dangerous, I may labor to prove it so, and to persuade him who embraces it to reject it; but a step further, I may not go. The man is and should be free to abide by his own convictions, and no man, no body of men, no community, holy or unholy, has the right to take cognizance of his belief, to breathe the least censure upon him for it, to cast the least impediment in the way of its free and full enjoyment.

He is no Christian, he is no man, who will not say to himself, "I will enter no dungeons framed for the soul, I will wear no chains forged to bind down the rising thought. I will be free to examine, to the full extent of my ability, heaven, ocean, earth, the world of matter, and the world of thought and feeling—ay, and I will be free to proclaim my honest opinions, comport they with the believer or the unbeliever, with the orthodox or with the heterodox, unlicensed, uninterrogated. This is my right. It is my duty and I will abandon it only with my life. What I claim for myself, I am willing all others should enjoy; and I will, to the full extent of my power, defend it for them, believe they, disbelieve or misbelieve they, what they may."

This is the sentiment and will be the expression of every man who has fully imbibed the free spirit of the gospel and become able to sympathize with the mind of its author. If all professed friends of Christianity had known this, felt it, obeyed it, you had not urged their conduct as an objection to religion.

But, be the conduct of Christians what it may, you will not, you cannot, exult over the crimes and follies of our fellow beings. These whom you condemn, belonged to the human family, they were your brothers as well as mine. It becomes you as much as it does the Christian to tread lightly on their graves, to leave their ashes to rest in quiet where they are inured. Together we may deplore their errors and weep over their mischievous conduct. We may draw from them if we can, the lessons of wisdom, but, instead of throwing them in each other's teeth let us rather try to forget that they ever were. That there has been wickedness in the church, I own; and glad were I if there had been none anywhere else. The black catalogue of man's crimes had then been shorter than it is, and the history of our race had been read with less of horror than it now is. Wickedness is not less wickedness out of the church than in it. That wars have been undertaken for religion I admit; yet there have been wars, and destructive ones too, which had no religion for their pretext; other passions, and other interests stirred them up and carried them on; and how know we that those other passions and interests were not in reality, at the bottom of those which were ostensibly religious? Some of the worst of the popes had no belief in the religion over which they presided; for a long series of ages the sacerdotal castes of the East and the South, had no real belief in the religion to which they chained the multitude they deceived and enslaved, and will you make religion answerable for the evils they occasioned? He who believes not in religion is an unbeliever, or a disbeliever; and if he professes to believe in it when he does not, he is a hypocrite. The popes and priests who did the most injury to man were at best unbelievers and hypocrites. Shall their misconduct be charged to the religion, I profess, and which they did not believe, or to the unbelief in which they and you are alike involved?

You say "the church has had its fanatics"; I own it, and ask in my turn if the church *only* has had them? Alas! they have been found everywhere. Philosophy has had them; unbelief has had them; tyranny has had them; freedom has had them; all parties and all causes have had them; and we must learn the lesson of mutual forbearance. Would you condemn liberty because a guillotine was erected in its name, and terror and death spread through France by its friends—republicanism, because it was disfigured by the cant and hypocrisy of the Puritans in England—science, because dreaming alchemists sought in vain the philosopher's stone, and the elixir vitae?[2] Why not be governed by the same just principle when you judge of religion?

We should always distinguish the essential from the adventitious, and always separate the cause from the character of its advocates. The defenders of religion may have been base and criminal: but surely, it is not beneath the philosopher to ascertain as nearly as may be, whether

---

[2][Ed. The "exilir of life" refers to a substance that can prolong life indefinitely, or to the quintessence and underlying principle of anything.]

that baseness and that criminality be produce by religion, or by some things which may have been mixed up with it or mistaken for it. The apparent is not always the true cause. There were mistaken disciples who would have called down fire from heaven to consume the enemies of their Master, but Jesus rebuked them, told them "they knew not what manner of spirit they were of" [Luke 9:55], and assured them religion's office "is to save, not destroy men's lives" [Luke 9:56]. When a man is seen acting inconsistently with this end, perhaps it were not wrong to say that he is not governed by a religious spirit.

You "deplore sectarian divisions," so do I. I own that they hedge up our love and often restrain our good offices to those of our own way of thinking. This is no trifling evil; but I see no religion in it. It is the want of religion, the want of those abiding principles, those pure and elevated sentiments which the wise and good call religion, that stirs up discord, divides us into petty factions and estranges our hearts. Were not these wanting, we were all of one heart, were all animated by a sweet and harmonious spirit, if not by a uniform faith. The unknown Agency that gives us our being, unites us by a common nature, by common wants, hopes, fears, joys and sorrows, and by common means of enjoyment; and religion commands us to "be kindly affectioned one towards another" [Rom 12:10], to "keep the unity of the spirit in the bonds of peace" [Eph 4:3], always having that "charity which is the bond of perfectness" [Col 3:14].

I dislike divisions; I dislike the distinctions which destroy the value of society. This eternal wrangling, this clashing of creeds, these conflicts of party interests and these shouts of embattled sectarians; what shall I say of them? Religion disowns them; humanity weeps over them; truth and reason abhor them. Do not charge them upon religion, for religion is of a mild and peaceful nature; it would throw around each, the sunny heaven of benevolence; it would calm the troubled spirit; it would steal through the heart, hush all its jarring elements, and give it a keen relish for all that is beautiful and lovely, for all that is generous and noble, pure and sublime. It would bind us together by a golden chain of love, give us the spirit of brotherhood and wed us indissolubly to the cause of virtue and humanity.

Such is the spirit of religion. If those who profess to have it are governed by a dark spirit, one that delights only in convulsions, in the storms and tempests of untamed passion, give them credit for being deceived or for being hypocrites, but honor them not by calling them religious. Distinguish, I pray you, between what men call religion, and what it really is, between the claims of its friends and its own, between their conduct, and that which it commands. It is your

duty as well as mine to make this distinction, for it is the duty of us
both to seek diligently after the truth. Obtain a clear idea of what is
true religion, obtain this yourself and for yourself, and I am confident that you will not again urge the misconduct of Christians, as a
proof of the falsity of religion. But enough.

NO. 3 (October 27, 1833): 170

Your next objection is of a serious nature. If as you say, "religion
degrade human nature and check the stronger and nobler exertions
of mind," every man of correct views and feelings, must pause before
he gives it his assent.

You refer me to our young aspirations, you ask if I "remember
when we sported together over our own native hills, or stood upon
those craggy cliffs so familiar to our childhood"; if I "remember the
spirit we there inhaled, that there when mind first began to unfold
and thought first dared trust its wing, we pledged ourselves to be
free, to be great, that we would test intellect to the full and rest not
till we had scaled the highest mount of truth?"

Yes. I remember those scenes, those youthful pledges. Time, distance, joy, sorrow, but bring them fresher to my memory, and make
me clasp them closer to my heart. Yes. I remember our young ambition, our dazzling dreams, the burning enthusiasm with which we
resolved that our names should go down to posterity honored by the
wise and blessed by the good. I remember it all and would spurn
from my embrace now as well as then a religion that should bring
down that ambition to the earth.

The ambition to be great is the mark of an elevated mind. You
need not have and I know you have not any sympathy with that
mean spirit which is contented to crawl on the earth and eat dust
with the serpent. No, give the soul an upward look: let it fix its eye
on the very son of greatness. It cannot swell with emotions too vast;
it cannot burn to perform deeds too great.

But when will you find the greatness after which you aspire?
What deeds will match your ambition? Would you

> That murder bare his arm and rampant war,
> Yoke the red dragons to her iron car,[3]

to enable you to gain renown by the blood of your brother? Do you
pant for the warrior's wreath,

> Blood-nursed and watered by the widow's tears?[4]

[3][Ed. Not able to identify quotation.]
[4][Ed. Not able to identify quotation.]

Has that a charm for your ambition? Can that fill up the measure of your wishes and make you feel that you are great?

Does your mind run on power? Would you triumph over the republicanism of our country, become a monarch—have millions for your subjects, to tremble at your frown—to rejoice at your smile? What would you be even then to be called great? After the novelty of the thing had worn off, what would you find in that painful preeminence to satisfy the cravings of the soul? Use your power for the good of your subjects? Ay, that you might; but that would be religion. It is religion that teaches or rather induces him who is so unfortunate as to be entrusted with power over his fellow beings, to use it for their good.

But waive this. Greatness depends not on place. It attaches to the mind. A king with a little soul is no better, is no greater than any other man with a soul of the same size. This outside, this pageantry, these robes of office make up no part of the man. They are but his gilded trappings, and he, after all, must be measured by his own mind and pass for what he is in himself.

But take something higher—not wealth—but knowledge, that after which you are now seeking with such untiring assiduity. Say that you have amassed all of ancient and modern literature and art and science, that you are familiar with men and things, know the world of matter, the world of thought and feeling, and can unravel all the mysteries of nature, what would it avail, if you must keep this knowledge locked up in your own bosom, uncommunicated, unused?

I will not deny that knowledge is worth pursuing even for its own sake; but I put it to your feelings, my dear friend, if ambition can have no higher object, than for one to obtain knowledge, merely for the pleasure of feeling that he has it, and that he knows more than the multitude around him? You might make the ignorant stare; but could you help feeling that their ignorance contributed as much to the effect as your knowledge, and that after all, if they knew a little more, they would know as much as you?

I know that you aim higher. You would acquire knowledge that you may be useful, that you may augment the sum of human happiness. It is for this that you pore with throbbing pulse and feverish brain over the relics of minds which were before you, and over the immense volume spread open round about, and within you. You would have knowledge—I do not misread your heart—that you may meliorate your fellow beings. In this you disclose true ambition. But to do good to others effectually, one should be good in himself, and to be good and to do good is the legitimate end of all existence and this is religion.

Whatever tends to make the heart right, to keep the soul vigorous and active, and to induce us to direct all our faculties to the promotion of others' good belongs to religion; and where, except in what has this tendency can you find anything to equal your ambition, the possession of which will make you feel that you are great?

The wise man is not amused with trifles. He is above the reach of mere applause; he values not the mere eclat of knowledge. This ambition is to have in himself a firm and pure spirit, to act a useful and honorable part in the interesting drama of life.

I call that man great who has struggled with every disadvantage, who has overcome difficulties all but insurmountable, who has mastered his passions and directed or aimed to direct all his faculties to the accomplishment of just and elevated ends. I call that man great who has borne without a murmur the poverty and neglect he could not avoid, who has retained his love for man and his relish for the beautiful and true, though compelled to dwell in solitude; who can bid defiance to the scorn or malice of the world and be happy, though compelled to lodge with his wife and children upon the bare ground and to subsist on the simplest food. Such a man is great in himself; he is superior to the world.

Look at *that* man, you know to whom I allude. He has been what the world calls unfortunate. He has been reduced from affluence to poverty. Death has carried away the companion that long shared his joys, and divided his sorrows; death has carried away, one by one, those children he had trained up to be blessings to society. Calumny has blasted his reputation. He stands alone, scathed by the lightnings of heaven, the mark of fate and the wrath of man; but he bends not. His look is assured, his step is firm, his soul is serene. There he is gathering up in himself a moral power that will prove more than a match for all outward might. Vain worldlings pity him, you and I stand in awe of him.

NO. 4 (November 2, 1833): 174

You must pardon me, my dear friend, for throwing back upon scepticism, the charge you bring against religion. I do this not in exultation but in sorrow. I write not to silence your logic, but to win your heart, and I should grieve to gain a victory over your reason at the expense of truth and good feeling. Friendship has not so often bloomed in my path that I can afford to trample it under my feet; no, not even when it grows on infidel ground.

Be religion as degrading to human nature as you suppose, you gain little by exchanging it for unbelief. The unbeliever's feelings are far from being pleasant, and his reflections anything but invigorating. While his notions are new and he is animated with a zeal to defend or propagate them, he may not feel to the full extent their withering influence; but as soon as that novelty wears off, and that zeal dies away, you know and I know, that they have no power to quicken the mind into vigorous action, or to maintain the soul in a firm and healthy state.

Here, you will allow that I may speak without presumption. I know too well what the unbeliever's feelings are, at least what mine were, and you must allow me to sketch them at some length.

When I first doubted, I felt but little uneasiness. I was inquiring—obtaining new notions—breaking out into new fields, and the newness of my sensations disguised their painfulness. But as soon as I had leisure to collect myself, look into myself, and ascertain what I must be if my new notions were true, I was, believe me, anything but happy. I had no compunctious stings of conscience. I had sought honestly for truth, and I had yielded only to what I deemed rational conviction. I did not then, I do not now, condemn myself for the scepticism in which I was then lost; but I felt that if I were right I was nothing.

I felt myself akin to the brutes and looked upon many of them with envy. I felt that I had more wants than any of them, and in myself fewer means of satisfying them. Of what use, said I to myself, is my reason? I am engaged in endless disputes. There is nothing the certainty of which is not questioned; morals by some are accounted a dream, conscience is pronounced a bugbear. I can think, but to what end? Can feel acutely, but to what good? I spring up, I receive my nourishment from the world around me, attain my growth, give my yellow leaf to the wind, fall, molder away, am—dust!

"For what"—continued I in one of those moments when reflection was forced upon me, "for what shall I labor?" Today I may commence some enterprise, and tomorrow?—I am not. Grant that I may live long, may labor with success; still, by the time I have attained the end I have in view, I shall be old: the juices of my body will be absorbed; my limbs will be stiff; my eye will be dim; my ear heavy; my heart cold; my sympathy dead; my relish for enjoyment gone, and those who could give to "pleasure the power to please," those with whom I might talk of the days of my youth, of the toils and struggles of my earlier life, with whom I might live over the past, will be few, and those, perhaps, far away. Old, worn out, ready to drop into the grave, what can I then say, but "I have lived and toiled in vain. I have extended my acquisitions, enlarged my possessions to no purpose. I had finished my new house, had filled it with every luxury to charm the eye, the ear, the touch, the taste; I was just ready to take posses-

sion—there it is, wrapped in flames! Thus perish the labors and hopes
of my whole life? I may as well die now, as after I have spent my
threescore years and ten, in toil and trouble."

"But I may find pleasure. What? and where? Indulge the senses,
feast on costly viands—task the vine[5]—drink, be drunk? What! lower
than the brute to be happy? Is it pleasure to forget? Ay, it may be. But
I may awake from my fits of forgetfulness. There may be intervals
between, filled with a morbid sensibility, with headaches, fevers; my
course may lead on to tremblings, to dropsies, to insanity, to death!
Alas! that is miserable pleasure whose best offer is death.

"But I may do good. To whom? To myself? I have no good. I am
as the brutes that perish. To others? Yes. I will labor to enlighten my
fellow beings. I will teach them great and important truths—what
truths? That they are but dust and vanity? No; I will leave the individual, I will ascend to the race; I will seek to be the benefactor of
nations; I will teach them to cultivate the arts of peace and industry;
I will persuade them to foster education, to diffuse knowledge, to
abolish their oppressive governments and barbarous customs; I will
make them "beat the sword into the ploughshare and the spear into
the pruning hook" [Isa 2:4]. I will bring together the estranged members of the human family, and make them feel that they are brothers
and sisters, and that they should love each other.

"But can I do this? Am I greater than Confucius, who, they say,
was banished for teaching his countrymen the practice of virtue? Wiser
than Socrates, who was poisoned for teaching the Athenian youth
wisdom instead of sophistry? More benevolent than Jesus who was
crucified between two thieves because he went about doing good?
But, they pronounced the writings of Confucius divine, they dedicated a chapel to Socrates, and they deified Jesus. True. But has China
practiced the lesson of her greatest philosopher? Did Athens obey the
instructions of her wisest son? Did Judea adopt the pure and peaceful
morality of her brightest luminary? Where are those nations now? China
is enfeebled by an excessive civilization. The proud Moslem treads in
scorn of the Jew where met the Sanhedrim, and binds his slave where
thundered the eloquence of Demosthenes, and where Plato taught.[6]

[5][Ed. "task the vine" replaces the original "taste the wine," according to
Brownson's correction in *Christian Register* 12 (November 16, 1833): 182.]

[6] This so far as Greece is concerned may not be strictly true at the present
moment, but whether in passing from the Turkish yoke to another she has bettered
her condition remains to be seen. [Ed. In 1821 Greek freedom fighters, led by the
Lavra Monastery of Patras, revolted against Turkish rule. With the aid of France,
England, and Russia, the Greeks won their political independence.]

Nations which were, are not. Silence reigns where rose the joyous din of gladdened courts; squalid poverty where wealth and industry smiled. Ignorance holds a "leaden" empire where science once shed its radiance and where art exerted its omnipotence. Gone are the great, the admired, the revered. Where now are the refinement, and learning, and science and philosophy attributed to ancient India? To ancient Egypt? Where the wealth and commercial activity of Tyre, of Zidon, of Carthage, the haughty greatness of Rome, once mistress of the world? Alas! Nations are and are not. They spring up, they flourish, they disappear. Africa, once the seat of learning, the nursery of arts and sciences, has long been a mart for slaves. Asia once so renowned is in its dotage, gone back to second childhood.

But the north of Europe has been quickened; a new world has been discovered. True. But the new is scarcely what the old was, and the new ay, the new, may one day be what the old now is. It is so. The individual is born, attains his growth, dies. The family starts up, has its day, give places to another. The kingdom or nation starts from the savage tribe or infant colony, puts forth its leaves, pushes out its branches, reaches its height—another is nourished from its moldering dust. The night bird now flaps his wings over the fallen columns and crumbling temples of Palmyra—calls to his fellow where stood, Babylon, Balbec, Persepolis, Ninevah, and who dare say the same may not hereafter be on the Seine, the Zuyder Zee, the Thames, the Potomac, the Hudson? It is so, nations go round. Knowledge and ignorance, greatness, civilization, decline and barbarism, follow each other in an eternal circle. A thousand ages hence, some philosopher like me, will weep over the follies and crimes and sufferings of man, and burn with the desire to "Reform." 'Tis in vain. The Reformer is the condemned Titan, struggling to roll the huge stone up the steep ascent, only to have it come back again to be rolled up, again to come down.

"Perhaps not so bad. The dark ages are passing away. Commerce has brought the most distant nations together, and established relations between them both pleasing and profitable. The invention of the printing press has given us the power to send our thoughts, discoveries and improvements almost instantaneously throughout the world. It is well."

But allow me to take breath, and reserve the rest of what I have to say on this point till my next.

NO. 4 Concluded (November 9, 1833): 177-78

"It is well. But the dark ages succeeded an age of light scarcely less resplendent than our own. Commerce indeed has brought all nations together; but it has as yet done little more than introduce slavery and oppression into one half and luxury and effeminacy into the other. Books are easily enough made; but, if they do not flatter prejudices, foster pride, encourage base passions and morbid tastes, few will read them.

"But good thoughts once written are in the world and if not read and appreciated when first published, the books which contain them, may afterwards be brought forth from their repose to quicken new minds and to introduce a new epoch. It may be such things are not often. People praise the good, condemn him who will not, and—continue their old errors. One may teach the world the most perfect system of morals and it avails nothing so long as the history of two thousand years proves that mankind can persecute each other in the name of a God who is love and of a religion which is charity.

I may let alone reforming the world. I will leave mankind to themselves. I will pursue knowledge. To what end? To learn that I am here for a few days, to toil, to struggle, to weep, to die, and then to drop into—nothingness? No. I am good enough, wise enough already, for the worm.

"What is then to be known? History? It is a record of wrongs, of man's crimes, follies, sufferings: cruelties, and why learn what man has been only to weep at what he must be? Government? It is a gull trap. Honest men do not need it; rogues disregard it. As I would neither ride my fellow beings nor be ridden by them, I have nothing to do with government.[7]

"True, there are Sciences and Literature, but what are they worth? This world is but a fortuitous jumble of atoms. A certain agglomeration or combination of atoms today makes the man; tomorrow, a dissolution takes place, and a new combination presents the plant, the fish, the bird, the beast, the reptile or the insect; all is an eternal round, ever changing, but forever the same: why seek to know it, merely to become more and more disgusted with what I am?

"Pass over this; suppose that there is something worth knowing, that I may rise to know more than all who went before me, that I burn for knowledge, feel the eternal thirst to know, that I rise early, sit late with thought intent, work up thought till thought is dizzy, till reason stands on the verge of insanity, till my bosom throbs with pair and my body reels and totters, to what will it all amount? I can then but exclaim, "alas how little can be known!"

---

[7] I beg pardon for this sentiment. It *was* mine, and *is* that [of] nearly all the leading unbelievers of our country with whom I am acquainted.

And then to keep this knowledge to myself, little as it may be, will not be easy. I may discover that which men will not like to hear told. If I tell it, I shall be called a heretic, become an outcast, be neglected, be cursed, and my wife and children be cursed because I dare be honest. Well, be it so. This I could bear. I could bear the loss of friends, of reputation, of property. I could follow to the dungeon or to the scaffold. It is not hard to be a martyr. But who could appreciate my lessons? Who could sympathize with the mind of their author? Who profit by his sacrifices?

"Away with all this. I will be rich. How? I am poor. I cannot begin with nothing and become what the world calls rich, without obtaining that which of right belongs to another, perhaps to the widow and the orphan. Would I have the widow's curse follow me? The cry of the fatherless upbraid me? Might not conscience—away with conscience. It is a bugbear, a whim, a dream. Every man is selfish, follows his own interest, gets all he can, and I may as well be selfish as others.[8] I will be rich. Wherefore? I want but little and to the selfish man there comes no pleasure from giving to others.

"No, it will not do. What will? Nothing. Well, said he of Judea, reported wisest of men, perhaps so of kings, 'vanity of vanities, all is vanity'" [Eccles 1:2].

Such, my dear friend, were some of my reflections while I was a sceptic. I recur to them with no pleasure; I have stated them with a chilling horror of soul. There were times when I could not summon up enough energy to engage in any pursuit whatever. My mind would roam from object to object, seeking someone on which to rest but finding none. Hope, the friend of the friendless, the only solace of the wretched, danced at so great a distance, that its light came not to my heart. "There was nothing to charm the eye or the ear. The flower seemed to have lost its fragrance, and the forest note its sweetness. I felt that earth was vanity, that all things were vanity, and there were times when I believed every person hollow hearted, truth, reason, virtue, all a dream.

Two things alone served to sustain me, and for which I was not indebted to scepticism. The first was a desire to effect a moral revolution, to reform mankind. This desire I had before I became a sceptic;

[8]Before I close I shall show that scepticism in religion inevitably leads to scepticism in morals so far at least as it is consistent with itself. Its termination is at complete selfishness, the worst possible conclusion at which man can arrive. It is this scepticism in morals which we have the most reason to deplore. The sentiment expressed above prevails to a greater extent than I am willing to believe, though I think it on the decline.

I may say it led me to scepticism. It has led me out of it, but it never pertained to it, and it suffered grievously by it. At first I did not perceive that this desire to reform was a noble inconsequence in my new system, and till I perceived this, I could rouse up something of energy. Long as I could fancy myself a redeeming angel sent on errands of mercy, I could be active. But this could not always be. My most serious lessons were ridiculed, I was treated as a visionary, as crazy, sometimes as something worse. And to own the truth, I became tired of seeming to myself wiser than all who went before me, wiser than all my contemporaries. It was a painful preeminence; one that shut me out from the pale of humanity. I might walk alone, feared or laughed at, but for me there was no sympathy, for me there was no friendship; for me not heartbeat in kindness, no cheering voice bade me go forward, no whisper of hope that if I did, I should be successful, and none of conscience that if successful, I should be beneficial. The withering influence of scepticism set in, and the zeal to reform died away.

The other sustaining consideration was the fact that I had a wife and children to whom I was attached. That I was saved from—I know not what—that I have now, while I am yet young, a prospect of usefulness before me, is under God, owing to the fact that I have strong earthly ties. The young man who has a feeling heart is most unfortunate in becoming a sceptic. It is seldom that he can come to any good. He must have a constant whirl of something to carry him out of himself or he will be most wretched.

He who has a family and retains enough of the man to feel the play of the warm affections of the husband and the father may not be quite so miserable. In indulging those affections and in discharging the duties they involve, he may find something which in some degree, may beguile the hell burning in his bosom. It is well that our affections are often stronger than our belief, or our want of belief. In them nature is more merciful to us than we are to ourselves. How the old man who has no faith in God, and whose earthly ties are broken, must feel, I know not. How he can fill up his thoughts with scepticism, how find in it a relief for the loneliness and darkness of old age, and the staff he needs to guide his tottering steps down life's decline, I know not, I dread to think!

Admit, if it must be so, that religion be all you suppose it, what must we say of scepticism! You know, and so do I, that scepticism cannot be loved for what it is in itself. Every sceptic feels that want of something more spirit-stirring—something more invigorating to the inward man—something which opens a wider prospect and permits the soul to linger on a richer and more extended landscape. Scepticism is left to be too confined. It binds us down to earth. It, at best, presents us only a dusky plain, skirted by no mountains, variegated by no inequalities, relieved by no herbage, watered by no streams, from which the eye turns away, wearied with its sameness and the heart chilled by its barrenness.

Scepticism makes all prospects alike desolate, alike useless. It presents us the "end of all things," exhibits man as altogether vanity, as a bubble on the ocean, which floats for a moment, bursts, and is no more! The sceptic sits down in sorrow and weeps over his nothingness, or wraps himself up in a sort of desperation and hides the workings of his soul beneath pretended scorn of the human race.

I have not exaggerated, but would to Heaven all I have stated were but the dreams of my own imagination. The picture is but too true. The individuals, to whom you may refer me as apparent exceptions, are persons in whom there are still remaining some traces of those moral and religious sentiments, which it is so hard entirely to obliterate from the heart. They have reasoned themselves into unbelief, but the heart retains recollections of religion. Hence the discrepancy between their reasoning and their feelings. But as far as scepticism touches the heart, and influences the life, it is what I have described. For proof of which I give my own experience and confidently appeal to yours.

NO. 5 (November 16, 1833): 182

I am far, my dear friend, from admitting that religion is unfavorable to the dignity of human nature and to the exhibition of the stronger and nobler exertions of mind. That some things have passed for religion against which your charge may be urged I pretend not to deny; but I believe them as repugnant to the gospel as they are to unperverted reason and to the native benevolence of the human heart.

Religion asserts the existence of one God. The conception which the believer forms of God, is not the conception of a mind "moldering earthward" in love with meanness and servility. God is all that we can conceive of the great, the wise, the good, the beautiful and the true. His moral character is the union of all the perfections. His energy created and sustains all worlds and beings, his wisdom controls all events; his bounty provides for all that live. He is the mind, the soul of the universe, the mighty Spirit that

> Warms in the sun, refreshes in the breeze,
> Glows in the stars, and blossoms in the trees,

> Lives through all life, extends through all extent,
> Spreads undivided, operates unspent.[9]

I say not that this is a true idea. I merely assert that it is the idea which the really religious man has of the God he adores. Be it false, there is still grandeur in it. Grant if it must be so that God is but a creature of man's dreaming fancy, he is still a splendid creation. It was an upward look that saw him; it was a swelling heart that felt him, a sublime spirit that communed with him.

Examine this idea of God. It is only when you turn the mind in upon itself, collect all its energy and compel it to make its mightiest effort that you can take it in. Poetry cannot reach it; language fails to give it utterance; the loftiest genius, and the most comprehensive understanding fall in adoration before it. It swells in magnitude as you approach it, becomes more and more boundless as you attempt to measure it, and forever enlarges in proportion as the mind enlarges that would comprehend it.

Now I am not willing to believe that continued efforts to take in this idea of God can enfeeble the mind. What is it that indicates a strong and noble mind but the power to take in great and sublime ideas? What idea surpasses in magnitude and sublimity this idea of God? Can you believe that mind is chained to the earth, wasting away in ignoble action, which is constantly engaged with this idea, laboring to comprehend it, and struggling to possess the excellence which belongs to it? It cannot be.

Religion pronounces man the offspring of God, the child and the image of Him who has all possible perfection. Does this assertion degrade his nature? Does it not raise him from earth to heaven—from a worm which crawls in the dust to a kindred spirit with Him who inhabiteth eternity? Be it a dream, it is one that gives in thought, at least, dignity to human nature. When once admitted to be real it must quicken the spirit, give grandeur to its conceptions and purity to its desires. Man is, nearly always, what he believes he is. If he believe himself a kindred spirit with the everlasting God, all the breathings of the soul will be after the excellence which best comports with that sublime relationship and he will not rest till he attains it.

I speak not now of the truth or the falsity of this relationship: but of belief in it. As long as the soul believes it, the very laws of mind are such that it must have an exalting and purifying effect. It opens to a new world, not to one naked and barren, but to one with everything to give power to thought and joy to sentiment. It makes

[9][Ed. Alexander Pope, *Essay on Man*, epistle 1, lines 271-74.]

us breathe a purer air, inhale sweeter fragrance and listen to softer music. It enables the mind to assert its supremacy, to rise from the low and the perishing, to dwell on the spiritual and the everlasting. Time and space vanish before it, and there are no deeds which seem to the soul too great to be done, there is no good too unbounded to be possessed.

Religion commands us to worship God. God is to us all that we can conceive of spiritual excellence, the very standard of all perfection. Worship implies submission, love and reverence. When we worship God, we submit ourselves to his will, love and revere his perfection. What we love and reverence we always seek to possess. Hence worship to God resolves itself in the end, into efforts to become like him, "perfect as our Father in heaven is perfect" [Matt 5:48]. Will it degrade human nature to struggle to possess the highest perfection of which the mind in its happier efforts can form any conception?

Let us dwell a moment on worship to God. This worship does not consist in burnt offerings in outward prayer and praise. Those outward acts which too many mistake for the worship of God have no worth any farther than they are the manifestation of internal sentiments. Submission to what is believed to be unerring reason, love of what is deemed unbounded greatness, reverence for the highest wisdom, the loftiest spiritual greatness of which the mind can conceive, are what constitute the worship. Wherever you find these you find true worship. They undoubtedly have a tendency to display themselves in outward acts but these outward acts are not the worship, they are only the efforts of the soul to embody what it inwardly feels. The question then becomes exceedingly simple; will submission to the demands of an unerring reason, the love and reverence of the most unbounded goodness, the most exalted wisdom, spiritual power, energy or greatness, depress the soul and prevent the free and full growth of mind?

What are the laws of the mind? How can the mind become great? Must it not be exercised? And to be exercised needs it not an intellectual object which will task all its powers and compel it to struggle for powers yet greater? Does not the idea of God present this object, and is not the worship of God the very exercise demanded?

You would have the sentiments of the heart generous, pure and noble. How will you make them so? By precept? You cannot. You must exercise them, and how will you exercise them but by compelling them to dwell on that which is generous, pure and noble? And is not this found in infinitely greater perfection in the idea the believer forms of God than anywhere else?

By a law of our spiritual nature, we always borrow something of that excellence which we adore. We dwell not on a scene of loveliness without obtaining from it a milder spirit, and without being filled with sweeter thoughts. We walk not amid ruins, over tombs, come not in contact with the wild and romantic, where nature sports in lawless grandeur, without catching something of the spirit which reigns around us. We gaze not upon the broad expanse of the ocean, cast not our eyes at night up to the deep blue vault of heaven and trace in our minds worlds rising on worlds through the infinitude of space without taking a tinge of sublimity and without becoming conscious of more elevated sentiments and holier aspirations. One cannot even converse with a master mind without borrowing something of his superiority, cannot leave him without being conscious of a new accession of internal energy. It is by conversing with that which is good, wise, great, by the meeting of mind with mind, and of heart with heart, that we obtain our inward power.

All here implied, I find in the idea the believer forms of God. I find in that idea all that can quicken mind, task the power of thought, call forth the most venturous imagination, stir up the heart from the very bottom and give full exercise to all its pure, generous and elevated sentiments. I reverse then your charge, and add, it is religion alone that can give dignity to human nature, and urge the mind on in its upward and eternal career of self- development.

NO. 6 (November 23, 1833): 186

As farther proof of the position of my last, I ask you now, my dear friend, to consider the doctrine of immortality. I am aware that you do not believe this doctrine but you cannot reasonably refuse to examine the influence it may have in the formation of character.

The belief that we shall live again cannot be depressing to him who has it. I have heard many a man regret with tears in his eyes his want of this belief. He who believes that he cannot die, that he will live on, renew his age, flourish in eternal youth, though the earth wax old and crumble to ruins, though the sun and stars grow dim and fade away, cannot but be conscious of a dignified existence.

There is in this belief something which makes us amends for the feebleness of these bodies, for the paucity of our knowledge, and the shortness of our stay. Be earth and all its joys vain and transitory, we can find a sustaining power in the belief that we are immortal. By this belief we are relieved from those gloomy reflections to which I referred when treating of the withering effects of scepticism. We feel that we are something, that our being has some object, that we are heirs of an inheritance incorruptible and eternal in the heavens, and we rise in conscious worth; we rise to the abode of spirit and borrow some of the sunshine of that fairer and better world to tinge with loveliness the one in which we dwell.

I am a progressive being, I am not confined to one spot, nor limited to one degree of acquisition. Eternity is before me. I may die before I have finished my present study. But I can take it up hereafter where I left it off and go on without fear of farther interruption. One never grows old, except in relation to his stay here; no one, therefore, need fear to engage in any pursuit after knowledge. Death will be only the delay of a night's sleep and we shall rise in the morning invigorated by rest, prepared to go forward with increasing ardor and ever enlarging power.

We often become unwilling to continue our efforts after knowledge. We gain one height and another and yet another, rises in the distance. For a time we press onward and upward. But gradually the ardor of youth subsides, the vigor of manhood departs, and we become discouraged with our slow and toilsome progress. We are oppressed by the much to be gained rather than cheered and sustained by the little acquired. The grave opens before us and we give over exertions, exclaiming "all is vanity and vexation of spirit" [Eccles 2:11].

Here the doctrine of immortality steps in, all powerful to relieve. Nothing can be lost. That little which we have gained and with which we are so dissatisfied is an eternal gain. It will set us so much the farther forward. On entering the other world we shall take rank according to our proficiency here. If we have advanced far here we shall take there a higher standing, and be permitted to go on to higher and more pleasing studies. We may have, too, abler teachers and more facilities for learning. The soul freed from its clogs of earth will be able to move with the celerity of thought, and to be wherever it wills to be. In a space of time almost inconceivably short, we can send our thoughts to an immense distance. Sooner than you can read the sentence I am now writing, our thoughts can survey the earth, make the circuit of the heavens and travel on, beyond the utmost verge of the universe. In a space of time equally short, the soul hereafter may visit all the points here indicated, make the whole of that immense journey here implied. It does not appear what we shall be, but we shall be something passing all conception now. Is not this encouraging? Will it not make us apply with new zeal and pleasure to our task?

You know, my dear friend, that it has always been our ambition to be among the greatest and best. We are neither of us willing to be outdone. In a moral as well as in an intellectual point of view, we shall take rank according to our several degrees of acquisition. If instead of improving our time and talents, we waste them in low objects, in vice or crime, or even in useless regrets, we shall find ourselves in the rear. It will be our mortification to see others occupying stations which might have been ours. We shall be compelled to see some who started behind us with fewer advantages, supplying by diligence their deficiencies, gradually coming up beside us; now shooting past us, and now on, far forward, out of sight. Can we bear this? Will not the thought rouse us from our indolence? Shall we loiter by the way? No, we cannot, we will not; we will enter the lists; we will stretch for our lives to gain virtue's highest prize. Ah! noble emulation. But what except the hope of immortality can kindle the requisite ardor, and call forth the needed energy?

The departed may linger around the scenes where they once acted. Who can tell the pleasure the good may receive from witnessing the result of the beneficent actions they performed? They labored, it may be, in obscurity; they were hardly known, or if known, perhaps scorned, treated as visionaries or as enemies to their fellow beings. The veil is now removed. Their worth is discovered and acknowledged. The lessons which cost them so much labor, so many days and nights of intense, often of painful, thought, are now read, approved, obeyed. That which they sowed amid scorn or neglect, in sorrow and anguish, they see now spring up, blossom with beauty and bear the rich and nourishing fruit.

The patriot had labored for his country; had fought her battles, had singly withstood her enemies in her senate chamber, had warned her of her dangers from her aspiring rulers. He failed. He was exiled, or atoned for the purity of his intentions, the depth and singleness of his devotion to her interests, in the dungeon or on the scaffold.[10] Now from his aerial seat he looks down upon the country he loved, upon the scene of his trials, his suffering and his death, where are all the fond associations of childhood and youth—he looks down and sees that justice is done, that his patriotism is acknowledged, that the liberty for which he struggled is triumphant, and the land he all but adored is free and happy. It is not easy to tell his joy. But will not the belief that we may hereafter witness the effects of our present actions, and be pained or pleased, as they are good or bad, have a powerful influence in prompting and sustaining just and beneficial action?

In this world success is not always the just standard of merit. Virtue is often clothed in rags while vice struts in embroidery. Worth is concealed in dungeons while obsequious crowds bow to the vil-

[10][Ed. Sentence as in original.]

lain. In the world to come all shall be righted. Humble virtue shall raise her drooping head; haughty vice shall be abashed, the tyrant dethroned, and the patriot recalled from exile. This is no trifling thought. It has no little power to sustain us in a course of well doing. The good we do shall be acknowledged. Though now neglected, though now compelled to stem the torrent of popular clamor or party invective; though now we have to plead with ignorance, to contend with obstinacy, to combat with prejudice, the day will come when the value of our labors shall be owned, and we rewarded by seeing them produce the results we had so cordially desired. You and I, my dear friend, have seen times when we had little else than this hope of a future adjustment of present wrongs, to light our darksome path and cheer us on in the way of our duty. And perhaps, notwithstanding your doubts, unsuspected by yourself, you still recur to it, and gather strength for your journey.

The future is represented by religion as a social state. The good and the bad will be separated by feeling not by place; their difference will be in state, not in location. We must then be eternally in the neighborhood of each other. We can never part. Does not this enforce the necessity of acquiring here that social character and that love for each other, which will make our meeting pleasant there? It will be pleasant to renew there friendships begun on earth, and which were interrupted a moment by death. It will also be painful to meet there those we had injured here. Thoughts of that meeting must come with inexpressible delight to the good, and with tremendous power of admonition to the bad. Find you in this nothing to prompt a virtuous life.

In reference to that great and solemn event which awaits us all, the doctrine of immortality proves its power. I do not mean in sustaining us in that trying moment, but in fitting us for just and beneficial action. To the unbeliever death is the total extinction of being. He looks for no life beyond the grave. What is undone when death comes, he believes is undone forever. This reflection, at times, comes upon him with a withering power. He dreads to think that he must die. He has an inward horror that goes with him wherever he goes, and palsies his arm in what ever he would do. He becomes gloomy, unhappy, misanthropic, and here is the end of his virtue.

Here again, the hope of another life proves its power. It takes away that inward horror by assuring us that we do not die, that what we call death is no more than passing from one room to another, that it is as natural and as desirable an event as sleep. We lie down in the grave—no, we deposit in the grave our clogs of earth, our infirmities, to uprise in power, glory and immortality. This quiets the soul and throws it into that state which is the most favorable to an elevated morality.

It is a law of our nature that what makes us unhappy makes us vicious, and what makes us happy is powerful to make us virtuous. Beware of the dark visaged man, on whose brow sits the stern resolve to bear. There may be moments when his heart will soften and his chilled affections show signs of returning life. But usually you will find him as unfriendly to others as he is miserable in himself. That which puts a man at ease with himself, calms his troubled spirit, smooths his ruffled passions, is that which opens his heart to virtue. The tendency of the doctrine of immortality cannot then be mistaken. As it has an influence in reconciling us to ourselves, to our lot, to death itself, it cannot be unfavorable to those actions which mark the elevated mind and the good heart.

Now, my dear friend, review what I have advanced in my last four letters on this charge of yours and say, not to me, but to yourself, if you were not wrong; if religion, instead of degrading, do not ennoble human nature, and, instead of checking, if it do not demand the stronger and nobler exertions of mind? You may say I have proved religion desirable, but that I have not proved it true. Be it so. If I have proved it desirable I have done something. Its truth will be the subject of my remaining letters.

NO. 7 (November 30, 1833): 190

Having, as I trust, my dear friend, proved religion desirable, I now proceed to offer some considerations which I think must go far at least to prove it true.

There is religion in the world. From time immemorial men have had some kind of religion. All ages, all nations, and nearly all individuals—all, whether Pagan, Jew, Moslem, Christian, Indian, Egyptian, Arabian, Chaldean, Persian, Chinese, Japanese, Greek, Roman, South Sea Islander, ancient or modern European, African, native American, all, whether savage, barbarous or civilized, ignorant or enlightened, have admitted a divinity and paid him some sort of religious worship.

I know this statement is sometimes contradicted; I am well aware, that it is pretended that some nations, some wandering tribes at least, have been found that had no kind of religion, and no word in their languages to express the idea of God. But this rests on the doubtful testimony of travelers, who understood not the language of the people they professed to describe. Later discoveries have proved those travelers in many instances wrong, and I think I am by facts which are now well known, fully borne out in my statement. I will reiterate it. Men have everywhere, in all ages and under all circumstances, had a religion of some sort or other.

Now is not this fact, this universal concurrence of mankind a phenomenon that must awaken the curiosity of the philosopher and command his serious attention? Whence came religion? How came all the world to embrace it? Neither you nor I can well avoid putting these questions; or refrain from laboring to ascertain their true answer.

The universal consent of mankind may not be full proof of the truth of a proposition, but it *is* a strong presumption. There must be something extraordinary in a deception, if deception it be, that imposes upon the whole world, and not for one age only, but for a long succession of ages. That must have a very strong resemblance to truth, which is mistaken for it, by men of every grade of intellect, and of every possible variety of taste, habit, education, mode of feeling, thinking and acting. Most singular is it, if it be a falsehood, that no one can prove it so, and make its falsity generally acknowledged.

But whence is the origin of religion? Will you ascribe it to education? Education may perpetuate, but it cannot originate. The father may teach religion to the son, but who taught it to the father? The present generation may have learned it from its predecessor, but where did the first generation obtain it?

Will you pronounce religion a trick of wily statesmen and crafty priests? Priests are ministers of religion. The very idea of a priest presupposes the existence of religion. For what should men appoint priests where they have no religion, no altars, to render their services necessary? Priests may have abused religion, they may have made a trade of it, but they could not have originated that to which they were indebted for their existence. Statesmen have no doubt made of religion an instrument. But what put it into the head of a statesman to invent religion as a means of accomplishing his unholy purposes? Finding a religion already existing, already having a strong hold on men's minds and hearts, on their fears and hopes, we can easily conceive that he might labor to turn it into the channel of his own ambition. But a religion proposed for the first time, proposed when men had never thought of it, when it was foreign to the human soul and all its habits, could have no power, and consequently could offer no temptation to the statesman, nothing to make him desire it for an instrument. Before it could have answered his purpose it must have long existed, have become deeply seated in the human heart, and obtained such an ascendency over it, that it would be retained though perverted to the base work of enslaving him who embraced it.

Will you ascribe it to imagination? I know imagination has a power almost unlimited. Its creations are numerous and often of surpassing beauty. But imagination always takes its coloring from the mind that sends it abroad, and its creations are molded and fixed by the peculiarities of each individual. Men do not imagine alike. Their dreams are as various as their tastes, habits and education. This may be seen in the strange and fantastic work imagination makes with the forms of religion. Every man has a form of religion peculiar to himself. One man's heaven or hell is by no means the heaven or hell of another. In no one point which belongs to the form of religion do men agree. But all or nearly all agree that religion itself, its sentiment, is true. In everything else that is left to conjecture, or to imagination, they are as various as possible; here is a point where all come to the same conclusion. Is it possible that both can be the work of imagination? Why is it so different in its operations? Indeed, if you will contend that it is imagination, I must add that an imagination that creates the same belief in all ages, in all countries, in nearly all individuals, cannot work at random. It can but be subject to some fixed and universal law and does in fact bear the stamp of truth.

Is this belief collected from surrounding nature? Could the outward, the visible, universe originate religion? I do not believe that it could; but admitting that it did, you must admit its correctness. What nature teaches is true. Her voice you allow is the voice of truth, her testimony the testimony of reality. We no more think of calling in question the lessons of nature than we do the sensations of our minds. If then the outward universe, visible and surrounding nature, originated religion, we are bound to receive it.

If you deny that the outward universe could give men the notion of religion, to what then will you ascribe it? You must ascribe its origin to something, and there remains only revelation or instinct.[11]

If the origin of religion be ascribed to revelation, that is enough. God could not reveal his existence, if he did not exist. And if he does exist and has revealed himself, and commanded us to worship him, there can be no question respecting the truth and propriety of religion.

If you deny to religion this origin, there remains for you only the position that it is instinctive, that is, a fundamental law of human

[11]The argument here introduced, is urged, in part, by Addison, in one of his Spectators. But his fondness for wit and humor prevented him from making as much of it as he might. [Ed. Brownson is probably referring to Joseph Addison (1672-1719), author and editor of *The Spectator*, originally issued from March 1, 1711 to December 6, 1712, and June 18 to December 20, 1714. For a reprint, see *The Spectator*, 10 vols. (Boston: Hastings, Etheredge and Bliss, 1809-10).]

nature. In this case we must admit its truth, for it rests on evidence as direct, as positive and as conclusive as the testimony of our senses, and can no more be doubted in a healthy state of the mind and the affections than can be our own existence. This last conclusion is the one I adopt, I consider religion a sentiment of the heart, a fundamental law of human nature.[12]

NO. 8 (December 7, 1833): 194

I stated in my last, my dear friend, that I consider religion instinctive, a fundamental law of our nature. In this case, it is not so much a matter of belief as of consciousness. We are not religious beings because we have been taught religion, nor because we have reasoned ourselves into a belief of its truth. We are religious because we were made to be religious, because religion is as much a want of the soul as food or drink is of the body.

Our approbation of moral justice is the result of no process of reasoning. Convince a man that what you propose is just, and his approbation will be invariably given. It is because he is so made that he cannot but approve what he believes to be just. He who should undertake to prove his own existence, would not be guilty of a greater absurdity than he who should undertake to prove that men ought to be just. No man doubts this. All the reasoning you want is to convince one of what *is* just and to persuade him to do it. It is the same with the religious sentiment. It is something within us, not dependent on our reason, immediate and irresistible in its action. No argument creates it, none can destroy it. It is natural to us, we feel it, know it.

I am led to the conclusion that this sentiment is natural to man from a fact already stated. That which is received in all countries, in all ages, by nearly all men, and of all races of beings by men alone, I think I have a right to infer, is natural to man. You cannot drive men out of nature. You may suppress many of the natural powers, but you

---

[12]The reader may perceive this is the ground assumed by Benjamin Constant in his invaluable work, "De la Religion," and he may also perceive in what will follow several positions and illustrations very similar to some in that work. But I am not indebted to it, as these Letters were written long before I read it. I may be considered then as an independent witness to the same truths. Since I have mentioned Constant, I would enquire whether his work has ever been translated into English? If not, I hope it soon will be for I consider it the best work ever written to establish religion in the minds of unbelievers; at least, setting aside Dr. Channing's works, it is the only one, I have ever found which was not better suited to make sceptics than believers. [Ed. Brownson is referring to Benjamin Constant's *De la religion, considérée dans sa source, ses formes et ses développements*, 5 vols. (Paris: Pichon and Didier, 1824, 1827, 1831).]

can add nothing to them. You cannot compel men to embrace that which is unnatural without having them give you unequivocal signs of its unsuitableness and of their impatience. But in this case almost all men not only embrace religion but cling to it. No arts, no persuasions, can, to any considerable extent, induce them to abandon it. Mankind are pretty generally agreed to treat the atheist with abhorrence. His arguments are usually pronounced sophistical and when unanswerable are unconvincing. Religion is cherished by those who are ridiculed for it, and even by those who are conscious that they are unable to defend it. There is something within stronger than logic, more powerful than ridicule. They have the sentiment, and since this is almost, if not quite universal, and peculiar, I may on the soundest principles of reasoning pronounce it natural to man.

The ease with which religion is received confirms my conclusion. Were it something foreign, unnatural, opposed to our spiritual constitution, we should find in it something repulsive, something demanding of us an effort to be embraced. But we experience nothing of this. The mind takes hold of it with ease. It slides at once into the midst of our most fondly cherished convictions, coalesces with all our tender, generous and elevated sentiments, receives from the heart a most friendly welcome, is embraced with a warmth of affection that increases with age, and a strength of attachment that triumphs over the grave.

This is worthy of remark. We require the creation of no new principle, no new molding of our natures. All is ready prepared for its reception. It comes to us as an expected guest, rather as a returning member of a beloved family, as that after which the heart had yearned. We embrace it, we cling to it as the child clings around its mother's neck. We find it a place in the heart. There we lodge it, as one of our dearest friends, and scarcely any reasoning, scarcely any circumstances whatever, can induce us to expel it, even for a moment. Were it unnatural would it be so cordially welcome, so fondly retained? Try this sentiment with some of the animals around us. Can you make the dog, the horse or the ox, religious? Why not? Why are they not religious as well as man? The beaver erects his house, why not the temple and the altar as well as man, if there be not something in man's nature that determines him towards religion?

The tenacity with which men cling to religion, and the sacrifices they make for it, proves to my understanding that its foundation is in a natural sentiment. There is nothing in nature which surpasses this tenacity. Men adhere to religion in sickness and in health, in prosperity and in adversity, in youth and in old age, in life and in

death. The strength of their attachment may be seen in their obedience to it even when associated with the most painful and revolting
forms of superstition. At its command they part with their most valued possessions, submit to the severest privations; the virgin sacrifices her modesty, the wife her chastity, and the father stretches his
only son upon the altar. That is no ordinary power that can do this.
That which can prove itself thus awfully strong, must have its seat in
human nature. Perverted it is, horribly perverted, but no human being would submit to it when making such demands were there not
something at the bottom inseparable from his very existence.

In our propensity to adore, I read the same truth. Men love to
adore. They look around for some object to worship. Even when we
doubt the existence of God, we feel this propensity. I thought myself
an atheist. I had adopted a mode of philosophizing which excluded
God from the universe. I was sorry that my speculations led to this
result, but I could make them lead to no other. And yet, when I
stood on the borders of the ocean, in the primitive forest, where
silence was unbroken save by here and there a wild note, or amid the
grand and the beautiful, I would long to fancy the universe a temple,
all nature an altar, and I would involuntarily look upward in silent
adoration. When I entered the house dedicated to the worship of
God, though it were but to find matter of merriment or indignation,
when I listened to the holy man in fervent prayer, offered, as I then
believed, to mere vacancy, I would often be surprised to find myself,
in spite of my atheism, filled with the spirit, and engaging with warmth
in the devotions of the place. When alone, in my study, in the silence
of midnight, devotional feelings would come, and come unbidden.
There were times when they fastened upon the soul, as a magic charm,
not to change but to heighten all my faculties. I would then seem to
myself to hold mysterious communings with some hidden intelligence. Feeling was then warm and rich, thought was clear, strong
and apparently almost unlimited. I could see truths of which I had
not been aware, had arguments full and irresistible, language of unrivaled beauty and eloquence, an enthusiasm swallowing up the whole
soul, urging her on to deeds of loftiest virtue. These were visions of
the soul. They came, they went, but always left the spiritual man
stronger and healthier. They were to me then unaccountable, but
always inexpressibly sweet. In their presence I always felt to adore,
and seemed conscious of some invisible spirit breathing fragrance
upon the soul. Whence came these visions? They were the efforts of
nature to rise superior to speculation, the struggles of the religious
sentiment to vanquish doubt.

If not, account to me for that propensity to adore. Tell me whence come these solemn feelings, these inward visions, these mysterious communings, of which we are conscious even in our doubts, and which no reasoning can prevent. It is not education that produces them. We are conscious of them almost from the cradle, and long before instruction on them could be comprehended, we have something of the deep and awful feelings of religion. I can account for them only by supposing religion is natural to man, that the religious sentiment constitutes a part of our own nature, that the great spirit is near us—within us—ever breathing into us notices of himself and secretly inviting us to a communion with him more tender and interesting than human friendship.

But enough till my next.

NO. 9 (December 14, 1833): 198

To resume the topic of my last. I see this propensity to adore and find evidences which convince me, my friend, that the religious sentiment is natural to us, in men's proneness to deify matter and to give a living spirit to every object of surrounding nature.

The human race delight to make the sun and stars, the air, the ocean and the earth, the rivers and the fountains, trees and plants, fruits and flowers, the day and the night, the spring and the fall, the summer and the winter—they delight to make each the residence of a god with whom they might hold intercourse. This is indeed the religious sentiment in its wildness, untamed by reason, but something deeply planted in human nature lies at the bottom of it. Even now, we half regret the Naiad, the Dryad,[13] the river-god, the wood and the ocean nymph. There is that within us which delights to multiply the Divinity around us, and in this I see that which bids man own and worship God.

The pleasure which we receive from indulging our propensity to adore, leads me to the same conclusion. The worship of God calls into exercise our holiest feelings and engages our sweetest and most abiding affections. There is no love so full as that which the soul may have for God. There is nothing of which the heart is susceptible, so sacred, so absorbing as adoration. It is a fullness of enjoyment that may be felt, but which no language can describe. The meeting of mind with mind, of soul with soul, the union of heart with heart, is sweet, beyond expression, but it gives one only a faint notion of the meeting of the soul with God, of the union of our spirits with the

[13][Ed. Naiad in Greek mythology was one of the nymphs living in and presiding over brooks, springs and fountains. The Dryad, a wood nymph, in Greek mythology was a nature divinity inhabiting or presiding over forest or trees.]

Father-Spirit. In silence we meet him, in the quietude of our own hearts, we find him a spirit, full of life and light, all that we can love, all that we can adore. Communion with him stirs up our love from the very depths, and we love on and on till we grow into his likeness and have our wills swallowed up in his. Were this possible if the exercise of adoration were unnatural? Could we find this pure, deep and lasting pleasure in worshiping God were not our natures fitted to worship him, were not his worship a want, a fundamental law of the soul?

If these considerations suggest, as I think they must, a train of reasoning which proves the religious sentiment natural to man, we can hardly escape the conclusion that there is a God, a Divinity in whom that sentiment finds the object it craves. Contend that there is no God whom we may love and adore, the teachings of this sentiment must be false. Its inspirations are then deserving no confidence, its promptings would only drive us into error. Is this the case with any other sentiment of our nature? Is not the language of all the other sentiments, so far at least as we can ascertain, the language of truth? How comes it that this is an exception? The others have never deceived us, why shall we then distrust this? The evidence of our sentiments is as strong and as worthy of confidence as the evidence of our senses or of our understanding. We admit that evidence and act upon it every day of our lives. In every case except this we make no question of its soundness, why shall we here? The sentiment of moral justice leads us to view actions and agents not merely as useful or injurious, but as just or as unjust. No man in his heart doubts that a man doing a good or a bad action differs essentially from a good or a bad knife. The knife is tried by the law of utility; but the man, if he be of a sound mind, is tried by another law and is always condemned if proved unjust, though his conduct have been in the highest degree useful. On this idea of the just as independent of the useful is founded the whole fabric of morality. But this idea of the just, or this senti-ment of morality belongs to the same category as does the religious sentiment. The evidence in both cases is precisely the same; why ad-mit it in one and not in the other? This sentiment compels us to worship God as irresistibly as the sentiment of morality compels us to bestow a lively approbation upon a good man or a virtuous act. And that which we feel is that which satisfies us the man is good, or the act is virtuous. Why should not that inward feeling, which satis-fies us that the God we worship is a reality, not be held as good logic here as there? If it be, we must acknowledge there is a God.

Without admitting there is a God a large portion of our faculties must remain unquickened, unexerted. We have all the faculties required to love God, deny his existence, and what is there to exert them? That capacity which we have to take in the magnificent idea of God, that capacity which we have to bind ourselves to him and to possess some of that superior excellence which the soul by its inward visions sees in him, must be counted for nothing if his existence be not admitted. All those sweet feelings, all those pure and abiding affections, which communion with Him quickens and employs, must be foregone, if there be no God, if we may not believe there is. The soul seems to have powers and capacities which are only for God. Nothing but God can fill its deep wants. This world is too small. The soul looks beyond the earth, beyond the heavens, beyond the fixed stars, beyond the farthest limits of space, beyond all time for something equal to what it is conscious of in itself. Deny it is a God of infinite perfection on whom it may fasten and to whom it may assimilate, and it turns back in disappointment, feeds in sorrow, grows sickly, pines away—dies.

You know, my dear friend, and so do I, what a blank there is in the world to him who sees no God. He is the poor friendless child looking around in vain for his Father. You and I have asked, "where is he?" and echo has answered, "where?" I cannot describe that sinking of the soul I then felt. All within me became dark. I saw not where to bestow my affections, I saw no object that seemed worthy of that fullness of love, of which the heart was susceptible. At times I loathed my being, in the bitterness of my soul cursed the unknown cause that gave me birth, and would, if I could, have blotted out the universe and laughed over its mighty void. These were feelings of a soul in ruins, but of one ruined, because its inward sentiment was deprived of the object it craved. They said I was mad. It may be they were right. Religion had been to me a source of deep and cherished feeling. It had sustained me amid trials to which youth are not often exposed. It had cheered my solitary path and been to me father, mother, sister, brother. It had been with me in my labors and my studies, had lightened the one and aided the other. But now a fatal eclipse had come over the soul, the torch of reason was obscured, and I no longer saw my Father-God, no longer heard his voice, no longer was conscious of that presence, which had been to me my all, and all I wished. I was alone, in a cold, dark world, "a friendless child without a sire."[14] No wonder if I was mad. Perhaps all are not affected in

---

[14][Ed. Not able to identify quotation.]

the same degree that I was, but all are deeply affected. And why? Because that which gave employment to the affections and sustained the heart is taken away. Those affections are now useless, the soul becomes desolate. That which made its life, supplied its wants, and filled its thoughts is gone, and it weeps its loss.

This clearly proves to me that we have a class of faculties which are only for God. To deprive them of their object is to leave them to prey upon themselves. Give them God and heaven and they find that which is wanted; they fall into their proper rank; the whole soul is engaged and moves on in healthy and harmonious action. May I infer nothing from this? If the soul cannot obtain the healthy exercise of all its faculties without God, and if by his presence all be healthy, all be employed, all move on in harmony, why shall we hesitate to pronounce the religious sentiment natural to man, or fear to clasp to our hearts the belief that God is and that we are made for him? In the love and worship of God, all our faculties may be employed; without them, they cannot be, but must remain useless, to stagnate, or to drive the soul to madness. Do you ask stronger evidence to prove religion is the natural element of the soul, and that the testimony of its inward sentiment is worthy of confidence? I think you cannot. For myself this is enough, I yield to the promptings of my own heart, trace the religious sentiment up to my heavenly Father, repose in confidence on the bosom of the Divinity and commit my doubts to the winds.

Whoever will attend to the workings of his own soul, to its deep wants and holy aspirations, to its yearnings and its sighings after a greater, a more substantial good than earth has given or can give, cannot mistake the religious sentiment. He who communes with his own heart, follows that inward light which he will discover whenever he looks steadily within, will hardly fail to find the pathway to God and heaven. It is not from abroad, but from within that we obtain the proofs of religion. They are not, cannot be, communicated from one mind to another. Each must, and I believe, each may, find them in himself. Look within. You have a noble nature; you are conscious of holy breathings and of lofty struggles; you are capable of deep and solemn feeling, of sacred and living love for all that is great and good. You see nothing around you equal to your power of love or the wants of the soul. Earth is too narrow, life is too barren, man is too poor in incident, too feeble in action, to stir all your energies, interest all your affections, and absorb the whole soul. You look round for something wider, deeper, higher, and lovelier; you have visions of infinitely greater good than any you find; you see no where realized the perfection the mind bodies forth in its upward tendencies. Dissatisfied you rise to the contemplation of the everlasting God, and there you find all that you can desire. You cannot wish beyond his goodness, think beyond his wisdom, nor imagine beyond his perfection. Follow out the train of thought here suggested, be just to yourself, mark accurately what passes in your own soul and you cannot fail to find yourself once more within the arms of the Divinity, within the embrace of your Father.

Here I must reluctantly close. To complete the plan I at first prescribed to myself, it would be necessary for me in addition to what I have done to point you to some more direct proofs of the being of God, to give you the grounds on which I hope for a future life and expect a future righteous retribution; also to discuss the important topics of inspiration in general and that of the Bible in particular. I have made some progress, collected some materials, and may, hereafter, perhaps, complete the plan. But not now. Others have done, or are doing the work, better than I can. To them I refer you, and in case they give you no satisfaction, I will refer you again to your own spiritual nature, with the request that you will venture a prayer to the Great Source of Light for that illumination of which you may feel the necessity. Farewell.

29.

CHRISTIANITY AND REFORM

Unitarian 1 (January 1834): 30-39

Thousands assure us that we live in a wonder-working age, and refer us for proof to man's conquests over the material world. We are told that man has attacked the elements and subdued them, made the most hurtful comparatively harmless, and the most stubborn ministers to his wants or his pleasures.

But man's moral conquests are far more striking proofs of his power and are infinitely more encouraging to the philanthropist. Moral events, which are to influence all coming generations, have succeeded, and are succeeding, each other with astonishing rapidity. It would seem that in these latter days a new spirit had been breathed into the moral world. Mind breaks its long slumber and begins to exert its energies. Men begin to feel the workings of a nobler nature, and to indulge, and labor to embody, visions of a higher and lovelier destiny for the human race.

A war rages—a war of opinion—between the past and the future, between the advocates of the old order of things, and those who demand new and better institutions for time to come. It extends to everything. Nothing is too sacred to be attacked. Nothing in politics, in morals, or in religion, is too venerable for its age, too well established by experience, to escape the hand of the ruthless soldier of the *movement* party in this new and fearful war. Blows are struck at the very foundation of the existing social order and the ruins of all once held sacred are exposed to the idle gaze of the multitude.

All over the world the war has commenced. All over the world the demand for reform is uttered; in some places, in sounds half suppressed and scarcely audible; but in others, in tones loud, determined, and startling. In all communities there is a deep feeling, there are full hearts, there are quickened spirits, that will dare improvements in man's moral and social condition, with the hero's courage, with the saint's singleness of purpose, and with the martyr's firmness. The millions awake. They begin to perceive, or imagine they perceive, that they have been trifled with, that they have tamely submitted to an order of things which a little well directed exertion on their part would have exchanged for one immeasurably better. Urged on by a sense of real or fancied wrongs, they are collecting their forces and nerving their souls to the battle.

Such is the rising spirit of the times. We may deny or seek to disguise it, but proofs meet the eye at every glance. We may denounce it, declaim or reason against it, call it dangerous, impious, blasphemous, or what we will; its course is onward, and no power on earth can stay its progress or scatter its gathering forces. It may pass over the earth with desolation and death, may sweep off everything well established in government, pure in morals, or venerable in religion, but it must and will have its course. Of this we may be assured, great and lasting changes will be effected. The day has gone by to prevent it. The work is too far advanced to be arrested. Will the changes to be introduced settle down into salutary reforms, or will they prove only mischievous innovations? This is no trifling question. The wise and the good ask it with solicitude, if not with alarm. What answer shall be returned?

I may be answered, that the results of the impending struggle will be good or bad, according to the alliances which may be formed. If the spirit at work ally itself to infidelity, nothing valuable will be gained; if to religion, the most satisfactory consequences may be predicted.

This article will therefore labor to prove that no salutary reform can be effected by infidelity, and that the spirit of reform is, in fact, the very spirit of the gospel.

Those who are acquainted with man's whole nature require no proof of the first position here assumed. But these are not many. Enough has been witnessed for a few years past in our own country as well as in other countries to convince us that those are not wanting who think they must commence reformers by making war upon the church, declaiming against the clergy, and breaking men loose from the restraints of religion. When the French reformer undertook to remodel society and to base his government on "the rights of man," he judged it necessary to reject religion. In England, at the present moment, many of the publications addressed to the laboring classes, publications, which are the boldest and most popular advocates of reform, are either avowedly infidel, or else, under the pretense of opposing the church establishment, use arguments which strike at the foundation of religion itself. In our own country, within a few years, we have seen start up a large number of publications professedly advocating a radical reform in the social institutions of all countries, and, without a single exception, all have openly or covertly, attacked religion. Almost every young man, who learns, for the first time, that all, which is, is not right, charges the wrong he thinks he has discovered to the clergy, and believes himself aiding a reform by opposing them, and, too often, the cause they were set apart to defend. It is true, that he is soon cured of this folly, but seldom without the loss of those generous feelings by which he was governed. These are facts not without meaning. They admonish us that it is no work of supererogation to prove that infidelity can effect no real reform.

To effect any real reform, the individual man must be improved. The mass of mankind is made up of individuals. There is no such thing as reforming the mass without reforming the individuals who compose it. The mass of mankind is often spoken of as if it were a real individual; but in itself it is nothing. It has no head, no heart, no soul, no character, but as these exist in its individual members. Each member of the great whole has a separate existence, will, powers, duties of his own, and which cannot be merged in the mass. The reformer's concern is with the individual. That which gives to the individual a free mind, a pure heart, and full scope for just and beneficial action, is that which will reform the many. When the majority of any community are fitted for better institutions, for a more advanced state of society, that state will be introduced and those institutions will be secured. What the reformer, then, wants is the power to elevate the individual, to quicken in his soul the love of the highest excellence, and to urge him forward towards perfection with new and stronger impulses.

Will infidelity supply this power? Does infidelity seek to reform individual character? It is folly to pretend that it does. It attacks institutions. It deals only with some of the forms under which the errors of individual character may have been manifested, while it leaves the errors themselves untouched. It pronounces religion false and its action on man's social relations mischievous. It declaims against government, but it does not propose a remedy for those depravities of individual character which render government necessary. Viewed in the most favorable light, it is powerless. Separated from what it often borrows from religion, it can present no motive to action. It has no power to kindle up a moral energy in the soul, and to arm it for a long and vigorous struggle for lofty and abiding virtue. The highest standard of morality it can recognize is expediency and expediency for this short and transitory life.

Till within a few years, the unbeliever dreamed of no social reform, advocated no moral progress, imagined nothing better for man than the long train of existing abuses, unless, indeed, it were, that he should go back to the condition of the "untutored savage." What visions of a higher and better social existence than that they found already sustained, ever flitted across the minds of such men as Hobbes, Mandeville, Hume and Gibbon?[1] What inward thirst, what promptings of the soul, had they for a purer virtue, a greater amount of human happiness—they, who seem to have had not the least sympathy with their fellow beings? Indeed, what inducement can he who believes merely that he is today, and tomorrow will not be, what inducement can he have to struggle with "the powers that be," to risk ease, property, reputation, perhaps life, to benefit those of whom he knows nothing, for whom he cares nothing, and who, like him, are only for a day, destined to flourish in the morning, to wither at noon, and to die ere it is night? Indeed, after the novelty of his disbelief has worn off, the unbeliever seldom troubles himself much about anything except his own immediate interests. He wraps himself up in his selfishness, looks in scorn upon the world, and bids it take care of itself. You often find him the loudest and most inveterate opponent of all useful changes. Where religion is popular, you may not infrequently see him in the garb of the church, consoling himself for his hypocrisy by saying, every man is selfish, following only his own selfish purposes, and that he must take the same course in self-defense. Long would reform sleep undisturbed, were it entrusted to the care of such as he!

[1][Ed. Thomas Hobbes (1588-1679) was an English philosopher who held that sovereignty, although derived from the people and not of divine right, is transferred from people to the king (monarch) by implicit contract and that power is absolute, but not of divine right. His greatest work, *Leviathan* (1651), was in support of political absolutism. He also supported psychological determinism against the free-will advocates. Brownson could be referring here to Bernard Mandeville (?1670-1733), a Dutch-English satirist and author of the *Fable of the Bees* (1705), a symbolic story of human society. For Mandeville progress and prosperity were not the result of virtue, but of such vices as egotistical ambition, desire for gain, and showy expenditure. He is said to have influenced Hobbes and paved the way for Jeremy Bentham's utilitarianism. David Hume (1711-76), Scottish philosopher and historian, was author of *Philosophical Essays Concerning Human Understanding* (1748), which contained his famous "Essay upon Miracles." That essay argued that "it is contrary to experience that a miracle should be true, but not contrary to experience that testimony should be false." To some extent by reducing reason to a product of experience he destroyed its claim to sole validity. His position could lead toward skepticism because of his view that beliefs in the existence of God and of the physical world, though a practical necessity, could not be proved by reason. Edward Gibbon (1737-94), historian of the later Roman Empire, was author of the famous *Decline and Fall of the Roman Empire*, 6 volumes (1776-88), which presented an anti-supernatural perspective on the rise and early growth of Christianity and all supernatural considerations were treated with bitter irony and ridicule. He was typical of an elegant eighteenth-century skepticism.]

It is true that infidelity, in these days, pretends to be a reformer. It speaks much of the debasement of the human mind, of the degradation of human nature, and makes loud and frequent demands for improvement; but, usually, without any clear conceptions of what would be an improvement, without any knowledge of what lies at the bottom of existing abuses, of man's wants and capabilities, or of what would supply the one or fully develop the other. One attributes all the wrong which exists to a mischievous government, another to the malign influence of certain indefinable, constantly varying external circumstances, another to the prevalence of religious belief, another to the priesthood, even where no priesthood exists, and so on to the end of the chapter. But in all their speculations, the idea of improving the individual man, as the means of improving the body of which he is a member, seems never to have come across the minds of unbelievers. They demand radical changes, but seem to have no suspicion that there can be no radical changes in society, or if there can, that none are desirable, any farther than they may be rendered necessary by radical changes in individual character. In France, the unbeliever, for a time, had an open field and fair play. He began by overturning the whole fabric of society, and then reorganized it according to his own mind. As he had modeled his new institutions after the principles of his ideal perfection, he was surprised to find that they did not produce the results he had predicted. It did not, at first, occur to him, that his new institutions and the character of the individuals for whom he had provided them were not in harmony; and when he did learn this, he believed the shortest way to remove the discrepancy was to destroy nearly all the then existing generation. Hence, his reform became a reign of terror and his efforts in behalf of free institutions have retarded the march of liberty for centuries. All this evil would have been avoided had he perceived that his work should begin with the individual, that he should first raise the individual and develop the powers of the individual mind. Had he done this, he would have elevated the standard of morality, and produced a discrepancy between individual character and—not his new institutions—but the old, and this would have inevitably involved their destruction, and have necessarily introduced new ones, as perfect as the new standard of individual excellence would admit. The notion that government and social institutions can produce and preserve any given description of individual character would never have been entertained and tyrants would not have been furnished with another plea for despotism to save society from the horrors of anarchy.

In this country, we established a free government, not because we had reasoned ourselves into a belief of its superiority to all others, not because we believed it would produce and preserve the virtues of individual character but because such were already the virtues and the intelligence of our citizens as individuals, that none other than a free government would have been in harmony with their character. That even a free government and comparatively perfect social institutions do not necessarily preserve a corresponding excellence in individual character, is obvious from what we are daily witnessing among ourselves. Our people, as individuals, in the high uncompromising moral virtues, are very little, if at all, in advance of what they were at the commencement of our glorious struggle for freedom and national independence. We have thus far depended too much upon a free government and enlightened institutions, and have vainly thought to legislate people into high-toned moral beings. The better informed among us are daily perceiving the necessity of paying more and more attention to the culture of the individual mind. They are daily becoming better and better convinced that the only way to set the mass of our citizens forward in the career of virtuous improvement is to develop the capabilities of the individual man; to induce him to employ all his faculties in the accomplishment of just ends, and to exert all his energies to the perfecting of his own mind and heart.

Nothing, it should be added, will reform the individual that does not appeal to his whole nature and give full employment to all, especially his higher faculties. This infidelity cannot do. It addresses us as animals, not as men. It has no concern with the soul. It recognizes no spirit in man, and, consequently, can appeal only to the body, to bodily appetites and bodily powers. It can give us no high and stirring views of our nature, no inducement to pure and elevated virtue, by assuring us that we are related to a Being who is infinitely great and supremely good, that we are kindred spirits and may attain to a kindred excellence with the everlasting God. In one word, it can make no appeal to the religious sentiment, can furnish nothing on which the religious affections can lay hold, and from which they may derive purity, strength, and delight. In this it leaves out a part and that the noblest part of our nature.

It is not necessary to prove that the religious sentiment is a part of our nature. We see this, we feel and know it. All ages, all countries, and nearly all individuals have the sentiment and manifest it in combination with some form of religion. True, some few of our race have not always felt the inward workings of the religious sentiment, but to infer from this, that it is not natural to man, would be as absurd as to pretend that hunger and thirst are not natural, because, in certain morbid states of the stomach, there is felt no appetite for food or drink. Take away God and religion from the soul, its moral life dies, as quickly as does the body when deprived of wholesome nutriment. The soul hungers and thirsts for religion. Religion is its meat and drink; its bread of life; and is as strongly craved, as much needed for its growth and healthy action, as is food or drink for the body. How, then, can we hope to find the individual man morally strong and healthy, when deprived of this nutriment of the soul? Without this he must inevitably pine away, wither into a mere animal, to vegetate, propagate its species, and die. Yet of this would infidelity deprive us and to this wretched fate would it abandon us.

No change, which does not tend to give free and full scope for the just exercise of all our faculties, can be a real reform. The only error of the present state of things is, that it infringes right action, supplies motives to wrong, and prevents the full development of the individual mind. What we want, are such changes, such improvements, as will develop, employ, task to their fullest extent, and rightly direct all the faculties of our common nature. But such, infidelity cannot effect. Denying the religious sentiment, it can assign no place for its development; discarding all the pious affections, it can afford them no employment in its new-modeled society, and shape nothing to their wants; contemplating only the human animal, it can make provision only for animal wants; and having no use for the spiritual nature, it must do all it can to break and destroy its power. Let any man ascertain accurately how large a portion of his nature finds employment only in that which belongs to religion, or is in some way dependent on the religious sentiment, and he may easily satisfy himself, whether infidelity would be likely to reorganize society, so as to give full scope for the free, vigorous and healthy exercise of our whole nature.

Now as infidelity does not propose to do this, has never done it, and never can do it, it can produce no salutary reform. The institutions it would introduce would always be opposed to the development of much of our nature, and to individual improvement; consequently, they would be mischievous. They would place the social and the individual man in a state of perpetual war; the spiritual and the animal nature in an eternal struggle. The bosom would be torn by contending factions; government would be one thing today, and another tomorrow, and nothing would be fixed but anarchy and confusion.

That infidelity and the spirit of reform have sometimes been found in alliance is not denied; but this alliance is unnatural and has never produced anything worth preserving. Reformers have some-times erred. Animated by a strong desire for human improvement, feeling an undying love for man, they have freely devoted themselves to his emancipation and to the promotion of his endless progress towards perfection; but they have not always had clear conceptions of what would be an improvement, of the good attainable, nor of the practicable means of attaining it. Their zeal may have flowed from pure hearts but it has not always been guided by just knowledge. They have often excited needless alarm, waged needless war, declaimed when they should have reasoned, censured when they should have pitied and consoled, awakened resentment when they should have gained confidence and attracted love. The consequence is that they have been opposed by their natural friends and this has obliged them to league with their natural enemies.

In the contest, the reformer has excited the alarms of the reli-gious and armed against himself the guardians of the faith. He has met the minister of the church commanding him in the name of God to desist, and assuring him, that if he take another step forward, he does it at the peril of his soul's salvation. When the French re-former rose against the mischievous remains of the feudal system and the severe exactions of a superannuated tyranny, he found the church leagued with the abuses he would correct. Those who lived upon her revenues bade him retire. The anathema met his advance and re-pelled his attacks; and he was induced to believe there was no place whereon to erect the palace of liberty and social order, but the ruins of the temple.

Yet his cause was most eminently a religious cause. It was not that the spirit of reform was an infidel spirit, that it was opposed by the professed friends of religion. All reforms come from the lower classes who are always the sufferers; and they are usually opposed by the higher classes who live by those very abuses, or who are the higher classes in consequence of those very abuses which the reformer would redress. These classes, whether hereditary, elective, or fortuitous, whether composed of the same individuals or of different ones, have always the same spirit and the same interests. The old order of things is that which elevates them; and that order of things they, of course, must feel it their interest to maintain. Hence it is that the upper classes of society, all who are under the direct influence of those classes, and all who hope one day to make a part of them are almost always opposed to all radical changes and consequently to all real reform. In most countries, the ministers of religion, especially the higher orders of the hierarchy, make up a part of the higher and privileged classes, and hence the reason why they oppose the reformer, and force him into the ranks of the unbeliever. They, from their position, feel no need of a reform in the moral and social institutions of the community and hope nothing from a change; and, as they are supposed to be like other men, they can but oppose it; they always have done so, and they always will do so, till they are made sensible that they must lose all their influence and their means of benefitting themselves or others by continuing their opposition.

It is because the ministers of religion have in most countries and in most ages of the world formed one of the higher classes or constituted one of the privileged orders that we have so uniformly found them in past times at least advocates of the stationary principle. Where a man's treasure is, there will be his heart; and they had their treasure, they always have their treasure, in the existing order of things. This were no subject of complaint were the existing order always the best order; were not progress a law of our nature and an inevitable condition of human society; were we able at any given time to reach the perfect, instead of being destined to be eternally approaching it. But such is not the fact. Man's course is onward. No state of society is perfect. No form of religion has ever yet been extensively embraced but it had its imperfections. Christianity has been everywhere presented under forms which ever have been and ever will be opposed, as mind advances and there is felt the want of something more liberal and more refined. Admit that the spirit of Christianity is always the same, yet its forms may be changed to suit the changes of individuals and of societies and were this done no difficulty would occur. But its ministers and its professed friends declare religion to be identified with forms which have become revolting and thus the reformer is driven from their company to that of the infidel.

It is never religion itself that the reformer opposes. He finds the gospel adulterated; he finds a foul and unnatural mixture presented him in the place of pure religion, and it is always those parts which are foreign to religion, but which are presented with it, that excite his hostility. Yet, in opposing the mixture, he may sometimes, innocently, because unintentionally, oppose the pure; in attacking the abuse, he may sometimes inadvertently strike the thing abused; in warring against the wrong-headed advocate, he may war against religion itself. He may not always clearly discriminate in his own mind; and if he should not, he is not more guilty than thousands who pass for good Christians. And should he make the proper distinctions in his own mind, he may fail to make others perceive them; for the vast majority of mankind identify religion with the abuses he would correct; and we need not, perhaps, be either surprised or angry, if, in his zeal for reform, wearied with effort after effort, opposed on every hand and persecuted by the servants of the temple, he come to the conclusion that it is best to cut the knot and reject religion entirely. Men have so done, they may continue to do so, but no genuine friend to man ever did or ever will come to this conclusion till driven to it by the professed guardians of the faith, "who neither enter into the kingdom of heaven themselves, nor suffer those that would to enter."

This should induce no Christian to decry reform. It should rather lead him to inquire if he be not supporting religion under a form which is opposed to the progress of mind. The "overflowing scourge," which will sweep off "every refuge of lies," is now passing over the earth and well doth it import us to surrender voluntarily whatever we love that is not based on eternal truth, that is not absolutely essential to the existence and free and healthy action of the religious sentiment. Well doth it import us all to return to the simplicity of the gospel, and to refuse, henceforth, to defend religion under any form not consistent with the endless progress of human reason and the ever advancing state of human society.

The consideration of my second position, namely, that the spirit of reform is in fact the very spirit of religion, is reserved for another number; as more room has been already occupied than was intended.

(February 1834): 51-58

In a former article, we attempted to show that no real reform in man's moral or social condition can be effected by infidelity. We now proceed to the consideration of our second point, namely, that the spirit of reform is in fact the very spirit of the gospel. This proposition may require some proof. Everybody may not perceive, at first sight, the identity of the spirit of the gospel with that spirit which now agitates "the millions." There are those who look only on the surface of things, and never have any notion of what lies at the bottom; let such as these suspend their judgment, till they have examined and collected facts to make their judgment worthy of attention.

The spirit which lies at the bottom of the movements among the people is the spirit of reform, of progress. It may seem to the superficial observer only the spirit of insubordination, of restlessness, of unnecessary, if not criminal, agitation. But discontent, insubordination, destructive as either may be, should not be condemned. Man is a progressive being. His uneasiness at his present condition is the result of an internal consciousness, vaguely defined, poorly understood, perhaps, that he is susceptible of something better. He has an inward thirst for perfection. The millions now feel the workings of this desire, this craving for a more perfect moral and social condition. They are conscious of wants which the present state of things cannot satisfy. They demand something better; they resolve and struggle to gain it. They may not clearly perceive what would be an improvement; they may even place perfection in that which would be a deterioration; but this alters not the character of the spirit which urges them forward. They wish something which will satisfy all the wants of the soul; and if they direct their exertions towards that which will not do this, the defect is not in the spirit that moves, but in the judgment which directs.

The spirit whose movements have encouraged some, alarmed and offended others, is, thus, the spirit of reform, of progress, a spirit always aiming at perfection. Is not this, in fact, the very spirit of the gospel? To answer this question, one should clearly perceive and fully comprehend the character of that work which the author of the gospel came into the world to perform.

That work has greatly suffered by not having been understood. He who reads the gospel carefully, bringing to his aid enlightened philosophy and just criticism, cannot fail to perceive that it was not, as too many have imagined, the primary object of Jesus to make us happy in the world to come. If the good he labored to effect was to extend beyond this life, into that which is eternal, it was only because the acquisition of holiness here sets one so much the farther forward in holiness hereafter. It was this world that he came to bless—man, in his earthly mode of being, that he preached, suffered, and died to make happy. He indeed alluded to another world; he promised the rewards of heaven to the good; he startled the wicked with fears of punishment in hell; but it was to reach the hearts and consciences of men, to reform the individual, and, through the individual, the mass. The world was wrong, was wretched; he came to meliorate it, to set it right. Hence, the first words which broke from his lips in public were, "Reform, for the reign of God approacheth" [Matt 3:2].

Are there those who deny this? What, then, does the gospel demand? What is it that Jesus requires? Did he not, in his mission, contemplate the production of greater purity of heart, a deeper sense of duty and of individual responsibility? Was not the gospel given to breathe new life into the soul, to urge it on by new and stronger impulses to a higher, a more abiding, an ever enlarging virtue? Did it not, does it not, appeal directly to the individual heart, and seek to kindle up a strong, undying love for all that is pure, useful, generous, and noble in character; and was it not expressly designed to impart the inward power needed to gain it? Is not here the spirit of reform, of a radical reform?

But this reform is not the production of a moment. It must be gradual, a progress, a growth. The gospel commands us to improve in knowledge and virtue, to "grow in grace, to press onward and upward towards the mark of our high calling" [2 Pet 3:18], "to become perfect as our Father in heaven is perfect" [Matt 5:48]. It is not with one degree of holiness, not with one step forward in the eternal career of moral progress, that the gospel is satisfied. It is the highest degree, the step farthest in advance possible, that it demands. It has no smile for mediocrity, no indulgence for the indolent. Its look is forward, and if it sometimes permits one to survey the ground over which he has passed, it is not that he may applaud himself for the progress already made, but that he may gather fresh courage and hope for the journey which still lies before. Is not here the spirit of progress, the spirit urging on to perfection?

Nor is it to one individual alone that the gospel appeals, not one alone it would quicken and urge onward in a glorious career of improvement. It appeals to all. What it demands of one individual it demands of every individual. It acknowledges no man's right to be a sinner—declares that no man can be exempt from the law of duty—declares, in terms not to be misinterpreted, to the high and the low, to the rich and the poor, to the bond and the free, that no one has the consent of his Maker to do that which is wrong or to neglect that which is right. The spirit of the gospel, then, requires a universal reform; it requires every individual to advance, to grow in grace, to press on towards perfection; and does not this identify it, in reality, with the stirring spirit of the times? With the spirit—not of the stationary—but of the movement party?

Does the gospel demand that which is impracticable? Does it demand this extensive, this radical reform, without permitting us to hope that it can be realized? So, indeed, it would seem, from the language of its professed friends. Even religious men brand him who proposes such a reform, a disturber of the peace, call him a disorganizer, and enough of other epithets of reproach. He who ventures to predict that it will be realized, is pronounced a visionary, and people propose a straitjacket, or physic and good regimen, as the only suitable arguments to be urged against him. "The evils of society," we are gravely told, "always have existed, and always must exist. Man has always preyed upon man and always will do so. It is in human nature to do so, and he but betrays his ignorance who dreams of a change." Perhaps so. Those who say so are doubtless wise men, men who are well acquainted with human nature in its diseased, if not in its healthy, manifestations. And yet, there is a singular inconsistency in these very wise men. They deny that the mass of mankind can possibly become virtuous; but point them to any particular individual of that mass, and they will admit, that that individual may, if he will, become a high-toned moral being. They thus deny of the whole, what they admit to be true of all its parts, and of parts, too, which are very much alike. For all men have, substantially, the same nature; all have within themselves all the elements of thought, of reason, of virtue. The greatest and best have nothing of which the least and worst have not the germs. And there is not an individual in whom those germs cannot be warmed into life and expanded into a generous virtue. Every man is commanded to love God with all his heart, soul, and strength, and his neighbor as himself. Single out one that cannot do this. Cannot *you* thus love God and man? Cannot your neighbor? His neighbor? And his? Where is there one who cannot? Nowhere? Then all can comply with the requisitions of the gospel. Each individual can reform, can improve, can attain a high moral standing. If each individual can, all can; and, of course, the great mass of mankind can become virtuous.

Should every individual become virtuous, acquire that purity of heart, that firmness of purpose, that love to God and to man, which the gospel demands, that moral growth which Jesus labored to produce, there could remain no institutions of an evil tendency. All that now bears man down to the dust and darkens his soul would be removed, all social as well as all private evils would disappear, and all governments would be so remodeled, as to have no longer a deteriorating influence. Bad governments, mischievous social institutions, are not to be attributed to the defects of rulers, to their ignorance, to their vices, nor to their crimes, but to the people. No people worthy of freedom was ever enslaved. When the majority of a community are really free in themselves, have pure and just principles, firm and manly characters, no tyrant can enslave that community, no mischievous government can possibly be established over it. Whatever political evils there may be in any community, they must disappear in the exact proportion that the growth of individual virtue demands. Make all men good Christians, and all can and should be, all governments would become free, all social institutions beneficial, and man's intercourse with man, harmonious, pleasing, endearing.

That Jesus came to introduce a new order of things, to change, to perfect, man's moral and social institutions has indeed been admitted by some, but so timidly, with such coldness of assent, that the admission has led to little vigorous and well sustained exertion. The great mass of the friends as well as the opponents of the gospel have had but a slight glimpse of this truth. They have said, and still say, that such could not have been his object, because he has not yet accomplished it. But we have seen too manythings effected during the last hundred years, which former generations would have pronounced impossible, to regard with much attention the reasoning that would measure the future by the past, that would infer that because a thing has not been it therefore cannot be. The work which Jesus proposed is not, indeed, yet accomplished. That work was immense. The gospel found the human race with false ideas of morality and religion, with mischievous governments, and institutions almost universally opposed to the interests of society. The prevalent modes of feeling, thinking, and acting were wrong. Things were valued in an inverse ratio to their real worth. Fame was obtained, not by real virtue, not by the preservation, but by the destruction, of human life. War was the business and the glory of governments and rulers. The useful arts were menial and were assigned to those who had and could have no share in what were esteemed honorable pursuits. The worship of God was an outward service, an observance of impure or debasing rites and ceremonies, performed, not at the command of conscience, but of the state or the priesthood. Now all this was to be changed. For the pompous was to be substituted the simple, for the external, the internal. The mere member of the state or of a sacerdotal corporation was to be converted into an individual, with rights, duties, responsibilities of his own. The useless was to give place to the useful, war to peace, the destruction of human life to its preservation, the false estimate of things to the true; and nothing was to be valued except in proportion to its power to add something to the well-being of man; nothing was to be accounted virtue which might not do something to develop the spiritual nature, to make man a more elevated moral being, a more pious worshiper of God, a warmer or steadier friend to his race. This was not the work of a day. Without converting man into a different order of being, it could be done only gradually; and because it is not yet completed, shall we rashly say it was never designed?

One great reason why Jesus has not effected more may be found in the contracted notions which have been entertained of his design. Of those who heard him most gladly, few comprehended his object. The ignorant multitude of that day did not and could not comprehend it. It far exceeded their stage of mental progress, to take in the idea of a reform so extensive and so radical as he proposed. They were incapable of understanding that it was an entire new order of things which he wished to effect. They degraded him in their minds, from the dignity of a moral regenerator of the world, to the littleness of a theological disputant. They supposed he had come to change a few items of religious belief, to alter or abolish a few of the forms of religious worship, that he had come merely to mend with a piece of new cloth a few of the rents in the old worn-out garment of the social and moral system; but they never imagined, notwithstanding they were so informed, that the new would tear away from the old, and the rent thus be made worse, and that the only rational way of proceeding was to throw off the old and to put on an entire new garment. Consequently, though Christ was nominally preached, for a long series of years his power was scarcely felt, and the great object of his mission was unperceived. People (to borrow, with a slight variation, another scriptural illustration) people "called themselves by the name" of Christ "to take away their reproach"; but they were "content to eat their own bread and wear their own apparel"[2]—they would fain be known by his name, but in regard to anything beyond this, to any change of life consequent thereupon, they cared not, they thought not. That he had power to touch the heart, power to quicken the soul, to give it the very life of virtue, power to change the whole face of the moral and political world, was not dreamed of in the philosophy which, for centuries usurped the schools and the churches.

Still, the spirit of Christ was in the world. Though the darkness of men's minds and hearts prevented it from being perceived, it was silently, gradually, effecting its work. It touched a heart, here and there. It kindled up the ethereal fire, now in this mind, now in that. It formed, here and there, little nuclei, around which began to gravitate the immortal atoms of a new moral world, pure and lovely in the sight of God and man. If its power was suspended in this place, repressed in this community, it burst forth with additional energy and glory in that. Meanwhile the world is agitated. Revolutions are daily occurring. All is in commotion. All is in a transition state, although to the spectator all seems settled. Letters revive. Science begins to shed its light. Young thought begins to feel its strength and to be ambitious of trying its wing. The past is recalled; the present is surveyed. Man sees himself in a new light. Views of his wrongs and sufferings, of his wants and capabilities, are taken from more favorable positions. Governments, religions, social institutions in general

[2][Ed. The citations may be biblical paraphrases of Acts 11:26, Luke 1:25, and 2 Thess 3:12.]

are summoned to the bar of infant reason. Speculation rushes into the future and dares picture forth worlds of ideal beauty and felicity for the human race. Practical spirits appear and resolve to embody what others behold in idea. Now the Son of God comes with power and glory. Now his Spirit, which has so long been trampled upon, which has so long been struggling in secret, looks forth upon the world and rolls back the clouds of mental and moral darkness. And there is a swelling of men's hearts; and there is hope stretching forth her arms, eager to grasp that greater good which the soul has beheld in vision. Mind redoubles its strength. The individual man now feels, almost for the first time, that he is not a mere cipher, nothing worth only as he is annexed to the state or the crowd, but that he is a man, with rights and prerogatives. The human race begins its upward and onward career in moral and social improvement. We call this the epoch of THE REFORMATION. It is that epoch when the power of Rome was shaken and the human mind was reconquered from her despotism. And the philosophical spectator might have then discerned at work all the causes which are to effect the mightiest revolutions, and to secure results inexpressibly grand and glorious for the whole human race. The gospel works silently but effectually. At times it may seem suppressed, and fearful souls may imagine the world abandoned to wretchedness and despair. But all this time of darkness and doubt, it is collecting its power for new and more astonishing victories. The gospel was compared to "leaven concealed in three measures of meal" [Matt 13:33; Luke 13:21]; though concealed its power was not destroyed. In what we now see, in these agitations, these new parties, these new demands throughout the world, we should recognize its slow but energetic workings to "leaven the whole lump" [1 Cor 5:6]. The gospel is the power of God unto salvation. The mass now feel it struggling within them and bear witness to its reforming energy; and we may "thank God and take courage" [Acts 28:15]. The time draws nigh when it will not be alleged that Christ did not propose to reform the world, because he has not yet done it.

Indeed, if all the glowing and majestic descriptions of the Messiah's reign be not so many rhetorical flourishes, changes of almost inconceivable magnitude are yet to be effected in man's moral and social condition. It was a glorious morning that which dawned on the birth of Jesus. If all Scripture be not a deceptive dream, then commenced a new age, that happy order of things which had been so often predicted, so rapturously sung by inspired bards, and so long desired by all nations. Then the Angel of improvement hovered with joy over the earth, and saw with rapture, as he looked down the stream of time, the all-comprehensive principles then introduced, gradually, but effectually, working their way through all opposition, subduing all enemies, surmounting every obstacle, and finally regenerating the whole moral world. He saw wrongs and outrages disappearing, ignorance, vice, and crime yielding up their empire, man rising from the oppressions of a hundred ages, and looking forth, the image of his Maker, upon a world of beauty. He heard the last note of discord die away in the distance, the tear which the mother shed for her son slain in battle was wiped from her eye, the sigh which bespoke unrequited affection was suppressed, man everywhere opened his heart and gave his hand to his brother. He beheld; and gave the shout of joy, which rung back from heaven's hosts: "Glory to God in the highest, on earth peace and good will towards men" [Luke 2:14]. The vision of the Angel shall be realized. Man shall yet be worthy of his origin and be able to rejoice in his destiny.

30.

THE WORKINGMAN'S PARTY[1]

Unitarian 1 (April 1834): 170-77

We have introduced this work, published under the auspices of
the Middlesex County Lyceum, not to pass any judgement upon its
merits, but because it gives us an occasion to devote a few pages to
the workingmen, for whose especial benefit it is designed.

We have long since taught ourselves to sympathize with human
nature wherever we meet it, in its humblest as well as in its proudest
manifestations. In the lowest and most abandoned of our race we
have learned to recognize a brother for whom Christ died—a mind
possessing all the elements of intellectual greatness—an immortal
soul capable of a generous and sublime virtue, capable of approaching the Deity himself by a kindred excellence. We must, therefore,
view with deep interest whatever affects for good or for evil any portion of our fellow-beings; and we do most heartily rejoice at every
effort made by the too long neglected workingmen, or for them, to
meliorate their condition and to give them their just influence in
society. And in this we are not alone. All who are conscious that their
own lot is bound up with that of the human race do and must sympathize with us.

The workingman is beginning to attract no little attention. Already, in some places, he assumes a degree of importance which the
most sanguine of his friends in former times would not have dared to
predict. Many of a class who once ranked him with the ox that aided
his labors, now admit that he is a human being, and suspect that he
has the common rights of man. He himself becomes conscious that
he has not always been true to himself. The thrilling words, "God has
created all men with equal rights," have reached his ears and penetrated his heart. He resolves to raise himself to an equality with

[1][Ed. A review of a new series of pamphlets under the direction of a Committee of the Middlesex County Lyceum, prefaced by Edward Everett, the president of
the Lyceum. The first two numbers of the series, called the *Workingman's Library*,
were by A. P. Peabody, *Address on Taxation* and Robert Rantoul, Jr., *An Address to
the Workingmen of the United States of America*, both of which were published in
Boston by L. C. Bowles, 1833. For an actual review of the texts, see "Library for
Workingmen," *American Monthly Review* 3 (March 1833): 247-53.]

305

those he long considered his superiors. This is what should have been expected, from the new impulse given to the human mind by the revival of letters, the invention of the art of printing, and that important—more important than commonly suspected—revolution which, by common consent, is called THE REFORMATION. That impulse has descended from the higher classes to the lower, from the learned to the ignorant. Knowledge has been wrested from the class which formerly monopolized it, and is now diffusing some of its omnipotence among the people. An intellectual day dawns on "the millions." True, the many, as yet, "see men only as trees walking" [Mark 8:24]; but to be able to see thus much proves that no little of their former blindness has been removed, and bids us hope that another washing "in the pool of Siloam" [John 9:7] will give them perfect vision. True, also, they know not yet what they would have. Their movements bespeak little more than uneasiness at their present condition, some undefined longings after something better, some dim and flitting visions of a higher good to be obtained. But these undefined longings, these dim and flitting visions, prove that some of the nobler faculties of man's nature, which have been for ages dormant within him, are waking, and beginning to be conscious of powers long unsuspected.

We have all heard, within a few years, much of "The Workingmen's Party"—that anomaly in the history of parties—a party professedly devoted to the interests of those who are engaged in the physical labor of cultivating the soil, or in someone of the useful arts. We all know that this party has been looked upon with alarm by some, and with contempt by others; but whatever it may be in itself, whatever may be the opinions formed of it, we see, at the bottom of the movements of which it is a result, much to encourage the philanthropist. This party has not been rightly comprehended. Those who see in it only insubordination, a desire to agitate, and the efforts of some demagogues to open, by means of a new party, a path to power which they despaired of attaining by any old one, may be right; but those who see *only* this are wrong. This party is linked with those great movements which are agitating the world, movements which in France have created a new dynasty, which in England obtained the Reform Bill and threatened to obtain much more, and which are now acquiring in Germany a momentum that will soon bear away everything that would obstruct their progress. It is one of the manifestations of a deep and settled conviction—soon to become general—that there is something wrong in men's social arrangements, that the evils embosomed in society are not inseparable from the social state, and that the workingmen deserve and can attain a higher rank than has ever yet been assigned them. It indicates an unwillingness on their part any longer to submit to the evils they have had to endure, and a determination to spare no pains to remove them. It is this view of the party that makes it animating to the friends of humanity, and which gives importance to its measures.

The party may be taken as a proof of the improved condition of the workingmen of our country. In those countries where the condition of the workingmen is the worst, the fewest efforts are made to meliorate it. There they know not their rights, are not discerning enough to discover the evils they endure, are not bold enough to attempt and scarcely capable of wishing to remove them. There they are peaceable, light-hearted, submitting to every species of tyranny, and receiving the blows of their masters with patience. But in those countries where their condition improves, where they rise in the scale of society, they become thoughtful, impatient, sensitive to the least neglect, unwilling to brook even the tone of superiority. The ignorant slave who knows not that he has rights makes no efforts to gain them, submits quietly to his condition, and dreams not that he is entitled to a better; but the one who knows that he has rights, that slavery itself though coupled with every luxury is a degradation, a crime against nature, will submit to it not without many a proof of his impatience, and many a struggle to shake it off.

When, therefore, we see a class of our fellow-beings, which long submitted patiently to wrongs of no small magnitude, taking measures to redress itself, we may be assured that it has already advanced. Formerly the workingmen made no complaint; they demanded no reform, dreamed not of attempting one. They knew not that they were created with equal rights; they knew that they had always been degraded, and they supposed, if they supposed anything about it, that it was just that they should be. Now they talk of their rights and form a party to obtain them; speak of their importance to the community, the wrongs they have endured, the justice they desire, and which they are determined to have. And indicates this no advance? Could this be expected from a degraded Russian serf? Is it no advance to become conscious that they have equal rights, conscious that they have not enjoyed them, and determined to submit to such a state of things no longer? Would the Russian serf ever dream of meddling with the political interests of his country? Would he ever dream of being able to control them? But in our country the workingman, the poorest workingman, grapples with the difficult problems of political science, and is influential in forming a party which not only proposes to protect the especial interests of his class, but to have an important bearing upon the welfare of the whole human family. Is not this an advance? Would the workingmen of our country, had they been suffering the evils endured by the workingmen of some other countries, ever have organized a party like the one we are considering? Certainly not. They would have had no mental power to comprehend it, no leisure to attend to it.

We may, as a general rule, then, take the movements of the people in their own behalf, their efforts to meliorate their condition, as a proof that their condition by some means or other has already been improved. Those outbreakings of a starving populace witnessed in some countries may be alleged to the contrary; but these outbreakings indicate no desire for a reform in the social state, the most they demand is one in the larder. They indicate no elevation of soul, no fitness for an advanced state of society, no thirst for a higher good, and consequently make nothing against our general position. There is something gratifying to a benevolent spirit in this view of the Workingmen's Party. It is cheering to contemplate its organization as the result, not of a worse state of society, but of a better—not of greater positive evils endured by the workingmen, but of less. In this case its demands for reform prove that one has already been effected; its exclamations at the depravity of the times prove the depravity lessening, for it is a great point gained, that depravity excites indignation; its denunciations of the evils of our social arrangements assure us that the greatest of those evils, unconsciousness of them, is removed. If this be correct, call the Workingmen's Party good or bad, suppose it adapted or not adapted to its avowed ends, its existence is a proof that light has increased, and the standard of virtue has been raised. That those who organized the party took this view of it we do not pretend. They thought the evils of society were increasing, but they thought so only because their eyes had been opened and their vision strengthened. They saw evil where before they had seen nothing, at least nothing bad. It is true that they had before seen the inequality in men's social condition, but they had supposed it a part of the plan of Divine Providence, and that they would be guilty of rebellion against his government, should they question its justice or its necessity. True, they did not exactly comprehend why it should be necessary, nor how it could be just for one man to sow and another reap, one labor and another enjoy, one be a master and another a slave, one the tyrant and another the victim; but those who had an interest in perpetuating old abuses soon relieved them, if at any time this chanced to give them any uneasiness. They were told that all the distinctions which disturbed them, all those evils of which they complained, were inseparable from the social state and could be avoided only by going back to the condition of the savage. The divisions into classes, of rich and poor, high and low, learned and ignorant, were said to be of the highest utility in promoting social order, in giving to society its just proportions, and in giving occasion for the display of some of the noblest virtues of which our nature is capable; and this, though wholly unintelligible, was perfectly satisfactory to the poor wretches who could be grateful for the crumbs which fell from the rich man's table, while their labor and their poverty made him the rich man. Reasoning like this had for ages satisfied one class with its usurpations and reconciled the other to its degradation.

We consider the organization of the Workingmen's Party a virtual rejection of this reasoning. The workingman had heard it, but could no longer be satisfied with it; he had learned enough to perceive its fallacy; he felt that an impartial Father could never have made such distinctions as he saw a part of his government of his children; and that it was charging him with great unkindness, if not injustice, to pronounce the evils of our condition inevitable. He now saw or thought he saw, himself and his class poor and neglected, though industrious and useful; while those who neglected him were rich and respected, though idle and useless. He saw that all over the world it was the same, that those who produced all the wealth, paid all the taxes, bore all the burdens of the community, maintained themselves besides maintaining all who were not of their number, were the "lower class," the "multitude," the "herd," the "mob," the "many-headed monster," called "the people"; while those who produced nothing, added nothing to the well-being of society, were considered beings of a superior race. "Is this right?" said he in the bitterness of his soul but with the stern resolve to be answered. "Is this right, that those who are alone the useful members of the community should be oppressed, be trampled upon, be the lower orders; while those who are useless shall be called the great, the higher orders? Here I am a hard-working man, I am honest, I am useful; but my presence commands no respect, my voice no attention, my wit excites no mirth. If I am sick, no one cares; if I am killed, there is little zeal to ferret out my murderer; if I die, none regard it. A rich man who has obtained his wealth by means which would have sent a poorer man to the penitentiary, is welcome, go where he will; does he speak, all listen; does he joke, all laugh; does he die, all mourn. Is this right?

We are the historians not the advocates of his reasoning. Whether it be correct, or incorrect, is not our present inquiry. We detail it as a proof of his progress. He must have advanced far before he dared arraign the justice of the present system of things, before he dared put such questions as we have repeated. And this is not all; the time when he put these questions gave them double power to startle. The same words may be repeated at one time with no effect, at another with tremendous power. The old mysteries arraigned the justice of Providence in terms far surpassing the boldness which is termed impiety in the author of "Cain";[2] but in them it was treated as a jest. Religion had so strong a hold on men's minds and consciences that nobody believed that anyone could seriously question its truths. In "Cain" the case was different. Passing from one form to another, religion was apparently weak, and every blow, however slight, became a serious affair. The progress of events had produced a similar state of things in reference to what were called the higher and the lower classes. The old aristocratic notions and aristocratic distinctions had received several severe shocks, and from the fifteenth century had been verging to the point where they must be entirely discarded. A war between the past and the future was kindled, and men's minds were agitated, men's hearts were open to a change great and important. This state of things gave to the words of the workingman a new and deeper meaning, permitted them to sink deep into the heart, and to become fruitful in effects. This is a reason why his party, his movements, which in a former age would have and should have excited only ridicule, now become and are to be treated as serious affairs, full of promise to his friends and of consternation to his enemies.

It is also worthy of remark to those who would fully understand this party, that the dissatisfaction of the workingman which led to its organization was not with mere local and temporary evils, but with the whole framework and texture of society as it is. He saw the few in possession of all knowledge and power, that the many were the vassals of the few, and that the few, having the exclusive control of everything, managed everything in accordance with their own interest, in opposition to that of the many. It was inquired by the workingman, "How happens this? How came the few to obtain this control? How do they preserve it? It is," he said, "that we have been and are too confiding. We entrust everything to the few; and this is the reason why they have power over us, and why they come to have an interest in opposition to ours. Were we enlightened, virtuous,

---

[2][Ed. More than likely refers to George Gordon Byron's (1788-1824) *Cain, a Mystery* (London: J. Murray, 1821).]

capable of governing ourselves, they would not be paid for governing us; should our minds become developed, our hearts duly cultivated, we might be their equals in knowledge and virtue, and that would destroy their superiority; and hence it is their interest to keep us ignorant, vicious, criminal, and enslaved. To avoid this we must hereafter attend to our own concerns ourselves. What one would have well done one should do ones' self; he who will not help himself will find nobody able or willing to help him. We must, therefore, help ourselves and take care of our own interests."

Having come to this point, he had come to the point where it was necessary to act; he must recover the control of his own affairs and prepare himself to manage them. For this object he organized his party; and hence the Workingmen's Party, the meetings, measures, that whole series of movements avowedly for the benefit of the workingmen.

These remarks show the light in which we contemplate this party and the movements of which it is a result.

31.

SOCIAL EVILS AND THEIR REMEDY[1]

Unitarian 1 (May 1834): 238-44

That the Messrs. Harper should give to the public an American edition of this work is nothing strange; but that a clergyman should be its author is more than we can account for, without a supposition which we are unwilling to make. The clergyman who really understands and is prepared to fill his mission is the workingman's true friend. The gospel is emphatically the workingman's religion. They were "the common people who heard Jesus gladly"; and it was because "the poor had the Gospel preached unto them" [Matt 11:5] that John was instructed to infer that the Messiah had come. By "preaching the Gospel to the poor," we are not to suppose was merely meant proclaiming to them its great truths, but that the gospel which contemplated the moral and social elevation of the poor, of the lower classes, was there proclaimed. This the gospel did contemplate and insured it when it proclaimed the fraternity of the human race; and it is this which makes it a religion for the many, peculiarly good news to the millions.

The author of the book before us gives us no evidence that he has ever suspected this. He seems not to be aware that by virtue of his office he is bound to be the poor man's friend and the unshrinking advocate of the equal rights of all men. He sees a broad line of distinction between the higher and the lower classes of society, but he sees no evil in it. He sees evil only in the uneasiness of the lower class, in its efforts to equal or to exchange places with the higher. This book, coming as it does from a clergyman, would, if anything could, justify infidelity and render indifference to religion a virtue. It breathes a spirit that would crush every effort of the people to meliorate their social condition. Its sentiments are worthy none but an antediluvian politician, such as none but a slave can embrace or a tyrant wish to propagate. Its language is, "Vulgar Mechanics, to your places. Stand ready bitted and saddled for your masters' pleasure. Be brutes, as you are, and dream not that you are human beings." Such is the lesson

[1][Ed. Review of Charles B. Taylor's *Social Evils and their Remedy. The Mechanic.* New York: Harper and Brothers, 1834.]

with which it would cure social evils and such the lesson its publishers would read to the liberty-loving workingmen of America!

With these remarks we dismiss this little production but not the subject it professes to discuss. That subject is one not to be lightly dismissed by him who is conscious that there are duties which he owes to his fellow-beings. We fear, however, that too many do lightly dismiss it. We fear there are those who would brand such as believe that there are great and grievous social evils which demand redress, as agitators, demagogues, Jacobins, or persons of desperate fortunes, who have nothing to lose but everything to gain by a change. We fear there are those and even clergymen too who, with their faces turned to the past, have no inward visions of a greater good for the human race, who dream not that as the professed disciples of Jesus they are bound to desire a progress and to labor to set their fellow-beings forward in knowledge and virtue. We fear there are those who, because they find this world "a vale of tears" to the many, confounding the actual with the possible, infer that it always must be so, that God decreed it, and that it is impious not to be resigned to it. We fear; God grant that we fear without reason! We wish not to complain. But we would to God that all, and especially every clergyman, felt that the gospel was given to effect a great moral and social reform in man's earthly condition, that Jesus was a reformer, that the apostles were reformers, that he and they suffered martyrdom as reformers, and that whoever would be a true disciple of Jesus must love all men, even the most abandoned, well enough, if need be, to die as he did, upon the cross for their salvation; that everyone felt that he owes a vast debt to the community—a debt which cannot be paid so long as a single human being is deprived of his rights, a single vice remains to be corrected, a single new truth to be promulgated, or the least additional good to be obtained for any portion of our fellow-beings. We should feel this. It should sink deep into our hearts and forbid us to desist from an earnest inquiry after a remedy for all social evils of whatever name or magnitude.

We say *remedy*. For we are not of that number who believe the evils of the social state are irremediable. We are not of that number who believe the earth is smitten with the malediction of heaven and that groans and tears are man's inevitable lot. We have seen suffering, we have heard complaints, we have seen and shared in man's miseries; but we never dared believe their cause was lodged in the bosom of the Divinity. We have seen the hand of God at work in the affairs of men; but we have seen it at work only for good. We have seen it pouring "oil and wine" into the wounded heart, binding up the broken spirit, and making the sufferer whole; but we have not seen it pushing man forward in a career of madness and compelling him to be "the greatest plague and tormentor of his kind." We have seen the factitious distinctions of society, and the tremendous evils they involve, but we have seen in them no marks of the wisdom and goodness of God; we have seen in them only the foolishness and wickedness of man. "The foolishness of man perverteth his way, and his heart fretteth against the Lord" [Prov 10:3]. If these evils are the work of man they are not imperishable. If man has made them, man can unmake them. At least, it can be no disrespect to the Deity to labor to remove them.

But what is the remedy for our social evils? Who is able to answer? Not he who, contemning first principles and what he calls abstract science, applauds himself for being only a *practical* man; not he who denies all disinterestedness, and judging from his own heart, pronounces selfishness the governing principle of everyone's life; not he who is unconscious of the great duties involved in the spiritual brotherhood of the human race; not he who has to learn that his nature is allied to the Divinity and is susceptible of indefinite perfectibility; nor he who sees in the gospel no great social principle, which in its progressive development must not only modify but recast society and place it upon an entirely new base. The remedy is in Christianity—in Christianity, not as a dogma, not as a system of belief, but as a grand, all-comprehending principle of moral and social action. It can be found only by carrying out into all the details of social and private life those great moral maxims which Jesus disclosed in his teaching and exemplified in his life. But how is this to be done? Not by saying, as it is said on either hand, it cannot be done; but by a full confidence that it can and *must* be done, and by engaging in earnest to do it. The pulpit alone cannot do it. *That* has spoken. Its voice, we trust, has alarmed many a one's conscience, arrested many a sinner in his mad career, called back many of the erring, and often consoled and confirmed the good; but alone it is too weak to check and roll back the full tide of depravity. It must be aided by education.

EDUCATION! He who pronounces that word pronounces the remedy for the evils of man's social condition. But not he who speaks only of intellectual education. Many know their duty, but do it not. Many a man's understanding is right whose feelings are wrong. Man's *whole* nature must be educated. *Educated*, we say; by which we mean the right exercise, training, or disciplining of man's whole physical, intellectual, and moral nature. The body must be so educated as to insure it health, active and vigorous limbs; the feelings should be so disciplined that those which furnish the energy for useful and virtuous action may always be predominant; and the intellect should be so developed that the right and the best means of obtaining it shall always be obvious.

Education should have a religious foundation. Those who propose a system of education which excludes religion propose nothing really practicable or desirable. Aside from that part of man's nature which finds its sphere of activity only in what pertains to religion, man is but an animal, or a mere creature of barren logic. In either case he ceases to be a human being who adds to his animal propensities and his reasoning powers those moral instincts which are the distinguishing characteristics and which constitute the real glory of human nature. All that is generous, touching, or sublime in our nature is intimately allied to the religious sentiment, and withers and disappears whenever that is struck with death. We would have all our systems of education recognize this truth. The great object of all our schools should be to reveal the mind to itself, to make the soul conscious of its lofty and deathless energies, and of its power to grow by an ever-enlarging virtue into the likeness of the Divinity. But in making religion the base of education, we should detach it from its various forms, disengage it from all its sectarian connections, and present it simply as a sentiment of the heart, a law of the soul, as the great principle which is forever urging man forward towards higher and more advanced states of living. In school we would consider it as the principle of perfectibility and occupy the young mind only with its spirit and results.

We know there are those who would exclude religion from our schools; but we believe it is only because they identify it with dogmas, and its instruction with sectarian strife and animosity. Did they view it as we do, they could not object to it. It does seem to us that no one not in love with depravity, no one who ever stops to gaze on an opening flower, to inhale its sweet perfume, or to catch the wild note of a forest songster, no one who feels the least emotion on beholding the distant mountains with harmonious outlines, the ocean where its "waves sleep on its bosom," or when the storm lashes them into fury, the deep blue vault of heaven lighted up with its thousands of evening fires, a generous sentiment, an act of heroism or of disinterested affection, can object to religion, which, as we view it, and as we would have it introduced into schools, is but the right exercise of our highest and most glorious faculties—neither more nor less than the perception of the beautiful and true, sympathy with the pure and spiritual, veneration for the holy, love for the good, gratitude for the munificent and the kind, and an eternal up-shooting of the soul towards perfection.

But however thorough, however religious, education may be made, the education of a few will not be enough. Egypt was the cradle of learning, of arts and sciences; but she has fallen. Greece was once the academy of the civilized world. Her philosophers sounded the depths of the human mind. Her poets and orators stand unrivaled. Her artists seized upon the idea of the beautiful, detached it, reembodied it, in forms which remain and will remain models through all coming time. But Greece has fallen. Rome, once the haughty mistress of the world, was rich in statesmen, heroes, learned men, poets, and orators. But she has fallen, and comparative solitude reigns upon the "seven hills" of her greatness. Why have all these fallen and veiled their glory in the dust? Not for the want of the educated few, but of the many—*for the want of an educated, enlightened population.* The lights which shot from the educated few were but flashes soon lost in the profound darkness which enveloped the mass of the people. The education of a few is not enough. The millions must be sent to school—not merely sent to school for two or three months in a year for half a dozen years, but must be educated in the fullest, broadest sense of the term. The whole population of a country and eventually of the world must be educated. This is the remedy for social evils, education, moral, intellectual, and physical, based on religion, and universally diffused, and this, too, is a remedy which can be applied.

Can be applied. The stationary philosophers may contradict us. They may allege such a thing never has been, therefore never can be; that children are born with unequal capacities and that it is folly to dream of making all equal; but they will not move us. We admit that children are born with different capacities, that education can never make all equal, but it does not follow from this that all cannot be educated. Education cannot create; we admit it can only unfold and aid the growth of the germs which nature originally wishes, but all except idiots have the genius and are susceptible of a spiritual as well as a physical growth. That all can reach the same size we do not pretend; but that all with proper culture can grow, will grow, is a truth we presume no one will controvert. Let this culture be given to all, let all have the means of attaining the largest growth of which they are susceptible; we ask no more.

To infer that all cannot be educated because all have not been is a species of logic long since superannuated. It is too late in the day to measure the future by the past. He who should wish to do it would have sided with the judges that condemned Socrates to drink the hemlock, would have joined the cry of the multitude in reference to Jesus, "Crucify him, Crucify him" [John 19:6]; he would have recommended the burning of Huss and Jerome and Bruno,[2] and the incarceration of Galileo; ridiculed Columbus for his new geographical notions, laughed at Franklin and his kite, and made sport of Fulton and his steamboat. Had this spirit prevailed, all those mighty discoveries and inventions which have given man his empire over nature would never have been made or would have been stifled in their birth. The melioration of laws for which humanity now justly applauds herself, the improvements in the science of government which in our case have taken a rapid stride towards perfection, would never have been effected, and instead of having the spectacle of a free people to contemplate, we should have had only masters and slaves. No. The past does not, cannot, in the sense in which the stationary philosopher alleges it, measure the future. There has been through all the past a progress, and this bids us look for still greater hereafter. If from the past it be allowable to predict the future, let it be from past improvements that we infer future ones.

We cannot dismiss this article without referring to the duty which one generation owes to another. The child must be "trained up in the way he should go" [Prov 22:6], but he cannot train himself. The education, at least its rudiments, must be *given*. Parents, guardians, or legislators must provide for it. The existing generation must bestow it on the rising. The rank the generation to come after us will hold, the advances in civilization which it will make, depend almost entirely on the education we give it. How, then, does our duty to educate *all* the children of our country rise in importance! How do almost all other considerations dwindle into insignificance compared with this! Who does not in this recognize an immense responsibility which rests upon him? Who would shrink from it and not do his duty?

For ourselves we are glad that the duty of educating one generation is given to another. It prevents us from feeling that we stand alone. It is an arrangement which connects us with all the past and

[2][Ed. John Huss (c. 1372-1415), a Czech religious reformer and popular preacher in Prague, was excommunicated (1411) by the antipope John XXIII, appealed to the General Council of Constance, and was burned at the stake at Constance. Jerome of Prague (1370-1416), also a Czech reformer, like Huss, rejected the right to property and the hierarchical organization of society and was burned at the stake at Constance. Giordano Bruno (1548-1600), an Italian philosopher, was burned at the stake in Rome for what was considered a heretical form of pantheistic immanence.]

with the whole future. We are an epitome of the vices and follies, the virtues and intelligence of all past ages; and our action, good or bad, upon the generation to follow us, will be felt by the remotest posterity. We occupy a commanding position. No action can be without its result. No word can drop idly to the ground. A word, little heeded when spoken, may kindle up a virtuous energy in some bosom, which shall pass from that to another, from that to still another, till there be collected a moral force sufficient to shake the empire of evil and then to create an entire new order of things. Every man may, in consequence of this law of our social development, be contributing something to the knowledge and virtue and happiness of the most distant generations. No one is too low, no one is too obscure, to be able to aid forward the glorious work of moral and social improvement. No matter how few or how apparently isolated from the world may be the friends of humanity, their exertions can never be lost. Their most private acts may prove to be the highest public benefits; their most secret devotions may be nourishing principles, cherishing a force of character which will one day pass from them to some beyond their circle, to increase in power and activity till the whole world feel and own their influence.

This is the grand secret of all human improvement, the action of man upon man and of generation upon generation. This is the principle by which Jesus accomplishes the grand reform he commenced. It was by the action of man upon man, of generation upon generation, that the germ of moral and social perfection which he deposited in the earth was to be nurtured into life. The nation in which he appeared has passed away. The conquerors of his countrymen have been conquered, and their conquerors in their turn have passed under the yoke, but that germ remains. It has sprung up, received fresh beauty and verdure from every storm which has passed over it, and it has now risen to afford shade and shelter to nearly half the earth; but that it has survived the revolutions of ages and reached its present growth has been the result of no other principle. Man has imparted something to man, and one individual has kindled up the soul of another. One generation has accumulated something that its predecessor had not, which it has imparted to its successor to be still enlarged.

Let us not overlook this grand principle of reform, and so long as we have it in our power thus to aid in setting the human race forward in the march of improvement let us not be discouraged. We have in our hands the lever which moves the moral world. Let us learn to use it with effect. Let us feel the sublime power with which it invests every individual of the human family. This lever is education; and when we see the mighty power it holds what importance does it not receive! What attention does it not demand! Let all our thoughts be turned towards the means of making it thorough, religious, universal, and with the least possible delay. We are called to do this by every consideration which can arrest the understanding or touch the heart. We are called to it by all our love of human happiness, by all our aversion to pain, by all our desire to share in great and glorious actions. Whoever we are, whatever our party, sect, creed, or mode of worship, here is a field broad enough for us all, and in which we may all labor in peace. Fathers and mothers! Religionists and politicians! Clergymen and legislators! Patriots, philanthropists, and reformers! Here is the object equal to your gentlest affections and to your loftiest ambition. Lend it the concentrated powers of all your minds and hearts, of your whole souls. God grant ye may!

32.

MEMOIR OF SAINT-SIMON[1]

Unitarian 1 (June 1834): 279-89, 350

Everybody has heard of the Saint-Simonians,[2] a new sect of philosophers, politicians, and religionists which a few years ago appeared in France. They made much noise and attracted no little attention for a time by the novelty of some of their notions and by the enthusiasm with which they supported them. It is said, how truly we know not, that they have latterly run into many wild and mischievous extravagancies, and that the day of their glory is past. However this may be, they have left indelible traces of their new system on the philosophical and religious opinions of France; and since they are now making their appearance in England, and since we have seen it stated that they intend visiting this country, we have thought it not too late to be both interesting and profitable to give a more detailed account of their doctrines than is within the reach of our readers generally. In this article, however, we can do little more than furnish some notices of Saint-Simon himself, the prophet of the sect, which we collect almost entirely from the works before us.

---

[1] [Ed. A review of *Doctrine de Saint-Simon. Exposition. Première Année. 1828-1829*, third edition, revised and enlarged (Paris, 1831); Hippolyte Carnot (1801-88), *Doctrine Saint-Simonienne. Résumé général de l'Exposition faite en 1828 et 1829.* Extrait de la *Revue Encyclopédique* [November 1830], second édition (Paris: Bureau de Globe, 1831); Jules Lechevalier (1800?-50), *Religion Saint-Simonienne. Enseignement Central.* Extrait de *l'Organisateur* (Paris: Éverat, 1831); *Lettre à M. le Président de la Chambre des Députés* (Paris, October 1, 1830).]

[2] [Ed. The Saint-Simonians were those French thinkers in the early nineteenth century who followed in the footsteps of Claude Henri de Rouvroy, Comte de Saint-Simon (1760-1825), a French socialist philosopher and reformer. Saint-Simon's philosophy inspired a "New Christian" movement after his death that propounded a gospel of brotherly love, concern for the poor, and the reconciliation of spiritual values with material progress and evolution. On this, see Martin V. Martel, "Saint Simon," *International Encyclopedia of the Social Sciences,* ed. David L. Sills, 17 vols. (New York: Macmillan, 1968), 13:591-94. For a history of the movement, see Sebastien Charléty, *Histoire du Saint-Simonisme (1825-1864)* (1896; Paris: Hartmann, 1931), and Frank E. Manuel, *The New World of Saint-Simon* (Cambridge, Mass.: Harvard University Press, 1956).]

Claude Henri Saint-Simon, son of the Duc de Saint-Simon, the author of the "Memoirs,"[3] was born April 17, 1760, of one of the noble families of France, which traces its descent, through the Counts of Vermandois, from Charlemagne. He had early a presentiment of his destined greatness, and from the age of seventeen he caused himself to be awakened in the morning with the words, "GET UP, COUNT, YOU HAVE GREAT THINGS TO DO." His heated imagination presented before him the royal founder of his family, who foretold to him that to the glory of having produced a great monarch should be added through him that of producing a great philosopher.

He entered the military service at seventeen, and the year after came into this country, where he made five campaigns with distinction, under the orders of Bouillié[4] and Washington. He became acquainted with Franklin and studied the political organization of our United States; for while here he busied himself much more with political science than with military tactics, for which he had no great fondness. It is from this period that he dates his philosophic tendency. "The war" [of the American Revolution], he says, "in itself did not interest me; but its object interested me very much, and this enabled me to support its labors without repugnance. 'I will the end,' I often said, 'I should then will the means.' But my disgust for the trade of arms was complete, so soon as I saw peace approach. From that moment I saw clearly what was to be my future career. My vocation was not to be a soldier. I was carried to a very different and, I may say, an opposite kind of activity. To study the development of the human mind, and afterwards to labor to perfect civilization, such was the object I proposed to myself, and to which I devoted myself without repose, consecrating to it my whole life. This new kind of activity began then to engross all my powers. The remainder of my stay in America was employed in meditating on the great events I had witnessed, in seeking to discover their causes and to foresee their results. I saw then that the American Revolution must signalize a new political era, necessarily determine an important progress in general civilization, and cause great changes in the social order then existing in Europe."

---

[3] [Ed. Brownson is probably referring here to *Mémoire sur la science de l'homme* (1813), in *Oeuvres de Saint-Simon et d'Enfantin*, 47 vols. (Paris: Dentu, 1865-78), 40.]

[4] [Ed. François Claude Amour Marquis de Bouillié (1739-1800) was a French general and veteran of the American Revolutionary war.]

Scarcely had he returned to Europe when he was called upon to witness the breaking out of the French Revolution. This spectacle, at once magnificent and terrible, could not fail to affect him deeply; but looking beyond the vulgar horizon, into the future as well as into the past, he was able to distinguish its causes and to appreciate its results. He saw in this grand event the practical application of the theories founded by the reformers in the fifteenth and sixteenth centuries, and popularized by the philosophers in the eighteenth century, the legitimate destruction of a moral and social order which no longer responded to the interests and the sentiments of society; and at the same time he saw that this crisis, called to prepare the soil for the seed, contained in itself no germ of reorganization and that it could be definitively terminated only by the production of a new principle of social classification. To discover this principle, bring it out, and establish it, was what he considered his mission. He viewed the French Revolution as having only a destructive mission, necessary, important, but incomplete for humanity; and therefore, instead of being carried away by its current, as were nearly all whose sympathies were like his, he applied himself to the accumulation of the materials required for the erection, on the ruins of the old, of a new social edifice, to remain, to improve in beauty, grandeur, strength, and symmetry forever.

His first care was to procure the pecuniary resources necessary for his work. To this end he engaged in some immense financial speculations, which were crowned with great success. "I desired fortune," he said, "only as the means of organizing a grand industrial establishment, to found a school to perfect science, in a word, to contribute to the progress of light, and to the melioration of the fate of humanity." The grand establishment was organized, but it failed; and his partner, who did not share his philanthropic, or, as some may say, visionary views, separated from him, much to Saint-Simon's disadvantage, whose ability to manage pecuniary matters alone does not seem to have been of the highest order.

However, faithful to the plan he had traced, he employed the feeble remains of his fortune saved from the ruin of the establishment, the attempted industrial and scientific school, to perfect his own scientific education. His object was to introduce into the French school a grand scientific theory which should embrace all the sciences and all the facts of science. But this required preliminary labors. It was necessary to know the actual condition of science and the history of its discoveries. Seven years were devoted to these preliminary labors. He did not confine himself to libraries. He sat down opposite the Polytechnic School; he contracted a friendship with several of its professors and employed three years with their aid in making himself master of the current knowledge respecting inorganic bodies. Good cheer, good wine, much attention to the professors, to whom his purse was open, seem to have made them communicative, and to have procured him all the facilities he could desire. "I had, however," he says, "great difficulties to surmount. My brain had lost its malleability; I was no longer young. But I enjoyed some advantages, extended travels, the intercourse of able men which I sought and obtained, an early education by d'Alembert,[5] an education which had woven me a metaphysical net so compact that no important fact could pass through it."

After three years, in 1801, he left the Polytechnic School and seated himself near that of medicine. Here he formed a connection with the physiologists and did not leave them till he had obtained a full knowledge of their general ideas on organic bodies. He then visited England, Switzerland, and a part of Germany. "My object," he says, "in going to England was to inform myself whether the English had discovered any new general ideas. I returned, assured that they had upon their stocks no new capital idea." His opinion of Germany was little more favorable. "I brought from Germany the conviction that general science was yet in its infancy in that country since it was there founded on mysticism; but I conceived a hope of its ultimate progress on seeing the whole of that great nation passionately engaged in a scientific direction."

Saint-Simon did not content himself with studying the sciences and the learned; he wished to know artists and their inspirations, and to compare their genius with that of scientific speculators. His house, thus, for a year, became the resort of the most distinguished men in Paris of both classes. Seven years had now been employed in forming an acquaintance with the various branches of human knowledge and he felt himself able to draw up an inventory of the scientific wealth of Europe.

But now commenced his severest trials, his greatest labors. His fortune, shaken by the failure of the "grand establishment," was wholly dissipated by his pursuit after knowledge. His friends deserted him. From this time he must live in want, in suffering, in humiliation. He must remain *alone with the consciousness of what he is*, and for a long

---

[5] [Ed. Jean Le Rond d'Alembert (1717-83) was a French mathematician, philosopher, Encyclopedist and anti-Christian free thinker involved in a number of religious disputes.]

324 THE EARLY WORKS OF ORESTES A. BROWNSON: VOLUME II

time this consciousness proved itself able to sustain his courage. His first occupation was to recast philosophy. Napoleon had said to the Institute, "Give me an account of the progress of science since 1789. Tell me what is the actual state of science, and what are the means necessary to make it advance." The Institute replied to this magnificent question merely by a series of partial, historical reports, which being tied together by no general view could give to science no real impulse. Saint Simon undertook to remedy this defect. He conceived and executed his *"Introduction aux Travaux Scientifiques du XIXe Siècle,"* in two volumes quarto, a great work, in which he deposited the germ of most of the ideas he afterwards developed. In this work he demonstrates for the human race what Bacon had for the individual, that intellectual activity has two general, alternate modes of operation, *analysis* and *synthesis,* the mode *à priori,* and the mode *à posteriori*; he makes it appear that science, considered in the assemblage of all the men who cultivate it passes successively, but at distant intervals of time, from *analysis* to *synthesis,* from the search after facts to the construction of theories; that the greatest step which the human mind can be made to take in the direction of the sciences is to determine the proper time to pass from one mode to the other; he takes it upon him to prove that the learned of Europe, for a century engaged in the paths of analysis, have sufficiently explored them, and that they ought to abandon them for a general or synthetic point of view. In a word, he required the learned to return to the point of view of Descartes, which they had entirely forgotten for that of Newton. "Descartes," he says to them, "had monarchized science. Newton republicanized it, he *anarchized it.* You are only learned anarchists, you deny the existence, the supremacy of a general theory." He afterwards enumerated the principal conceptions of the learned during the 17th and 18th centuries; particularly that of Condorcet[6] on the progressive development of the human race. He furnished the means for the study of this development, a study elevated by him to the rank of a positive science. The learned did not regard him, but the future will comprehend him.

But it was chiefly in reference to a social and political end that he sought to stimulate the zeal of the learned. The destructive wars which followed the French Revolution made him feel every day more vividly the necessity of reorganizing a general doctrine and a central

[6] [Ed. Marie Jean Antoine Nicolas de Caritat Marquis de Condorcet (1743-94) was a representative of the French Enlightenment who advanced the idea of progress, but with a sensitivity to the challenge that idea encountered in the face of one's individual death.]

European power. Preoccupied, as he was at this epoch, with the importance of the sciences, it was to the scientific that he addressed himself to realize his project. He wished to elevate them to the height of such a mission. "From the 15th century up to this day," he says to them, "the institution which united the European nations, and curbed the ambition of people and of kings, has been successively enfeebled. It is now completely destroyed. A general war, a fearful war, a war which threatens to devour the whole European population, has already existed for twenty years and harvested many millions of men. You alone can reorganize European society. Time presses—blood flows—hasten to declare yourselves." But he spoke in vain. The learned were as little moved by the anarchy of Europe as by the anarchy of science. Saint-Simon did not know, at this moment, that it was from HIMSELF ALONE must proceed the doctrine and the men capable of reestablishing unity, order, harmony.

The year eighteen hundred and fourteen arrives. Always ardent to pursue under the most suitable form the object from which he never in any circumstances allowed himself to be diverted, he abandons the direction essentially speculative, which till now he has followed, to engage in political labors. He soon perceives the new character which the development of industry must impart to society and to the forms of government. He speaks no longer, as before, to the learned. He turns to the industrious classes and devotes then years to the work of making them comprehend the new social rank they are destined to hold. He writes and publishes successively several works but they produced no great sensation. He who labors for the industrious classes does nobly but he must not expect to be very readily comprehended nor very cordially thanked. But let no one on this account desert them. They curse the hand that would unloose their fetters only because they fear its design is to rivet them firmer. At this period of his life Saint-Simon presents himself in a touching attitude. He lived in poverty, in want, in neglect. He labored incessantly in his own opinion for the good of his fellow-beings; yet no one thanked him; no one aided him; no one cheered him onward; but all united in loading him with obloquy and abuse. "These fifteen days," he writes, "I have lived on bread and water. I have labored without fire. I have sold everything, even to my wearing apparel, to defray the expense of some copies of my work. It is the passion for science and public happiness, it is the desire to find the means for terminating, in a gentle manner, the fearful crisis in which all European society is engaged, that has plunged me into this distress. It is therefore with-

326 THE EARLY WORKS OF ORESTES A. BROWNSON: VOLUME II

out a blush that I avow my wants, and solicit the assistance needed to put me in a condition to continue my work."

One day, one single day, in this terrible situation, scorned and abandoned by the very men for whom his life was a perpetual sacrifice, his courage fails him. He doubts his mission; he is in despair; he asks, he wills, he seeks to die. His hand is armed against himself; the ball grazes his forehead. "But his hour is not yet come" [John 8:20]. His work must not be left incomplete. He has created a philosophy of the sciences, a philosophy of industry; he must live long enough to find the religion destined to unite the two creations. He must now be the prophet of the law of love. "God," say his disciples, in apostrophizing him, "God has left thee to fall only to prepare thee for a still grander initiation; and see, from the bottom of the abyss he raises thee, exalts thee even to himself. He sheds over thee the religious inspiration which vivifies, sanctifies, renews thy whole being. Henceforth it is no longer the learned man, no longer the workingman, that speaks. A hymn of love escapes from his mutilated body. THE DIVINE MAN IS MANIFEST. 'New Christianity' is given to the world! Moses *promised* to mankind universal brotherhood; Jesus Christ *prepared* it; Saint-Simon *realizes* it. The church *really* universal is about to be born. The reign of Cæsar ends; a pacific takes the place of a military society; and the universal church governs the temporal as well as the spiritual, in the outer as well as in the inner court. Science is holy, industry is holy, for they seem to improve the condition of the poorest classes and to bring them near to God. Priests, the learned, the industrious, these are the whole society; chiefs of the priests, chiefs of the learned, chiefs of the industrious, these are the whole government. And all *good* is the *good* of the church, and every profession is a religious function, a grade in the social hierarchy. To each one according to this capacity, to each capacity according to its works. The reign of God is at hand. All prophecies are fulfilled. Saint-Simon, now thou mayest die, for THOU HAST DONE GREAT THINGS."

Saint-Simon closed his career with his religious work called "*New Christianity*." He died the 19th of May, 1825, in obscurity, in want, attended by his only disciple, who received his last revelations and who became the chief of the sect. If we may believe his disciples, Saint-Simon was a man of exalted worth. His only passion, according to them, was the public good. Liberty, industry, philosophy in all that it has of the sublime were the constant themes of his meditations. He had an almost unequaled nobleness of soul and of sentiment. His conversation was clear, lively, brilliant, able in a few hours to make perceptible and palpable, ideas which it would require volumes fully to develop. He never talked of himself. He discarded all the factitious distinctions of society, and shone by himself alone, by the man that was in him. His genius was great but his heart was greater. All his ideas passed through his heart. He was never known to complain of a single human being, although he had made many ingrates. He had an inconceivable simplicity of manner, always seized the tone and placed himself within the reach of the one who enjoyed his conversation; and such was his flexibility of mind that while the wisest carried away the hope of returning to profit by his conversation, the ignorant left him with the idea that they had instructed him. He was lavish of his thoughts, cared not who profited by them, provided they were diffused. It was his delight to collect around him young men, the men of the future, and to procure them the means of opening to themselves an honorable career by their labors or their writings. No selfishness was discovered to sully the beauty of his character. He knew how to acquire wealth, had acquired it more than once, but his regard for the interests of others and little care for his own made him diffuse it faster than he could obtain it. "If there were not generosity in the heart," said he, "it would always be a good calculation."

His enemies, indeed, allege many things against him. The most important is that he was a very troublesome beggar. His disciples do not deny the charge; they allege that it was his desire to do mankind good that reduced him to beggary. They, however, do not pretend that he was perfect. They consider him not as the type of perfection but of an eternal progress towards perfection. They see in him an advance prophetic of the advance of humanity. They think he ascended high the ladder whose steps, through the infinite, lead up to God. He leaped an immense chasm and now lends a helping hand to his disciples to leap the same and to place themselves by his side. He ended a thousand times greater than he began; and death does not interrupt his eternal progress. "Great God!" say his disciples, "he is and always will be before thy face; he is and always will be *with us, in us*. It will always be by him that we shall develop ourselves and make our way to thee. The being of Saint-Simon, growing more and more perfect, is at each moment made up of all that we can conceive of love, of wisdom, and beauty under a human form. It is to the being composed of these that our worship, our admiration, and our souls are devoted. Old religions, wholly *stationary*, have the type of what they reverence in the past; our religion, wholly *progressive*, places it in the future; and one of the finest results of our progress is that we every day become able to represent our type to ourselves under a more attracting and a more perfect form."

This may be a little mystical to those of our readers who have long had thinking made easy to them. It is not the *man* they worship. It is not the man Saint-Simon they reverence. They pay their homage to the progress he manifested, to the truths he disclosed, and to the passionate love of humanity which controlled him. They revere him as a model for them to imitate only in his progress and in the object towards which he directed his labors. They do not look at him as he was in the past, to see what they should be; they look at him where his continued progress has elevated him and thus gather strength to press onward and upward after him.

With the Saint-Simonians everything is progress, everything changes to man's conception as he advances. God enlarges, becomes pure, wise, and beautiful, in proportion as the mind that contemplates him enlarges, becomes pure, clothed with wisdom, and adorned with beauty. This idea is undoubtedly just. The God of the ignorant is not the God of the enlightened. Every man has a God of his own, exactly proportioned to his degree of mental and moral progress. That which a man worships is always the highest worth of which he can form any conception. The Negro ascribes to his ill-shapen *fétiche* the highest excellence he can conceive, and you must enlarge his mental and moral capacity before he can worship a God of higher and more moral attributes. You change not the object of man's worship by changing the name of his God. The Jew, who ascribed to his Jehovah no higher qualities than the Greeks did to Jupiter, was no more a worshiper of the true God than they. The same is true of the Christian. If mankind worship the true God now any more than formerly, it is because there has been an advance, because the human mind has grown and become able to take in the idea of a purer, sublimer, and more beautiful Divinity.

We delight to apply this thought to Christianity somewhat as the Saint-Simonians apply it to their prophet. Christianity is to every Christian the type of moral and religious perfection; but that type varies in different ages, in different individuals, and even in the same individual at different epochs of his life. Christianity, in the minds of those who embraced it in the early centuries, was a low thing to what it is now. No matter what it was in the mind of its Author; where it was embraced it was measured not by his mind, but by the minds of those who embraced it. It can never in any mind mean a greater degree of moral and religious perfection than that mind is capable of receiving, understanding, appreciating. There must be almost an in-

finite difference between Milton's Christianity and that of the Abbé
Paris.[7] Still, one was a Christian, as well as the other. One age, one
sect is Christian, as well as another, when compared with itself. Each
is modeled after the same type, each takes in the highest worth of
which it can form any conception. But the type stands for an amount
exactly proportioned to the progress which has been made. Christianity, then, can never be outgrown. We may pursue an eternal career of progress and at each step will the term Christianity enlarge its
meaning, and the word Christ designate purer, lovelier, sublimer
worth!

But to return. Saint-Simon, viewed as he may be, was undoubtedly no ordinary man. His views are those of no ordinary mind.
They bear the stamp of originality, of a mind in pursuit of variety, in
love with the beautiful, and, in its own estimation, wedded to humanity, and longing to redeem, exalt, and make it happy and forever
more happy. We have dwelt long upon his career, perhaps too long
for the patience of our readers; but we delight to trace such a character, we find instruction in its very extravagancies. We shall take up
his system as developed by his disciples, as we find time and room.

[7] [Ed. Perhaps the reference is to Matthew Paris (c. 1199-1259), a monk of St.
Albans in England and a medieval chronicler whose claim to fame was his *Chronica
Majora*, a history of the world from creation to 1259.]

33.

REV. MR. BROWNSON'S ADDRESS[1]

Christian Register 13 (June 28, 1834): 101

I see here a cause of gratulation and hope in the fact that this society is composed of young men. In old states where all is fixed, in these epochs where all is stationary, old men are at the head of affairs. They spread a calm glory over the past of which they are the representatives, impose a salutary restraint upon the spirit of innovation, and compel the young to keep back. But, when things are moving onward, when men's minds and hearts turn towards the future, when society believes in the future and longs to advance, young men come forward, to lend their unexhausted vigor and the ardor of their undamped hopes. When society is young, its measures young, it delights in young representatives. When, therefore, we see young men coming forward and making themselves felt, we may infer that the society in which we see it, has a long future, and that grand and noble moral improvements are to be made. . . .

"I see here also homage paid to that principle which leads one out of himself, to seek the good of others. You have not associated for your own benefit. Yours is not one of those associations, one of those corporations, prompted by the love of gain, and which see in men only the instruments of their wealth or their power. It is an association for the good of others. It is a witness to the spread of philanthropy, to the fast-spreading conviction of the age that men owe duties to their fellow men, and that they are bound to labor for a good of which self is not the center. It is one proof among others, that the empire of selfishness is shaken, that the morality of "interest well understood," has been weighed and found wanting. It is an assurance to those who have sighed and yearned for an increase of human happiness that there is witnessed the rising glory of a new order of ideas, of an order of ideas which gives ample room to all that is elevated, generous and touching in human nature.

[1][Ed. The address published here included some excerpts from an unpublished address delivered by Brownson before the Young Men's Bible Society in Boston, at its anniversary, 20 April 1834.]

"Be assured men are beginning to be moved by a nobler spirit. "The Divinity stirs with them." We see it in the universal agitation of men's minds, in that eternal thirst after something which we have not, in that constant grasping at that which lies off in the unknown. We see it in the movements of the church—in the church which for ages was the type of immobility, and the personification of the stationary principle. The church awakes from its dream existence, becomes conscious of a new mission, feels that it is called to do great things. It feels that it is called to go forth and evangelize the world, render good and happy the whole human race. Indeed there is a kindling spirit of philanthropy hovering over us, impatient to dart new life into our souls. Man feels that he is made for man, and instinctively begins to labor for man. To this all your Bible Societies, colonization and anti-slavery societies, your missionary, Sabbath school, and Education societies, your Temperance and your prison Discipline societies can bear witness. I will not say that all these societies are equally useful; I will not say, that some of them do not require important modifications, but I do say that in the spirit which has created them, I see that spirit which longs for human happiness, and which can engage in earnest, and do, and suffer much, to promote it.

"I do not dream. There is a new principle at work in the affairs of men. Not new in itself, but new in the minds of the people and in its application. The Christian world for a long series of years after the zeal of its youth had died away felt that its mission was ended, that its work was done. It had received the true faith, found the true church, and it was satisfied. It had the form of godliness, but it dreamed not of a spirit to animate it; it had the name of Christ but it had no suspicion that there was in that name a power to quicken the heart. It rested in the form; it slumbered in the name; and vice raged, crime left its concealment, all the ministers of Satan roamed at large over the earth, and the few who dared inquire, asked, "What has Christianity done for the world?" The movements we now see prove that it has awaked from its death-slumber, and that it feels a young life circulate in its veins. It opens its eyes; sees a world lying in wickedness, and all the virtues weeping over it; it hears the cries of oppressed humanity and it feels its heart kindle with the desire, and its arm filled with the power to remove that wickedness and to let in the virtues to weep no more.

It is beginning to be felt that to be a Christian one must be aware that he does not live for himself alone, that he must identify himself with man, devote himself without reserve to humanity, and labor unremittingly for its highest good. It was this feeling more or less distinctly perceived, more or less rightly appreciated, that led to the formation of your society, and this is wherefore it does homage to the principle which leads one out of himself to seek the good of others. You saw evil around you; you saw around you good to be done, and there was that within you that said, "go and do it." The sense of duty came home to your bosoms; and you dared not be found unfaithful. It was a noble spirit whose movements you felt. It was the movements of a spirit which is now passing over the world with power, breathing new life into men's souls, and preparing to fill, one day, the whole earth with peace and to cause every heart to sound with a holy joy. It is engaged in the service of the Almighty, it marches with humanity, it responds to the deep wants of the soul, and heaven and earth shall pass away, and the universe be as if it had not been, sooner than it shall not succeed. . . .

(July 5, 1834): 105

"Your society deserves to be approved and supported, not only because it does homage to the spirit of philanthropy, but because it is designed to benefit the poor—ay, the poor, that most numerous part of our race which so many ages have overlooked, scorned or oppressed. "Go tell John," said Jesus, that "the poor have the Gospel preached unto them" [Matt 11:5]. It was then a proof that the Messiah had come, and when I see associations formed to benefit the poor, I seem to see the proofs that he has come again with greater power and glory. Christianity is emphatically a religion for the poor; for it recognizes their rights and declares them equally with the rich and the great members of the vast brotherhood of humanity. In laboring for the poor you are following out the spirit of the gospel and finishing the work Jesus came to perform.

There is nothing in the movements of the day more cheering to the friends of man than the increasing sense of duty which is felt to labor for the poor. In nothing does the new spirit show itself more lovely, or more powerful, and in nothing is it more clearly distinguished from the spirit which ruled the past. Not that I would say the ministers of Jesus, during the ages which have passed away since the introduction of Christianity, have felt no obligation to labor for the poor. All Catholic Europe would rise to contradict me, were I to utter an assertion so false. The numerous hospitals, foundations, brotherhoods, and sisterhoods of the middle and late ages devoted to the poor would rise to contradict me. The Servants of Jesus, the Sis-

ters of Charity,[2] by the bedside of the suffering, in spite of the horror
and disgust of loathsome hovels and disease, administering to the
poor, the sick and the dying, the last consolations of religion, and the
most painful and assiduous attentions, can bear witness that in no
age has the Christian world entirely mistaken its mission. But up to
our days, the great principle on which all institutions for the poor
have been founded has been almsgiving—falsely called charity. In
past times, this was well. Almsgiving had its mission. The day of
emancipation had not come. It was well, it was but humanity to
render insensible those who were incurable.

But times have changed and their changes have brought with
them other duties. We are entrusted with a different mission. Mere
almsgiving ceases to be a virtue. We owe to the poor another and a
higher duty. It is not merely to help them but to put them in a condition to help themselves. This is the new duty which is imposed
upon us. In this is the principle which must govern our future labors.
And this, if I mistake not, is the principle which lies at the bottom of
your society. You labor not for the body alone. You recognize in the
poor, minds, souls, to which you would furnish the bread of life. You
would raise the moral tone of the poor, give them a moral consciousness that would fit them to act a higher and a nobler part in the social
drama. In this you hit the true principle. Mere almsgiving is but a
temporary and often a deceitful relief. For a moment it may blunt
the sharpness of hunger, guard against the wet or the cold, but it
reaches the bottom of no soil, removes no disease from the social
body. I will not say to the rich "cease to give"; but I will say, "rely not
on almsgiving." If you really wish to do the poor good, develop their
minds, quicken their moral and religious sensibility, and give them
that firm and manly confidence in themselves, which will make them
feel that they are something and that they can do something. Kindle
up within them the conviction that they *can* and *must* help themselves, that they can and must work out their own salvation. On this
principle, I believe you act, and if you do, you cannot fail to be benefactors to the poor, and through them to the human race.

That you do act on this principle, I infer from the fact that your
object is to supply the poor with the Bible. Here is also witness borne
to a grand conviction, to the conviction that religion is a blessing to
the poor. There are few convictions better founded or more important than this. There is no good in which religion does not mingle;

[2][Ed. The Servants of Jesus and the Sisters of Charity are two communities of
women religious (i.e., nuns) in Catholicism.]

there is no evil which anything but religion, or that which pertains to religion, can remove, and there is no part of community more in need of religion than the poor, I will not say, with a proud European Aristocracy, to keep them in order and to make them submissive to their masters, but to minister to them its encouragements, its consolations, and to spread over their dark and dreary habitations its hallowed and heavenly light.

In making this broad assertion, I know I contradict much of the philosophy of the last century, and oppose myself to the prevailing convictions of but too many of our own times, and of our country. There is a widespread feeling that religion ought to confine itself to the sanctuary and that it should not mingle, as it is not needed, in the affairs, in the joys, nor in the sorrows of life. There are those who laugh at religion's consolations, at its rich hopes, and exalting and purifying influences upon the soul. But "there is a laughter which is madness." He who laughs at religion is mad. This smile is that horrid unearthly smile of the maniac. I know there are those who consider religion an illusion, a trick of crafty priests or wily statesmen, an ingenious device to monopolize power and profit; I know there are those who talk of science, of knowledge, of philosophy, and yet, tell us that we are left to toss rayless, hopeless, Godless, upon the tumultuous ocean of skepticism and despair! I know there are such, for I have been with them and have prophesied in their midst. I know their pretensions, their disdain for religion, their contempt of immortality, their loathing of the Bible; but with the same voice from which they once heard their praises, I tell them they are mad. That restless eye, that withered heart, those cold and calloused affections, that hell of blasted hope burning within them, bear witness for me that they are mad; at least, that if not mad, they have forsworn the exercise of all that can give to existence a charm, to creation a beauty or to the heart power to warm at sight of a generous sentiment, or an act of heroism. The skeptic mock at religion and scorn its proffered aid! The skeptic! He who can see no glory in yon sun and stars, no majesty in yonder ocean, who can see in the world around him nothing to admire, no loveliness on which the heart may linger, no living, breathing spirit with which he may hold secret and mysterious communing—the skeptic that wreck of humanity rotting upon a tideless ocean, he disdain religion and scorn its hopes! O my God, forgive him. The worm gnawing within him, the despair and anguish which have consumed his soul, plead for him. Go, poor skeptic, I will not taunt thee. Go, from my heart I pity thee, and I could weep tears of blood would it save thee from withering away into a mere animal, a mere vegetable that propagates its species and dies. Go weep in silence thy loss, deplore in secret thy want of faith in the great and living Spirit of the universe!

(July 19, 1834): 114

It is not for man, weak and changing man, to scorn the aids and consolations of religion. It is not in the nature of things for spirit to be satisfied with matter, for the immortal mind to be contented with mere physical objects—with mere dust. The soul asks a good peculiarly its own associates with whom it can sympathize, and aims at pleasures congenial with its own spirituality.

We may toil for wealth, fill our store houses with rich merchandise and our coffers with gold, and the wants of the soul may remain. The spiritual man, poor and desolate, may wither away beneath the embroidered garment and in the midst of the glittering retinue. We may ask for fame, court this one's caprice, be deaf to that one's scorn, while rising to the honors of state; we may see our names in each gazette, hear them eulogized by the orator or sung by the bard, but, after the intoxication of the moment has subsided what is all this to the heart? There may be still a solitude within, a wilderness of the soul, dark and dreary, and notwithstanding all that wealth, that fame, that pleasure can give, we look eagerly round for something to sustain the spirit, to enable it to pursue its journey with courage and hope or to repose for a moment on the few sunny spots which may lie in life's pathway.

Strike from your minds the idea of God, separate in your thoughts this world from its Author, from the Father and the fullness of Spirit, and the universe will seem to vanish, its beauty and glory will fade away and its magnitude dwindle down into nothingness. You will feel alone, alone, with an endless blank around you. Everything to the sickened soul will be too little to be seen, or vague, indistinct as the traces of a forgotten dream. . . .

O, how different is it to him who believes in God! To him, who believes in God, who draws near to his Father, who sees the Divinity within him, who reads earth by the light of heaven reflected from the Bible, this world is no longer dull, senseless matter. It lives, it breathes, it speaks to him with a living voice that cheers and gladdens his heart. To him it shadows forth the eternal Father in whose wisdom, simple sublimity, unchanging love and unbounded goodness, he finds ample room to expatiate forever with expanding thought, increasing strength, admiration, love and joy. . . .

O say not religion is not needed. Mark that old man on whose head have lighted the frosts of four-score winters. The companion that long shared his joys and divided his sorrows has gone; his children, one by one, have gone down to the tomb. There he stands, by the new made grave of his last, his youngest, alone like an aged oak upon some barren heath, scathed by the lightnings of heaven with its branches broken off and moldering at its feet. Lone and withered he casts a look upward, light breaks upon his grief-worn features, his heart is full: "*No, they are not gone forever.* My wife, my children, I shall meet you again." O would you take away that book whence the old man derives that hope?

Go to that obscure dwelling where poverty seems to have erected her throne. Mark that half-famished mother giving her last morsel of bread to her starving children. What is it that can make amends for that neglect she endures, or "chase the world's ungenerous scorn away?" Ah, it is that her thoughts stray beyond this earth. She appeals from this cold, unfeeling world, to another and a better world. She sees her afflictions here, opening into a world of joy; and as she sees her dear loved little one drop piecemeal into the grave, she sees its young spirit, escaping from a world of pain and sorrow, to rise in glory, and to shine forth a bright angel in the kingdom of heaven forever and ever. O who would not carry to the poor the book that gives this consoling hope, this last solace of the wretched, that when the world abandons them and want chills them, they may read the precious words which go beyond the world and reveal a region where all wrongs shall be righted and all wants be satisfied.

You see that mother pale and wan with watching, bending over the faded form of her child. She marks its failing pulse, its closing eyes, hears its throat rattle, its last gasp—it dies. The terrible truth rushes upon the mother's heart, but, while she exclaims, "My child, O my child, would to Heaven I had died for thee," she meekly bows her head, and adds, "The Lord gave and the Lord hath taken away, blessed be the name of the Lord [Job 1:21]. My child is not dead. It lives. I shall see it again, again clasp it to my heart." Go, skeptic, take away the book whence the mother derives that hope. Go, tell her that hope which makes her see her child still living, is a dream, that her faith

> Which builds a bridge from this world to the next
> O'er death's dark gulf and all its horror hides,[3]

is but a delusion. Tell her this—O you *cannot.* The words would blister upon your tongue before you could utter them. . . .

[3][Ed. Not able to identify quotation.]

We all need religion as a guide, a friend, a consoler. There are times when we are nothing without it. There are times when the spirits sink and a mingled feeling of weariness and dissatisfaction comes over us; when the earth seems vanity, the world empty, every person hollow-hearted, truth and virtue a dream. A dark, heavy cloud rolls over our horizon and shuts out all prospect of future good. Thick, impervious gloom gathers round the heart. It is then we sigh for some sunbeam to dissipate that cloud and to disperse that gathering gloom. Religion is that sun-beam, which coming down from the Father of lights, makes a glorious day in the soul, cheers the heart and leaves a track of light along the darkness through which we must pass. . . .

We not only need religion to sustain us in the dark and gloomy periods of our lives, not only need it to impart to us strength to bear our trails and sorrows, but we need it to give confidence to virtue and vigor to benevolence. Take away religion and man ceases to be man. He becomes but a selfish animal. He wraps himself up in himself and seeks, regards only his own interest. All those emotions, all those sympathies which carry him away from himself die. He no longer listens to the claims of humanity. The wants of the afflicted widow and the starving orphan do not move him. The beings around him are but the plant that blossoms in the morning, fades ere it is noon, and is withered and dry ere it is night. And why should he labor to do good to such frail and perishing and worthless things. It is only he who sees in the human soul the image of God, only he who sees and feels the immense worth of the soul of a human being that will labor for another's good. Philanthropy without religion is an unmeaning term. Take away the truths religion discloses and there would be in man nothing to love, nothing to benefit. . . .

The age demands reform. Men's minds and hearts are anticipating great and important changes. Visions of a greater good for man come to a thousand minds, and millions of stirring thoughts are leaping forth from men's souls to realize them. But where is the power? Where is the grand lever of reform? Look over history. Examine ancient and modern institutions and you cannot mistake it. The ruling thought, which had led to all our social and moral improvements, is found in that book your society propose to furnish to the poor of this city. Christianity is the grand lever of reform. Its spirit is the very spirit of reform, and where that and the Bible go, reform will follow.

Gladly would I dwell upon this thought, one dear and consoling to my heart, but time fails me. I can only add, young men of Boston, you have done well. In forming this society you have borne testimony to some grand and comprehensive truths, truths which are marching over the earth with a constantly increasing power, which will eventually revolutionize society and bring about that period when all the earth shall be peace, when "the groans of this nether world" [Ps 116:3], shall be hushed, when every man "shall sit under his own vine and his own fig tree with none to molest or make afraid" [Mic 4:4].

Young men, you have done well. Whether you would act as Christians, as patriots, as philanthropists, as reformers, or simply as human beings, you have done well. You have begun right. You have begun with the poor, to elevate their moral feelings, to make them religious, to give them the word of life, to cheer them in their solitude, to console them in their sufferings, to strengthen them in their trials, to prepare them for a higher rank here and immortal felicity hereafter. You have begun right. Go on, and if there be a young man in this city who feels that he belongs to the great brotherhood of humanity, who has a soul that thirsts to do great and deeds, he will long to be of your number and to aid you liberally in this, and in every enterprise that like this would confer a spiritual and everlasting good upon any portion of the human race.

34.

AN ADDRESS, DELIVERED AT DEDHAM,
ON THE FIFTY-EIGHTH ANNIVERSARY
OF AMERICAN INDEPENDENCE,
JULY 4, 1834[1]

Friends and Fellow Citizens,

We must have cold hearts if they do not beat with warm emotions on the return of this day; we must have dull spirits if they be not stirred by the proud recollections of the anniversary we have met to celebrate.

No party victory, no triumph of ephemeral interests, calls us together on this day. We have met to commemorate an event dear to humanity—an event in which man throughout the world has a deep and lasting interest, in which he may find matter for sympathy, gratulation and hope. We have come together to celebrate Freedom's Birthday. Not the Birthday of Freedom merely for this country, but for the world, for man universally.

There was a deeper meaning in that Declaration of the Congress of '76 to which we have just listened than that of the political independence of this country. That independence was indeed declared, that independence has indeed been won and defended by deeds of heroism and self-sacrifice, unsurpassed in the world's history, but it enters for only a small affair into what should occupy our thoughts on this day. The struggle between the then feeble colonies and the mother country deserves all the eulogies it has received, but we are not here merely to recall it. A higher and a holier triumph than that of arms, or even that of the political independence of any country, excites the warm emotions of our hearts and calls forth our sympathy. We celebrate the triumph of humanity. No limited horizon con-

---

[1]Dedham: H. Mann, 1834. [Ed. Some, like the editor of the *Christian Register*, believed that this address tended to excite the "prejudices of the poor against the rich," a charge against Brownson that would continue in the next few years. Some identified Brownson with the Trades' Union Party, charges Brownson denied, asserting that his ideas of reform were addressed to the good of all classes in society. On this, see *Christian Register* 14 (August 23, 1834) and 14 (August 30, 1834): 10-11 for editor's original criticisms of Brownson and Brownson's response.]

fines us today. A boundless heaven spreads out over us and the whole human race comes within the scope of our vision.

I pray you, fellow citizens, not to take a narrow view of the American Revolution. There was more in that Revolution than the American and British armies. The past and the future were there. The spirit of immobility and the spirit of progress met there in terrible conflict; humanity all entire, was there, and ours was but the battleground where it conquered the power to take another step forward in its eternal career of improvement. In that Revolution there were debated not merely the interests of a few colonists and their descendants, but man's whole future was debated and decided. We should then look beyond the battleground, beyond the contending armies, to the cause then in question, to the principle which came out from the battle triumphant. To that cause, to that principle, sacred be this day. Sacred be this day, not merely to military triumph, not merely to deeds of heroism, nor of patriotism, but to the progress of the human race, to the political redemption and social installation of humanity.

The cause in question fifty-eight years ago this day was that of the human race, the principle then declared was the equality of mankind. "All men are created equal," is the noble sentence that embodies the doctrine contended for by the Congress of '76, maintained and triumphantly established by the revolutionary army. I will not say that at that epoch, the assertion "all men are created equal," was suspected of the deep and full meaning we now assign it. I am not certain that the signers of the Declaration of Independence intended to assert by it anything more than the political equality of different communities, and the right of each community to choose its own form of government. But Providence makes men the unwitting instruments of advancing his designs, and often puts into their mouths, words big with a meaning they little suspect, and sometimes with a meaning they are little able to appreciate. The time had come for the great principle of equality for which Christianity during so many ages had been paving the way, to be ushered in and set to work in the affairs of the world; and Providence so overruled it, that our fathers in asserting the rights of communities, asserted those of individuals, and in declaring one community's rights equal to those of another, uttered that soul-kindling truth, man equals man, man measures man, the world over.

I know of no topic more appropriate to this day than this great truth of man's equality to man. I therefore ask your indulgence to some desultory, perhaps commonplace, comments upon it, which I am desirous to bring before you and which I should be glad to bring before the whole American people.

In speaking of equality, I pray you not to misinterpret me. There is a sense in which it is not true that "All are created equal." It is not true that all men are born with the same capacities. There are original differences, intellectual, moral and physical, which no education that ever has been and which I venture to predict, none that ever will be devised can overcome. One child is born weak and sickly, another strong and healthy; one is quick and another is slow to learn; one can take in only isolated facts, dwell only on the minuteness of detail, another rises to causes and delights to trace first principles; one has no perception of the beautiful, sees nothing in nature to admire, and never rises to contemplate anything higher than food, clothing and shelter; another seizes upon the ideal of the beautiful, detaches it, re-embodies it, in forms before which all real beauty grows pale; one from the earliest moment is sweet tempered, another is sour tempered; one from a very early period is deeply affected by religious considerations, draws all his delight from meditating on God, the human soul, heaven and eternity, another cannot be made to think seriously of anything which goes above or beyond this present life. In these and a thousand other instances men are not, and we do not believe they ever will be, equal. We infer this from all experience, and from all acquaintance with human organization, and with the reciprocal action of mind and matter. And I by no means mean to assert that in these respects and in others of a like kind, "All men are created equal."

When I contend for equality, that all men are created equal, I mean that all have a common nature, are brothers of the same family, heirs of the same inheritance, having the same general faculties, the same general wants, and the same general elements of knowledge and virtue. I mean that all have equal rights, that in all our social intercourse and relations, in all our governmental and educational provisions, man should be considered as measuring man. In a word, I mean that one man has no rights over another which that other has not over him, and that no one should have the power to derive any benefit from another without giving to that other a full, an exact equivalent.

I here mean something more than that specious kind of equality which English and French statesmen and some even in our own country would give us, that is, simply equality before the laws. There are too many at home and abroad who have no higher notions of equality, or at least who contend that no other equality is practicable or consistent with social order. I am not able to express the abhorrence I feel for this doctrine. It is plausible, but it has no soundness. Its terms are popular, but its spirit is consistent with a very gross system of privilege. It is by doctrines like this that the enemies of the people contrive to mislead and enslave them.

There may be a great and most mischievous inequality, even in those countries where no man is above the laws. Laws may be framed so as to be very unequal in their influence upon different classes of society, and that too, without bearing on their face the marks of the least inequality. One class of community may have no temptations to steal, but very great temptations to defraud, to overreach, to oppress the poor; another class may be strongly and almost exclusively, tempted to steal; a law then punishing fraud, overreaching, or oppression, with a simple fine, while it punished stealing with death or imprisonment, would be anything but equal in its practical effect. And in fact, even in those countries where equality before the laws is recognized, the laws are generally framed so as to fall with the most tremendous weight upon offenses to which the poor are almost exclusively exposed.

Imprisonment for debt is a case in point. The rich, the poor, the honest and the dishonest are before this law, so far as its face is concerned, equal. But the rich man cannot be imprisoned for debt unless it be his choice; the dishonest have generally address enough to escape, and consequently to all practical purposes, it is a law exclusively against the honest poor man. Is there not here, and in cases like these, a distinction, and a most odious distinction tolerated by government? Yet in these and a thousand other cases that might be mentioned, all are equal before the laws. He who transgresses the law incurs its penalty. And what boots it that it is so, if the laws are made so as to strike only one part of community, and that too, the part it ought especially to protect?

I mean then by equality, if not that all men have equal capacities, at least something more than equality before the laws. I not only ask for equality before the laws, but for equal laws—for laws which shall not only speak the same language to all, but which shall have the same meaning for all, the same practical effect upon all. All have the same rights, and I ask that these rights be in no instance invaded, that all be in a situation to demand them, to defend them if attacked, and to enjoy them freely and fully.

Those of our orators who have no higher ambition than to flatter the people, inflate national vanity, and show themselves off in rounded periods, tell us that equality, even in this broad sense, is already gained in this country. But no such thing. We have equality in scarcely any sense worth naming. Will you pretend that we are equal as long as a large portion of our community lies at the mercy of any political demagogue who knows how to veil his liberticide designs under a pretended love of the *dear* people? Will you say that we are equal while all our higher seminaries of learning are virtually closed to all except the rich? Equal while we have those who are born with the right to live in luxury and idleness, while there are others who are born with only the right to starve if they do not work? Equal, while one part of community can and do lay under contribution the labor of the other, make it the means of their wealth and power, and the means too of riveting the firmer the chains of those who perform it? I allude not here to Negro slavery. I allude to that marked distinction which exists all over the world and which is every day becoming more glaring in our own country between the workingmen and the idlers, between those who produce and are poor and those who produce not and are rich; between those who perform all the productive labor and those who are crafty enough, *enterprising* enough, to obtain all its fruits. I allude here to what may seem to you no evil, but to me it is an evil, an evil of immense magnitude, one which lies at the bottom of nearly all the social evils which exist amongst us. And as long as this evil exists we are not free. There is a worm gnawing into the very heart of that tree of liberty which our fathers have planted.

Is my language severe? Be it so. I am not here to flatter. I stand not here to boast what a free, enlightened and virtuous people we are. I would not utter a note of discord to mar the harmony which the recollections of this day should always produce; but I cannot avoid saying that we are not that free, enlightened and virtuous people our Fourth of July orators and our political demagogues have made us believe we are. We have boasted too much. We must become more modest. Our freedom is written on paper, our equality is registered in our Constitutions, but of what avail is that, if it be not written in our hearts and registered in our souls?

We have a constantly besetting sin. We compare ourselves not with our own future, but with the people and institutions of the old world. Because in some respects we are really less wicked than they, we infer that we are as good as we can or ought to be; because our institutions are really better than theirs we conclude they are the best we ought to desire. We flatter ourselves that because we have taken one step, that we have run the whole career of improvement; that because we have begun well, that we have nothing further to do but to applaud ourselves for what we have done. Here is our besetting sin. Here is the rock on which we are liable to split. We look backward, not forward; to what we have done rather than to what we should do, and compare ourselves with what others are instead of comparing ourselves with what we may and ought to be.

God, in his providence, has assigned to the American people an important mission. He has given it us in charge to prove what man is, to develop his whole nature, and show of what he is capable. As the first step towards the completion of this mission, we are to bring out and carry into practice that grand, comprehensive principle, "All men are created equal." This we have not yet done. Our mission is only begun. We have only started in the race, and let us not sit down and fold our hands as if we had reached the goal and won the race. But let us be aware that we have done nothing, if we stop where we are. Our motto must be—"Onward, onward, till the work be done."

And do not, I entreat you hastily conclude, that all is done that can be done. Beware how you infer, because there never has been a greater degree of equality in any country than already exists in ours, that none greater is desirable or attainable. Beware, how you set bounds to human improvement. Providence, nature, nor grace has ever yet said to man in his progressive career, "Hitherto shalt thou come, but no further." We are in but the infancy of the world, in but the first, faint dawnings of civilization. Time and the progress of events have it in charge to unfold and nourish in that creature man, now so weak, so contemned, a moral and social growth not yet dreamed of by the firmest of the believers in his indefinite perfectibility. There are wrapped up in the bottom of his soul, the germs of lofty and deathless energies, which go beyond, immeasurably beyond and above the strongest, the sublimest, he has as yet been able to exhibit. Far, far is he from having attained his full height. Let thought stretch its pinions and soar to the highest point it can reach and man in his upward flight shall yet rise above it.

Let not this be doubted. There is in the belief of this a kindling power, a something which gives us a lofty enthusiasm and creates within us the energy to realize it. Let no one forget that one law of our nature, one which distinguishes us from the brute, is IMPROVEMENT. The beaver of today builds not his house with more skill, makes it not more convenient than did the beaver of four thousand years ago. He has not surpassed the first of his race. He knows no progress. But man has outstripped his ancestors. Generation improves upon generation, and the schoolboy of today is above the wisest of the Greeks. Let us not overlook nor underrate man's power of progress. Let us not, when a noble object is proposed, one for which all the better part of our nature cries out, let us not be deterred from pursuing it by the objection, "It never has been, therefore it cannot be." This is the cowardly sluggard's objection. What! Has there been no progress? Has there never been gained at one epoch nothing which did not exist before that epoch? What! Have I only dreamed of the creations of science, of industry, and genius? Is it a dream, that mariner's compass which opens a pathway in the deep and brings together the most distant corners of the earth? Is it a dream, that ART OF PRINTING, an art that electrifies the mass of mind, creates a universe of thought and opens a medium of intercourse between all nations and all ages? Is it a dream, that bold navigator who discovered this new world and led the way to this mighty republic and to all the civilized life on this western hemisphere? Is it a dream, those proud triumphs of science which have subdued nature, disclosed to us new worlds embedded in what were once counted simple elements, which have snatched the lightning from the clouds and guided the harmless fire? Is it a dream, the discovery and application of the wonders of steam which makes the ships walk the sea regardless of wind or tide? Is it a dream, this free government, this splendid creation of human wisdom, which we so loudly and so justly boast, whose origin we this day commemorate? And yet all these are modern things. None of the ancients knew them. They have come out from Christianity, and some of them have come up into life within our own memories. Either these are dreams, the flitting visions of a distempered fancy, or things may take place at one epoch, which had no existence before it. In other words, there has been, there is, there may be, a progress. Man even in his infancy has done wonders, what will he not do in his manhood?

Let us then bid adieu to the arguments of those who have eyes only for the past, and who exert themselves only to keep the human race from marching to its end. Let us bid adieu to the spirit of immobility and imbibe the spirit of movement, the spirit whose look is upward and whose motion is onward. The equality I have designated is not impracticable. It is a truth which we must bring out of the abstract and clothe with life and activity. God never made one portion of mankind to live in idleness, in uselessness, and in luxury, and another part to live in toil and want; he never made some to be masters and some to be slaves, some to live and grow rich by skillfully, not to say dishonestly, availing themselves of the labors of others— the many to be "hewers of wood and drawers of water" [Josh 9:21] to the few. God has never done this. He created all men with equal rights and made one capable of measuring another. He created all of "one blood," made them to be brothers, fellow beings, to aid, not to worry and devour each other. This is a truth taught us from heaven. It is a distinguishing doctrine, as it is one of the brightest signatures of the divine origin of Christianity. Christianity teaches it by declaring him alone the greatest who best serves the human race. "He who would be greatest among you, let him become your servant" [Luke 22:26]. And dare we say that here is a truth taught us, a duty enjoined upon us by religion itself, that is impracticable? And what is it that makes it impracticable, if it be so? It is nothing but our conviction that it is impracticable, nothing but the continual cry that it is impossible. It is this that unmans us and keeps us back in a condition we should have long since outgrown. To him that believeth all things are possible. If ye had faith as a grain of mustard seed, ye might remove mountains. It is the want of faith, the want of full conviction in its practicability that renders it impracticable. Take hold of the work with both hands, let your minds, your hearts, your very souls be in it, and no matter how difficult it is, you will accomplish it; mountains will give way before you, and your path will become smooth and easy. Men can—ay, men must, men will realize the equality for which I am contending. I see them pursuing it, I hear them crying out for it, and heaven and earth shall pass away sooner than they shall not obtain it.

But they will gain it not by a miracle. It must, as must all improvements in man's moral and social condition, be obtained by natural means, by the exertion of those powers which God has given us. Our present work is to realize this equality. How shall it be done? Important question have I asked—one on the right answer to which much depends for our country's future and for the future of humanity. How shall we realize, not in our professions and in our paper constitutions, but in our social condition, intercourse and relations, that equality is recognized—I will say taught, enjoined, in Christianity, and adopted as the basis of our political institutions? We have not yet done it. There is a striking discrepancy between our practice and the theory we avow. We have borne witness to a degree of equality which we have not yet created. How shall we do it?

Not by government alone. We cannot legislate our citizens into the equality we desire. Government, in fact, is much more limited in the sphere of its operations than is commonly imagined. In its best state, its mission is mostly negative. It is charged merely to prevent one man from invading the rights of another; to maintain an "open field and fair play" to individual genius and enterprise. In countries overrun with despotism, a free government may seem to be the greatest good to be desired, the greatest that God can bestow; but our own experience may teach us that it does not embosom and necessarily bring along with it every good. We have a free government. Here all offices are open to merit alone, and the whole body of the people are free to elect whom they will to be their servants or the agents of their power. But look at the men who sometimes fill high stations. Can you believe they are, one half of them, the choice of the people? I know the people may be deceived, but never so as to prefer some men who have filled some of the highest offices in their gift. We all know that party management, the intrigues of party leaders render the right of suffrage in perhaps a majority of cases where it is worth having a nullity. A few individuals of one party get together and make a nomination, a few individuals of another party make another nomination and my boasted right of suffrage is dwindled down to a choice between these two nominations. I may dislike them both but unless I choose not to vote at all or throw my vote away I must vote for one or the other.

But pass over this, let all party management and party sins sleep in forgetfulness, suppose the people select the men they really prefer, always elect the very best men in the state or nation, and very little is gained. No matter how good laws are, they will remain on your statute books a dead letter unless demanded by the public; and the public if ignorant or immoral, or but feebly moral, will not be very likely to demand any very good laws. A community in which privilege obtains, in which inequality prevails, will not often be very unanimous, in demanding or in obeying laws which have an equalizing tendency, which seek the good of the poorest and most numerous class instead of that of the richest, smallest and most highly favored class.

I value a free government, a popular government, ay, if you will, a democratic government, for I have not a feeling about me that is not democratic. But a free government is powerless without a free people. No matter how much freedom you incorporate into your paper constitutions, you can never have any more practiced than is written in the hearts and on the characters of the people. I therefore expect little from government, I ask little, but to be let alone. Its nature is never to lead, but to follow. The people must precede it, opinion must go before it. If the people go right government cannot go wrong. If the people love right character, liberty and equality will be maintained, let what will be the character of the government, and whoever may be the men entrusted with its management. We sometimes express fears for our government, we sometimes fear that our free institutions may become a prey to some aspiring demagogue who will succeed in erecting a throne of despotism on the ruins of our temple of liberty. It may be so. But it will not be so because that demagogue is wicked, is talented and powerful; but because the people will have become corrupt, because liberty will no longer be written in their hearts and because they will have ceased to have any freedom in their souls. It is, then, of comparatively little consequence, that fierce contention we witness among politicians. I view with almost perfect indifference the contests between the great leading parties which now distract our country. They are only struggles between those who *have* and those who *want* office. The country, humanity, moral and social progress are not in those struggles. We must leave them and to a certain degree, legislative enactments, take our stand upon higher and holier ground, and speak directly to the people as moral, intelligent, religious and social beings. We must dare look on truth and dare hold it up, that by its light there may be formed just such characters as we need to support our free institutions.

I know of but one means of introducing the equality and of effecting that moral and social reform in our country and throughout the world, which every good man sighs and yearns for, and that means is education. I do not mean ability to read and write, and cipher, with a smattering of geography and grammar, and the catechism in addition. I mean EDUCATION, the *formation* of *character*, the moral, religious, intellectual, and physical training, disciplining, of our whole community. Our common schools do not do this. They are better than nothing, but they do not educate us. Our higher seminaries may do something towards educating us, but little towards fitting us for our mission. They educate us to be fond of distinctions, to be fond of popularity, and to look with contempt on the people. And glad am I that no more of our community are able to give their children *such* an education.

We want a republican education, an education which shall accustom the child from the first to see things valued according to their worth—not in the market—but in themselves; an education which shall raise our children above the factitious distinctions of society, which now pervert our judgments, and which shall teach them to value every man according to his intrinsic worth, without any regard to his position in society, and even without any reference to the length of his purse or to the fineness of his coat. In a word we want an education that shall breathe into the child that very spirit which dictated the assertion, "God has created all men equal"; that very spirit which filled the hearts, nerved the souls of our fathers and made

them stake life, property and honor, in defiance of a transatlantic
tyrant and in defense of the rights of man—which shall breathe into
the child the very spirit of that gospel which is glad tidings to the
poor, which declares, "Blessed are the poor for theirs is the kingdom
of heaven" [Luke 6:20] that we all have one Father, and that we all
are members of the same vast brotherhood of humanity—an education which shall make us feel that man wherever seen is our brother,
woman wherever found is our sister, and he who injures a human
being commits an offence against us, he who wrongs a man wrongs
us, the arrow that wounds another's heart has sped deep into our
own—an education that shall make us good Christians, give us
firm and manly characters consistent with truth and full of love
to mankind.

The education we now patronize, teaches us no doctrines of equality, none of philanthropy. Our first lesson is to make a good bargain,
our second to get rich, our third to look out for ourselves, and our
fourth and last is that if some are unhappy, if our wealth has been the
occasion of others' poverty, if unholy distinctions prevail, we must
thank God we are not among the wretched, and the wretched must
believe for their consolation, that the distinctions in society of which
they complain, are, as a writer in a popular periodical has it, "the
express appointment of God."

We have now no such education. We have indeed little support
for liberty or morality. We have established a free government, but
we have done comparatively nothing to preserve it. We have declared
ourselves in favor of freedom and left that freedom to take care of
itself. There is no such thing amongst us as educating our children *in
reference* to their moral and social destination, in reference to those
duties which devolve upon them as citizens of this republic—of this
republic which God in his providence has appointed to be the school
whence are to go out the doctrines and the men destined to regenerate the world.

The education we now patronize, teaches us no doctrines of equality, none of philanthropy. Our first lesson is to make a good bargain,
our second to get rich, our third to look out for ourselves, and our
fourth and last is that if some are unhappy, if our wealth has been the
occasion of others' poverty, if unholy distinctions prevail, we must
thank God we are not among the wretched, and the wretched must
believe for their consolation, that the distinctions in society of which
they complain, are, as a writer in a popular periodical has it, "the
express appointment of God."

Long as such an education is the best we have, we cannot accomplish our mission, we cannot perform that grand and beneficent work
which Deity has assigned us. The fact is, we forget the millions; we
fix our eyes and the eyes of our children on the few. We covet and
teach them to covet their wealth and their distinctions. We legislate
for the few, not for the many. Our legislators seem not aware that
there are such creatures as workingmen in existence, except in the
penal part of their legislation. They legislate for capitalists, landhold-
ers, stockholders, corporations, master mechanics, and those generally who make use of the labors of others, but very seldom for the

journeyman mechanic, the laborers in your factories, and those generally who perform the physical labor of community, unless indeed they have some law with a severe penalty to enact; then, indeed, the workingman is by no means neglected. But in this I blame not our legislators. They seldom know any better. They do not know that such a thing as the people exists, or if they do, they know that they were raised to their dignity of legislators by deserting the people and that they must continue to desert or neglect them or lose it. This is an evil, and one that cannot be removed unless our children are taught that the people are the human race, and that he alone has any moral worth who devotes himself without reserve to their greatest good; unless we give to our children that republican education I have pointed out, and form them, not to despise the people, not to be masters of the people, but servants of the people, to raise themselves and to carry the people up with them.

And not only a few children must be educated in this way, but all the children of our whole community. All need it, all have a right to it, all may demand it. Society is bound to give it, and if it does not it forfeits its right to punish the offender. And not one sex alone must be educated, but the children of both sexes. Woman's is the more important sex, and if but one half of our race can be educated, let it be woman, instead of man. Woman forms our character. She is with us through life. She nurses us in infancy, she watches by us in sickness, soothes in distress, supports us in adversity and cheers us in the melancholy of old age. The rank determines that of the race. If she be high minded and virtuous with a soul thirsting for that which is lofty, true and disinterested, so is it with the race. If she be light and vain, with her heart set only on trifles, fond alone of pleasure—alas! For the community where she is so, it is ruined! Let all then, all the children of both sexes, have this republican education for which I contend. And all the coming generations may have it. We have only to will it. There is nothing we cannot do if we but will to do it. We talk much about education. We speak of its vast importance, of its absolute necessity, but seem to imagine that talking is enough. But we must will it. We must act. We must take hold of the work, take hold of it in earnest, put forth all our energies, and rest not till it be done.

Let there be once established a system of equal, republican education, of an education for all the children of our land, whether rich or poor, male or female, an education which shall be such as our position in the moral, political, religious and philosophical world demands, and the equality on which I have dwelt will be obtained, our government will be firmly established, our free institutions will begin to unfold their beauty, man will prove that he is capable of self-government, humanity will disclose its mighty power of progress, and we shall have accomplished our mission. The light of our example will then reach the darkest corners of the earth, all nations will then turn towards us with admiration and for guidance. Freedom will be vindicated, liberty will become universal, all the world will be free, all will be peace, love, and progress towards perfection. Noble result! By the eye of faith I see the auspicious day when it shall be so, dawn on the world. I see the moment draw near when man shall no longer see an enemy in man, when wars shall end, tyrannies be abolished, and oppression cease, and "every man sit under his own vine and fig tree with none to molest or make afraid" [Mic 4:4].

Young men! Ye who are full of the future, whose souls are full of energy, and whose hearts burn to do grand and glorious deeds, 'tis yours to hasten that day. Your fathers have done nobly. They have begun a magnificent work, but it is yours to finish it. The mission of your fathers is ended. They have departed. Gone are they who so nobly dared, so bravely struggled, to gain you a country and liberty for the world! Gone are they who signed that immortal paper which has this day been read in our hearing. Gone are they who stood firm, in those days which "tried men's souls."[2] I see but here and there one lingering behind as if unwilling to quit the scene till they can bear some good tidings from you, their children, to those who have preceded them. And gone too is HE whose soul was full of chivalry, whose heart was full of the love of humanity, liberty's representative and champion in two worlds! He is gone! And you are left alone. Alone, young men, to your own energies and philanthropy. A grand and comprehensive work is bequeathed you. The men of the revolution have given it you in charge to regenerate the world. Prove yourselves equal to your mission. And ere long free principles and just practice will become universal; man will prove himself equal to his destiny, act worthy of his lofty nature and heavenly origin. Imbibe the spirit which animated the hearts and nerved the souls of your fathers fifty-eight years ago, and you will extend your influence from circle to circle till it spread over the whole of human society—and the song of freedom, of peace and love resound from every corner of the earth and rise in swellings strains to mingle with the full chorus of angels and the blest above.

[2][Ed. A reference to Thomas Paine's famous "These are the times that try men's souls," in *The American Crisis* 1 (December 19, 1776).]

Young men! Look forward with full faith to such a glorious consummation; fix your eyes upon it; march towards it, as steadily and as firmly as your fathers did to win the political liberty we now boast. Contemplate the inspiring vision; let it fill your souls with a noble enthusiasm, and believe nothing gained till you have realized it. Feel that you live only for man, and that your mission is to set him forward with more rapid strides towards that perfection after which his soul hungers and thirsts. Make this the end of all your exertions, and never tire in this work of philanthropy. Do this and you will preserve your country free; do this and you will regenerate the world. Do this and all posterity shall bless your memories, and God himself approve your conduct and welcome you to heaven.

35.

SPIRITUALITY OF RELIGION—
GOODWIN'S SERMONS[1]

Unitarian 1 (September 1834): 405-13

There is a conservative principle in a good man's name that prevents it, whatever the sphere of his activity, from being soon forgotten. Virtue embalms it and preserves its freshness forever. The author of these *Sermons* was a quiet, unobtrusive man, spending most of his time and concentrating most of his energies in the circle of his ministerial and parochial duties; but the fragrance of his worth was wafted beyond that circle and will long continue to refresh the pious and to make the good regret his early departure.

We have not introduced these *Sermons* to review them. We have read them with pleasure and with regret that they are the last we shall have from one who seldom wrote or spoke but to make men better. They seem to us to be *Christian* sermons, to breathe peculiarly a Christian spirit, to view things in peculiarly a Christian light, and to estimate them in peculiarly a Christian manner. Their effect is purely religious. While we read them, they seem to spread a calmness over the soul, to hush the turbulence of passion, and to introduce us into the sanctuary of our hearts, to meet our Father God, to derive virtuous energy, pious feeling and holy resolution from sweet but mysterious communings with his holy Spirit.

Mr. Goodwin was remarkable for his spiritual views of religion. He was a Spiritualist—we do not mean in a metaphysical, but in a religious sense. It is this that makes us love to dwell on his memory, and that increases our debt of gratitude to him for his services to Christianity. We are heartily sick of the frigid philosophy of our times, and especially of our own country. There is a coldness in our religious and philosophical speculations, that chills the heart, and freezes up the very life blood of the soul. Disguise it as we will, the philosophy of the times, especially that whose results govern the mass of the people, is materialism. Not, perhaps, materialism, full grown, dis-

[1][Ed. A review of *Sermons by the late Ezra Shaw Goodwin, Pastor of the First Church and Society in Sandwich (Mass.) with a Memoir* (Boston: Benjamin H. Greene, 1834).]

tinctly perceived, and openly avowed, but secret, almost wholly un-suspected, yet not the less fatal.

The last century and the first fourth of the present have been distinguished by the progress made in the physical sciences, and in the application of them to the purposes of life. Men's thoughts have been turned almost exclusively to external nature. They have pushed their investigations into the world of matter to a degree all but mi-raculous; but they have been so engrossed with that world, so de-lighted with the discoveries they have made in it that they have al-most entirely neglected or denied the existence of that mind without which it were to us as though it were not. They have been so occu-pied, so filled with the material world, that they have materialized everything. The heart has been thrown aside as useless or inconve-nient; moral nature has been laid up as having no employment. And judging from some of our schoolbooks, we might be led to infer that it is believed, that "children may be trained up in the way they should go" [Prov 22:6] by oxygen, azote, carbon, feldspar, or greywacke, that religion may be sent into them by the Galvanic or Voltaic bat-tery, and that they will be good or bad as they are positively or nega-tively electrified.

We do not object to the physical sciences; we acknowledge their utility. We see it in the increased power of production given to indus-try, and the increased facility of transportation and exchange given to commerce. We are grateful for this; for we would be grateful for every good, however great or however little. But this is only a mate-rial good. It only makes us able and comfortable animals. It provides for only the lower wants. This indeed is well. It is desirable to be able and comfortable animals, but it is still more desirable to be human beings. We have no disposition to reject the physical sciences, we do not regret the attention which has been paid to them. Exclusive as that attention has been, it has been beneficial. But we think the time has now come to throw them into their proper rank, to place them at the lowest round of the objects of human study, not at the highest. The moral, religious, and intellectual sciences are as much superior to them as man is superior to a lump of clay.

There are those who conclude when they have ascertained the cause of an evil that it is not an evil; such persons may infer that materialism should not be considered an evil because it is easy to account for its prevalence. But we do not think that prevents it from being an evil of no small magnitude. We are aware that but few per-sons would be willing to acknowledge themselves materialists, we do not even know one individual in our country of any very extensive influence that would risk his reputation in the defense of a well defined materialism. This, indeed, proves that we are not intentionally, understandingly, materialists; but still we very seldom meet anything like true religious spiritualism. Indeed, our spiritualism is only a less gross materialism. It goes no farther than the understanding and is spiritualist only so far as some ontological questions are concerned. Our metaphysics are as cold and as meager, as the grossest materialist could desire. Indeed, we have no metaphysics properly so called; we laugh at everyone who has a fondness for them; indeed, we laugh at every attempt to explain or to give some rational account of the mental phenomena. And why is this, but simply because we have no faith in mind? Because we do not believe that anything certain can be known about it? Certainly to have no faith in mind is not to be far from materialism. And we not only have no faith in mind, but we have faith in matter. Who doubts the calculations of the almanac maker, the experiments of the chemist, the principles of mechanics, or the laws of optics? What passes among us for metaphysics is what might be expected when men's religion makes them nominally forswear materialism, but where there is no faith in mind, but full faith in matter. It is a metaphysics that allows nothing to be true or worthy of the least regard that cannot pass under the observation of the five senses, or at least, that cannot be thrown into a formal proposition, tangible to the understanding and susceptible of a logical demonstration. The testimony of the sentiments is discarded. All our mysterious emotions, our interior cravings, vague longings, and undefined and undefinable instincts are allowed to count for nothing; and philosophy, which should be full of life, warm with a glowing enthusiasm and a generous love is dwindled down into freezing dialectics.

In our prevailing morality there seems to be no perception of the beautiful, of the true, the right, the just. There is only the perception of the useful. The right is indeed enjoined, but not as an end; it is enjoined only as a means; not because it is obligatory, but because it is the only sure means of conducting us to happiness. The basis of our morality is selfishness; its measure is our own happiness; its law calculation. If it take a step further and attempt to come out of self, it attains only to general utility, which is nothing but selfishness on a broader scale, or rather a juster calculation, selfishness better understood.

In religion all is outward, objective; nothing inward, subjective. God is placed at an infinite distance from the human soul, deprived of spirituality, or at least clothed with a materiality that prevents him from reaching men's hearts, but by the aid of the understanding or through the medium of the cumbrous machinery of a formal revelation made to one man to be by him communicated to others. Faith is in something foreign to the soul; in something arbitrary, in that which has no necessary relation to consciousness. Revelation instead of being the inspiration of God is supposed to be the written word and is so treated, that one can hardly help inferring that it is believed that heaven or hell depends upon "a various reading," or the rendering of a Greek particle. Protestantism, instead of being viewed as a protest against the authority of the Pope and the traditions of the church would seem to be considered a protest against all light which does not come to us through the written word. It seems to be the prevailing conviction of the Christian world that all wisdom was confined to the Jewish nation and is to be found only in the Jewish writings. And not content with thus disinheriting all nations except the Jewish and with cutting off all communication between God and the rest of mankind, we take even those writings in their gross literal sense, instead of studying for their true spiritual meaning. We busy ourselves with the symbol, without looking to the thing signified, with the forms rather than with the essence of the doctrines taught us.

We know not whether there are many to sympathize with us, but we do grieve over this want of spirituality, over this materializing of the gospel, and this converting the inspirations of the Almighty into cold doctrines and formal precepts that can be written on paper. For ourselves, we should as soon think of seizing the winged lightning and of writing it out with pen and ink as of recording the inspirations of God in a book. Men have spoken, men may speak, as they were, and are, moved by them, but what they speak is something very different from the inspirations themselves. It is not the word of God, for that word is "quick, and powerful, sharper than any two-edged sword, piercing even to the dividing asunder of soul and spirit, and of the joints and marrow, and is a discerner of the thoughts and intents of the heart" [Heb 4:12]. Can men speak that word? Can it be written in a book?

The Christian world seems to us to deny the inspirations of God into the human soul, and to disbelieve in the word of God. We do not mean to say that they deny that God once inspired men, that he once spoke to them; but they deny that he inspires them, speaks to them, now. They indeed allow that once God tabernacled with men, was with them their guide, instructor, keeper, friend; but now he is ascended into the heavens and the earth is forsaken of his presence.

Once men heard his voice and it was to them authority; but now for that living voice we have only what men—wise and good men, yet not the less men—what men say, or rather what they wrote, ages ago, that it uttered. We are not satisfied with this. We would not feel ourselves abandoned by our God. We would not feel that He has turned us over to those who may be deceived themselves, and who, if not deceived themselves may deceive others. We cannot be content with the cold voice of an ancient book or with the erring voice of mortal men, where our fathers had the living and true voice of God. We would hear God speak. We would feel his spirit pass over our hearts bringing order out of confusion and light out of darkness.

And we may hear God now. He speaks to all ages, to all nations, to all individuals, and to "every man in his own tongue wherein he was born" [Acts 2:8]. Whoever will enter into the sanctuary of his own heart, into the innermost recess of his soul, shall meet God there, shall hear God speaking to him in a "still small voice" [1 Kings 19:4] that shall thrill through the whole man. God has not left us. "There is a spirit in man and the inspiration of the Almighty *giveth* him understanding" [Job 32:8]. We may not hear, but it is because we are not still—because we do not listen. We may not meet God now as the sages and patriarchs, the prophets and apostles of old met him; but it is because we go away from ourselves, because we look abroad for him. We do not go where he is. We must enter into ourselves, go into our own hearts. There, if we will but wait in silence, in the quietude of the soul, with the world shut out we shall meet him, as sensibly, and hold as sweet, as instructing, and as invigorating communings with him, as did the "holy men of old, who spake as they were moved" [2 Pet 1:21] by his spirit.

We trust that we shall not be misinterpreted. We do not underrate the written word. We yield to no one in our reverence for it as the record of the views which wise and good men of the Jewish nation took of the revelations made to their souls by the inspirations of the Almighty. But that written word is not a revelation to us. It is only a record of the views taken of a revelation made to others. It is valuable; it is of immense importance; but it is not alone sufficient. We want the spirit of God to breathe into our hearts now, to "reprove us of sin, of righteousness, and of judgment" [John 16:8], to "beget us unto a lively hope" [1 Pet 1:3], to invigorate us for our spiritual progress, and to "bear witness with our spirits that we are born of God" [Rom 8:16]. We *assent* to the truth of the written word, that is an act of the understanding, one in which the heart has nothing to do; but we *confide* only in the inspirations of the Almighty, made to our own souls, only in that "true light which enlighteneth everyone that cometh into the world" [John 1:9].

For ourselves we believe strongly in the internal operations of God's spirit upon our spirit, that there is an intercourse between God and the human soul; and we are unable to separate in our own minds the idea of religion from the idea of this intercourse. Religion is no deduction of reason; it is no calculation of interest; it is a sentiment, an inspiration. It is the poetry of the soul.[2] It enables the soul to call up and solve by a sort of intuition, all the great problems relating to God and to human destiny, and to solve them, not by reasoning, not by reflection, but by faith, sincere, and so firm that it is to the soul like knowledge, only a knowledge of which it can give no account. It opens the eyes of the soul and gives it power to see truths of the utmost importance to the conduct of life, but to see them as sentiments, as influences to be felt, rather than as distinct doctrines, which may be brought out and subjected to the action of the understanding.

We believe this, the power of religion, is the direct influence of God upon the human soul. We see no objection to this belief. It is but an influence of spirit upon spirit. The human soul is an image of God, bears a real likeness to him, and has in itself traces of all his attributes. God is wise, and so may be man, and the difference between wisdom in God and wisdom in man is a difference in degree, not a difference in kind.[3] God is good, merciful, just and holy, and so may be man. Now this spiritual likeness which we bear to God paves the way for an intercourse between him and us. One man imparts wisdom to another, in like manner God may impart wisdom to us. We can infuse our own spirit into the minds of others, and God may infuse his spirit into us, and that spirit may become the power which shall quicken within us, wisdom, justice, mercy, goodness, truth.

Indeed, for God to impart to us his spirit, he has only to awaken and cause to be exerted in us, those spiritual attributes which liken us to him. There is no difficulty in understanding what is the influence

---

[2][Ed. The association of religion and poetry was of course a recurring theme in the Romantic era. For Victor Cousin, upon whom Brownson relied during this period, poetry was "the necessary form, the language of inspiration." On this, see his *Introduction to the History of Philosophy*, trans. Henning Gottfried Linberg, 166.]

[3][Ed. Brownson seems to be drawing here upon William Ellery Channing's *Likeness to God* (1828) where Channing indicates that the difference between human and divine attributes is in the degree of perfection. For a recent edition of *Likeness*, see *William Ellery Channing: Selected Writings*, ed. David Robinson (New York: Paulist Press, 1985), 146-65, especially 152.]

he may exert over us. An assembly has met. Heavy responsibilities rest upon its deliberations, and its decisions are big with the fate of millions. Each member is free to offer his own opinion and to follow his own determination. A giant mind discloses itself. One rises who has a clearer conception of the danger to be dreaded, a greater stretch of vision, a mightier grasp of thought; who is more prudent in counsel, firm in resolve, bold and persevering in action. He speaks; his words flash conviction; he infuses his own mind into the minds of those that hear him. All now decide with his wisdom, lean on his advice and follow his direction. Here is an influence of mind over mind, of spirit over spirit; and it is an image of the influence God may exert over the minds of men, and of what we term the inspirations of the Almighty. He thus gives us some glimpses of his own all-powerful, all-comprehending and eternal mind; by the breathings of his spirit, he exalts ours to the exigencies of the condition in which we are placed, infuses into us the needed faith and energy and gives the impulse which carries us forward to the work to be done.

We believe there are few who have not been sensible of the inward breathings of God's spirit upon their souls. Who of us has not often when conversing with the works of our Creator, when admiring their beauty and grandeur, their loveliness and utility, been conscious of purer feelings and holier thoughts; of an inward power and a freedom of soul to which we are ordinarily strangers? When alone, in the silence of nature, in the stillness of night, when wrapt in contemplation, when the soul looks in upon herself, and we commune with our own feelings, have we not seemed to hear a sweet and thrilling voice discoursing to us on the loveliness of virtue, and to be conscious of some spirit unveiling all the attractive charms of goodness, and inviting us by motives as sweet and as powerful as heaven to become holy? And have we not at those times resolved that we would? And has there not been then a swelling of the soul, and has not the heart seemed to enlarge, thought to become sublimer, and all our good affections sweeter and stronger? Now that voice we seemed to hear was the voice of God, that spirit was the spirit of God, and that inward movement, that new energy given to the whole spiritual man, were the breathings of God's spirit into the soul.

But let us not be misunderstood: This voice is soft, to hear it we must be still, to understand it we must listen. This spiritual influence rushes upon us not like the mountain torrent. The great and strong wind rent the mountain; God was not in the wind. There came the earthquake, the Lord was not in the earthquake. There came the thunder, the fire which wrapped the mountain in flames; the Lord was not in the thunder, nor in the fire. There came a still small voice, and God was in it. Silent, with noiseless step, and scarcely perceptible is the approach of the Lord; but the prophet who awaits his coming, recognizes it, wraps himself in his mantle and goes forth to meet him. Weak man is prone to err. He asks for some noisy display of the Almighty. But God's ways are not ours. He walks in majesty, but he walks in stillness; he wheels the spheres in their orbits, but he wheels them in silence, by agents imperceptible, but not on that account the less powerful.

And let us not be prejudiced against this internal operation of God's spirit, this immediate inspiration of the Almighty into the human soul, because some pretenders to it, have been guilty of wild extravagances. We have detected those extravagances, and by what power? By our reason? If reason be adequate to prove that those practices we pronounce extravagant, are extravagant, will not its exercise be able to prevent them? Those pretenders to this inspiration, whom we condemn, were exclusive mystics, they supposed that the inspiration of God should supersede reason. This was their error. We must avoid it. The inspirations of the Almighty are given, not to supersede reason, but to aid it, to purge its vision, to increase its power, and to give to the soul an impulse, an energy, an enthusiasm, which reason cannot give; and an intuition, or an inward sentiment of moral truth, of which reason can take no cognizance. God inspires us, but he inspires us as rational, not as irrational beings, to aid us in the work of perfecting our whole nature, not to make us foreswear the exercise of a part.

36.

BENJAMIN CONSTANT ON RELIGION[1]

Christian Examiner and Gospel Review
17 (September 1834): 63-77

Why is man affected by religious considerations? Why has he, wherever found, some kind of religious worship? Why does he, by turns, embrace and abandon that vast variety of religious forms, which range from the loathsome fetishism of the savage to the simple and sublime monotheism of the Christian? Is it by accident, or in accordance with certain invariable and indestructible laws? If in accordance with certain laws, what are these laws? Such were the questions which passed through the mind of Benjamin Constant, and produced the works placed at the head of this article, which if they are not so perfect as to leave us nothing to desire on the topics they treat, open a new route to the philosopher, and let in light upon many a dark passage in the history of religions.

In these works, Benjamin Constant attempts to reduce our religious history to a science, and to verify its laws. He brings forward a striking and important theory, develops and sustains it with much felicity of style, with great beauty of language, power of argument, and extensive erudition. He may not, indeed, always convince the understanding, but he never fails to enlighten the mind, to warm the heart, and invigorate the religious sentiment. In going through his volumes, he compels us to run over the errors and the follies, the vices and the crimes, of a hundred ages; but he spreads over them such a warm sun-light, from a benevolent heart that they lead to no discouragement, excite no misanthropic emotions, but increase our love for mankind, and inspire us with new zeal and confidence in the noble work of setting the human race forward in the march towards perfection.

He begins his work with the position that all beings created or uncreated, animate or inanimate, rational or irrational, have their

---

[1][Ed. A review of Benjamin Constant, *De la religion, considéré dans sa source, ses formes et ses développements*; *Du polythéisme Romain, considéré dans ses rapports avec la philosophie Grecque et la religion Chrétienne*, Introduction by M. J. Matter, 2 vols. (Paris, 1833).]

laws. These laws constitute the nature of each species, and are the general and permanent cause of each one's mode of existence. We do not know, we cannot know, the origin of these laws. All we know, or need know, is, that they exist, and in all our attempts to explain any partial phenomena, we must assume their existence, as our point of departure.

Man has his laws, laws which constitute him what he is, that is to say, man. By one of these laws, he is led to seek some object to venerate, to adore, between whom and himself he may establish mutual relations. That this is by a law of his nature is inferred from its being peculiar to man, and common to nearly all men, in all ages, and in all positions, being always reproduced with the new generation. It follows from this that man is not religious by accident, has not religion because he is weak or timid, or through the influence of wily statesmen, as some have asserted, nor because he has reasoned himself into the belief of its truth and utility; but because he is man, and must be religious or divest himself of a part of his nature. It is no longer a question, then, whether we ought to preserve or destroy religion. That matter is settled. Religion man has, and will have. He is determined to it by an interior sentiment, by a fundamental law of his being, a law invariable, eternal, indestructible.

But if man is determined to religion by a fundamental law of his being, how comes it that men, even wise and virtuous men, at various epochs, are either indifferent or opposed to it? To solve this problem, we must distinguish between the religious sentiment and religious institutions. The sentiment results from that craving, which we have, to place ourselves in communication with invisible powers; the institutions, the form, from that craving which we also have to render the means of that communication we think to have discovered, regular and permanent. The consecration, regularity, and permanence, of these means, are things, with which we cannot well dispense. We would count upon our faith. We would find it today what it was yesterday, and not have it seem ready at each moment to vanish and escape from us like a vapor. We demand the suffrage of those with whom we have relations of interest, of habit, or of affection; for we take pleasure in our own sentiments only when they are attached to the universal sentiment. We do not love to nourish an opinion which no one shares with us. We aspire, for our thoughts as well as for our conduct, to the approbation of others; and we ask an external sanction to complete our internal satisfaction. Hence the necessity of religious institutions, the reason why the sentiment is always clothed with some form.

But every positive form, however satisfactory it may be for the present, contains a germ of opposition to future progress. It contracts, by the very effect of its duration, a stationary character that refuses to follow the intellect in its discoveries and the soul in its emotions, which each day renders more pure and delicate. Forced to borrow images more and more material, in order to make the greater impression upon its adherents, the religious form soon comes to present man, wearied with this world, only another very little different. The ideas it suggests are daily narrowed down to the terrestrial ideas of which they are only a copy, and the epoch arrives when it presents to the mind only assertions which it cannot admit and to the soul only practices which can no longer satisfy it. The sentiment now breaks away from that form, which, if one may so speak, has become petrified; it asks another form, one which will not wound it, and it ceases not its exertions till it obtains it. Here is the history of religion; but without the distinction between the sentiment and the form, it would be forever unintelligible. The sentiment is lodged in the bottom of the soul, always the same, unalterable, and eternal; the form is variable and transitory.[2]

But if the form be variable and transitory, it is not by accident that the sentiment combines now with this form and now breaks from it to combine with another. That which we worship is always the highest worth of which we can form any conception. We always embody in our religious institutions, all our ideas of the true, the beautiful, and the good. Consequently, the object of our worship, and the religious institutions we adopt, or the form with which we clothe the religious sentiment, will always be exactly proportioned to our mental development and moral progress. At every epoch, there is cherished and defended, as pure a form of religion, as the general civilization of that epoch will admit. The lowest, the grossest form of religion is fetishism. But, low and gross as this form of religion is, it is the purest and the most elevated, which the minds and the hearts of the tribes who adopt it can grasp, and nothing better, more spiritual, can be received, till there be an advance in civilization. Yet this form, miserable as it may seem at more advanced stages of mental and moral progress, is good and useful when adopted. It then responds to the wants of the soul, is in harmony with the lights of the understanding, and has a binding tie upon the conscience. It is at that epoch desirable, has an important mission to accomplish.

[2][Ed. The distinctions here are similar to those of Theodore Parker's famous *A Discourse on the Transient and Permanent in Christianity . . . May 19, 1841* (Boston: Printed by author, 1841).]

But the correspondence between this form and the wants of the mind and the heart is soon broken. Man is a progressive being. The institutions which he adopts today help him onward, but as they do not advance with him, he has soon outgrown them, and begun the work of exchanging them for others. The religious sentiment itself is the very spirit of progress. It labors unceasingly to purify the form with which it is combined. It is forever struggling to enlarge the sphere of its activity. It demands a broader horizon; it shoots off into the unknown, rises to the infinite, and seizes upon the perfect. Left to the workings of this interior sentiment, man would march onward with an uninterrupted progress, and every day become able to conceive a nobler object of worship, and to embody more of excellence in his form of religion. The unyielding nature of every religious form, combined with the influence of the sacerdotal corporations, which always have an interest in perpetuating the existing order, whatever it may be, interrupts, however, this regular progress, and keeps him wedded to the low and the worthless form from which he should long since have been divorced. But, if interrupted, suspended, progress cannot be wholly prevented. Fetishism ceases to be in harmony with civilization. Its mission ends and a new religious form is demanded. Polytheism is elaborated, improved, perfected, but in its turn it must yield to theism, to the theism of Christianity.

Each religious form has three epochs. At first, man seizes upon a religion, that is, following his instinct, directed by the lights of his understanding, he seeks to discover the relations which exist between him and invisible powers. When he believes he has discovered these relations, he gives them a regular and determinate form. Having provided for this first craving of his nature, he develops and perfects his other faculties. But his very successes render the form, which he had given to his religious ideas, disproportioned to his developed and perfected faculties. Now begins the second epoch. From this moment the destruction of that form is inevitable. The polytheism of the Iliad no longer comporting with the age of Pericles, Euripides, in his tragedies, becomes the organ of a nascent irreligion.[3]

If the old creed be prolonged by institutions, sacerdotal corporations, or other means, the human race, during this factitious prolongation, is furnished only with an existence purely mechanical, in which there is nothing of life. Faith and enthusiasm desert religion and there are left only formulas, observances, and priests. But this forced state

---

[3][Ed. Pericles (c. 493-429 B.C.) was an Athenian statesman, orator, and general. Euripides (c. 480-406 B.C.) was a Greek dramatist and author of nineteen extant plays.]

has its limits. A conflict commences, not only between the established religion and the understanding which it insults, but between it and the religious sentiment, which it has ceased to satisfy. This conflict brings about the third epoch, the annihilation of the form, which stirred up rebellion; and hence the crises of complete unbelief, crises, disorderly, sometimes terrible, but inevitable, when man wants to be delivered from what has become, and hereafter can be only a bar to improvement. These crises are always followed by a form of religious ideas better suited to the faculties of the human mind, and religion comes forth from its ashes, with a new youth, purer, and more beautiful.

This distinction between the religious sentiment, and the religious form, is very necessary to be made. It explains many of the phenomena, which occur in the history of religion. This explains wherefore it is that men of virtuous lives, of ardent enthusiasm, of generous devotion to liberty, and to the welfare of their fellow beings, have at times opposed themselves to religion. They are men who have outgrown the established form. It no longer responds to the wants of their souls, no longer comports with their understanding, nor comes up to their ideas of the perfect. They rebel against it, and the religious sentiment itself in them is found combating a religious form, which galls it, and restrains its free and healthy action. This explains the existence and the great influence of certain infidel writers. Writers are the organs of their age. They collect and bring out the ideas of their times. Had Lucian been placed in the age of Homer, or merely in that of Pindar,[4] had Voltaire been born under Louis IX, or Louis XI,[5] Lucian and Voltaire had not even attempted to shake the belief of their contemporaries or would have attempted it in vain. They were less indebted to their own merit for the applauses which they obtained from their own times and for the eulogies which encouraged them than to the conformity of their doctrines to those which began to be accredited. They said plainly and unreservedly what everybody thought. Each, recognizing himself in them, admired himself in his interpreter. Men must begin to doubt, before one can have much success in shaking their belief, and certainly before one can gain celebrity by attempting it. This explains why it is impossible at some epochs to disseminate doubt, and equally impossible, at others, to establish conviction. This is not accidental. It is not by mere

[4][Ed. Lucian was a second century B.C. Greek satirist. Pindar (c. 522-443 B.C.) was a Greek lyric poet.]

[5][Ed. Louis IX (1214-70) was a king of France (1226-70) who was canonized a saint by Pope Boniface VIII in 1297. Louis XI (1423-83) was also king of France (1461-83).]

caprice that people are devout or irreligious. When the religious form is in harmony with the religious sentiment, and with the faculties of the mind, doubt is impossible; when that harmony no longer exists, belief is equally impossible. A believing epoch marks institutions which respond to the wants of the soul, and of the understanding; an unbelieving epoch marks a growth, an advance, which has left those institutions behind, a search after new institutions, which will answer to the new wants that have been developed, and with which the faculties of the human mind may unite and gather strength to take another step onward in its endless career of perfectibility.

From Benjamin Constant's theory, slightly and imperfectly as we have now presented even its most prominent traits, we may derive much to soften our indignation at the past, and to inspire us with hope for the future. All the great institutions of former times have been good in their day and in their places and have had missions essential to the progress of humanity to accomplish. The Catholic institution, Catholicism, which still excites the wrath and indignation of many a religionist as well as of many an unbeliever was a noble institution in its time. It was a mighty advance upon the paganism which preceded it. It was suited to the wants of the age in which it flourished and we are indebted to it for the very light which has enabled us to discover its defects. Its vices, and they need not be disguised, appertain to the fact that it has lingered beyond its hour. It has now and long has had only a factitious existence. Its work was long since done, its purpose accomplished, and it now only occupies the space that should be filled with another institution, one which will combine all our discoveries and improvements and be in harmony with the present state of mental and moral progress.

Protestantism cannot be said to supply the place of Catholicism. Protestantism is not a religion, is not a religious institution, contains in itself no germ of organization. Its purpose was negative, one of destruction. It was born in the conflict raised up by the progress of mind against Catholicism, which had become superannuated. Its mission was legitimate, was necessary, was inevitable; but may we not ask if it be not accomplished? Catholicism is destroyed, or at least, is ready to disappear entirely, as soon as a new principle of social and religious organization, capable of engaging all minds and hearts in its service, shall present itself. And this new principle will present itself. Men will not always live in a religious anarchy. The confusion of the transition-state in which we now are must end and a new religious form be disclosed, which all will love and obey.

But we need not go out of Christianity to find this new principle. Christianity contains the germs of many new principles, which wait only the proper hour to develop themselves. We have, as yet, seen but little of Christianity, suspected but little of what it is, and what it contains. Christianity is unalterable, eternal, indestructible as to its foundation; but it is exceedingly flexible, as to its forms. In one stage of spiritual improvement, it unites enthusiastically with Catholicism, and, in another, it unites no less enthusiastically with Protestantism, and urges it on in its career of destruction. A great excellence of Christianity and one of the most striking proofs of its divine origin is the fact that it is wedded to no form, but can unite with all forms and exist in all stages of civilization. Indeed, in the last analysis, it is little else than the religious sentiment itself, detached from all forms, exhibiting itself in its divine purity and simplicity.

We think the time has come for us to clothe the religious sentiment with a new form and to fix upon some religious institution, which will at once supply our craving for something positive in religion, and not offend the spirituality which Christianity loves, and towards which the human race hastens with an increasing celerity. We think we see indications that this presents itself to many hearts as desirable. And we think we see this especially among our own friends. Every religious denomination must run through two phases, the one destructive, the other organic. Unitarianism could commence only by being destructive. It must demolish the old temple, clear away the rubbish, to have a place whereon to erect a new one. But that work is done; that negative character, which it was obliged to assume then, may now be abandoned. The time has now come to rear the new temple, or a positive work, and if we are not mistaken, we already see the workmen coming forth with joy to their task. We already see the germ of reorganization, the nucleus, round which already gravitate the atoms of a new moral and religious world. The work of elaboration is well nigh ended, the positive institutions, so long sought, will soon be obtained, and the soul, which has so long been tossed upon a sea of dispute or of skepticism, will soon find that repose after which it so deeply sighs and yearns.

Here, perhaps, we ought to close; but we cannot let the occasion pass without offering some remarks upon a point very distinctly recognized in the interesting Preface to the first volume of the first of the works we have named. The point to which we allude is that religion and morality rest not on the understanding, not on logical deductions, but on an interior sentiment. Here is an important recognition, a recognition of two distinct orders of human faculties. This recognition is not always made by metaphysicians, but it never escapes popular language. It is found in the distinction between the head and the heart, the mind and the soul, the understanding and the affections, which obtains in all languages. And this is not strange. One cannot have made the least progress in psychological observation without being struck with internal phenomena, which can by no means be classed with the operations of the understanding. There belong to human nature, passions, emotions, sentiments, affections, of which, the understanding, properly so called, can take no account, which pay no deference to its ratiocinations, and even bid defiance to its laws. The feeling which we have when contemplating a vast and tranquil sea, distant mountains with harmonious outlines, or, when marking an act of heroism, of disinterestedness, or of generous self-sacrifice for others' welfare, rises without any dependence on the understanding. We feel what we then feel, not because we have convinced ourselves by logical deductions that we ought so to feel. Reasoning may come afterwards and justify the feeling; but it did not precede it, and, if it had, it could not have produced it. The understanding cannot feel; it cannot love, hate, be pleased, be angry, nor be exalted or depressed. It is void of emotion. It is calm, cold, calculating. Had we no faculty but those it includes, we should be strangers to pity, to sympathy, to benevolence, to love, and, what is worse, to enthusiasm. Bring the whole of man's nature within the laws of the understanding and you reduce religion, morality, philosophy, to a mere system of logic; you would, in the end, pronounce everything which does not square with dry and barren dialectics, chimerical, and everything which interest cannot appropriate, mischievous.

But we not only contend for the distinction of the mental phenomena into two different orders, but we contend, that the sentiments are as worthy of reliance as the understanding; that, to speak in popular language, the testimony of the heart is as legitimate as that of the head. We are aware that the philosophy of sensation will condemn this position. Be it so. The philosophy of sensation reigned during the last half of the last century, and it is, as far as we have any philosophy, still the philosophy of our own country; but it is no great favorite of ours. It undoubtedly has its truth; but, taken exclusively, freed from its inconsequences, and pushed to its last results, it would deprive man of all but a merely mechanical life, divest the heart of all emotion, wither the affections, dry up the sentiments, and sink the human race into a frigid skepticism. The testimony of the senses requires an internal sanction, and, in the last analysis, that of the understanding is not credited till it is corroborated by that of consciousness. Neither our senses, nor our understanding, can prove to us, that we exist, and yet it is impossible for us, in a healthy state of mind to doubt our existence; neither our senses nor our understanding can prove to us the existence of an external world, nor the objective reality of anything, yet we should justly regard him as insane who should not believe in the existence of an external world, and there is no one, who, listening to the sweet strains of music, will not believe they come to his heart from some objective reality. It is a law of our nature, of which reasoning cannot divest us, that in these, and in a vast variety of cases, we must believe on the simple testimony of consciousness, or, in other words, we believe so, because our nature, the very laws of our being, compel us to believe so. But the moment we recur to the testimony of consciousness, to the laws of our nature, we desert the understanding, we leave the power of ratiocination, and have recourse to an entirely different order of testimony.

We may be told that to admit that the feelings, the sentiments, are worthy of reliance, is to go off into the mysterious, to stop we know not where. We know many are very coy of mystery. We know there are many who say, "Where mystery begins, there religion ends"; and we know, also, that in saying it, if they mean what is inexplicable to the understanding, properly so called, they pronounce a general sentence of condemnation upon all that is elevated, generous, and touching in human nature. We can explain to the understanding, none of the workings of the sentiments of the heart, none of the emotions, the affections of the soul. Indeed, we do not wish to explain them. We are not afraid of the mysterious. It is one of the glories of our nature and one of the strongest pledges of its immortal destiny that it delights in the mysterious; that it has cravings which go beyond what is known; that it dares rush off into the darkness, trusting to its own instincts for guidance; and that it has powers, which can out-travel the understanding, and which can seize and shadow forth to its own eye a perfection, which reason cannot comprehend, of which it does not even dream. To condemn the mysterious, were to bring the soul down from the beautiful and the holy, to the merely useful, were to kill poetry, to wither the fine arts, to discard all the graces, for all these have something of the mysterious, are enveloped in mystic folds, offensive it may be to the understanding, but enchanting to the soul. We say, again, we are not afraid of the mysterious. We love it. We love those mysterious emotions, which we feel, when we survey the magnificent works of nature, or the creations of genius; when we hear the wind sigh over ruins; or when we walk among the dead and think of those who were and are not, of the hearts which once beat but which are now still, of the sweet voices which once spoke but which are silent now. We love those emotions, which start within us when we think of God, of the human soul, of its immortality, of heaven, and of eternity. Reasoning is then still and the soul, asserting her supremacy, half escaping from the body which imprisons her, catches some glorious visions of her native land, her everlasting home, and of those sublime occupations to which she feels herself equal. It is to us, then, no objection to say, our doctrine leads off into the mysterious. All to us, human beings, is mysterious, except the little that we know, and it is only that interior craving of our nature which keeps us forever hovering beyond the horizon of what we know, that enables us, by conquests from the dominions of mystery, to enlarge the boundaries of our knowledge.

But we would not merely rely on this order of our faculties, which we call the sentiments. We would have them appealed to, as the most essential part of our nature. We do not mean to depreciate the understanding; we would not underrate the power of ratiocination, nor, in any case, dispense with sound logic. We value man's whole nature; man's whole nature is essential. We should think clearly, reason closely, powerfully; but we should also feel justly and energetically. We should retain and develop all our faculties, each in its place, so as to preserve unbroken harmony through the whole man. But if we do this, we shall find, that the sentiments, the feelings, are entitled to a much higher rank than it has been customary to assign them for the last century. To us the sentiments seem to be peculiarly the human faculties. They give to man his distinctive character. They supply him with energy to act and prompt him to the performance of grand and noble deeds. We fear that their power is seldom suspected, that little attention is paid to the mission which is given them to accomplish. We have schools for the intellect. We take great pains to educate the reasoning faculty, but we almost, at least so far as our schools are concerned, entirely neglect the sentiments. We cannot but regret this; for knowledge when not coupled with just feelings, strong reasoning powers when not under the guidance of pure and holy sentiments, only so much the better fit one for a career destructive to the best interests of humanity. And, let it be understood, men are not reasoned into good feelings, for the feelings do not depend on the intellect. Just sentiments are not the result of just knowledge. A man may know the truth, be able to defend it in language and with arguments that fix attention, and flash instantaneous conviction, and yet have no just, honorable, or benevolent feelings. It is an old saying, that men know better than they do;

Video meliora, proboque;
Deteriora sequor.[6]

It will be so as long as we trust to merely intellectual education to
give right feelings. We would, therefore, without in the least neglecting the intellect, turn attention to the sentiments, appeal to them on
all occasions, and make it the leading object of all education to develop them, to fit them for strong and beneficent action.

We would appeal constantly to the sentiments, for all that we
have of the disinterested and self-denying pertains to them. Destroy
the sentiments and we should never support any cause, however just,
dear, or essential to humanity, when the nicer calculations of interest
assure us that we have nothing to gain for our individual selves. Destroy the sentiments and we could never identify ourselves with humanity, and at times come forth in its behalf with the reformer's zeal
and with the martyr's firmness. There is nothing great or good ever
won without sacrifice. No man will devote himself to the defense of
liberty, of justice, of his country, of religion, or of the welfare of his
fellow beings in any shape unless he has within him the power of self-
denial and is prepared to make almost any sacrifice. Had the apostles
not had this power of self-denial and of self-sacrifice, they never would,
they never could, have established Christianity. Had it not been for
this, the reformers of Germany would hardly have succeeded, the
Puritans would not have withstood the prelates, left their homes, and
all the fond recollections of childhood and youth, to brave the dangers of the deep and of a new and hostile world, to maintain liberty
of conscience; nor would our fathers have staked life, property, and
honor, to gain a country for their children, and liberty for the world.
But this power, or rather spirit of self-denial and self-sacrifice, which
Christianity was sent into the world to cherish and clothe with omnipotence, pertains solely to the sentiments. The understanding knows
nothing of it. That, at best, knows only the self-denial of calculation,
of temporary pleasure to obtain a lasting good, which is nothing
more than selfishness would every day command.

We are not willing to dismiss the topic of self-denial without a
farther remark. We speak not now of its necessity. We have already
shown that. But we would refer to man's love of self-denial, of sacri-

[6][Ed. Latin for "I see the better and I approve; but I follow the worst." Quote
from Ovid (i.e., the Roman poet Publius Ovidius Naso, 43 B.C.–17 A.D.) *Meta-
morphoses* 7:19. The quote is sometimes associated with Rom 7:19. John Cassian
uses the two texts together in his *Collatio quarta*. On this see the *Patrologia Latina*,
49, col. 592A.]

fice, and to the power of that principle on which it depends. It is, perhaps always was, extremely fashionable to speak of interest as man's strongest, man's governing principle of action. If there is a good thing to be done, a religious institution to be patronized, a moral or political reform to be accomplished, appeal is almost invariably made to interest, to selfishness. But in this we do not show our deep knowledge of human nature. Paradoxical as it may seem, men will do more from a disinterested than from an interested motive. It has been asked how could Christianity, a self-denying religion as it was, be established without a continual miracle? Had it not been a self-denying religion, its establishment would have required a miracle indeed. Once awaken the sense of duty in a man and it is infinitely stronger than his sense of interest. Men will see everything dear to them die, see their children drop into the grave, have their own flesh torn off by inches, sooner than they will abandon duty, we mean those in whom the sense of duty is not dormant. But has interest ever shown itself equally strong? And what is the sense of duty, but another name for the spirit of self-denial, of self-sacrifice?

There is a standing proof of the weakness of men's sense of interest, obvious to every eye, in the indifference shown to religion. Who is not convinced that it is for his highest interest even in this world to be religious? And does everyone follow this conviction? Far from it. You may go into the pulpit and speak with the tongue of an angel, you may prove, beyond the possibility of a doubt, that it is for the highest good, the greatest possible interest of everyone of your hearers for time and for eternity to be religious, and induce no one to forsake a single sin, no one to cleave to a single virtue. Your success would be immeasurably greater would you insist on self-denial, and show clearly that heaven is not to be won without a struggle, without a costly and painful sacrifice. The successes of different religious sects clearly evince this. With all the drawback of a most irrational creed, those sects among us who insist most upon self-denial and sacrifice, spread much faster than those sects, albeit they have a much more rational creed, who attempt to show that religion demands no sacrifice, no self-denial.

We do not, in this, shut our eyes upon the fact that a large proportion of mankind are selfish, governed by a sense of their own interest. We admit the fact and we can account for it. Our own good has its place. The faculties which lead us to seek it are on the surface of our nature, and are almost the only ones to which appeal is ever made; consequently, the only ones much developed, and the only ones suspected by those who never penetrate beneath the surface.

BENJAMIN CONSTANT ON RELIGION

But let us go deeper into human nature, let us go down into the depths of the soul, and stir up from its bottom the sense of duty, of the good, the beautiful, the true, and the holy, the spirit of disinterestedness, of self-denial, and of sacrifice, and we shall find a power infinitely stronger than our sense of interest.

To be sure, it costs us an effort to awaken this sense, an effort to obey it. But so much the better. The sentiments all demand an effort, a self-denial, a sacrifice; it is their very nature to carry us away from ourselves, to seek a good which does not center in ourselves. But this is their praise. It costs us an effort to obey them, we own, and we are glad that it is so. Men love to make an effort. There is that in man, which delights in the struggle, which disdains repose, and pants for strong, varied, and continued action. The sailor on land feels its workings, and longs to be on his loved ocean, to be again amid the fury and excitement of the storm. The old soldier proves it; though he have lost a leg, an eye, or an arm, in battle, still, as his ears catch the strains of martial music, he is ready to rush into the conflict. Why? Because there is excitement there, because there is danger there, because there is a struggle, an effort, there. Take away the excitement, the danger, the struggle, and men would lose their passion for war. This shows us there is something within us, that loves the conflict, that delights to war with danger, to grapple with the enemy, even to the death-struggle. This at bottom is a noble principle. It is one which belongs to all men. We were made for war, to brave danger, and to face the enemy with a dauntless courage. But it was for a spiritual war, a war of the spirit against the flesh, a conflict with sin and Satan, not with our fellow beings. Now this principle which delights in the struggle, pants to put itself forth in strong and continued effort, is very nearly allied to the spirit of which we have been speaking, if indeed it be not the same. This, then, explains wherefore it is that self-denial is so powerful, and wherefore it is that the cause which demands it will always have adherents.

Let us not, then, overlook the sentiments; let us rely on their testimony in their own sphere of action; let us appeal to them, educate them, and depend on them to support us in all that is elevated, generous, or good. Let us venture to trust them for the support of religion. We may rest its cause securely on the disinterested and self-sacrificing affections. We shall not be disappointed. They will avail us immeasurably more than appeals to interest, for all experience will prove that it is infinitely safer to league with the good than with the bad in human nature.

37.

PRINCIPLES OF MORALITY[1]

Christian Examiner and General Review
17 (January 1835): 283-301

We refer again to these *Sermons* for they possess no common degree of interest. They come not within the ordinary range of sermons. Their aim is higher and broader; it is not their object so much to throw new light on specific moral duties as to bring out and set to work those great and immutable principles of right, which are the source and the life of morality itself. This, to us, is their chief excellence. It is of little use to dwell on the mere details of duty. In these, men need but little instruction. It is not in these but in those first principles that would make morality something living, controlling, and abiding that they are most deficient.

We are aware that there has gone abroad a deep and obstinate prejudice against all disquisitions that touch first principles. Such disquisitions are termed "abstract reasoning," "metaphysics"; and that, in this age of steamboats and railroads, is enough to stamp them with reprobation. The great cry of the times is for something "practical," something material, something that will spare the labor of thinking. But we can have no practice worthy of reliance without correct first principles. When not attached to first principles, our morality is only the fragment of a morality, without power to touch the heart and kindle the spirit, to make itself loved or its obligation felt. We have no true morality till we have a living fountain within us from which it may unceasingly flow.

We look in vain for a moral community where first principles are disregarded. Where nothing is said concerning first principles, where there is instruction only in the details of duty, there is only a routine of decencies or of heartless conventionalisms. Only a low standard of virtue is adopted, only a depressed moral tone obtains. But where first principles, principles broad and comprehensive, are brought out and insisted upon, we witness a result wholly different.

---

[1][Ed. A review of William Johnson Fox's *Sermons on the Principles of Morality inculcated in the Holy Scripture, in their Adaptation to the present Condition of Society* (Boston: Leonard C. Bowles. 1833).]

At first, indeed, they may not be obeyed, they may touch only the understanding; but they become subjects of thought and conversation; gradually they find their way into the very heart of the community, become the mainsprings of its actions, the controlling influence of its measures.

Nobody is better convinced of this truth than Mr. Fox. He therefore rises into the philosophy of morals and attempts to furnish us or to direct us where we may furnish ourselves with first principles, which we may always bear about us not only to point to right actions but to create the will and the power to perform them. He may not always succeed but we give him our hearty thanks for his aim and the example he has given us. He considers himself a utilitarian, but his utilitarianism is so modified by enlightened thought, liberal feeling, and just sentiment, that he scarcely deserves the name. It is true, he makes happiness "our being's end and aim," and commends us to consult general utility, as the only means of securing it; but he understands by happiness little else than the development and perfection of our intellectual faculties and of our moral and religious sensibilities. In this there is not much to disapprove, except the application of the terms of one system to another, which sometimes confuses and misleads him.

The utilitarian scheme of morals, however, as it generally is, and almost inevitably must be understood, is very far from being satisfactory to us. Like the selfish scheme, it takes it for granted that happiness is the only legitimate object of pursuit. But this is a point by no means self-evident. The Deity, so far as his designs see manifest, seems very far from having made this system of things, of which we are a part, expressly for enjoyment. It, at best, is but a mixed state. It may have its smiles but they are smiles through tears. Pain grows by the side of pleasure and often springs from the same root. Bitter waters are everywhere mingled with the sweet. When we propose happiness as the end of our exertions, we never obtain it. It invariably and eternally flies from those who pursue it and no people are more miserable than those who try the hardest to be happy. It is with happiness as with health. He who is always nursing his health, making its preservation the end of life, is always sickly. He and the one who pursues happiness alike fail; and is it not because both make that which God has not made the end of existence?

The misery, however, which attaches to this system of things, does not necessarily detract from the goodness of God. The end he proposes is not happiness, but spiritual growth; we were placed here, not to enjoy, but to perfect ourselves. Nothing then, which contributes to this end can, relatively to this system, be an evil; and to this end pain contributes full as much, often more than pleasure. The only question, therefore, respecting the goodness of God, is, whether the end he proposes be a good one. Good or not, we can conceive nothing better. There is nothing but mind to which we can attach any real value. This outward universe, with all its furniture of worlds and beings, is valuable only as it displays the marks, or ministers to the wants, of mind. It is mind that seizes upon the idea of God, that is, that image of God in which we were created and that enables us to "be followers of God as dear children" [Eph 5:1]. Nothing so completely fills us with admiration and awe, as the strong, varied, and continued exertions of mind. We do them homage, and secretly desire them, although coupled with the greatest possible sufferings. The unconquered and unconquerable mind, which Milton ascribes to Satan, and which sustains him, makes him a greater favorite with almost every reader of the "Paradise Lost," than Michael, with all his glory, and obedience, and happiness; and would, were it not for his guilt, be a rich indemnity for the "lowest hell" to which he is condemned. We look with infinitely warmer emotions of approbation upon the brave man, struggling with adversity and converting all he may suffer into the means of enlarging his mental and moral power than we do upon the quiet, prosperous man, who never meets a cross incident to disturb his tranquillity, and knows not what it is to have his course run roughly. And is not this because we never entirely lose all sentiment of the end for which we were made? Torture me with pain, load me with afflictions, and I can thank my God for it, if it become the means of the growth and maturity of mind.

That happiness is not the end of existence, few people who reflect on the nature of our ideas and duties, will be disposed to deny. Whenever happiness, whether it be our own or that of others, comes in collision with the right, it is pretty generally agreed that the happiness should be sacrificed and the right maintained. This proves that we have the sentiment of something superior to happiness, to which happiness must always be held as subordinate. Can that be the end of existence which is itself subordinate to another end, to one which we are to seek, let the consequences be what they may?

But were happiness the only legitimate object of pursuit, it might still be a question, whether consulting general utility would secure it; and this too, whether it be our own happiness or that of others that we would promote. Mankind are made happy only by satisfying their desires. But, however great our exertions, new desires will be pushed out, faster than we can satisfy the old ones. He who is starving may fancy a good supper will make him happy; but should you provide him a supper and then leave him to lodge in the street, he would hardly thank you. Could we multiply physical comforts a hundredfold, satisfy a hundred desires where now we satisfy but one, we should in no degree lessen the amount of misery. There would be remaining the same, if not a greater number of desires unsatisfied, to prey upon the soul and fill it with torment. Indeed all experience proves that we cannot be more successful in laboring for others' happiness, than we are in laboring for our own.

Our prospect is not more flattering, to say the least, if general utility be consulted as the means of making ourselves happy. Mr. Fox tells us, and it is the language of all utilitarians, that our duties are interests and that we should seek the happiness of others as the only means of securing our own. What he has in mind is doubtless true. The pleasures of benevolence are the most exquisite and the most lasting of any which are allotted to mortals; but they are pleasures only for the benevolent. He who loves only himself can find no pleasure in laboring for the happiness of others. The malicious, the envious, do not find their own happiness increased by seeing others happy. To be made happy by making others happy, we must love them and make their good the end of our exertions. But he who seeks the happiness of others as the means of promoting his own, makes his own happiness the end to be gained; and, consequently, throws himself out of the condition in which seeking the welfare of others could give him pleasure; he is selfish, not benevolent, and therefore cannot, although he do the deeds, taste the pleasures of benevolence.

We know that it is customary to urge people to the practice of benevolence, by the consideration that the benevolent are happier than the selfish; and, although this is an appeal to selfishness, and might, if made the motive of action, defeat itself; still, under a certain aspect, it is very proper. People are all in the pursuit of happiness, but they fail, and this is merely telling them the cause of their failure. It assures them that if they would be successful, they must cease to be selfish and become benevolent. It has an influence in fixing attention upon benevolence, in quickening the desire and in promoting exertions to become benevolent. Appeal may be made to men's hopes and fears. We may hold out the promises of the gospel to allure men to holiness, and its threatenings to make them pause in their downward course, and inquire the demands of duty; but he who has no higher principle of action than fears of punishment or hopes of reward is not virtuous. Hopes and fears may be useful means to prepare men to be virtuous, but they cease to influence in proportion as they become perfect.

True, it is said that Jesus acted with a view to the "joy set before him" [Heb 12:2]; but we see no necessity for supposing that he had respect to any personal reward, nor to any joy that he himself was to receive. There is a higher reward, a nobler recompense to the good, than anything which can be bestowed on themselves. The philanthropist, whose soul is wedded to humanity, who "hungers and thirsts" [Matt 5:6] to set mankind forward in holiness and happiness, smiles in exile or in death if he see them reaping as the fruits of his exertions the good he wished them. A just conception of the character of Jesus would, it appears to us, assign him a reward similar to that of the philanthropist. The "joy," to which he looked, was not his but that which was to "be unto all people" [Luke 2:10].

That the internal joy of Jesus, as he beheld in prophetic vision the immeasurable good he was procuring the human race, was great, we do not deny. The internal joy of the good man, on seeing literally, or by the eye of faith, others benefitted by his exertions, although he be expiring on the cross for having made those exertions, is unspeakable and unimagined by him who has not within himself the moral power to be a martyr to the cause of humanity. But why is it so great? Simply because it was no matter of calculation, was not proposed as an end, was not anticipated, and is no subject of distinct consciousness. His soul is full of joy because he thinks only of the joy of others, and because it does not occur to him to ask himself whether he be happy or miserable. He who *could* turn away from the happiness of others, and say to himself, "How happy I am! how richly am I rewarded for the sacrifices I have made!" would prove that he could not be happy by suffering to make others happy. Where there is this return upon self, there is not the disposition to be delighted with others' joy.

The mistake of the utilitarian on this point is not that benevolence does not insure a reward, or that duty does not prove itself man's interest, but that he does not distinguish between deeds of benevolence done for the sake of others, and done for the sake of ourselves; between duty performed as duty, and duty performed as interest; between the right pursued as an end, and the right pursued as a means. And yet here is a very obvious and a very important distinction. It is not easy to mistake the difference between one who pursues duty because he believes it to be duty, and one who pursues it merely because he believes it for his interest. The two men are governed by very different, not to say wholly opposite, principles.

One of them is governed by principle that bids him do his duty at all times, under all circumstances, and at all hazards; the other by a principle that, in case duty demanded a sacrifice, would bid him abandon it, desert his post whenever it became dangerous, and prove himself a coward on the approach of the enemy. He who is governed by this principle will never be a martyr.

To confound these two is to confound the idea of the useful with that of the just, a thing which nobody in his senses is likely to do unless compelled by a theory. A steamengine may be useful, but who thinks of calling it just? A man is just or unjust, according to the principles by which he is governed, without reference to the utility or inutility of his life. There is a marked difference between the emotion one has on viewing a steamengine, however useful it may be, and that which he has on reading the Life of Howard;[2] between the one excited in us by contemplating the assassin and the one excited by contemplating his dagger. The difference between these two emotions shows the difference between the idea of the useful and the harmful and that of the just and the unjust.

The utilitarian, as his name imports, is one who is governed solely by the idea of the useful. The just, the true, the beautiful enter for nothing into the considerations which influence his conduct. It is nothing to him that his course violates what he terms "abstract right," if he be satisfied that it is useful. He sees no men around him, no moral beings, with duties not to be neglected, with rights to be consulted and never abridged; but simply human machines, concerning which he has only to inquire what is the most advantageous manner in which he can employ them. Whatever is difficult, whatever demands a sacrifice, if it have nothing but its justice to recommend it, is abandoned as inexpedient. He may see his neighbor's house on fire and his family in peril, but before running to assist in extinguishing the flames or in rescuing the family, he must ascertain the bearing the assistance he might lend would have upon the useful. His brother may be sinking in the wave; but if, upon a full and impartial discussion of the matter, he be convinced that his brother's death will be more useful than his life, he leaves him to drown. Murder, robbery, theft, and all those acts, which the world has agreed to call crimes, are very good things in his estimation if they promote what he believes is general utility. He would have recommended the Athenians

[2][Ed. The reference may be to *The Life of John Howard: Abridged from Authentic Sources* (New York: B. Waugh and T. Mason, 1833). John Howard (?1726-90) was, among other things, a British prison reformer.]

to follow the advice of Themistocles,[3] which Aristides declared useful, but unjust.

Doubtless the utilitarian would recoil with horror from these conclusions; but they belong to his system and he reasons inconsequently when he rejects them. In refusing to admit them he goes out of his system and declares it "too strait" for him to dwell in. He, indeed, talks of the sentiments, the emotions, the affections, of the pleasure to be derived from diffusing love and joy among mankind; but, whenever he does this, he is away from his utilitarianism, in a different order of ideas, where, instead of restricting himself to the useful, he appeals to the right, the benevolent, and the humane. We do not censure him for this inconsequence, which proves him better than his system; for it is inevitable. No one can pay the least attention to what is passing within him, without being conscious of ideas and wants that are forever carrying him beyond the narrow circle, and away from the mechanical life, of the merely useful.

Let it not, however, be inferred, that we condemn the useful. The useful is a real element of our nature and in its place it is as proper and as important as any other. We merely object to making it comprise man's whole nature and to regarding it as the rule and measure of morality. We do not make it the basis of morality for we do not find that it necessarily involves any moral consideration. We base morality on the moral sense and what we term the idea of the just, or of the right. The idea of the just is common to all moral beings. He who has it not is no more accountable for what he does than the assassin's dagger for the act of assassination. This is not a derivative, but a primitive idea, a constituent element in human nature itself, whose destruction would involve our annihilation. It reveals to us that law of eternal justice, anterior to all other laws, on which all other laws depend for their authority, and which, as Marcus Antoninus says, "binds both Gods and men."[4] He who has the sentiment of this law is moral; he who has it not is out of the pale of moral beings. He who obeys this sentiment is virtuous; he who disobeys it is guilty. We know no objection that can be brought against this, for it recognizes a law which is known to all moral beings, and which is immutable, eternal, and universal, the same in all nations and in all ages.

If we are asked, why we are bound to obey this law, we send the interrogator to his own conscience and consciousness for an answer. But no man was ever yet by his own wants induced to make the

[3][Ed. Themistocles (c. 527-460 B.C.) was an Athenian military and political leader famous for his victorious battle at Salamis.]
[4][Ed. Marcus Aurelius Antoninus' *The Meditations*, 8.2.]

inquiry. Theorists may have attempted to find a reason why we should obey the right, as geometricians have attempted to define a straight line, but it has been labor lost. Convince a man that what you propose is right, and he will hardly ask you to prove that it is obligatory. No man ever yet doubted that he was bound to do right. Indeed, there is no real difference between the idea of right and that of obligation. To say that a thing is right is the same as to say that it is obligatory.

Moralists have thought differently and have therefore attempted to show why we ought to obey the right. They have usually alleged authority or utility. But authority, that is, the command or the will of the Deity, cannot create the obligation. Nobody is bound to obey an unjust command. It is not the command but its justice that constitutes its obligation. The commands of God do not make the obligation, they merely declare it. Even the will of the Deity does not constitute the obligation for it does not make the right. A thing is not right because God wills it; he wills it because it is right, because it is in accordance with the decisions of his wisdom, of his own infinite and unerring reason. Nor can the obligation be derived from the idea of the useful. Grant the right always involves the useful, the very moment you assign that as the ground of its obligation, you transfer the obligation from the right to the useful; and prove, so far as you prove anything, that the right is not obligatory and that we are bound to consult only utility. And why are we bound to consult utility? Is not the evidence on which it rests precisely that on which rests the obligation of the right?

But in basing morality on our inherent idea of right, on the moral sense, we would guard against misapprehension. This moral sense is not a perception, but a sentiment of the right. It is that which constitutes us moral beings but is not itself a code of ethics. It craves but it does not see the right; it makes us feel that there is a right, that it is obligatory, but it does not give us clear perceptions of what the right is, much less of all its bearings, of all its specific duties. This is done only by the aid of the understanding. Nature, or rather God in nature, has laid the foundation of a moral edifice, but its erection depends on us, and the just proportions of its parts, its beauty and strength, depend on the harmonious development of all our faculties, intellectual as well as moral.

There must, then, always be a difference between the morality of the cultivated and that of the uncultivated man. The savage has the same nature, the same elemental wants, as the civilized man; he is carried away towards the right by the same inward sentiment; but the right which he is able to body forth as his ideal of excellence, falls far below the ideal of him whose mind and heart are well cultivated. Not that nature decides differently in one case from what she does in another, or, that she ever pronounces that right which is not right; but the one sees only a little of the right, while the other takes broader and more comprehensive views of it, and, consequently, is able to form to himself a less defective morality. In the case of the savage, the faculties, not having been exercised, are weak, and therefore able to take in but a little of the right, to see it only under one of its aspects; the faculties of the civilized man having been strengthened by exercise, he is able to see the right under several aspects, and to take in vastly more of it.

This same remark is applicable to Christian morality. Jesus Christ did not give us a body of morals, he merely gave us the law of morality. This law is the law of love, of love to our neighbor, which is merely the realization of the idea of the right, the moral sense clothed with a practical form. But this love varies, according to the mental and moral progress of him who harbors it. To him of narrow views and uncultivated soul, love to our neighbor will have a low and narrow meaning. It will, indeed, mean the greatest good he can conceive, but it will not be the less low and narrow on that account. The Western Indian's ideal of good is the happy islands where his fathers have gone, where no bad Indian intrudes, where there is plenty of game and the hunter is never weary or hungry. Yet in wishing his neighbor a reception into those happy islands, he is as sincere, is as obedient to his sense of right, follows the dictates of as pure a love, according to the measure of his light, as the Christian who would raise a fellow being to his sublimer and more spiritual heaven. Give the Indian the Christian's cultivation, the Christian's spiritual growth, and his simple heaven "behind the cloud-topt hill,"[5] will no longer be the measure of good his love would bestow upon the object beloved. But without that cultivation, that spiritual growth, although he might adopt the Christian's creed and the Christian's law, he could give to the terms of that creed and of that law, no higher meaning than he assigns to his own rude moral code, and to the simple religion he has received from his fathers. His ideal would not be changed by a change of names. Every man's ideal of excellence, whether he be savage or civilized, Christian or Pagan, Jew or Mussulman, is measured by his spiritual progress, and must be as different as is the degree of that progress; and that difference would remain the same,

---

[5][Ed. Alexander Pope, *An Essay on Man*, epistle 1, line 99.]

although all might come to bear the same name and nominally profess to worship the same God.

This is a consideration of which we should never lose sight when
we cause past generations or the less civilized portions of the present
generation to pass in review before us. Each must be measured by its
own ideal, acquitted or condemned as it comes up to it or falls below
it. The savage should not be tried by the ideal of a Fenelon,[6] the ages
before Christianity by that of the Christian, nor the early ages of the
church, by that of the nineteenth century. Those who in the infancy
of Christianity gave to love to our neighbor all the meaning in their
power are not to be condemned because it falls short of the meaning
we can give it, any more than he who is just commencing simple
arithmetic is to be condemned for not being able to solve the more
difficult problems of the higher branches of mathematics.

It is also very important to bear this consideration in mind whenever we attempt to estimate the service Christianity has rendered the
world. We are exceedingly prone to underrate that service. We look
back and down upon ages which seem to us sunk in vice and crime,
in barbarism and wretchedness, without reflecting that it is to Christianity that we are indebted for our advance beyond them, and for
that moral elevation from which we look down upon them. It is
because Christianity has been long at work, strengthening, purifying, exalting, that is, educating the mind, that we of the present, are
able to see as low and comparatively worthless, what wise and good
men in their day in the past saw as elevated and ennobling. When it
was first disclosed by its author, the world could not take in those
loftier ideas of excellence which are common to our times; but it
contained the very spirit of progress, and it constantly exerted itself
to bring the mind up so as to perceive more and more of its worth;
and, had it not been for the influence its exertions have had in setting
us forward in our career of improvement, we have no reason to suppose that the ideal of this age would have been superior to that of the
age of Nero.

And this superiority is not trifling. In examining the monuments
of the moral grandeur of the past, we are very likely to shed over

[6][Ed. François de Salignac de la Mothe Fénelon (1651-1715), Catholic archbishop of Cambrai, was politically an anti-absolutist (as in *Télemaque*, 1693-1711)
and religiously a quasi-quietist, attracted to the pure love doctrine of Madam Guyon
and to a mystical spirituality (as in *Explication des maximes des saints*, 1697). Many
of his devotional writings were popular among American Unitarians and Quakers.
Quakers William Backhouse and James Janson translated some of his works in *A
Guide to True Peace* (Philadelphia, 1813, and many subsequent editions).]

them something of that purer and stronger light which belongs only to the present. When we meet among the ancients the same terms that are in common use among ourselves, we ascribe to those terms something of that deeper and fuller meaning which we alone can comprehend, a meaning which was not, and which could not have been, suspected without that additional growth of mind which it has taken Christianity nearly two thousand years to effect. In fact when it is our object to discover, not the worthlessness, but the worth of past ages, we almost invariably ascribe to them a degree of wisdom and moral grandeur which is theirs only as it is thrown over them from our own more truly enlightened minds. If we guard against this too favorable estimate, common to the wise and the good, who read almost everything by the benevolent light of their own pure and gifted minds, we may easily satisfy ourselves that our ideal of excellence is almost infinitely superior to that of the age in which Christianity was first proclaimed. Individuals then, indeed, might have stood out from the great mass, the representatives of the future rather than of their own times; but the age, taken as a whole, was immeasurably below the one in which we live. The advance has been great, has been, if we view it rightly, almost miraculous. Christianity has not been wanting to its mission; it has thus far fulfilled it nobly.

Indeed, it is refreshing to the philanthropic soul to dwell on the progress Christianity has effected. It has enabled us to take broader views of the right. Love to our neighbor means vastly more than it did. We have learned also to give to the term *neighbor* a broader meaning; we begin to comprehend something of that parable of the good Samaritan, so simple, touching, and sublime; and in proportion as we comprehend it, anyone, albeit our bitterest enemy, to whom we can be useful, becomes our neighbor; and, as the means of usefulness open to us, as we see new methods and opportunities of benefitting millions, the term *neighbor* comes to mean a greater number. He cannot help thanking God, who observes how this age has enlarged the neighborly feeling and multiplied the number of neighbors. National prejudices are fast yielding to the influence of constantly increasing international intercourse; sects, classes, and parties are gradually losing something of their asperity, as they come to mingle with one another, and to know one another better. Indeed, sects, classes, and parties become brothers, nations become families, and a quarter of the globe a neighborhood. Men become less and less vain of factitious distinctions, titles, and decorations, and more and more ambitious to appear in the simple dignity of human beings.

And this dignity of human beings means vastly more than it did formerly. Human nature, or that which passed for human nature, was formerly a small affair. It was, we suspect, no better than those, who, to show their superiority, speak slightingly of human nature, have pronounced it. What history presents us for human nature is in most instances nothing but that part of our nature which we possess in common with animals. In the individual we see the animal before we do the man. It is not in childhood or youth that we see the peculiarly human faculties predominant but in mature age. So is it with the race. It has a growth of its own, laws of development precisely analogous to those of the individual. The animal propensities are developed first and it is not till childhood and youth have passed away that they cease to be predominant. Up to the present, history has been concerned only with the childhood and youth of mankind. It has not yet presented us the full grown man of a ripe age; and surely it is no great stretch of charity to absolve those who are acquainted only with the weakness of childhood, or the fiery, impetuous passions of youth, from any very aggravated offence in pronouncing human nature a worthless thing. He who had never seen any human beings except children before they could walk or talk, might very innocently infer that to walk or talk does not pertain to human nature, unless he should *happen* to reflect that he can do both, and that there was, however, a time when he could do neither. We could pardon him who had seen the human body only when wasted and distorted by disease, for smiling to hear us talk of its beauty, its symmetry, and its vigor; but his smile would not be less the smile of ignorance, because we could absolve him from guilt. So it may be with those who form their estimate of human nature from acquaintance merely with its infancy, imperfect developments, or its diseases. Their estimate will be natural, but hardly just. There may be more things wrapped up in human nature "than is dreamed of in" their "philosophy."[7]

Although up to the present, the animal in our race has predominated, the man has not been wholly out of sight. There have been at all times in all nations exhibited proofs that we have within us higher powers something, weak and half suppressed it may have been, that is forever looking towards the infinite and craving the perfect. Individuals in all ages have appeared to enlarge our conceptions and give us higher ideas of the capabilities of our race. And these individuals

[7][Ed. Shakespeare, *Hamlet* I, v, 166. "There are more things in heaven and earth, Horatio, than are dreamt of in your philosophy."]

are not now, as they once were, held as prodigies, as exceptions, but as an earnest of what all may become, as a sort of first fruits, the sure pledges of the glorious harvest to follow. We do not now look to the multitude on whom tyrants have trampled, whose holy breathings are repressed, whose cries for liberty are stifled by misguided priests, to learn what human nature is, and what man may be; but to the Aristideses, the Socrateses, the Platos, the Confuciuses, the Pauls, the Alfreds, the Fenelons, the Penns, the Miltons, the Lockes, the Hampdens, the Howards, the Washingtons, the Lafayettes.[8]

This new mode of judging human nature has been introduced by Christianity and is not the least of the proofs that it has been faithfully executing its mission. The effects of this new mode of determining what human nature is and what man may be are not small. Man assumes a new dignity and enlists purer and nobler feelings in his service. Love to our neighbor takes a deeper and broader meaning. It is no longer a mere instinctive feeling or the cold and formal obedience to a positive command; but a reverence for human nature, a heartfelt conviction of its worth, a kindling desire for the lofty excellence it may attain, and the power to devote one's self unreservedly to aid it in accomplishing its destiny. It not only takes in a broader horizon of worth, but it discovers new and more effectual methods of promoting the good it sees, desires, and wills. It involves new duties, and duties immeasurably more comprehensive. The greater worth we discover in human nature makes us feel a deeper and a more abiding interest in every individual who shares it. In the poorest, in the most worthless, the most abandoned, we do not now see the vile sinner alone, but a lofty and deathless nature, that links him with the world of spirits, and gives him the image of God.

The duty of preaching the gospel to the poor has always been admitted and considered one of the most important of the duties enjoined by Christianity; but the higher estimate we now form of human nature, gives to it a fuller meaning, and makes it, as Jesus declared it, one of the most striking proofs of the divinity of his mission. It now means something more than merely proclaiming to the poor the facts of the gospel, and efforts to make them submissive to their unfriendly condition; it now means proclaiming to the world those doctrines, inculcating those principles, that make the poor, as a

[8][Ed. Alfred the Great (849-99), King of Wessex from 871, defeated the Danes and preserved the presence of Christianity in England. John Hampden (1549-1643) was a British political leader of a revolutionary movement of tax resistance to King Charles I. Hampden was also a member of Parliament and served in the Parliamentary army in the 1640s prior to his death.]

class, feel that they belong to the common brotherhood of humanity, have the same rights, the same duties, and in themselves the same image of God requiring to be developed as the rest of mankind. Almsgiving, which once meant giving money, food, clothing, or shelter, to some few of the poor, now means infusing into the whole body of the poor that moral tone, moral courage and energy that will enable them to elevate themselves to their proper level in the social scale.

We are unwilling to dismiss this topic without a further remark. If we do not misread the signs of the times, this duty of preaching the gospel to the poor is about to be felt as it never was felt before. The great doctrine of the fraternity of the human race is beginning to make itself believed and comprehended; and hundreds and thousands are lamenting the low, degraded, and suffering condition to which so many of their brethren are sunk. There are those who do not believe that the condition of the poor as a class, or that social policy of which they are the victims, is approved by the Deity or that it is irremediable by human agency. In a word, there are those who see no necessity for so wide a disparity in the condition of members of the same community and brothers of the same family, and who are exerting themselves to lessen it. No one can mistake the tendency of the times. Everything is verging towards equality and men are beginning to feel an interest in the masses which they never felt before. We rejoice in this tendency. It is to us a proof that Christianity has not been preached, that great and good men have not sighed, and labored, and suffered, in vain. But even this tendency, glorious and promising as it is in our eyes, may not bring all the good we could wish. The boasted "reformers" of the age, have, in many instances, more zeal and benevolence than just appreciation of the work they should perform. They do not penetrate deep enough. They would introduce equality in our external circumstances; but this, admitting it practicable, would hardly deserve the name of a reform. Poverty is not itself an evil, it is only the symptom of an evil. The inequality which now obtains is in itself a small affair; the mere physical suffering it involves, great as that may be, is hardly worth lamenting. The real evil lies deeper and is infinitely greater. That evil is the injury done to mind. The waste of mind is that over which the philanthropist weeps. The immortal mind, on which God has stamped his own image, is suppressed, is prevented from unfolding even the least of its mighty powers in the vast majority of our race. Nine tenths of mankind are so situated that they have neither the time nor the opportunity of attending to anything but the wants of their animal nature.

This is the real evil; and the real work for the reformer is to put into the hands of the whole, not equal wealth, but the means of spiritual cultivation and growth. This is no slight work. Much has been done, much is now doing, but vastly more remains untouched. It is painful to reflect how many are born every day who must live and die mute, inglorious, and forgotten, who yet, had opportunity been afforded them, would have displayed as much power of mind, loftiness of soul, strength of purpose, and even creative genius as the greatest and most venerated of our race. The great end of existence, we have said, is spiritual growth; and, though we are far from believing that all men are born with equal capacities, we do believe that all are born susceptible of a growth. To aid this growth to the full extent of our power, in the humblest as well as in the most gifted of God's offspring, is the aim of all enlightened philanthropy; and to this end, instead of being wasted on efforts to accomplish that comparatively slight affair, equality in men's external condition, we hope will be directed the exertions of all those who have the sentiment of something better for man than what he now has.

We have here touched upon some points in which we think the ideal of our age is superior to that of the age when Christianity was first preached. It seems to us, that the great law of love, the distinguishing law of our religion, is now more fully comprehended than it ever was before. But that it is so we attribute to the influence of Christianity, which has been silently but effectually exerted, strengthening our minds, shedding new light on our duties, and bringing them home with more energy to our hearts. If it has done this, let us not say that it has not thus far faithfully and successfully executed its mission.

We also think that the influence of Christianity in enabling the mind to form to itself loftier ideals of excellence has not been confined to those who have believed themselves Christians. When men break away from the reigning form of Christianity and look down upon it with a sort of contempt, it is because that form does not come up to their ideas of the perfect; and that it does not, is owing to the fact that they have outgrown it and become able to form to themselves a more perfect ideal. But it is not necessary to suppose that these are enemies to Christianity, as Christians are apt to suppose them nor that they are what they are without the influence of Christianity as they are apt themselves to imagine. Christianity demands a progress and it invariably deserts those who refuse to advance. When its professed adherents become stationary, it breaks out in new sects, and sometimes joins with its professed opponents. This should teach us to listen to every new sect with interest and candor, and to hear without prejudice all that unbelievers have to offer in their own behalf. It may be they have in some respects had some more perfect visions of truth and that we may by their aid enlarge our ideal of excellence. This should also admonish unbelievers that their work is to reform, improve, not to destroy; that, if they have discovered any truth which Christians generally have not, they have only discovered a little more of Christianity than others, and ought therefore to be its warmer friends. Infidel philosophers have told us some truths, but they were Christian influences that enabled them to discover those truths; and as Christianity is not stationary, but always advancing, always meaning more, it can receive them without any injury, but with great benefit to itself. Unbelievers, that class of unbelievers, we mean, who are so because they desire a greater good for mankind, should return to the church; because it is that which has given them that desire, it is that alone which can give them power to gratify it, and because the desire which governs them is the most peculiarly Christian desire of any which Christianity has quickened in the human breast.

One consideration more and we close. If Christianity has aided past progress, if it be to Christianity that we are indebted for that loftier ideal of excellence which belongs to this generation than that of the generations which are gone, who shall say that it has no power to aid a future progress; who shall say that love to our neighbor will not mean two thousand years hereafter as much more than it does now, as it now means more than it did two thousand years ago? May not the generations to come after us improve as much upon our ideal as we have improved upon the ideal of those who went before us? Shall we say that Christianity has spent its force and that it has done all that it can do for the world? Great changes in men's views of the rectitude of specific actions have taken place and are there none to take place hereafter? War was once deemed the business and the glory of nations and was made the principal end of the most admired political and legislative institutions of antiquity. Armies could once be raised to fight for conquest and for glory; but that time has passed away. Wars can now be carried on only under pretense of securing or maintaining national or individual rights or of obtaining peace. Armies cannot now be raised to fight for the mere honor of fighting nor with the avowed object of stripping a neighbor of his territories. There needs some plea of right. Some even go further and declare the resort to arms in all cases anti-Christian and unjustifiable. There is greater advance still. When Christianity was introduced, slavery was deemed right. Cruelty to slaves was condemned, but slavery itself was not even considered as requiring an apology. But now, in a vast majority of cases, it is declared a crime, and it is nowhere tolerated except on the ground of expediency and that miserable plea bids fair not to be available much longer. The slave-trade, which almost within our own memory was deemed honorable, is now ranked with piracy; the traffic in ardent spirits, in which the best of men a few years ago saw no evil, promises soon to be considered no better than the slave-trade. And why have all these changes taken place? Why do we condemn practices which our fathers approved? Simply because we form to ourselves a loftier ideal of excellence. Christianity means more with us than it did with them. But do we not tolerate practices which a more comprehensive view of Christianity, a clearer perception of the right, would condemn? Are there now no methods of gain, of applause, of promotion, approved and deemed honorable by us all, and even recommended by parents to their children, which are not sinful, only because we have not reached that degree of moral progress which would disclose their iniquity? And who among us dare say that degree of moral progress will not be attained and that even the best of us are not approving that which after generations will view as we do war, slavery, the slave-trade, and as we shall soon the traffic in ardent spirits? We believe it will be so; but *in that belief we do not see the condemnation of the present, but its duty to be continually exerting itself to take more and more comprehensive views of the right, and to form to itself a less and less defective morality.*

The belief of the possibility of this would perhaps dictate a change in our treatment of a class of individuals who are generally condemned. We allude to those who in every age demand reform. We have individuals of this class amongst us now. We call them "visionaries," or brand them as disorganizers; and this may be true of some; but perhaps the only fault of many consists in the fact, that in them the far-glancing sentiment of the future has some dim and shadowy visions of what generations to come will prove to be glorious realities. They may be the prophets of humanity. Half mad, it may be, as all prophets are to their contemporaries; but they should be listened to with interest and their "burdens" should be received with respect.

38.

ESSAYS FOR BELIEVERS AND DISBELIEVERS

Boston Observer and Religious Intelligencer
1 (January 1, 1835): 2-3

I think, Mr. editor, that I may assume it to be true that we live in an unbelieving age and that the great want of our times is faith in the reality of a spiritual world. If I may assume this to be true, no inquiry can be more important than that which has for its object to produce and strengthen religious convictions. But before we can ascertain these means, it is necessary that we understand accurately the position of the believer in religion and of the disbeliever, the real difference and the agreement between the two, together with the cause of the difference. This, although only a preliminary inquiry, is undoubtedly the most difficult. I cannot flatter myself that I am able to do justice to it, but I have thought that a few brief, and, in some degree, desultory essays on the subject might be the means of drawing the attention of others to the real problems to be solved, and thus eventually lead to their solution. With this view I send you some, which you may, as you please, publish or return. I commence with

NO. 1 — THE DIFFERENCE BETWEEN THE BELIEVER AND
THE DISBELIEVER IS THE DIFFERENCE
OF THEIR POINTS OF VIEW.

That is truth or falsehood to us human beings, which, when clearly perceived and fully comprehended by us, is believed or disbelieved.

We can believe or disbelieve only what the human mind was originally fitted to believe or disbelieve. All systems of religion, morals or philosophy, which have been believed, have found in the human mind, in human nature itself, something to respond to them and vouch for their truth.

And the internal voucher is enough. At least, it is all that we should demand, for it is all that we hang on in cases where demonstration is the most complete. The whole process of demonstration is but stripping a proposition of its envelops, presenting it to the mind in its true character so that it may be seen as it really is. If, when we have thus presented it to the mind, it be believed, we say we have demonstrated it true; if disbelieved, we say we have demonstrated it to be false.

To say of a proposition that it is one which the human mind is fitted to believe, that it is one that can be believed, that it is one that has been believed, is the same thing as to say it is true. It follows, then, that falsehood is never believed and that truth is never disbelieved. To deny this conclusion were to plunge us into universal skepticism. For admit that the mind can believe or disbelieve indifferently, truth or falsehood, and we are deprived of all criterion of distinguishing between them.

Religion has been believed. It is therefore true. It has been disbelieved also, it is said; is it therefore false? Most assuredly, just so far as it has been or is disbelieved. But, if what we have premised of truth and falsehood, be correct, it never has been, it never can be, disbelieved in precisely the same sense as the one in which it is believed. The same thing is not both believed and disbelieved. That which is disbelieved, though it bear the same name, is never precisely that which is believed. The disbeliever believes that he disbelieves religion; but that which he takes to be religion is something totally different from religion in the mind of the believer.

The believer and disbeliever occupy different positions. They have different points of view. They do not both look upon the same side of things. Both report correctly enough what they see and both see things as they really are from their respective positions, but they do not both see the same objects. That which the believer sees as religion is true; that which the disbeliever sees as religion, or religion on the side on which he sees it, is false.

Both, then, are right; that is, as far as they go. They both see and tell us *some* truth; so far they are right. But neither sees and tells us the *whole* truth, and therefore both are wrong. This error is in their exclusiveness; not that one takes that to be true which is false, but that each takes his own to be the only point of view, and that what he believes is precisely what the other disbelieves.

This is the error to be corrected. We all see and believe some truth, but we ought to see and believe the whole truth. We ought to see religion upon all sides and from all positions. To do this, the believer must abandon some of that righteous horror which keeps him aloof from the infidel, and approach him, ascertain his mind, his habits of thought and feeling, in a word, take the infidel's position, see things from his point of view, through his medium, and judge them with his feelings and his understanding. He must seek the elements of infidelity and the elements of human nature which respond to them. For, let him be assured, that infidelity is founded in human nature, and that it could not subsist one moment if it were not, and if it had not truth for its support.

The disbeliever must also lay aside a little of his sovereign contempt for the believer, and seek the believer's point of view. He should become acquainted with the believer, with his mind, his heart, his spirit, and try to see things as he sees them. He should be aware that what appears to him false, absurd or mischievous, cannot be that which the believer really means by religion. A moment's reflection is sufficient to teach him that the believer sees something in religion which he does not see and he should look at it in all lights till be does see it.

This mutual exchange of positions is greatly to be desired. Infidels now write against religion; but they do little besides proving that religion in their acceptation of the term is something really different from the believer's acceptation of it; Christians, too, write against infidels, but they seldom touch one of their difficulties. Both shoot aside the mark, and for this very good reason, neither sees it, or has any suspicion where it is. Both fight in the dark, and harm their adherents about as much as their opponents. It is time to end this worse than folly. It is time for believers and disbelievers to understand each other and when they do they will themselves both be of "one mind."

NO. 2. THE POSITION OF THE DISBELIEVER
(January 15, 1835): 17

Instead of denouncing the disbeliever and dwelling upon the odiousness of his character, we should seek for this point of view, ascertain why he is a disbeliever, and what it is that he disbelieves.

This is not easily done. The believer and disbeliever are each other's antipodes. They not only see through different mediums, but they really see different things. It is extremely difficult for the believer to forget his belief, at least to lay it aside, to divest himself of himself, so to speak, for a time, and to make himself a disbeliever, to call up the disbeliever's feelings, to see things with the disbeliever's eyes, and to judge them with the disbeliever's eyes, and to judge them with the disbeliever's understanding. And yet this he must do before he can do him or his disbelief the least justice.

To do this requires a knowledge of mind and habits of discrimination, which few possess. One needs a clear understanding of oneself to be able to distinguish, with accuracy and precision, what he believes from what is connected with it, which he neither believes nor disbelieves, because it is not made a subject of distinct consideration. And yet it is this something which is connected with what he believes and which is made no account of by the believer, that stands in the foreground of that picture of religion, which is present to the eyes of the disbeliever. The position of the believer is such that he does not see it. Objects of greater prominence attract his attention and absorb his thoughts; while the position of the disbeliever is such as to conceal these more prominent objects of the believer and to prevent him from viewing them distinctly, if, indeed, he views them at all.

Mind is imperfect. Its horizon is bounded. Its view, correct enough far as it extends, must always be defective. It can never take in the whole of truth. Consequently all our notions of religion, just indeed as far as they go, must be defective. Beyond the truth seen and believed, there lie boundless regions of the unknown. Now the believer looks solely upon that little portion of truth which the mind has discovered, and seeing in that nothing but truth, he is filled with satisfaction and delight; but the disbeliever looks beyond the limited horizon of the known, off into the boundless regions of the unknown regions which have not yet been conquered by the mind and annexed to the domains of truth. He sees that off in that immense world there is needed a stronger light than the believer has yet obtained, a guide which the prevailing system of religion, whatever it may be, has not supplied. He becomes conscious of a want which that system does not meet, and which he gradually comes to believe it cannot meet. His confidence in it is therefore impaired; his ardor for it cools; he becomes indifferent to it, and if any circumstances transpire to awake him from his indifference, he may think it false, mischievous and therefore become a disbeliever, an opponent.

This result is in some degree inevitable and must be so long as mind remains imperfect, or only imperfectly developed. So long as mind remains imperfect or only imperfectly developed, our notions of religion cannot be perfect. They can only reach to a certain extent. The boundless space beyond that extent, will if filled with anything be filled with error. But mind is progressive. Its power of vision is forever enlarging, and it every day becomes able to see farther and farther off into the unknown and to make new conquests to truth from the dominions of error. Our notions of religion, consequently are forever becoming more and more perfect, that is, forever embracing more and more of truth. But this progression is made only under the condition that men become dissatisfied with that portion of truth already obtained; for, as long as men are satisfied with that they will seek for nothing more.

Now there are some individuals who have the sentiment of the insufficiency of the amount of truth obtained in a much greater degree than others. Why we know not. But that it is so we do know, and the result of this is the separation of the human race into two grand divisions. One division, which I shall term the *movement* party, is always governed by a sentiment of the insufficiency of what is, and generally, though not always, of something better to be obtained; the other division, I shall call the *stationary* party, a party satisfied with what is, and of course, deprecating all change. In some epochs the movement party is little numerous; men's minds look back rather than forward and seem to believe in the past and the present, rather than in the future. These are epochs of belief, epochs the absence of which many wise and good men are perpetually lamenting. But they are epochs in which the human mind makes little advance. They are the night of the intellect, in which it slumbers; but in which it, indeed, is refreshed and invigorated to make, on its awaking, more powerful exertions to achieve new and more glorious victories. In other epochs the stationary party is small. Nearly the whole human race is carried away by the spirit of movement. The past is condemned; present institutions are examined; fixed order is broken up; all the elements of society are thrown into confusion, and nearly all minds are turned towards the future, and look to it with eagerness and hope. These are infidel epochs, but they are epochs of progress. Epochs in which the mind leaps forward and grasps a truth, a good which it had not before possessed, of which it had not dreamed.

The position of the disbeliever, of right, is in the movement party. His disbelief may, indeed, be a barrier to his progress, because he is to himself a disbeliever in religion, without which there can be no progress; but still, it is his sentiment of the insufficiency of what is, and perhaps, thirst for something better, that make him a disbeliever, and these constitute the very foundation of the movement party. Having thus found the position of the disbeliever, I may add, that he is not, upon the whole, without use to society. He had his mission and an important mission. It is his mission to keep the mind forever looking beyond the acquisition it has made, and to be forever urging it forward to new ones. So far he is right. So long as the mind shall have the power of progress, and so long as it shall not be desirable to remain contented with a small portion of truth, so long will it be desirable for him to look off into the unknown and urge us forward to new conquests. In a word, he is needed to look at the errors connected with any particular system of religion; instead of its truths, for were it not for him there would be no advance.

NO. 3. THE POSITION OF THE DISBELIEVER. — CONTINUED
(February 5, 1835): 42-43

That my last essay assigned the disbeliever his true position, must be obvious, I think, to all who comprehend modern infidelity. But unfortunately these are few. Some details on its origin, character, and real objects will therefore be necessary.

Of Christianity in its internal character, as to its foundation or essence, I shall hereafter treat. I will only add now that as to its external character it sprung out of disbelief or rather availed itself of disbelief, in the religious systems which prevailed before it. It was the triumph of infidelity over Judaism and paganism. It was a conquest gained by the movement party; and its first fixed form, that of Catholicism, was the purest and most elevated form which the majority of minds at the time when it became fixed could appreciate. Up to the moment of its becoming triumphant and fixed, it satisfied the spirit of progress and was the object of its exertions. But the moment it became fixed, became the settled order, it ceased to satisfy the movement party, and became satisfactory only to the stationary party. This party was then, however, much the largest, comprehending nearly the whole of the religious community, consequently Christianity under the form of Catholicism, may be said to have satisfied the wants of that age.

But the movement party, till the triumph of Catholicism much the largest, though now become a very small minority, was by no means extinct. There were even in the best days of Catholicism, minds which had a sentiment, if not a perception, of its insufficiency and is something altogether more true, beautiful, or useful. These showed themselves in sects, and were branded as heretics. Their notions were suppressed as heresies by the strong arm of authority; but if suppressed they were not extinguished. If persecuted in one place they appeared in another, in one shape, they assumed another. The party of the present labored in vain to keep out the party of the future. All its exertions militated against itself. The more it persecuted, the more did men become dissatisfied with it, the more rigorous its measures the more did it revolt men's minds and hearts; and consequently the more did it weaken its own power and resources. The longer it remained the more minds there were that had out-grown it, and the more confident, too, did it become in itself. Its utility became less in proportion as the opposition to it increased, and its corruptions kept pace with its decreasing utility and with the growing opposition to it; at length it became too gross to be longer tolerated, too depraved not to be detested, too superannuated not to be discarded.

Now had arrived the epoch in which the movement party, kept alive by various sects, continually persecuted, had become, though unknown to itself, the largest and the strongest. At this epoch it rises in open rebellion against the stationary party, or things as they are, and determines to put down Catholicism. Now is the struggle. The present disappears. There is only the past and the future in mortal combat. In this struggle modern infidelity is born. It is a revolt at Catholicism, a dissatisfaction with the order of things which it finds existing, a sentiment of its insufficiency and a craving for something— it scarcely knows what—that shall be better.

It was not religion that was opposed, but Catholicism; not the authority of God that was resisted, but that of the Catholic priesthood. An authority which was felt to be offensive, galling to the mind, was resisted, shaken and attempted to be put down. In this moment men did not think of the good Catholicism had done, of the truth the Catholic priesthood might still have; they thought only of what they felt, and that was an intolerable burden, an unholy restraint, which they were resolved, come what might, to shake off. They saw, they felt the evils, the errors, the injustice which were connected with Christianity under the Catholic form and with these they waged a war of extermination.

The whole movement party, known as the Protestant party, was infidel. The very idea of Protestantism is not that of religious belief, not merely that of unbelief, but that of disbelief. The Protestant declares his *dissent* from the existing order, his *disbelief* in its justice or its obligation. Although all Protestants were really disbelievers in Christianity according to the most approved definition of it at the time their party was organized, some went further in their disbelief, than others, or rather took stronger and shorter methods than others, for removing what they all disbelieved, for destroying what they all in common hated. Some having a strong sentiment of order combined with their desire for progress, a strong sentiment of religion combined with their hatred of Catholicism, and of the Catholic priesthood, became Protestant Christians, Lutherans, Calvinists, Episcopalians, Socinians; others having in a less degree the sentiment of order, and the sentiment or religion, but in a greater degree hatred of Catholicism and Catholic priests, a still stronger desire for progress, more restlessness of disposition and greater delight in change, became, if the expression be not tautological, Protestant infidels.

Still, it was not that these last were opposed to religion; they were opposed only to the great religious institution which had so long held Christendom in slavery and so long waged unrelenting war with the rights of the mind. They thought of science and of the friends of science persecuted, of philosophers burned, imprisoned or compelled to disavow the glorious truths which their genius had discovered, they thought of the galling chains thrown over the intellect, of the iron that ate into the soul, and all the manlier, better, and holier principles of their nature rose indignant at the iniquity and called down vengeance upon the institution guilty of it. That inequity seen from their position was so great as to entirely conceal the truth and excellence there might still be in that institution, or at least to make it appear so very small as not to be worth a moment's serious consideration. They therefore resolved to sacrifice what there might be of good to escape the evil that accompanied it, and which, if they thought upon it at all, they deemed inseparable from it.

But let me not be misinterpreted. What I have alleged is an inevitable result of the spirit of movement. But let it not be inferred that this result is foreseen and designed. All who belong to the movement party do not see whither they tend, nor do they know the spirit which controls them. Many are carried along by an impulse of which they can render no account. They have no clear perception of the errors against which they war, nor of the good they would obtain. They do not comprehend their own movements; they know not what they want. But they want something which they have not, they are impatient of what is, of the authority to which they must submit, and are carried onward by a vague sentiment of something better in reserve. Such is the general character of the movement party, till someone appears who comprehends it, embodies, impersonates its sentiments. As soon as such a one speaks, all who are affected by the spirit of movement, hear, listen; hear a voice responded to from the bottom of their hearts and they rally around him and from him learn what they are, from him learn to comprehend themselves.

Nor is it true that all who are found in the stationary party are opposed to progress viewed as a separate question. They may even see and acknowledge evils in their present condition, they may even wish to remove them; but falling into the common mistake, into the same mistake into which the infidel falls, they fear to attack them lest they also attack that which they hold sacred. They fear to pull up the tares, lest they also root up the wheat. They cannot separate in their own minds the good from the bad, the true from the false, the necessary from the contingent in the existing state of things, and they think it better to submit to what is painful than to hazard the good by attempting to remove it. Such is the character of many who are found with the advocates of things as they are; but they are misplaced. They would readily join the movement party could they be convinced that the removal of what is painful would not sweep off what they embrace as religion and which they love more than they hate the other.

But they see not the possibility of doing this. They make not the proper distinctions. The disbeliever does not make them, and from the position he occupies cannot be expected to make them, as they defend indiscriminately the whole system which he finds at war with the spirit of progress. He sees in that system an authority to be put down. That authority is all he sees. All the parts of that system seem to him homogeneous, and in his estimation, necessarily conspire to uphold that authority. That system then in all its parts must be destroyed. He sees a priesthood exercising a power that offends him. But that priesthood could not exist without Christianity, or as it was at the epoch of the Reformation, without Catholicism. Catholicism or Christianity, which he identifies with it, must be destroyed. But Catholicism depends on the Bible and the traditions of the church, supports its authority on their authority. The authority of the Bible and the traditions of the church must be destroyed. The Protestant Christians destroyed that of the last, and he would complete what they begun by destroying that of the first. But here it is plain that his hostility is not originally against the traditions, nor the Bible, nor Christianity, but against the oppressive or offensive authority which he finds or believes he finds them combined to uphold, and he attacks them only because in his mind they are inseparably connected with that authority. Now, if religion be distinct in reality from that authority, he does not in reality oppose religion. He is at war with an evil which he indeed believes to be religion or inseparable from it, but which is in fact only an arbitrary authority of the priesthood, unwarranted alike by pure religion and the progress of the human mind. His opposition to that authority is just, it is needed for the welfare of religion itself, is needed for the advancement of civilization, for the best good of the human race. Disbelief in its origin then is good, and thus far we absolve the disbeliever. He opposes an authority which is inimical to progress, and why? Because he is dissatisfied with it, because he is dissatisfied with the order of things which he finds, and has a craving for something better.

NO. 4. OPPOSITION TO AUTHORITY
(March 5, 1835): 73-74

Modern infidelity, under an active form in its most general expression, may be defined [as] opposition to authority.

The Catholic church claimed absolute sovereignty over ecclesiastical and civil policy, over the mind and the conscience. It, therefore, excited against itself a threefold opposition, ecclesiastical, political, and philosophical.

Of the ecclesiastical opposition, I need not treat. Its members seldom, if ever, became infidels in the common acceptation of the term. They did not oppose authority in the abstract. It was with them, for the most part, a question of more or less, how authority should be distributed, or in whose hands it should be lodged. This is true, unless we except the Congregationalists or Independents, who of all the opponents of the authority of the Catholic Church, have been the most consequent.

The political opponents may be divided into classes. One class opposed the authority of the church in behalf of the king or state, the other in behalf of the people. Catholicism ruled the state, kings were its vassals, and held the stirrup of its chief. Humanity does not complain of this. The pope was as good a depository of authority as the kings, perhaps better. But they thought otherwise. Their pride was offended and they placed the state in opposition to the church. Those who loved the state better than the church joined this opposition. Still there was here no question of authority itself; Henry VIII of England, who gives us an example of this kind of opposition, would probably have had no objections to the popedom had not the pope claimed to be his master.

The second class of political opponents did not appear at the epoch of the Reformation, at least not distinctly. There was no people then, or if there was, it was too insignificant to be consulted. The people is a child of the Reformation. Ecclesiastical freedom to some extent, and the independence of the state being achieved, the movement party turned its attention to a new object, and called into existence the people. With the people there sprung up friends of the people, these saw the people degraded, the wretched victims of an imperfect social organization and they wished to meliorate their condition. But as their point of view was political, they sought to do it by modification of the state. But the church met them and commanded them to desist.

Every church, Protestant or papal, when fixed, is attached to the stationary party, and opposed to all change, except proselytism to itself. Before the Reformation, the state was the servant of the church, afterwards the church became the servant of the state and labored to sustain it by opposing all innovation. Those in whom the spirit of progress was predominant, arrayed themselves therefore against the church, and attempted to destroy its authority. Some attempted this without touching the question of the truth or the falsity of religion, others despairing, or not dreaming, of reforming the church, imagining no way to break its authority but by the destruction of its creed, attacked religion itself, or what they supposed to be religion, and became open, avowed, disbelievers, propagandists. Such were many of the French infidels in the last century, such are some of the English reformers now, and such too, echoing bygone arguments, without considering their present applicability, are some in our own country.

The philosophical opponents, however, are those who most interest us. I do not call them philosophical opponents because they were philosophers but because they felt the want of philosophy. The discoveries of philosophy do not make infidels, in point of fact, they all tend to enlarge and confirm religious truth; but it is the want to philosophize that makes them. The philosophical want is of all times and of all countries for it is a want of human nature itself, although it may be more deeply felt and more powerful in its action in one individual than another, in some epochs than in others. But it is indispensable to philosophy that it be free. It can make no compromise with authority. It will be first, above and over all, or it will be nothing. It goes beyond the question of more or less, in whose hands power shall be lodged, and questions the authority itself, to which it is equally opposed whether it be deposited in the papal or episcopal hierarchies, in a Presbyterian synod, or in an independent church; in the Thirty-Nine Articles, the Westminster Confession, or in the Scriptures of the Old and New Testament. It attacks every species of authority, wherever lodged, whoever or whatever may be its representative that would place an interdict upon thought and set bounds to inquiry.

But this unlimited freedom is permitted by no church. The Catholic Church prescribed rules to the mind, to a certain extent men might think, but they could venture beyond only on pain of the vengeance of the church here and the wrath of God hereafter. This is seen in the practice of the old schoolmen. They thought and they thought acutely, but not freely. They must think according to the church. They had their bounds. They were like the horse in the mill, compelled to grind forever in the same circle. The same remark to a certain extent applies to all Protestant churches. They all have their creeds, expressed or implied, beyond which reasoning and reason must not venture.

Here lies the objection. The Bible is opposed, but not on its own account. Its alleged inconsistencies, its alleged cruel or absurd doctrines of which infidels make so much parade, are not the cause of infidelity. It is the authority of the Bible that produces revolt, and these are after thoughts, adduced to justify the revolt, and to gain recruits. Most of the doctrines of the Bible would be admitted by infidels; I believe all would be admitted could they be presented disembarrassed of the question of authority. But they allege they cannot believe because commanded. They ask a reason, you give them authority. Is that authority legitimate? Is it the authority of the universal reason, if so, you place the book you call authoritative in the same category with any other book that might be admitted, or rejected as found to be true or false, and of course it ceases to be in itself an authority for any of the doctrines it contains. In that case, each doctrine must stand upon its own foundation and be received or rejected for other reasons than that of the record in which it is found. If you allege any other ground for its authority than that of the universal reason, which is the authority of absolute freedom, the legitimacy of that ground is denied.

Atheism has the same origin. It is not the difficulties which are alleged to be in the way of theism, that make men atheists. They cease to be theists before they feel those difficulties, and allege them to justify their atheism. On the idea of God is built up an authority which offends them; and, desiring freedom more than they desire to believe, taking it for granted that freedom and the belief in God are incompatible, they cease to believe, and in their own opinion become atheists. In the case of rejection of the Bible, a complete answer to all the objections brought against it would not make it admitted, so long as it was alleged as an authority; so in the case of atheism, no answer to the objections against theism, can make atheists believe in God, till they are convinced that they may be believers in God and yet be freethinkers or till they change their notions of authority.

39.

A SERMON,
DELIVERED TO THE YOUNG PEOPLE OF THE FIRST CONGREGATIONAL SOCIETY IN CANTON ON SUNDAY, MAY 24TH, 1835[1]

"But seek ye first the kingdom of God and his righteousness; and all these things shall be added unto you." Mt 6:33.

This morning I preached to the children: I now address myself to the young people of my congregation. I address myself to you, my young friends, because yours is the season of preparation and because you are soon to be the acting members of society. He who addresses you and those who are now active with him will soon be laid in yonder graveyard, and you will be left alone to fill their places. In a few days you will be the existing generation. You will then have duties to the church, duties to your country, duties to God, duties to humanity; and I would have you early feel them and prepare yourselves to discharge them with promptness and fidelity.

The first thing I would impress upon your minds is the importance of determining in the outset of your career what shall be the great object of your lives. You must have some object. You must not go through the world objectless, without end or aim, floating in the direction of every wind like the leaf severed by the frost from its parent branch. You will be nothing, you will succeed in nothing, unless you fix your minds upon some object, concentrate upon it all your energies, and resolve to gain it, let its acquisition cost what it may.

What shall be this object? To what will you devote yourselves, your lives, your bodies, minds and hearts? Your own pleasure? Will you wrap yourselves up in yourselves and say: "Let the world take care of itself; I care not for others, let them take care of themselves; enough for me to please myself?" Will ye propose an object completely selfish, and never suffer a thought or a wish to stray beyond

[1][Ed. Dedham, Mass.: H. Mann, Printer, 1835. This sermon was given extemporaneously and later put in its current form at the request of the young people Brownson addressed.]

your own narrow self-interest? I can conceive of selfishness in the aged; I can almost pardon it in the old man who has been for three-score years the sport of a hostile world, who has seen all his plans fail, whose hopes are blasted, heart made cold and desolate, and whose affections are withered by adversity; but I can hardly conceive it possible for the young man or young woman in the fullness of life, seeing everything through the sunny medium of a beautiful spring day, open to all generous emotions—I say I can hardly conceive it possible for the young man or young woman, with affections unchilled by the cares and disappointments of age, to become so completely selfish as to dream of regarding nothing but his or her own selfish pleasure. Cold, colder than the dead body, must be the heart of that young man or that young woman who is contented to be doomed to seek only a selfish pleasure, a merely selfish interest! Selfishness in the young! I have little hope for those who in the morning of life have no regard for others' welfare. I see in them proofs of a depravity so deep-rooted that I fear its cure is hopeless. I can but weep over them as over fallen angels.

But if you resolve on your own pleasure that your own selfish gratifications shall control all your wishes and exertions, be it so. Be selfish, if you will; feel that your own dear individual selves are all that deserves a moment's consideration in the universe of God; but be careful and not complain should not your success respond to your expectations. You resolve to please yourselves and if you seek only to please yourselves will you succeed? You disregard others; you will not weep with that afflicted mother; you will not watch by the sick-bed of that brother or sister; you will wipe no tear from that eye of woe, pour no oil and wine into that wounded heart, make no exertions to bind up that broken spirit and relieve that distress. Be it so. Go on your way and think only of yourselves. But, when sickness lays its withering hand on you, when you are parched by the burning fever, who will watch by your side? Who will moisten your lips and by gentleness and assiduity relieve the tedious hours of illness? Ye have not done, ye have refused to do it, unto others, and if they adopt your principles, they will refuse to do it unto you. Let selfishness become universal and ye would soon sigh in vain for love and sympathy, for generosity and disinterestedness.

But talk no more, my young friends, of selfishness, of pursuing only your own pleasure, of sporting mere butterflies in your hour of sunshine and then—to die. Ye are made for something higher. God has made you social beings. He has linked, all over the earth, man with man, society with society, and made the good of each consist in the good of the whole. He has given you faculties which are forever leading you away from yourselves, giving you an abiding interest in others, and enabling you to weep with those who weep and to rejoice with those who rejoice. The most miserable beings on earth are those who seek only to please themselves. They deny the noblest part of their natures; they forswear the exercise of their purest and sweetest affections, and though made in the image of God they live and die mere animals.

You will not, I am sure, my young friends, consent to live and act merely for your own selfish pleasure. What then will you seek? What will you fix upon as the great object of all your thoughts, wishes and labors? Shall it be wealth? Will you live and toil simply to become rich?

Wealth is the leading object of a great portion of our countrymen. To become rich is apparently the "one thing needful." Most of our young men, whenever they look around them and ask what they shall pursue, answer, wealth. Soon as they begin to inquire, it is, how they may become rich, where is a good chance for speculation, the best opportunity for making money. This or that place is preferred because it affords an active young man the best means for becoming suddenly very rich, this or that profession because it is the most lucrative.

But are there no more important inquiries? Is wealth the greatest good possible to be obtained? I do not condemn wealth. I say not that you should not seek to possess some portion of this world's goods. I ask no one to choose poverty. Wealth is good, everything God has made is good, when sought with right motives and directed to right ends. But why seek to be rich? It can hardly be for the riches themselves. It must be for the purpose to which they may be applied. What shall be this purpose? The gratification of your own appetites and propensities? That is a low object and one which we have already condemned in deciding that you should not seek merely your own pleasure. Will you seek wealth, then, as the means of distinction, as the means of fixing you in what are termed the higher classes?

This, my young friends, were still proposing an object purely selfish. In seeking it your minds are fixed upon yourselves and never escape to dwell on the good of others. But let this pass. Can you conceive of no higher good than the rank and distinction in society given by wealth? What is the value of such rank and distinction? How long will they last? Go to that graveyard and read your answer. "The grave is the grand leveler of distinctions." "The small and the great are there." The rich and the poor sleep there, side by side. The petty distinctions which obtain on earth, and which are often determined by the texture of a coat or the length of a purse, go not beyond the grave. Be rich, be distinguished as you may, in the grave you will be as destitute and as unheeded as the poorest. You will carry none of your possessions with you. A winding-sheet and a small spot of ground, in which your bodies may molder back to their native dust, is, at most, all you can claim. Naked ye came into the world and in relation to wealth naked ye must leave it.

No, no, my young friends, ye are not to seek wealth to give you rank and distinction. There is a higher good, one to which wealth, your own pleasure, everything which can affect you, must be subordinate. What is it? My text answers, "Seek first the kingdom of God and his righteousness." Here is the greatest, the supreme good. Here is your object. Seek the kingdom of God and his righteousness with your whole hearts, with your whole strength.

This phrase, "Kingdom of God," may mislead you. As it is commonly interpreted, it may induce you to believe it the great object of your lives to gain admittance after death into the place where reside the blest. This under a certain aspect is indeed true, but as it presents itself to you, it is too far in the distance to act upon your hearts with its full force. Something nearer by is wanted to gain the attention and fix the mind.

Instead of *kingdom* of God, the phrase should be, *reign* of God. The Greeks expressed by one word both the exercise of the kingly authority and the territory or country over which it was exercised. We have a word for each. We call the first, *reign*; the second, *kingdom*. In my text the original word is used in the sense of reign. We are not commanded to seek the country where God reigns, but his reign itself; and that may be here, within us, for Jesus says, "the reign of God is within you" [Luke 17:21].

By the "reign of God" should be understood the reign of his moral attributes or perfections. The reign of these is the same thing as the reign of righteousness or moral goodness. It was to establish the reign of God *on earth* that Jesus came into the world, suffered and died. It was to extend the reign of God that the apostles labored, exposed themselves to a thousand perils, and endured martyrdom. It is for the reign of God, or of goodness that the wise and good in every age and in every clime sigh and yearn.

The gospel was the annunciation of the moral reign of God in a new and peculiar sense. The time had come for men to be governed by a new principle, for them to pass under a new moral order and to shape their actions by a new moral code. Jesus announced this new moral code. He termed it the reign of God. To seek to have God reign in each of you, and over all men, is what you are to understand by seeking the reign of God. God reigns in you when you are governed by his spirit. His spirit is the spirit of love, of goodness. When you love what God loves, desire what God wills, labor to accomplish what God proposes as the end of his works, you are governed by his spirit; you then submit yourselves to him; you then love his reign and desire all to come under it.

The reign of God is the reign of love or goodness. When then, love or goodness, reigns in you, God reigns in you. To have love or goodness reign in you, is the same thing as to be good yourselves, the same thing as it is to be just in all your actions, pure in all your wishes, benevolent in all your feelings and aspirations. When you are good yourselves you will delight to do good to others. When love reigns in you, you will love all men and labor for their well-being. To seek, then, the reign of God and his righteousness, may be defined, to seek to be good and to do good. To be good and to do good, this is your object. Hold this up to your mental vision. Never lose sight of it for a moment. Let all your wishes, all your exertions, all your sighings and yearnings point to this as faithful as the needle points to the pole.

Be good and do good. You must possess in yourselves the righteousness of God. You must have pure hearts, hearts that love all that is beautiful, that is true, that is good, that is holy; hearts that yearn for the perfect and keep you forever struggling to "be perfect even as your Father in heaven is perfect" [Matt 5:48]. And you must not only be good, possess right feelings, right wishes, but you must do good, diffuse goodness over your fellow beings to the full extent of your power.

Here, my young friends, is a good to be obtained, infinitely superior to that of merely sensual pleasure, or that which wealth can purchase. Here is a good not for the body merely, but for the soul. In seeking this you are laboring for that part of your nature which allies you to the Divinity. In seeking wealth or pleasure you are seeking only the gratification of appetites and propensities, which you have in common with the animals around you. In seeking the one you are seeking to be like God, in seeking the other you do not seek to rise above the beasts. In seeking this superior good you seek durable riches; you are not laboring for the meat that perisheth, but for that which endureth unto everlasting life.

Goodness, righteousness, my young friends, is the riches of the soul. You will not leave it behind you at the mouth of the tomb. You will carry it with you. Your souls are not like your bodies. These are but for a day. They are of the earth and to the earth they must return. But those are forever. Your souls do not die. They live, and will live though the earth wax old, the stars fade away, and the outward universe itself molder into ruins; and whatever they acquire they may retain through everlasting ages. Seek then to enrich your souls with righteousness, a wealth that will abide and be forever increasing. In comparison with this how poor and paltry is mere worldly wealth! What indeed does it concern the wise man what he shall eat, drink, or wherewithal he shall be clothed? Give me a soul rich in the righteousness of God, a soul in which God holds undisputed empire, and I care little for what may affect this clog of clay, my body. I have then that within me no calamity can touch, no reproach can sully, no change destroy; that which will resist the ravages of death, and rush off with fearlessness and joy into the darkness beyond the tomb. Is wealth your object, seek it here. Let it be moral wealth, for that is everlasting. Is pleasure your object, seek it here. Let it be the pleasure of being and doing good. It is a pleasure as much superior to the gratification of the appetites and propensities, as the soul is superior to the body, or as God is superior to the animals around us.

"And all these things shall be added unto you." We wrong God's providence. We are prone to think the path of virtue is obscure and pleasureless. This is wrong. God has not made the road to distinction and pleasure lie through the fields of sin. Virtue, after all, is the surest road to them. Nothing worth possessing is ever gained except by seeking to be and to do good. Honesty is the best means, after all, to gain worldly prosperity. Virtue, high, uncompromising, moral virtue is that which gives men their fame. It is false to suppose that wealth alone gives distinction. Humanity is too true to itself. He who has labored in its behalf is remembered, is honored; while the selfish, those who have lived only for themselves, pass off and are forgotten, or remembered only to be execrated. Look around you, look over history, those who are most revered, in whose names there is a magic spell to wake the spirit to noble deeds, are, and were, often the poorest of earth's many sons, in this world's goods. Wealth, at most, gives but a momentary distinction to its possessor, and that too only in the estimation of the weakest of mankind, while virtue confers immortality.

Poverty is far from preventing men from being useful to their race, far from being able to prevent the good from being held in everlasting honor. Look at Jesus, the author of our religion. He was poor—more so than the foxes of the earth for they have holes, than the fowls of the air, for they have nests, but he had not where to lay his head. The rich and the great of his time scorned him; he was persecuted, rejected, crucified; and yet, we on this day, in this house, eighteen hundred years after, are met together in his name, to pay homage to his worth. To human appearance a Jewish peasant, put to death as a malefactor, has created a new moral world, and throughout all civilized nations the people meet on this day in their thousands of temples to honor his example and bear witness to the power of his moral excellence. Who thinks the less of him because he was poor, because he was not, in his day and generation the idol of the great, because only the "common people heard him gladly" [Mark 12:37]?

But take another example, one more strictly human, that of Socrates. He was poor, so poor that he begged a cloak. And, was not only poor, but he refused to be rich. He was so unpopular, if I may use the term, that he was put to death as a criminal. Yet his name lives. It has come down to us through more than two thousand years, and it will live forever. Every man who wishes to know himself and be a philosopher is proud to bestow an eulogy upon his character. And why? Socrates felt that his powers belonged to humanity, that he was not placed in this world to pursue only his own pleasure, that God had made him to be useful, and he exerted himself to improve the world in knowledge and in virtue. He sought to be good and to do good, and became the father of philosophy. Hence his fame.

Were there no rich men in his times? Where are they? Will ye tell me their names? Will ye point me to their monuments? Look ye round for them? Ye will not find them. The rich men who had nothing but their riches to distinguish them are forgotten. Their names have perished; but the philosopher, the man of mind and virtue, lives and seems to us as one of our familiar acquaintances, as one of our personal friends. Which would ye prefer, the momentary distinction of the rich, and the long silence which comes over them or the everlasting remembrance which awaits the good?

Aristides, called the Just, is another name that has come down to us from a time still more remote. What has preserved his memory? His wealth? Who knows, or thinks of asking whether he was rich or poor? He was a brave warrior; but others have been as brave, have been greater in battle, but they are forgotten. Why is he remembered? He was Just. He was remarkable for his strict virtue. That has given him his fame and ranked him among the real nobility of our race. That embalmed his memory, has transmitted it to us, and will transmit it to the latest posterity. Thousands of other examples might be adduced to prove that it is the good alone who really are honored, that real distinction is acquired only by real worth, by unreserved devotion to God and humanity.

And, my young friends, have you no ambition to have your names live after you, to be held in everlasting honor by the generations which are to come? Do you not wish for a fame like that of a Socrates, or of an Aristides? Have it then. You can. You can all be just, be virtuous as Aristides was, and if so the world will not let you die. You will survive death; you will live in your works, in the services you render to humanity, in the gratitude of a posterity honoring your examples and blessing you for their happiness. But even should men forget you, you will be remembered in heaven. Worth, however concealed from human eyes, never escapes the notice of our God. He sees it, he honors it, however lowly it may be, however obscure the retreat in which it seeks to hide itself. And is not the notice of your Creator worth more to you than that of men? Can you desire any greater distinction than to be honored by the great and eternal God?

Would you be useful to your fellow beings, would you have the world the better for your having lived in it, would you, in fine, have power over men to induce them to pursue their own good, be virtuous, be righteous. Goodness is never lost. While you are acquiring good feelings, the Christian virtues, in comparative solitude, with no eclat, unknown, you may be conferring the greatest possible benefits upon your race. While fitting yourselves for the indwelling of God, you are fitting yourselves to exert the greatest power that man can exert over the destinies of his race. And should you never be called upon to display your worth in public, it will not be lost. It will quicken some heart, influence some mind, aid in forming some character, and that will do the same by another, and that by still another, and thus on till the whole earth comes to feel its power.

The little stone cut from the mountains without hands, grew to be a mountain that filled the whole earth.[2] Every good man is a little stone cut from the mountains without hands, has within himself a principle of growth that will fill the earth with benefits. No man is fully conscious of the power he may wield. No one fully comprehends the advantageous situation he occupies. He who exemplifies, in its perfection, a single moral virtue, he who discovers and places in the world, a single new truth in morals, in religion or in the philosophy of mind, outdoes the proudest of earth's heroes, exerts a power greater than any king or emperor ever did or ever can exert. He com-

[2][Ed. Perhaps a reference to Dan 2:34; 2:45.]

mences a new creation, forms the nucleus of a new world round which atom after atom shall gravitate till it becomes a new heavenly body to revolve forever in a new moral orbit.

My young friends, forget never, I pray you, the infinite power of virtue, of moral worth. It gives you all you can desire for yourselves; it gives you lasting riches, the purest and highest pleasure, confers upon you immortal honor, and distinguishes you for time and for eternity with men and with God. Carry this lesson with you. Whatever you would have, whatever you can desire, wealth, pleasure, fame, lasting and wide extended usefulness, know that you gain them but by "seeking first the kingdom of God and his righteousness." All that is worth having is in God, and you gain it only by studying and exerting yourselves with all your might to be like him.

My young friends, I cannot close without reminding you again that you are soon to be the active generation. On you is our dependence. On you is the dependence of the church for her earthly support. She looks to you for new sons and daughters. On you too rest the hopes of our country. Our country will ask much of you. Your voices must aid in deciding its destiny. You will soon be called to influence, in various ways, the laws to be enacted and the general measures to be adopted. Among you are those who are to be the fathers and mothers of future lawgivers and rulers of a free country. Even some whom I address may be called upon to fill offices of the highest honor and responsibility.

On you too, as an integral part of the human family, rest in some degree the hopes of humanity. The human race is not always to be sunk in vice and crime as it is now. Human society is not always to be as imperfect as it now is. Man is not always to be the foe of man, the greatest plague and tormenter of his kind. The whole family of man is to be brought together, to form one body, to have one soul, and to feel the pulsations of one universal heart. Here is your work, to fill the world with love and joy. See here too, in reference to the church, to your country, and to humanity what tremendous responsibilities rest upon you. In church, in state, in humanity, there is to be a progress and you are sent into the world, endowed with intellect and feeling, the power of reasoning and of sympathy, to aid it. Be faithful to your mission. Prove yourselves equal to your responsibilities; prove yourselves superior to the generation preceding you; be able to say in your dying hour, that the world has been the better for your having lived and may God bless you both now and forever. AMEN.

40.

REMARKS ON G. E. E.

Boston Observer and Religious Intelligencer
1 (May 1835): 146-47

Mr. Editor. Your correspondent having closed his "Comments on O. A. B.,"[1] some remarks from me I presume are expected. I shall not reply to him fully because I am recasting and preparing for publication, the series of essays I originally contemplated, and which I suspended in consequence, of the inconvenience attending the detached manner of publishing required by a weekly newspaper.

Your correspondent says I am much better qualified to do justice to the subject discussed in my essays than he is. I shall not dispute this; but if he so believed, he should have suspended his strictures till I had finished my essays. Such a belief would have naturally inspired sufficient distrust in himself, and confidence in me, to have heard me at least to my conclusion.

I have read his comments with attention and interest. He writes very well; expresses very handsomely what the community very generally will approve because it meets its views. When he shall have gone deeper into his subject and become better acquainted with what lies at the bottom of the unbeliever's heart, he will, I do not say, write what will be more generally applauded, but what may come much

[1][Ed. G. E. E. wrote three articles, "Comments on O.A.B.," for the *Boston Observer* 1 (March 5, 1835): 75-76; (March 19, 1835): 90-91; (April 16, 1835): 122-23, reacting to Brownson's "Essays for Believers and Disbelievers." G. E. E. charged that Brownson had failed to explain his use of terms sufficiently (using terms like infidelity in a very uncommon way) and thereby laid himself open to much misconstruction "among the uninformed." He was also afraid that Brownson's apparent support for the unbelievers would be misinterpreted as support for some Boston unbelievers (e.g., Abner Kneeland) whose infidelity was not a mere rejection of the forms and doctrines of Christianity, but a rude, erroneous, impious, attack upon Christianity. Brownson used the term infidel in a sense "totally different from that which is commonly attached to it." Contemporary disbelievers, G. E. E. asserted, deny the very nature of humanity by denying the natural religious tendencies of the human constitution. Brownson was too abstract in his approach to unbelief, and was not sufficiently conscious of the concrete and local nature of modern infidelity. Modern infidels were not just free inquirers. Brownson misrepresented the current situation and therefore his articles must be challenged.]

nearer the truth. He writes as every intelligent well-meaning man must write who views the subject from the position he does, and who does not suspect that there is another and a higher view to be taken of it.

In treating of unbelievers, he adopts the popular notion that it is their depravity that makes them unbelievers. This is a delusion. Depraved, infidels no doubt are; but, in point of morals—understanding by the term, honesty of heart, and general duties from man to man, viewed simply as a social being—I have no reason to believe that they fall below the members of Christian societies of a corresponding rank in life. They give by the very fact of avowing their opinions, unpopular and abhorrent as they are, no mean proof of honesty, and of moral courage; two things which rank very high in my catalogue of the moral virtues.

I know what is said against them; but absence of exaggeration, not to say false accusations, is not a characteristic of any party when speaking of its opponents. I have learned to receive with very liberal allowance what one party says against another, and especially what Christians allege against unbelievers. It is my deliberate opinion, that the overcharged statements of Christians respecting them, and their unchristian treatment of them, make more infidels than all the exhortations of infidels themselves. When you misrepresent the advocates of any particular opinions, you do harm; they appear so different on acquaintance, that there is almost always a revulsion of feeling in their favor. I have schooled myself into treating unbelievers as I would be treated by them, that is, as men and brothers. I respect every man's opinions in that they are his opinions and compel myself to treat them, if I treat them at all, as I would wish to have my opinions treated.

G. E. E. complains of me that I use words in an improper or an unwarranted sense; and intimates that though he may understand me, your readers generally will not. He has, therefore, labored to develop the meaning which he presumes I did *not* intend to convey, and to prove that if I had so meant, my meaning would have been false. I wish that, instead of doing this, he had had compassion on me and my readers, and endeavored to carry out, to the common understanding, what he supposes was my meaning. True, I could not have exacted this of him; but it would have been a Christian act, if, through the obscurities of my style and the difficulties of my language, he could decipher my meaning, to have translated it into plain English, for the benefit of the unlearned.

That I use words in an improper and unwarranted sense is very possible. I am an uneducated man and cannot aspire to the classical use of language. Words are commonly used in a loose and indeterminate sense; and it requires the profoundest philosophy to collect and fix that sense. Yet this I was obliged to attempt, and to attempt it where I had no guide but my own judgment. The process by which I came to my conclusions, I did not state in my essays. I merely used terms in the sense which I had determined in my own mind to be the true one. I may have erred; and it may also be that my supposed error was merely in using a word so that it must have a definite meaning, whereas it had received only a vague one before.

My use of the terms infidel and infidelity is that to which your correspondent most objects. I mean, by infidelity, the rejection of religion, or disbelief in religion. I believe this is the popular meaning of the term; and the popular meaning of any word, I consider its true meaning. But what is this meaning? Before this can be answered, we must know what religion is, and in what sense it is, or can be rejected.

The term religion, if I mistake not, has a twofold meaning, as the thing it names has a twofold existence. The word designates both the ideal and its realization. Religion exists first in the reason; and as it exists there, it may be defined, with sufficient accuracy for my present purpose, with M. Cousin,[2] the idea of the holy. In this sense, religion is ideal, subjective, inseparable from the being we call man. In this sense, religion is never rejected or disbelieved. But religion does not always remain dead in the reason, barren idea; it has a tendency to realize itself, to assume some form, an outward expression, a symbol. This form is constructed by the understanding, and constitutes religion for the understanding, as the idea of the holy constitutes religion for the reason.

The idea, existing in the reason, is invariable, eternal, indestructible; for the reason never changes, never retrogrades nor advances.

---

[2][Ed. For Cousin the perception of God is intuitive. The idea of God—like the idea of beauty, the idea of the just, the idea of the useful—is a light that illumines the soul. The idea of God realized itself in worship and created a world that transcended nature. On Cousin's views on religion, see his *Introduction to the History of Philosophy*, trans. Henning Gottfried Linberg, 16-17, and *Course of the History of Modern Philosophy*, trans. O. W. Wight, 2 vols. (New York: D. Appleton, 1852), 1:21-22. I could not find in Cousin's works the identification of religion with the "idea of the holy." But Cousin would certainly have been amenable to such a phrase. Rudolf Otto (1869-1937), of course, made the phrase famous in his *Das Heilige* (1917), translated in 1923 by John W. Harvey as *The Idea of the Holy*.]

The form, being the work of the understanding, varies as vary the lights of the understanding. The understanding is progressive, and it is forever becoming able to realize a more perfect form or symbol for the religious ideal. But one form is never obtained but by the destruction of its predecessor. This destruction of a religious form is what I call infidelity. The form, the symbol, what M. Cousin calls *un culte*, is that only which can be rejected or disbelieved. Infidelity never strikes at the ideal; it strikes only the symbol. It is the rejection, the destruction, if you please, of a religion. This is the sense in which I have used the term infidelity in my essays, and it is, if I mistake not, the popular meaning of the word determined.

I made two statements, to which your correspondent objects; "Christianity was the triumph of infidelity over Judaism and paganism," and that "the whole movement party, known as the Protestant party, was infidel."

With regard to the first, G. E. E. did not quote me fairly. I distinguished between the internal character and the external of Christianity, and stated that Christianity, "in its *external* character, sprung out of disbelief, or rather availed itself of disbelief in the religious systems which prevailed before it." I, of course, meant by Christianity, in this sense, Christianity as a religious establishment, a *cultus exterior*. Was not my statement correct? In this outward sense, Christianity could be established only by displacing Judaism and paganism. Judaism and paganism were both religions, and as they could be displaced only by being rejected, the displacing of these, which Christianity effected, was certainly infidelity, if infidelity be the rejection of a religion.

If we look to facts, my assertions will be sustained. Christianity, in the sense I am now speaking of it, was a victory, I perhaps should not have said a triumph, of the movement against paganism, commenced by Socrates, and continued by his followers. Nobody, I think, can doubt that the Greek philosophy prepared the way for the introduction and triumph of Christianity, if, indeed, it was not its elaboration. But the whole movement of that philosophy was infidel. It was Euripides who was the favorite poet of Socrates, and in Euripides is seen, as Benjamin Constant has remarked, a nascent irreligion. Socrates himself was put to death for attacking and teaching others to attack paganism. From the day of his dispute with the divine on sanctity, up to the coming of Christ, paganism, or polytheism, was unceasingly and so successfully attacked that all faith in it was nearly destroyed. It was from those who had become disbelievers in it, or those whom they induced to disbelieve it that the early Christians collected in the pagan world their adherents. Where, then, is the impropriety in saying that they availed themselves of disbelief in paganism? And if they did do this, and if Christianity was established by the success of the party which rose against paganism from the birth of the Grecian philosophy, and which party was certainly infidel, where is the impropriety in saying Christianity was the triumph of infidelity over paganism? When it had triumphed, become established, it of course was not infidelity; it was then a religion.

My assertion is proved by the various defenses of Christianity, offered by the early Christians. They are, so far as they are known to us, attacks on paganism, rather than any development of the truth and excellence of Christianity. The early Christians hated paganism full as much as they loved Christianity; and they triumphed as much by their intolerance as by their truth. In reference to Judaism, allowance being made for difference of circumstances, similar remarks might be made. Paul, indeed, at the advice of friends, from prudential considerations, or because he was a Jew and owed allegiance as a subject, did conform to the Jewish law on a certain occasion; but his epistles are full of arguments and statements of the utter insufficiency and complete nullity of that law, at least so far as all Gentile converts were concerned. Everybody knows the hostility of the Jews to the Christians, which could hardly have been the case, had there been no attack upon Judaism.

With regard to my statement respecting the Protestant party, all I need say is that it was correct, if two things be admitted: 1st, that Catholicism was a religion, and 2nd, that the Protestants, in their character of Protestants, wished to destroy it. It is true, on another consideration. The dominant sentiment of the Protestant party was freedom of mind, and unaccountability of man to man for his belief. And this is the dominant sentiment of modern infidels, and that which makes them infidels.

These few remarks, I think, will prove that I had some semblance of reason, at least, for the manner in which I used certain words. That I was wrong is possible; let those to whom my statements are not new, be my judges. I close, but I pray you not to consider this communication anything more than a few hints upon the topics it touches.

41.

PROGRESS OF SOCIETY[1]

Christian Examiner and General Review
18 (July 1835): 345-68

This is a valuable work on a very important subject. It is the production of no commonplace mind. Every page of it bears the proofs of strong, independent, and original thought. Whoever thinks at all on his own moral nature, or on the destiny of mankind, will read it with deep interest, and find much in it to prompt inquiry, to warm his heart, and guide his thoughts.

The object of this essay, as stated in the preface, is, "to show that mankind collectively, or society, was destined to grow from infancy to maturity in the same way as individuals are, and that the due consideration of this truth explains the origin of moral evil, the cause of its prevalence under varied forms and extent, and the means of its cure"; and also to consider "as connected with the actual progress of society, the means of its *education*, provided by Divine Providence, in the different revelations he has given to mankind. These were completed, doctrinally, by Christianity; but the world being incapable, at the first promulgation of the Christian religion, to comprehend, still more to practice its lessons, the time had not yet arrived for the actual success of the doctrine; nor has it yet arrived; but the era is approaching."

The author's point of departure is progress. Man does not come into the world full-grown. Individually and collectively, he is designed by Providence to pass from rude and feeble beginnings, to maturity, to the strength and perfection of which he is capable. Knowledge and virtue are to be acquired, by slow and toilsome effort, often at the expense of temporary suffering and evil.

The individual and the species are both subject to the same law of development. In attaining maturity, each passes successively under the dominion of different sets of faculties. In infancy the individual is a mere animal, affected chiefly by the appetites, instincts, and passions of animal life. These are all essentially selfish, having for

[1][Ed. A review of *An Essay on the Moral Constitution and History of Man* (Edinburgh: W. Tait, 1834)].

their object the preservation, nutrition, and health of the individual. To these succeeds the imagination. Under the dominion of the imagination the individual has a great curiosity to learn the causes and the uses of everything; but he is credulous, particularly charmed with the wonderful, and becomes the easy dupe of every tale that is told him.

The intellectual powers come next in order, and assume, or try to assume, the mastery; but the remains of preceding influences and habits, together with the circumstances by which the man is surrounded and which tempt or compel him to fight his way through the world, prevent this mastery from being complete, often from being even predominant. Under the reign of the intellect the follies and prejudices of childhood and youth are surmounted, knowledge and strength are gained, but not wisdom and happiness. There remains another set of faculties to be developed, the moral sentiments. These are last in order; their predominance constitutes the maturity, the perfection of human nature, and gives moral wisdom, which is the proper attribute of age.

Society comes under each of these different sets of faculties in the same order. The infancy of society is the savage state, in which the animal passions predominate as in children. Savages are wholly occupied with the means of self-preservation, and the gratification of their natural appetites and instincts. The next epoch in social progress is marked by the predominance of the imagination. This is the age of superstition. The imagination, usurping the prerogative of reason, attempts to account for all the phenomena of nature by its own conceits. Whatever is extraordinary it imputes to some mysterious influence; it peoples the world with imaginary beings—some above, some below men, some good, some bad—who are forever interfering with the affairs of mankind, and with the ordinary course or general laws of nature; and, when it has exhausted itself with these fanciful creations, it resorts to the supposed influence of occult qualities, of charms, and of magic. Under a more seductive form, it gives rise to the fables of the poets and to the sublime reveries of the Platonic and oriental philosophies.

Childhood and youth cannot comprehend the reason of their duties, they must therefore be commanded. They must be governed by *authority* and the rule of their duty is *obedience*. The social epochs, which correspond to childhood and youth in the individual, require, therefore, a different code from that which may be introduced at a more advanced stage of society. They find their moral expression in the code of authority, which appeals, not to conviction, nor to love, but to *fear*, and, in cases of obstinacy, resorts to *force*.

To the imagination succeeds the predominance of the intellect. This epoch begins by "chopping logic," attempting, by dint of syllogisms and hypotheses, to penetrate the secrets of nature, or to illustrate the teachings of divine revelation, and ends by hitting upon the true method of philosophizing, of which Bacon[2] is the representative; but which can be successfully followed in this epoch, only in the department of physics. The intellect, being in advance of the imagination, requires a more perfect moral code. It demands the code of justice, which finds its expression in law, a rule of right between equals. This code, at first, like that of authority, appeals to fear, and resorts to force; but, after its precepts come to be established in the reason and the habits of men, they are voluntarily obeyed, and its appeal may be said to be to honor.

The fourth epoch—the golden age of the poets, which however, was not in the infancy of the world, but which shall be in the latter day—is to come. We are now in a state of *transition* from the age of matured intellect to that of mature wisdom or moral sentiment, with more of the former element as yet than of the latter, and more occupied with the laws of nature than with those of humanity, but ready to pass to the last stage, which is analogous to that of experienced age in the individual. In this last stage, however, the wisdom of society will rise superior to that of individuals. It will not be tarnished by any of the physical infirmities incidental to individual life. It will not be deteriorated by the personal bad habits of former years. All the evils of former generations may and will die with them, all the good may and will survive; because their posterity will have acquired the wisdom to reject the one and to cherish the other,—to profit by the experience, knowledge, and accumulations of their fathers.

This social epoch will have for its moral expression the code of benevolence. The precepts of this code may be easily distinguished from those of authority, or of justice. Authority commands, and the one commanded has no right to ask why he shall obey; justice says, do no wrong to others, submit to no wrong from them. But this cannot be the maxim of a definitive state of society. It is liable to perpetual misconstruction. We may think we are doing no wrong to others when we are doing them great wrong; and we may believe others are doing us a wrong which we should redress when they are not. It will always make a great difference in our estimate of any

[2][Ed. Francis Bacon (1561-1626) was a philosopher, essayist, orator and lawyer. He is perhaps most famous for authoring *Novum Organum* (1620), the Bible of empiricism and the inductive method. Lord Bacon was a guiding light among many antebellum American intellectuals.]

particular action whether it be done to us or by us to others. All efforts to obtain a perfect state of society by the rules of justice must prove ineffectual because the rules themselves are imperfect. Something higher and broader is demanded. This will be found in the code of benevolence, which says, do *more* than justice to others, submit to *less* than justice from them. This, on the one hand, requires us to *forgive* those who injure us, and, on the other, to inquire not what others may claim from us as a matter of right but what good we are able to do them.

This is the natural order of individual and social progress; but it is not effected by man's unaided powers. The child is set forward by the education it receives from the father; so is society by divine revelation, designed to educate not the individual merely but the species. Revelation, like education, does not seek to supersede the natural powers but to develop and strengthen them. Education must regard the age and capacities of its subject, at first give the most simple and easy, and gradually proceed to the more complex and difficult; so God does not communicate all truth at once, but gives it in different portions at different times as the wants and capacities of society demand or allow. His object in all his revelations is to prepare men for the reign of benevolence. To this end the whole series of revelations points from that made to our first parents in Eden to that made through Jesus Christ. The first revelation was of the simple elements of religion and natural science, and the last was of that sublime code of morals destined to govern the last epoch of society. Between these two, society had received all the great truths of natural religion and the precepts of justice; the object of Jesus, who closed the series of revelations, was not, therefore, to reveal any new religious doctrines nor to give any new sanctions to the precepts of justice, but to introduce and establish the moral code of benevolence. The peculiarity of the gospel, then, is in its morality, in the fact, that it bases morality, not on fear nor honor, not on authority nor justice, but on love. "Thou shalt love thy neighbor as thyself" [Lev 19:18; Matt 19:19].

We have here given but a meager outline of this very interesting essay; but we cannot give a fuller analysis of it without exceeding our limits. We may add, however, that the development of the system we have sketched exhibits the marks of a master. The limitations which some of the general principles require, and which we have not room to notice are in most cases stated; and the objections which may occur are in general taken up and satisfactorily answered. We would mention especially that brought against the triumph of benevolence, from the supposed inherent depravity of human nature. It is admitted that man brings into the world with him the seeds of evil, but it is contended that he also brings with him the seeds of good. That he is subject in some degree to error and liable to sin is not denied; but he has also the capacity to feel and act liberally and may be brought under the dominion of benevolence. The position that its morality is the only peculiarity of the gospel is supported with much earnestness and strength of argument, and the causes which have aided or retarded its progress are treated with great ability. Nearly two thirds of the essay are taken up with these, and evince a patience of research, a philosophical candor, and a Christian tenderness in discussing opinions which are deemed false and mischievous, that cannot be too much commended. That the author is always correct, that he gives to all opinions and events their true influences, or that he always assigns them their true origin is more than we are willing to assert. We have noticed, in the perusal of his work, a number of points, mostly subordinate matters, on which we should disagree with him; but when he errs, he, for the most part, sheds a light that will enable others to correct him.

But, however much we might object to some things in the work which we have introduced and which we commend to our readers, we are happy to agree entirely with its general theory. That society has a growth analogous to that of the individual; that Christianity, as well as all other revelations, was designed to aid that growth; that its morality is the only peculiarity of the gospel; that its morality is based on benevolence, and forms a code under which the whole human race must ultimately pass is our fixed belief, and has long since been ranked by us with those truths which we make our governing principles of action.

In a former article we spoke of the progress which Christianity has effected.[3] We advanced the doctrine of the essay before us that mankind collectively has a growth precisely analogous to that of the individual. This is a doctrine which enables us to recall the past without wrath or bitterness. All past social institutions have had and fulfilled their mission. They are not to be tried by the present but by that epoch in the progress of society to which they belonged. Tried by this standard, most of the institutions which we now condemn will be found to have been good in their day, and the evil which is charged against them belonged, not to their origin, but resulted from their lingering too long, from their outliving their time.

[3][Ed. Brownson is probably referring to "Benjamin Constant *On Religion*," *Christian Examiner and General Review* 17 (September 1834): 63-77.]

Judaism is almost infinitely below Christianity, viewed either as a social or as a religious system; but who will contend that Judaism was a bad institution in its day? It was adapted to its age and country, and was better for that age and country than Christianity would have been. Christianity would have been too pure and spiritual to be comprehended. It could not have reached the consciences of the people upon whom Judaism was to act, and would have been to them only a system of license. Despotism, justly abhorred by all free men, was in its origin a victory achieved by humanity. The condition of those who live under the severest despotism is preferable to that of those savage hordes who submit to no authority but that of an extemporary chief chosen to lead them to war or plunder. There is no society in the savage state; there is aggregation, but not society. The elements of society are indeed there, for they belong to human nature; but they are isolated, and for the most part inoperative. But under a despotism, there is society, rude, imperfect, we admit; still it is society with its look upward and its step, slow indeed, but onward.

Similar remarks might be made of all other systems of religion, of government, of legislation, and of philosophy which have reigned in the past. None of them, perhaps, would be good now because we are in advance of the respective epochs of their usefulness; but in the time and country when and where they were adopted, they were salutary reforms, important victories gained by the progress of society. Each of them, if compared with its predecessor, will be found to have been a forward step in the march of improvement. That they were all imperfect, nobody who comprehends them will deny; but they were as perfect as their respective stages of social progress would admit. It is impossible to give to the child the perfect notions of things which become the man; so is it impossible to give to the infancy of society those perfect social institutions which are suitable only to its full age; or, if we could, it would be like clothing the infant in the dress of a full-grown man.

But, if we acquit the past, we must not forget the duty of the present. We must neither feel nor act as if all progress was ended, and man had attained all the perfection of which he is capable. There is to be a progress through all the future, as there has been one through all the past; but the future progress must always be elaborated in the present. The child prepares the youth, the youth prepares the man; and in like manner this generation must prepare its successor, and that must prepare the one to come after it. The duty of the present, then, is great; its position is one of great consequence; it can act on all future time, and hasten or retard, in some degree, the progress of society through all coming generations. It will discharge its duty very much in proportion to its estimate of itself and its hopes for the future. If it be satisfied with itself or if it believe that nothing better is possible its exertions will be feeble, and its contributions to future progress will be hardly worth naming. For ourselves, we believe the present greatly superior to whatever has gone before it; but it does not satisfy us. We do not declaim against it, we attempt to comprehend it; we contemplate it with gratitude to God but it does not come up to our idea of good. There flit across our mental vision the shadows, at least, of something immeasurably better.

That all will agree with us in our estimate of the present or in our hopes for the future is more than we expect. Men's notions of society are much influenced by the position from which they view it. He who is at ease himself, rich, enjoying ample leisure, and associating only with the most favored individuals in the community, will call society as it is, very nearly, if not quite, perfect; he will be prone to forget, or not to suspect, the vast amount of suffering that lies beyond him; and, unless perchance he has learned something more of Christianity than its dogmas, he will be very liable to look upon the manual laborer, not as a fellow immortal, with rights, duties, interests, and feelings, sacred as his own, but as a mere instrument of his wealth or pleasure, made to be used for his service, and sufficiently provided for if fed and clothed and comfortably lodged. It will be difficult for him to comprehend any measures taken to benefit the workingmen as a class, and any interest shown in their behalf will seem to him to flow from a Jacobinical spirit or from an over-refined sentimentalism. But the poor man who trudges daily to his toil, feeling himself hardly more respected than an implement of husbandry, and able, with all his exertions, barely to keep his wife and children from starving, will believe society as it is, very imperfect; he will call this a bad world, and hard and bitter thoughts will pass through his mind, as he gazes on the palace of the rich or sees its lordly owner roll by him in his carriage.

We do not censure or approve either. The views of both are natural, if not inevitable, if we take into the account their respective positions. The guinea often slips between men's eyes and the truth; and, from not seeing the truth, it is very natural that they should come to deny it. For ourselves, we share fully the views of neither of the two individuals we have introduced as the representatives of the two extremes of society. It has been our lot to see society on more than one side. Indeed we have seen it on all sides. We know what it can give, and what it requires to be endured, and we say again, it does not satisfy us. We cannot avoid dreaming, if dreaming it prove to be, of something greatly its superior. We see endured by all classes a vast amount of evil, to which we cannot reconcile our love of humanity. We see noble energies misdirected, false modes at judging adopted, factitious distinctions to obtain and be defended. All over the world, even in its most favored portions, there is an inequality in wealth, in moral, intellectual, and social advantages, which we believe wholly inconsistent with the full exercise of Christian love. Everywhere one part of our fellow beings are wasting away in luxury, indolence, listlessness, and dissipation; and another part pining in want and neglect, devoured by discontent and envy; and when we see this, we can call it neither good nor necessary. We ask that it may be cured and we turn to the future with full faith that it will be.

But, in expressing ourselves thus decidedly against the present and in favor of the future, we would guard against being misinterpreted. We are not among those who believe society, as it is now organized, is radically wrong. Its roots are in human nature itself and a society radically different cannot be obtained till we procure another human nature. We would not destroy present society; we see in it the germs of all that we desire should be; but we would carry it forward to its perfection. The work, in which we would enlist the friends of humanity, is one of improvement, not of destruction.

In speaking against inequality, we do not propose that all the members of the community should be in precisely the same condition. This is not a world in which all things and all men can be reduced to one dead level. The Creator everywhere delights to put himself forth in variety and it is variety that makes up the charm of life. Life were a dull scene were we all in precisely the same condition, of precisely the same size, and of precisely the same way of thinking and feeling. Better, far better, were all the storms and tempests which rage from the greatest inequality than such a dead and deadening calm. Were such a state of uniformity, of monotony, once brought about, gone were all our enterprise, all motives to exertion, all hopes of further progress; society would be dead and would rot, as it is said the ocean does when the long calm has hushed the tide and the wave on its bosom.

There are different classes in the community and there always will be so long as there shall be a diversity in men's natural gifts or in the business of society. But diversity is not inequality. The shoemaker differs from the blacksmith; but he is not, because he is a shoemaker, necessarily inferior or superior to the blacksmith. A division of labor is undoubtedly necessary to civilization and to the progress of society, but this says nothing in favor of inequality. The arguments usually adduced to prove that inequality is an essential element in civilization, merely prove the advantages of a diversity in men's talents and of a division of labor. We see a necessity for different classes, but none for a *subordination* of classes. We know not why the mechanic or even the common day-laborer should not so far as his trade or occupation is concerned claim equality with any member of the community; and certainly we cannot understand the justice of excluding him from any of the means of becoming so far as his native talents admit a great and a good man. There should be nothing in labor to degrade the laborer or to operate to his disadvantage. Whatever is necessary to be done should be counted not only honest but honorable. No man should be estimated by his employment or his social position, but by what he is in himself, independent of all adventitious circumstances whatever; and the means of moral and intellectual growth, so far as society can furnish them, should be within the reach of the humblest as well as the proudest member of the community.

But we are willing to admit, because we believe it true, that mankind are not and cannot be equal. Men are born with equal rights, but not with equal capacities. All have the elements of the same nature, but these elements are more developed in some than in others. Some will be leaders, others will only follow. Go into any family or school, when the external circumstances are as nearly equal as possible and you will find someone who is the leader, some two or three who arrange and control the play and the pleasures of all the rest. Nature has given us an aristocracy, though it has left its particular character, under a certain aspect, to accident. When war is deemed the business and the glory of society, the best warriors, heroes, constitute the aristocracy; when religion fills men's minds and hearts, the ministers of religion, priests, are the aristocrats, or, to borrow a Saint-Simonian expression, the chiefs of the people; when learning is the public passion, the aristocracy is based on literature, as it is said to be now in China; when wealth is counted the supreme good, and money-getting the chief end of man, the accumulators of wealth, businessmen, are the aristocrats, the leaders of mankind. In a word, the aristocracy is always based on the spirit of the age or country and composed of those who best represent that spirit.

But against this, which we consider the order of nature, the appointment of God, we have nothing to urge. It is a wise and beneficent appointment and would involve no evil if the aristocracy were based, as it one day will be, on the morality of the gospel, and composed of those who best represent the spirit of Jesus. Some, even then, would be greater than the rest, but there would be no subordination of classes, no exclusive privileges, no monopoly of social advantages. All would have the same object, be in the same path, and engaged in the same work. If some received a higher reward than others, it would be only relatively higher; compared with his capacity, no one would receive more than another, and each would receive in proportion to his capacity to enjoy. It would be in that case an aristocracy of real virtue; an aristocracy taking the lead in true excellence. Give us such an aristocracy and we will fall contentedly into our rank; and, if there are many above us, we will adopt the sentiment of the old Grecian patriot, who, on losing an election, rejoiced that his country had three hundred better men than himself.

We admit then an original inequality in men's capacities; we believe that the Almighty has established an aristocracy; but this is something very different from admitting, that all the distinctions and their attendant evils, which now obtain in society, are of Divine appointment. They are the natural but not the necessary result of the original inequality in men's capacities. A man may sow tares in his field; if he does, they will grow there as naturally as wheat, and grow too by a law of God; but the law of God does not compel a man to sow tares instead of wheat. If the aristocracy be based on anything else than Christian morality, it will occasion more or less of evil; but this is because the aristocracy rests upon a wrong foundation, bears a wrong character. Now, unless we are prepared to say that God has ordained that the aristocracy shall rest upon that wrong foundation, bear that wrong character, and to say it would be virtually saying that he ordains all sin, we must abandon the notion that all the distinctions and the evils consequent upon them, which obtain in society, are of Divine appointment.

But, in charging them upon the aristocracy, we have not traced them to their origin. The aristocracy does not make the people but the people the aristocracy. Show us your people, and we will tell you who are your aristocrats. They are those who represent the spirit of their times and country the best of all their contemporaries. In censuring them we censure the predominant spirit of their epoch, a spirit which controls the lowest as well as the highest. The aristocracy then is not alone in fault. It but shares a common error. The whole people, individual exceptions of course, are wrong, and the evil complained of can be cured only by infusing a better spirit into the whole mass of society.

The aristocracy of our country is based on wealth. The accumulators of wealth are our leaders. But why are they so? These are leaders only by virtue of a spirit in those to be led, which responds to the spirit in those who would lead. Did we not all love wealth, bow to it, cringe to it, the poor even more than the rich, and estimate a man's worth by the length of his purse, wealth could create no aristocracy amongst us. Were the great mass of our population able to say with him, in the Revolution, to whom the British commissioners offered a large sum to desert the cause of his country, "Tell your master, I am poor, but the King of England is not rich enough to buy me," wealth would have no power over us. But so long as we make it the god, at whose shrine we pay our devotions, it will govern us, and our leaders will be those who engage in its accumulation with the greatest energy and success.

But we have extended these remarks, designed to prevent us from being misapprehended by our readers, too far. We return to the duty of the present in relation to the future. This duty is to labor for the future progress of society. We do not stop to prove that society may be carried forward to greater perfection than that to which it has now attained. There are few who cannot form to themselves an *ideal* vastly superior to it. That ideal will be realized. God has not given us the capacity to form to ourselves loftier and yet loftier ideals, merely to mock us with our impotence. The power of execution may, indeed, fall short of the power of conception; but both can grow, and the growth of one always strengthens the other. Progress there will be. The loftiest ideals of the most gifted of men will be realized. Man is made for a higher destiny than he has yet attained. And he will attain it. That is written. But how? What are the principles by which he should be governed in his efforts to do it? This is the question to be answered; and to answering this question we shall devote the remainder of this article.

Our hope for the future progress of society is not exclusively, nor mainly, in government. This is the age of political economy; the point of view of most of those who would be reformers is political. And their hope is in the action of government upon the masses. The agency of government in the progress of society is not to be overlooked; but it belongs not to government to take the initiative. Government is the creature, not the creator, of any particular state of society; and its mission is to collect, concentrate, and facilitate the operation of the spirit of a people.

All social reforms must be the effect of individual reform. Any change in the public institutions of a country, not demanded by a corresponding change in the individual character of those whose opinions can influence government, will be injurious instead of salutary. Joseph the Second of Germany[4] attempted some reforms in his empire, reforms which could have proceeded only from a sincere regard for the well-being of his subjects; but, being mistimed, they miscarried, and served merely to disturb the peace of his reign, to increase the prejudice against innovation, and to retard the cause he had so much at heart. Declare a race of ignorant, degraded slaves, free, and your declaration will not make them free; give them all the forms of a republican government, with all the guarantee of the most clearly defined constitutions, and they will not be less slaves, and slaves with the disadvantage of being in want of a master to keep them in order. Vain are all the forms of a free government, where freedom is not in the hearts and the habits of the people, as individuals.

A notion has prevailed to some extent, and, perhaps, is not yet wholly abandoned, that man is the creature of external circumstances, and that any given description of character may be produced by a proper modification of external circumstances. Government, as having the most control over external circumstances, has, therefore, been considered the great agent of reform. The whimsical, but philanthropic Owen[5] has pushed this theory to its last results, and thus furnished the means of its refutation. It is a theory which springs from a sensual and superficial philosophy, a philosophy that overlooks the most important element of human nature, man's power to originate action of himself, by his own internal energy. Man acts upon circumstances, as well as they upon him; and it depends mainly on him, whether they control him, or he them. Were it not so, were he indeed a spinning-jenny, then we admit that the modification of external circumstances might make him a spinning-jenny of the most approved fashion.

[4][Ed. Joseph II of Austria, Holy Roman Emperor from 1765 to 1790, was an Enlightenment figure who promoted civil and ecclesiastical reforms that included religious toleration, the right of the state to regulate ecclesiastical affairs and to reform abuses, and the right of the state to limit the authority of the pope over the local church. These eighteenth century reforms are usually characterized as "Josephism" by historians of modern Catholicism.]

[5][Ed. Brownson refers here to the Scottish industrialist, socialist, and reformer Robert Owen (1771-1858). Owen was a utopian who tried to create a "new moral world." He articulated his philosophy in, among other texts, *A New View of Society* (1816), a book that Brownson had read with some interest. On Owen see Arthur Eugene Bestor, Jr., *Backwoods Utopias: The Sectarian and Owenite Phases of Communitarian Socialism in America, 1663-1829* (Philadelphia: University of Pennsylvania Press, 1950).]

It was thought at one time, that a free government could go alone, that it had some magic-working power by which it could at once convert the rudest materials into polished stones for its social edifice. Experience is correcting this error, as it will correct many others. We are beginning to perceive that it is not a free government that makes a free people, but a free people that makes a free government. No people will be more free, wise, or just, in its collective capacity, than it is in its individual capacity. What is called the collective wisdom of a nation, when it speaks through public institutions, is only a compromise between the most and the least advanced of the individuals of which it is composed. It is only an average of the wisdom of private individuals. If some fall below it, others rise above it. The wisest and best men of a nation are always in advance of the government. Government cannot come up to their ideal without losing sight of the many. The wise and the good must labor to bring the many up to their ideal, and in proportion, and only in proportion, as they do it, may government advance.

We admit, however, that government is a powerful agent in the progress of society. It has done much, and we trust it will do much more; but it is not omnipotent. It must bend to the spirit of the people. Could we get a legislature mad enough to enact a community of goods or an equal division of property, their enactment could not become a law. It is not the legislature, nor the court, nor the sheriff and his *posse*, that can give to a legislative act the power of law. It is the spirit of the people on whom it is to operate. Look at our people, with a strong sense of property, appreciating to its full extent the value of the *meum*,[6] and do you believe they would submit to a community of goods, or to an equal division of property? Or suppose a statute limiting the amount of property which may be held, could it become a law? Every businessman in the community would trample it under foot; or if not, every species of fraud would be resorted to, for evading it and concealing the amount of property actually possessed. Where such a statute could become a law, it would not be needed, for there the love of wealth would not be too strong. That the love of wealth is too strong in our own country, as well as in many others, is true; that it is the source of many evils is also true; but the remedy is not in legislation, not in government, but in calling into exercise a higher and a purer principle of action.

This purer and higher principle must be sought in the gospel of Jesus Christ. In our efforts to effect the future progress of society we

---

[6][Ed. Latin for "mine," or what I own.]

must be guided solely by the principles of Christian morality. There is no way to carry society forward to its perfection but by making its individual members good Christians. We know that some will smile at this answer. No matter. It is possible that we have given as much of study, brought as great a love of humanity and as strong a desire for progress to the problem we have proposed as those who will smile in contempt at the solution we have offered.

We repeat it; the grand lever of reform, the mighty power that is to carry society forward to its perfection, is Christian morality. In making this assertion, we do not plunge into the arena of theological warfare, we touch not the field from which ascend the battle-shouts of conflicting sectarians; we rise to higher and broader ground, and plant our footsteps, not on the dogmas of the gospel, but on its simple, sublime, and universal morality. We leave the dogmas about which theologians wrangle; they have their truth, have had their use, but they do not constitute the peculiarity of the gospel. They are nowhere made by the author of the gospel the direct object of his instructions. Even the doctrine of the Divine unity, great and glorious as we view it, although recognized by Jesus, is never recognized as one that he was sent to teach but as one already known and believed. The same remark is true of the doctrine of a future state of existence. Jesus alludes to it, but not as a doctrine of his own, whose revelation made a part of his mission; he assumes it, illustrates it, and makes use of it to enforce his morals, but does not make it an object of direct instruction. When questioned respecting it, he refers the interrogator to a previous revelation. It is the same with all the great doctrines of theology. We say not that they are not true, are not important, but they had been revealed previously to the coming of Christ, and needed not to be revealed again.

We assert without fear of denial from anyone who has made this a subject of distinct investigation, that all the great theological doctrines, properly so called, which are connected with Christianity and considered essential to it, were known and believed at the time of our Savior. The unity of God, it is well known, was a distinguishing doctrine of Judaism. We meet in the Old Testament, also, the doctrine of God's paternity, and distinct intimations of his sin-pardoning character. It is true, God's justice reigns in Judaism, but his mercy is also there. "Let the wicked forsake his way, and the unrighteous man his thoughts; and let him return unto the Lord, and he will have mercy upon him; and to our God, for he will abundantly pardon" (Isa 55:7). There may be some question, whether the Jews, in the time of Moses, believed in a future state and a righteous retribution after death; but there can be none that they, or at least a portion of them, believed in both long before the birth of Jesus. Socrates and Plato certainly believed in a life to come; and indeed no people have ever yet been discovered, of whom it could be said with certainty, that they did not believe in some kind of a life beyond this life. The most savage tribes have their land of shadows, their world of spirits, where are their fathers, and where they hope to rejoin them when they die. How men came to the knowledge of these doctrines, whether naturally or supernaturally, by a deduction of reasoning, by the unfolding of a law of their own nature, or by a direct communication from God himself, we do not now inquire. It is sufficient for our present purpose that they were known before the coming of Christ. This we assert. They may all be found in religions existing before the gospel was given, if not in precisely the Christian form, at least the same in their elements, in their foundation.

It is important that we do not forget this. We believe in the originality of the gospel; but if the gospel be asserted to be the revelation of a mere system of theology, its originality remains to be proved. Its originality, and its only peculiarity, in our opinion, is in its morality. We find its theology, at least "for substance of doctrine," elsewhere; but nowhere else its morality. We find in one place a morality based on selfishness; in another, one like the Jewish, "an eye for an eye, a tooth for a tooth" [Exod 21:24; Matt 5:38], based on justice; but nowhere one on the broad, omnipotent, and indestructible principle of love. This is peculiar to the gospel, this distinguishes it by broad lines from all other religions, and this, and this alone, is the direct object of its instructions. Nothing else is taught in that simple and sublime Sermon on the Mount; and, when Jesus alludes to the love of our heavenly Father for his children, it is to deduce from it motives for them to love one another. His leading object, whether taken from his own words or from the commentaries of his apostles, obviously was to establish the reign of love or benevolence. His first words were, "Repent for the kingdom of heaven is at hand" [Matt 3:10]. The "kingdom of heaven" and the "kingdom of God" mean precisely the same thing; and by the kingdom of God, we must understand the reign of God. God is love; the reign of God, then, is the reign of love. God reigns in that heart where love reigns. He dwells there. "He that dwelleth in love," says John, "dwelleth in God and God in him" [1 John 4:16]. Jesus expressly declares, that the new commandment he gave, or the addition he had come to make to the reigning code of morals, was that his disciples should love one another. "A new commandment give I unto you, that ye love one another; as I have loved you, that ye also love one another. By this shall all men know that ye are my disciples, if ye have love one towards another" [John 13:34]. Now that which should distinguish the disciples as the disciples of Christ, must be considered the peculiarity of what he taught. This was love one to another; and this, we think, fully authorizes our assertion, that the peculiarity of the gospel was in basing its morality on love, or benevolence.

This "love one to another," which Jesus enjoined, was not a narrow love, to be shut up within the inclosure of his professed followers. It was the broad principle of universal philanthropy. "Ye have heard that it hath been said, Thou shalt love thy neighbor and hate thine enemy; but I say unto you, Love your enemies, bless them that curse you, do good to them that hate you, and pray for them that despitefully use you and persecute you, that ye may be the children of your Father who is in heaven; for he maketh his sun to rise on the evil and on the good, and sendeth rain on the just and the unjust" [Matt 5:33-35]. It is not then a meager system of morals that the gospel enjoins. Its principles extend beyond the outward act, beyond the narrow circle of our friends or our own sect; they go deep into the heart, and quicken a love for universal man. They command us to love one another, to love even our enemies, as well as Christ loved us; that is, well enough, if need be, to die for our fellow beings as Christ died for us. Here lies our hope, in this grand principle of love to man, and we expect the progress of society only in proportion as men come to love one another better.

Existing social evils have their cause. What is that cause? Say, with our radical politicians, that it is in bad government, and the question is only removed one step, not answered. What is the cause of bad government? If it be in the depravity of rulers, whence that depravity? "They are chosen from the wrong class," say our workingmen; "they should be chosen from our ranks, and then they would take care of our interests, and, if our interests were taken care of, all social evils would vanish." Perhaps so. We have great tenderness for the workingmen; we have mourned over their depressed condition, and we rejoice to see them making efforts to elevate themselves to the social rank to which they are entitled; but we have no great respect for their moral or political philosophy. Admit that all the officers of government were taken from the working classes, or from those who really and preeminently have their interests at heart; and does it necessarily follow that the interests of those classes would always be promoted? Do the workingmen never mistake their own interests in their private capacity? Who will assure us, then, that they may not mistake it, in acting in a public capacity? And is this the way to cure the evils of society, to have every man and every class pursue his or its own interest, regardless of that of any other, to support a system of universal competition? This is the very system now in operation; and we may answer the question, What is the cause of social evils? by saying, It is in the fact that each man, whether rich or poor, is pursuing his own interest, or what he believes his own interest, without regard to that of his fellow. And why does he do this? Because he is selfish, does not love his neighbor as himself. All the social evils of which anybody complains, may be traced to the predominance of the selfish propensities. The standard of morality is too low; men's notions of duty fall infinitely below the Christian standard.

Are we wrong? What is the morality of the world? In its best possible shape, it is "Look out for yourself; take care of *Number One*; but," it added in a lower tone, "do no wrong to others." This is all that is aimed at, and more than is accomplished in practice. In practice, the clause spoken in a low tone in theory is sunk, and the maxim runs, "Look out for yourself, keep what you have, and get all you can." In all the varieties of trade and business transactions, every man means to enrich himself, to make his own end of the bargain as much the best as he can; and, if he makes it a great deal the best, he boasts of it, however much the one with whom he trades may suffer. Such we say is the spirit of trade, the predominant spirit in all business transactions, and with a vast majority of the community, though there are no doubt many honorable individual exceptions.

Now what better is to be expected from this morality, than that which we already have? Here is the morality of self-interest; and, in the monstrous inequality in wealth, in learning, in moral and intellectual culture, which glares upon the stranger on entering this city, we see the best it can effect; and even better than it can effect, for benevolence has been here, and in no city on earth has it been more active. It is in vain to expect anything better without a higher standard of morality. If we make interest the governing motive, we must expect all individuals and all classes to be governed by their views of it. These views will always be partial and conflicting. The carpenter and the timber-merchant will contend, that all houses should be constructed of wood; the brick-maker and the brick-layer will prefer brick; the fur-cap manufacturers will encourage the wearing of fur caps; but the hatter will complain that in so doing, they injure his business and take, as it were, the bread out of his mouth. All the trades will be mutually opposed, and perpetual clashing must be the result. There is no such thing as reconciling all classes, all the divisions of labor, and making society harmonious without having men aim at something higher than the morality of selfishness.

Existing social evils, we have said, may be traced to the predominance of the selfish propensities; it is evident, then, that we must have recourse to the predominance of the benevolent affections for a cure. The predominance of these is what the gospel contemplates, and what we mean by the morality of love. Now we love ourselves, if not exclusively, at least chiefly; but the gospel commands us to love our neighbor as ourselves. Here is a higher principle than selfishness, a broader principle than justice. Selfishness is satisfied when self is provided for; justice contents himself with doing and receiving no wrong; love goes beyond both, and can be satisfied only by doing good, not by doing some good, but the greatest good in its power. It does not wrap itself up in itself, but it goes out of itself; with its hands filled with benefits, it goes out into the streets, the lanes, the by-paths, into the humble shed of poverty, and into the loathsome dungeon of the prisoner, to find objects to bless; and it returns not as long as it can find a single human being borne down by a burden too great for his strength, a single tear in a human eye to be dried, a single wounded heart into which it can pour the "oil and wine," or a single bruised spirit that it may bind up.

Such is love. Such is the principle that would reign were Christian morality predominant. All crimes would fail, all wrongs would cease. There would be no unmitigated poverty, no ostentatious display of wealth to increase the vanity of the possessor and the discontented envy of him that has it not. There would be no *exploitation de l'homme par l'homme*,[7] as the Saint-Simonians happily express the reigning vice of the past; no encroaching; no turning of one's superior knowledge to one's own exclusive advantage, but to supplying the deficiencies of others; trade would become, what it should be, the mutual exchange of benefits; everywhere would reign peace, harmony, and joy; man would give his heart and his hand to his brother, and society would present a picture on which even God himself might look with approbation.

Such were society, were love once to become predominant, to run through all our actions, and to preside over all the intercourse of man with man. "*Were it* predominant, ay, were it," it is said; "but it is not, it *cannot* be. Men are selfish, each one for himself, no one for his brother, and it is folly to expect that all will come under the influence of the law of love." We have heard this objection to our hopes of

---

[7][Ed. French for "exploitation of man by man."]

future progress, at least in substance, in the humble shed of poverty, in the palaces of the rich, in the shop of the mechanic, in the fields of the agriculturist, behind the counter of the merchant, in the halls of legislation, from the bar, the bench, and the pulpit; but we dare not give utterance to the outraged feelings with which we have always heard it. We never hear it but with deep abhorrence. Let it never proceed from the lips of a professed disciple of Jesus. Whoever thou art, if thou hast no more faith in human virtue, no more faith in the power of human nature to come under the government of the pure and godlike principle of love, than this objection implies, blush to enter the pulpit, to speak in the name of one whose disciples are to be known only by having "love one towards another" [1 Thess 3:12], in the name of one who commands all men to love even their enemies, and whose avowed object was to turn men from their iniquities, to bring them to God, and to make them perfect as their Father in heaven is perfect!

Do we use strong language? We know it, and we mean it. The interests of religion, of humanity, demand it; and he who does not bring out the great principle of the gospel, and insist in strong terms on its being admitted, preached, and obeyed, seems to us to fail in his duty to God and to man. He is a poor missionary, who begins by saying to those to whom he addresses himself, "My brethren, the religion I bring you is an excellent thing. Its morality is of the purest and most elevated character. If obeyed it would have the most happy effect; but then you must not be so foolish as to suppose it generally practicable. A few gifted individuals alone can ever come under its influences; the great mass of mankind can never be governed by it." Suppose one of our missionaries to the Indians should thus address his heathen audience, and what would be the influence of his preaching? What the answer that would be returned him? "Go back to your own country; if your gospel morality is impracticable, why come ye here to disturb our minds and the state of our society by proclaiming it?" Or, if he should not tell them that it is impracticable, if he should so feel, with what success would he preach? Would he be likely to speak in those earnest and thrilling tones, which go to the heart and the conscience, fasten conviction and lead to reformation? He who would go forth to convert the world should go in faith; he should believe what he preaches, and not only believe it true, but practicable.

The question between us and those who urge the objection we are considering is not, whether we are visionaries, dreaming of social perfection which can never be realized, but, whether the gospel be or be not a practicable scheme of morals. We throw ourselves upon the gospel. We have stated its morality, and what would be the social result, were it obeyed. Nobody, who reflects a moment, will accuse us of misstating that morality, or pretend that our inferences are illegitimate. There is, then, no escape for the objector but in arraigning the gospel itself. The blow with which he would demolish us, he must reserve for our Master. Was Jesus a visionary, preaching a morality which only a few, if indeed any can practice; or did he proclaim a moral law adapted to universal human nature, and consequently one which all men have the power to obey? This is the question. To this question we wait a reply, leaving the objector to settle it with one who "needed not that any should testify of man, for he knew what was in man" [John 2:25].

We are aware that we have presented the subject in a light in which it is not usually contemplated; but we are confident that we have presented it in its true light. We believe that one great reason why the Christian ministry has not been more efficient is that it has not had full faith in the practicability of the gospel morality. It has, we own, labored with great diligence and fidelity in its calling; but it has often left the people where it found them—dead in a worldly policy, or consumed by a crackling fanaticism or an unmeasured zeal for dogmas of faith. It has had no just conception of the extent of the morality it was called to preach, and of course no belief in its practicability or in the state of society which it was destined to introduce. It has therefore been unable to speak as its Master spoke; its words have been powerless, and its tones lifeless. It could not go to the people in the fullness of faith, and consequently it could not adopt the tone and manner of reality, which alone can make a preacher successful.

We mean not to apply these remarks to the Christian ministry in its relation to religious dogmas. These have been believed, and at times so believed that the idea of proving them could not find admittance into the head of him who preached them. They have been to the preacher, not opinions, but realities; and when they have been so, he has spoken with power and fastened conviction. But it was not a moral conviction. No man has yet gone forth and preached the great law of love as the peculiarity of the gospel, and preached it in full faith of its universal obligation and practicability; for it has not yet been so believed, except by here and there an individual. But those who do not so believe, are so far unbelievers in the gospel, and in their influence in some respects the most fatal class of unbelievers. Here is the call for reform. Men must be brought to believe the gospel; not its theology, for that the majority of the civilized world already believe, but its morality.

We do not make these remarks to condemn the past, nor to censure the present, but to point out what is our duty for the future. There is a time for all things. We know that men move slowly, and that the progress of ideas is like that of the apparent motion of the sun; we cannot see the sun move, but, after a while, we see that it has moved. We do not complain, because the great truth for which we contend has not been brought out distinctly before. It required time to wear out the old morality, to exhaust theological discussions, and to fix the basis of our ever progressing religious theory. That is now done, and the epoch has arrived for extending our views, and making the exclusively theological element, with which the religious world has been engaged for so many ages, give place to the moral element, which alone constitutes the peculiarity of the gospel. The Christian world is now distracted, torn into contending sects, and exhibiting a spectacle saddening to the hearts of all the real friends of humanity. These sects must be brought together, these alienated hearts must be united, and these scattered and inoperative elements must be brought into one grand and complete whole. But this cannot be done by any system of theology whatever. It can be done only by striking a chord which shall vibrate alike through all moral nature. We can do it only by a new and a higher view of Christian morality. We have cleared away the rubbish of a false and mischievous theology; we have brought men back, at least in theory, to the simple doctrines inculcated in Scripture, to those which are based on everlasting truth, which are in perfect harmony with man's intellectual nature, those on which Jesus based his morality; and now we must bring out that morality, and hold it up to the admiration and love of all hearts.

The first step to this is to comprehend the extent of that morality, and to obtain the conviction of its practicability. We have said that it is the law of love, a law that requires us to love one another as Christ loved us, that is, well enough, if need be, to die for our fellow beings as Christ died for us. This is the principle of Christian morality. It is, we believe, practicable. Jesus preached it, commanded his disciples to preach it to "every creature," and that too without ever intimating that all men could not obey it. Let the preacher, when he reads the discourses of Jesus to his congregation, when he calls upon his hearers to love God with all the heart, mind, and strength, and their neighbors as themselves, catch the meaning of what he utters, and he will want no arguments to prove that men can "have that mind in them which was also in Christ Jesus" [Phil 2:5]; and, when he comes once to believe that they can, he will speak with such firm persuasion of the truth of what he utters, that "his words will be with power" [Luke 4:32]. Let him comprehend his mission, and its grandeur will waken all the higher and better principles of his soul, kindle up a moral enthusiasm that will carry him through every difficulty, and make him mighty in the work of turning men's hearts to God. This is what is implied by the ministerial office. It is a practical answer to the objection brought against our hopes; and, till men will admit, that the preacher is inducted into his office to preach an impracticable scheme of morals, we shall consider a further answer, at least to professed Christians, as unnecessary.

INDEX OF BIBLICAL REFERENCES

INDEX OF NAMES AND SUBJECTS

443

449

and removal of vice, 72-73
and social equality, 346-47
and unbelievers, 267
Granger, Frank, 6
Gray, Thomas, 118n
Greeks, 328
Guyon, Madam, 383n

H

Hamlet (Shakespeare), 385n
happiness, subordinate to right, 376
Harvard University, 56
heart
    locus of religion, 281
    and moral truth, 256
    over creeds, 213
    source of virtue, 213
hell, 61
Henry VIII, 400
Herald of Reform. See *Genesee Republican and Herald of Reform*
history, of religion, 30-31
History of Redemption (Edwards), 62n. 4
Hobbes, Thomas, 291
Holley, Myron, 48
holiness, 230-31, 246-47
Homer, 132, 365
honesty, 170-71, 209
Howard, John, 379, 379n
human dignity, doctrine of, 273-74
human nature, 279-80
    corruption of, 61
    and equality, 341
    as image of God, 138
    and its potential, 386
    and unequal capacities, 425
    See also human dignity; humanity; man; nature; perfectibility
Human Nature in its Fourfold Estate (Boston), 62n. 4
humanity
    dignity of, 9, 273-74, 305-11
    divinity within, 9
    as social beings, 404
    triumph of, 339-40
    See also human dignity; human

nature; man; perfectibility
Hume, David, 291
Huss, John, 317, 317n

I

"idea, of the holy," 21
idea, of the just, 380
idealism, 19
idleness, cause of intemperance, 219
ignorance, cause of poverty, 10
imagination, and origin of religion, 279
Imitations of Horace (Pope), 219n
immortality, doctrine of, 273-77
imprisonment, for debt, 48, 342
incarnation, of God, 61
Independence, American, 66
Independents, and ecclesiastical authority, 400
industry, and Saint-Simon, 325, 326
infidelity, 9, 10, 12, 13
    Brownson's use of, 2
    and Calvinism, 203-4
    and Channing's *Discourses*, 215-17
    and clerical indifference to the poor, 312
    as destruction of religious forms, 415
    and the future, 395
    and human nature, 33, 392-93
    and ideal, 415
    modern, 397, 399
    and paganism, 396, 415
    and progress, 21
    and reform, 289, 294
    as rejection of religion, 414
    spread of, 215
    as uncommon definition, 412n
    See also atheism; disbelief; doubt; Protestantism; skepticism; unbelief
injustice, as cause of poverty, 10
inspiration
    divine, 356-57
    and doctrine, 95
    immediate, 360

W

Walpole, New Hampshire, and
  Brownson, 16-26
Walpole Temperance Society, 23,
  227
Wannay, George, 15n. 34
war, 301, 389
Washington, George, 46, 77, 321
Watts, Isaac, 62, 62n. 3, 79, 79n. 3,
  87, 110, 110n
wealth, 160-61, 335, 405, 427
Weed, Thurlow, 6n. 14
Westminster Confession, authority
  of, 401
Whitman, Bernard, 20
wisdom, 358, 381, 419
Wisner, William, 15, 85n. 1, 85-
  116, 137n
Wodin, 140
women, education of, 350
Word of God, as internal revelation,
  137. *See also* Bible; revelation
working class, 9
workingmen, 183-84, 432
  and Brownson, 10
  cause of, 1, 10-11
  and the idlers, 343
  interests of, 47
  movement of, 2, 10, 24
  protests of, 39-43
  Salina, New York, state conven-
    tion of, 58-59
  unbelief of, 10
  See also laboring class;
    Workingmen's party
Workingmen's party, 2-7, 24, 54n,
  305-11
  and Brownson, 59
works, and faith, 230-53
worship
  and assimilation of object
    worshiped, 273
  external, 168
  of God, 144, 282-83
  implications of , 272
  as moral perfection, 145
  mystical, 169

  as natural law, 362
  of progress (Saint-Simonians),
    328
  and Protestant Reformation, 237
Wright, Fanny, 4, 5

Y

Yale University, 56
Young Men's Bible Society (Boston),
  330n
youth, and aims, 403